Canadian Corrections Second Edition

Curt T. Griffiths
Simon Fraser University

THOMSON

NELSON

Australia   Canada   Mexico   Singapore   Spain   United Kingdom   United States

THOMSON

NELSON

Canadian Corrections,
Second Edition

By Curt T. Griffiths

Editorial Director and Publisher:
Evelyn Veitch

Executive Editor:
Joanna Cotton

Marketing Manager:
Lenore Taylor

Senior Developmental Editor:
Edward Ikeda

Senior Production Editor:
Bob Kohlmeier

Copy Editor:
Sarah Robertson

Proofreader:
Margaret Crammond

Indexer:
Dennis A. Mills

Production Coordinator:
Hedy Sellers

Creative Director:
Angela Cluer

Interior Design:
Gabriel Sierra

Cover Design:
Ken Phipps

Cover Image:
Ric Evans

Compositor:
Carol Magee

Permissions Coordinator:
Karen Becker

Printer:
Transcontinental

National Library of Canada Cataloguing in Publication

Griffiths, Curt T. (Curt Taylor), 1948–
Canadian corrections /
Curt T. Griffiths. — 2nd ed.

Includes bibliographical references and index.
ISBN 0-17-622476-9

1. Corrections — zCanada. I. Title.

HV9507.G74 2003   364.6'0971
C2003-902301-X

To the kids,
Collin and Lacey,
Two of the brightest stars in the universe!

CONTENTS

CHAPTER 8 CLASSIFICATION, CASE MANAGEMENT, AND TREATMENT 286

CHAPTER 9 RELEASE FROM PRISON 336

LIST OF BOXES

LIST OF FIGURES

LIST OF TABLES

LIST OF 'AT ISSUE' FEATURES

PREFACE

This text is designed to provide a comprehensive overview of corrections in Canada. It attempts to capture the dynamics of corrections in this country and to explore the unique attributes of the Canadian correctional enterprise. The materials presented in this text are descriptive and analytical. In writing this text, I have endeavoured to present the materials in a way that will stimulate your thinking about corrections and capture the intensity of the issues surrounding the response to criminal offenders by systems of corrections.

The public, criminal justice and corrections personnel, and offenders have expressed a considerable amount of frustration, anger, and disappointment with the response to criminal offenders and the operations of correctional systems in Canada over the past 200 years. It often appears that, despite the expenditure of considerable time, effort, and money, we are no further ahead in our quest to find successful strategies for preventing and correcting criminal behaviour. Given the pessimism that often surrounds corrections, it would have been quite easy to write a text that focused only on the failures, of which there have been enough to fill volumes. However, to have done so would have been to tell only part of the story. In recent years, there have been some exciting initiatives in corrections, many of which hold great promise.

This text avoids the doom and gloom that so often characterizes discussion of corrections. It describes community-based and institutional programs and, as well, includes the latest research findings. No doubt, the text may raise more questions for you than it answers. This is the nature of scholarly inquiry and of any study of corrections.

It is also important to keep in mind that corrections systems have been given a very difficult role to play: to sanction offenders while providing programs and services that are designed to reduce the likelihood that the offender returns to a life of crime. The response of correctional systems to offenders in carrying out this mandate has ranged from the brutal to the humane. Nearly always, it has been controversial.

This second edition of the text updates materials from the first edition as well as highlights some of the recent trends and challenges that have emerged in recent years. One of the more significant trends is the "Americanization" of corrections, as reflected in the shift in correctional policy and practice at the provincial level in the province of Ontario and, to a lesser extent, in Alberta and British Columbia. This has involved the implementation of a tough, no-frills correctional policy that includes the expansion of mega-institutions and an increased focus on community safety. This approach to corrections contrasts with that of the federal Correctional Service of Canada that continues to be based on a liberal, European model of correctional practice. Public–private partnerships are also be developed in corrections and the first efforts at privatizing correctional institutions are under way in Ontario. The monetary costs of confining offenders in correctional institutions continue to escalate, providing further impetus for efforts to develop alternatives to confinement and to expand various programs and interventions centred on the principles of restorative justice.

Correctional institutions continue to be beset by violence, and HIV/AIDS, hepatitis, and an aging inmate population are among the more significant health-related challenges confronting systems of corrections. For correctional officers and inmates, correctional institutions continue to be unsafe places in which to work and live. The breakdown of the traditional inmate code of conduct has created more unpredictability, and a considerable amount of violence—much of it related to the illicit drug trade—continues as a feature of daily life in correctional institutions.

On the treatment side, Canada continues to be a world leader in the development of effective correctional programs and there has been success in implementing programs for Aboriginal offenders and for female offenders. The research evidence is substantial that correctional treatment programs, if properly implemented, can reduce the rates of re-offending. The release and re-entry of offenders into the community remain areas of concern, with increasing scrutiny of parole board decision making and efforts to meet the needs of and to manage the risk posed by special categories of offenders, including sex offenders.

In addition to presenting current research findings and updating statistical materials, the second edition of *Canadian Corrections* contains the following new material:

Chapter 1

- Identification of new trends in Canadian corrections:

  1) the "Americanization" of corrections and the emergence of a U.S.-style approach to correctional policy and practice in several provincial jurisdictions, particularly Ontario

  2) the development of public–private partnerships (P3s)

3) the adoption of private-sector practices in correctional planning and operations

4) the increasing role of information technology and the rise of "technocorrections," involving the application of high technology in the surveillance of offenders

Chapter 2

- Update on correctional history, with a section entitled "1990 to the Present: Competing Models of Correctional Practice," which focuses on the emerging split between the federal and provincial models of correctional practice. The federal model of corrections is still firmly rooted in the liberal European model, while several provincial systems of corrections, led by Ontario, have adopted a no-frills, get-tough approach patterned on the American model.
- A box that sets out the commissions and inquiries into systems of corrections, indicating the year of the commission or inquiry and the focus and impact of the initiative.

Chapter 3

- Updated information on crime and criminal justice, victims, and the public and corrections.

Chapter 4

- Update on alternatives to confinement programs, including diversion programs.
- Insertion of widely used documents, including an actual completed Pre-Sentence Report, a completed Community Risk/Needs Assessment, and an actual Probation Order.
- Update on the challenges to probation in the early 21st century and suggestions for improving the effectiveness of probation.
- Update on the use of electronic monitoring by provincial systems of corrections.
- Additional materials on restorative justice, including a discussion of the Collaborative Justice Project in the Ottawa-Carleton judicial district and an actual case handled by the CJP, designed to illustrate the use and effectiveness of restorative justice in the urban context.

Chapter 5

- Update on the eras of prison architecture, including materials for the early 21st century, illustrating the split between the "new American school of architecture," reflected in the development of no-frills mega-institutions in Ontario, and the European model, reflected in the architecture of federal institutions.
- A list that outlines the initiatives taken by the CSC in response to the Arbour Report (1996).
- Updated information on the profiles of institutional populations.
- A box that profiles an Aboriginal woman serving time in a federal institution.
- Updated information on privatization of corrections in Canada.

Chapter 6

- Updated materials on recruitment and training of correctional officers.
- A new typology of correctional officers.
- Updated materials on sources of stress for correctional officers.
- An At Issue box on the issue of cross-gender staffing in women's correctional facilities.

Chapter 7

- An account of a day in the life of an adult offender.
- Updated information on inmate social systems and the inmate code, inmate gangs, the drug trade, and violence in correctional institutions.
- Updated information on inmate grievances and complaints, including a new box on the most frequent types of complaints made by federal inmates, 2001–02, and the most common types of complaints made by inmates against the provincial system of corrections in Ontario, 2001–02.
- New cases from the files of the provincial ombudsman in Ontario.

Chapter 8

- Several instruments used for risk assessment of inmates, including the Static-99.
- Updated materials on the effectiveness of correctional treatment.

Chapter 9

- Updated materials from the three provincial parole boards.
- Materials on community assessment, prepared for the parole board, and a copy of an actual completed community assessment form.
- An actual decision made by the B.C. Board of Parole and an actual completed Certificate of Parole.

Chapter 10

- New materials on community-based treatment centres.
- New boxes detailing the activities of a CSC Team Supervision Unit, a High-Risk Offender Community Notification for a sex offender in Alberta, the community notification process in Manitoba, and the execution of a Warrant of Suspension and Apprehension by federal parole officers in Toronto.
- An actual completed Critical Incident Report from B.C.
- Updated figures and charts on conditional release at the federal and provincial levels.

Appendix A

- Updated chronology of corrections.

Every attempt has been made to make this text student-friendly and to ensure that the text complements the well-taught corrections course. At the beginning of each chapter, a number of objectives are identified. Boxes highlight research findings and present important issues. Key words are highlighted and included in a glossary at the back of the book. Questions for review are located at the end of each chapter. Liberal use is made of figures and charts to illustrate important information. There are also a number of appendixes that provide additional information on corrections.

You will note that the text has not been written within any one theoretical framework. It is my view that Canadian corrections is best studied from a perspective that combines description with critical analysis of key issues and concepts. There is no one theoretical or conceptual framework within which materials on corrections can neatly fit. Consequently, the text should be viewed as only one resource in the study of corrections. It should be supplemented both by information from local jurisdictions and regions and by any additional theoretical/conceptual materials that instructors may want to introduce.

I hope that I have been successful in my efforts. Should you wish to offer comments on any aspect of the book or have suggestions on how it can be improved, you can reach me via the Web page for the book at **www.cancorrections2e.nelson.com** or by e-mail at griffith@sfu.ca.

ACKNOWLEDGMENTS

Many people contributed, directly and indirectly, to the production of this second edition of *Canadian Corrections*. At the outset, I would to acknowledge Alison Cunningham, my co-author on the first edition. Over the years, Alison has challenged me to think critically about many facets of the corrections process and I have benefited from collaborating with her.

I would also like to thank the reviewers whose comments and suggestions on the first edition of the text provided guidance in preparing the current edition: Doug Heckbert, Grant MacEwan College; Vicki Ryckman, St. Lawrence College; Martin Silverstein, University College of the Fraser Valley; and Kevin Wong, Brandon University.

A number of correctional professionals have influenced my thinking on corrections and contributed ideas and materials for text. I would like to thank Kelly Chahal, probation officer, and correctional officers Jack Trudgian, Deneen Jones, and Nick Walsh, all with the B.C. Corrections Branch. In the Pacific Region of CSC, Morgan Andreassen, Unit Supervisor, Kent Institution, and Randie Scott of the Regional Office continue to share their experiences and insights on corrections.

I have benefited greatly from serving as a member of the B.C. Board of Parole. I thank my colleagues on the board for sharing their insights and experiences, and I thank Tracey Thompson, chair of the B.C. Board of Parole, for her support and assistance in making materials available. Special thanks to Fae Chato-Manchuk, my colleague on the board, who has enlightened me on the various subtleties of corrections and correctional treatment.

I would also like to acknowledge the students in my corrections courses in the School of Criminology. Over the past two decades, they have made the teaching and study of Canadian corrections an exciting endeavour, and their curiosity and criticisms have been a continual source of inspiration. A further debt of gratitude is owed to those offenders and correctional officers and administrators who shared their experiences and observations of corrections over the years.

As always, it has been a pleasure to work with the outstanding publishing team at Nelson: Edward Ikeda, Joanna Cotton, and Bob Kohlmeier. All brought a high level of enthusiasm, energy, and professionalism to the project.

Curt Taylor Griffiths, Ph.D.
Simon Fraser University
Burnaby, B.C.

CHAPTER 1
SYSTEMS OF CORRECTIONS: AN OVERVIEW

CHAPTER OBJECTIVES

- *Define corrections.*
- *Discuss the legislative framework of corrections.*
- *Discuss the structure of contemporary corrections.*
- *Identify and discuss the challenges to corrections.*
- *Identify and discuss the trends in corrections.*

KEY TERMS

Corrections
Noncarceral
Carceral
Probation
Conditional sentence
Conditional release
Canadian Charter of Rights and
 Freedoms (1982)
Constitution Act (1867)
Criminal Code
Corrections and Conditional
 Release Act (1992)

Two-year rule
Correctional Service of Canada
 (CSC)
National Parole Board (NPB)
Office of the Correctional
 Investigator
Remand
Provincial ombudsman
Exchange of service agreements
Split personality of corrections

Corrections is perhaps the most fascinating and controversial component of the criminal justice system. Nearly everyone is interested in crime and criminal offenders and has an opinion to contribute to any discussion that arises; for example, try bringing up the subject of capital punishment with your friends or family members over dinner. This interest has not been lost on the media, which present an endless supply of police dramas and crime news. In the study of corrections, sorting fact from fiction and sifting through the sensational to discover reality are not always easy tasks. In fact, most Canadians know little about their correctional systems, other than what they hear on the evening news.

Regardless of your particular philosophy of corrections, whether your opinions lean toward the punishment of offenders or toward treatment and rehabilitation, you should be concerned with how our correctional systems operate. This is true not only because of the enormous outlay of tax dollars— approximately $2.5 billion a year in direct expenditures—but also for reasons closer to home. The majority of people convicted of criminal offences will never serve a day in prison. Instead, they will be fined, discharged, or subjected to some degree of supervision by correctional authorities while they live at home. Those who do go to prison may well be "out of sight, out of mind," but almost all of them, including virtually everyone sentenced to life imprisonment, will eventually be released into the community. They will live in our communities, be our co-workers, stand in line behind us at the grocery store, and attend college or university with us or with our children.

These facts alone require an examination of how correctional systems, from the sentencing stage onward, respond to people convicted of violating the law. Just as important is the need to reflect on a question asked of C.T. Griffiths by an 18-year-old facing a 25-year minimum sentence: "When I get out of here in 25 years, do you want to be my neighbour?" In addition to the need for scholarly study of this topic, each of us has a stake in our correctional systems. If only out of self-interest, it is crucial that we understand not only how these systems operate, but also how they can be made more effective.

Chapter 1 presents a brief overview of correctional systems in Canada. This material should get you thinking about the different dimensions of the correctional enterprise and provide a backdrop for the more detailed discussions throughout the text.

WHO AND WHAT IS CORRECTIONS?

The term **corrections** describes such a wide range of structures and activities that it is often difficult to determine what is being discussed. Many people equate corrections with prisons (and many college and university texts have pictures of prisons or inmates in cells on their covers). This image is perpetuated by the popular media, which generally take a "crime of the week," "men in cages" approach when presenting information on criminal justice and corrections. This approach not only presents a false image, but also ignores the large part of corrections that is unrelated to institutions and their inmates.

All correctional systems have both **noncarceral** and **carceral** components. Noncarceral systems include offenders, correctional personnel, and programs that are outside an institution, and carceral systems include those that are inside institutions. Most correctional personnel and convicted offenders are involved in noncarceral programs and services, such as probation. The "who" of corrections is relatively straightforward: correctional systems include all people involved in sanctioning, supervising, and providing services to convicted offenders. The "what" of corrections includes all of the programs and facilities through which these sanctions and services are provided.

The "Who" of Corrections

Well over 100,000 people are employed or volunteer in systems of corrections. About 150,000 offenders are subject to correctional programs or supervision, and 80 percent of offenders are under some form of supervision in the community. People involved in noncarceral corrections include sentencing judges; probation officers; probationers; staff of nonprofit organizations, such as the John Howard Society, the Salvation Army, and the Elizabeth Fry Society; staff of treatment and counselling programs; community service coordinators; Aboriginal organizations, such as friendship centres; community volunteers; religious organizations; the offender's family; parole board members; parole officers; parolees; and staff in community halfway houses.

People involved in carceral corrections include sentencing judges; superintendents and wardens; correctional officers; program staff; volunteers; the offender's family; treatment professionals; health-care providers; spiritual advisers, such as chaplains and Aboriginal Elders; Aboriginal organizations, including Native prison liaison workers; the inmates; and oversight agencies, which receive complaints from inmates.

Some of these people are employed by the government, either federal or provincial/territorial, whereas others work for private, nonprofit organizations, which may be partially or fully funded by the government and may operate with the assistance of trained volunteers. Recently, there has been increased interest in for-profit, private contractors who provide correctional services for a fee. Note that both of the above lists include criminal court judges, because the correctional process really begins when the sentence is passed.

The "What" of Corrections

The "what" of corrections is somewhat more complicated. Correctional systems can be described in a number of ways.

Corrections as a Subsystem of the Criminal Justice System

Systems of corrections, together with the public, the police, and the criminal courts, provide the foundation of the criminal justice system. Being interconnected, the activities of each component of the criminal justice system affect the others; for example, the patterns of police enforcement and arrest affect the number of cases Crown counsel must handle, and the case-screening decisions of Crown counsel determine the caseloads of the criminal courts. The sentencing decisions of judges in criminal courts influence the caseloads of probation officers and determine the number of admissions to correctional institutions, while the decisions of parole boards affect both the numbers of offenders who are incarcerated and the caseloads of parole officers (see Figure 3.1 on page 71).

Corrections as a Philosophy for Responding to Criminal Offenders

The term *corrections*, as the name implies, can refer to the approach taken in responding to convicted persons. As the discussion of correctional history in Chapter 2 will reveal, several philosophies have, at different times, provided the basis for the response to persons designated as criminal. These responses have ranged from the death penalty and corporal (physical) punishments, to treatment and rehabilitation. The particular philosophy that has guided the response to offenders at any time in history can generally be traced to social, political, and economic developments in society. Chapter 2 will consider the various correctional ideologies that have influenced the response to crime and criminals from the early days of settlement to the present.

Corrections as a Range of Programs and Services Delivered in Community Settings

One fact that is often overlooked in discussions of corrections is that the majority of convicted offenders are *not* incarcerated. Rather, they complete their sentences under some form of supervision in the community, which is less expensive than incarceration and better suited to addressing the program and treatment needs of most offenders.

There are three primary strategies used to supervise and provide programming to offenders in the community: probation, conditional sentence, and conditional release.

- **Probation** is a sentence that a judge in the criminal court imposes on an offender to provide for supervision of the offender in the community by a probation officer.
- **Conditional sentence** is a sentence that a judge imposes on an offender who would otherwise be incarcerated for a period of less than two years, but whose risk to the community is deemed by the court to be so low that the offender can serve the term at home, abiding by prescribed conditions and subject to imprisonment should he or she violate the conditions. Probation and conditional sentences will be examined in Chapter 4.
- **Conditional release** from confinement allows offenders in confinement to serve the remaining portion of their custodial sentence under supervision in the community. The various types of conditional release will be discussed in Chapter 9.

Corrections as a Range of Programs and Services Delivered in Institutional Settings

Correctional systems also offer programs and services to the relatively small number of offenders who are sentenced to a period of custody. Many programs are designed to address offenders' problem areas, such as substance abuse, anger management, and antisocial values. Other programs attempt to convey skills that will help inmates avoid reoffending after release, such as communication, problem solving, relationship skills, life skills, educational upgrading, and vocational training. There are also programs that target offenders convicted of specific offences (e.g., sex offenders or men who abuse their female partners). Institutional programs for inmates will be examined in Chapter 8.

Corrections: A Definition

Combining all of the above dimensions, corrections can be defined as *the structures, policies, and programs that are delivered by government, nonprofit agencies and organizations, and members of the general public to punish, treat, and supervise, in the community and in correctional institutions, persons convicted of criminal offences.* Needless to say, corrections involves much more than prisons.

THE LEGISLATIVE FRAMEWORK OF CORRECTIONS

Correctional systems operate under a variety of federal and provincial/ territorial statutes that establish the authority of correctional officials, set out jurisdiction, and provide the framework within which decisions are made and programs are administered. Among the more significant pieces of legislation are the following:

- **Canadian Charter of Rights and Freedoms (1982).** The Charter is the primary law of the land and guarantees fundamental freedoms, legal rights, and equality rights for all citizens of Canada, including those accused of crimes. Until passage of the Charter in 1982, Canadian courts were reluctant to become involved in suits against systems of corrections, particularly those brought by convicted offenders. However, over the past decade a number of decisions by Canadian courts, including the Supreme Court of Canada, have had a significant impact on the operation of correctional systems.

- **Constitution Act (1867).** This Act, formerly known as the British North America Act, sets out the respective responsibilities of the federal and provincial governments in many areas, including criminal justice. The federal government is assigned responsibility for enacting criminal laws and for establishing the procedures to be followed in criminal cases, while the provincial governments are given the authority to establish the necessary structures for the administration of justice. However, this is only a general division of responsibilities, and some boundaries remain ambiguous. For example, the Royal Canadian Mounted Police (RCMP) is a federal police force that is also involved in the administration of justice under contract as a provincial and municipal police service.

- **Criminal Code.** This is a federal statute that defines most criminal offences, the procedures for their prosecution, and the penalties that sentencing judges can hand down.

- **Corrections and Conditional Release Act (1992).** This is the primary legislation under which the federal system of corrections operates. The Act contains three parts. Part I is entitled "Institutional and Community Corrections" and includes sections on the purpose and principles of the federal correctional system, provisions for managing convicted offenders in community and institutional settings, and special measures for female and Aboriginal inmates. Part II, "Conditional Release and Detention," sets out the purpose and principles of conditional release; eligibility criteria and review processes for the various types of release, including day parole and full parole; the supervision of released offenders in the community; and the structure and operation of the parole board. Part III, "Correctional Investigator," sets out the legislative framework for the federal Office of the Correctional Investigator, which is the federal ombudsman for offender complaints; the functions of the office; and the procedures for receiving, reviewing, and reporting on offender grievances.

- *Provincial legislation, including correctional statutes.* Each province and territory has legislation setting out the framework within which its correctional system operates. In Ontario, for example, the Ministry of Correctional Services Act pertains to inmates, parolees, and probationers, as well as to those held in detention before trial and young offenders who are 16 and 17 years of age. The ministry's mandate, set out in section 5 of the Act, is "to supervise the detention and release of inmates, parolees, probationers and young persons and to create for them a social environment in which they may achieve changes in attitudes by providing changes, treatment and services designed to afford them the opportunities for successful personal and social adjustment in the community."
- *International agreements and conventions.* The federal government is a signatory to a number of international agreements and conventions that affect its operations, including the Transfer of Offenders Act, the United Nations Standard Minimum Rules for the Treatment of Prisoners, and the International Covenant on Civil and Political Rights.

CORRECTIONAL SYSTEMS

Correctional systems in Canada are operated by the federal and provincial/territorial governments, who together spend approximately $2.5 billion a year on personnel, programs, services, and infrastructure. Correctional services in Canada are delivered in a wide variety of community and institutional settings. Canada's unique demographic attributes of a large land area and a small population present challenges to service delivery. Although the majority of correctional personnel and offenders are concentrated in or near large urban areas, services must also be delivered in remote and rural areas of the country. These challenges are particularly acute for correctional personnel who supervise offenders on probation or in other noncarceral programs, such as parole. The difficulty of delivering effective correctional services in remote and rural areas has been one catalyst for the development of innovative alternatives to confinement. These alternatives will be examined in Chapter 4.

The Split in Correctional Jurisdiction

A unique feature of Canadian corrections is the **two-year rule,** under which offenders who receive sentences of two years or longer fall under the jurisdiction of the federal government, while offenders receiving sentences of two years less a day are the responsibility of provincial/territorial correctional authorities. The historical record indicates no clear rationale for the two-year rule, which was established at Confederation, but researchers have offered the following explanations: (1) the federal government was interested in strengthening its powers, (2) only the federal government had the resources to establish and maintain long-term institutions, and (3) offenders receiving short sentences were seen as in need of guidance, whereas those receiving longer sentences were seen as more serious criminals who had to be separated from society for longer periods (Ouimet, 1969).

The split in correctional jurisdiction has a number of implications for offenders and correctional authorities. The relatively short period that offenders are confined in provincial institutions means there is a high turnover of the population, which makes it difficult to provide treatment programs. As well, there is considerable variation among the provinces/territories in the noncarceral and carceral programs and services offered. Many offenders spend their entire "careers" in provincial/territorial facilities, and others spend time in both systems. The consequences of the split in jurisdiction will be alluded to many times throughout the text.

THE FEDERAL SYSTEM OF CORRECTIONS

Correctional Service of Canada

The federal system of corrections is operated by the **Correctional Service of Canada (CSC),** which is part of the federal Ministry of the Solicitor General. The CSC is divided into five regions (Atlantic, Quebec, Ontario, Prairie, and Pacific), with headquarters in Ottawa. With an annual operating budget of $1.5 billion (in 2001–02), the CSC provides correctional services from sea to sea to sea and operates a variety of facilities, including 53 federal penitentiaries, halfway houses, healing lodges and treatment centres for Aboriginal offenders, community parole offices, psychiatric hospitals, reception and assessment centres, health-care centres, palliative care units, and an addiction research centre.

The CSC has also partnered with not-for-profit organizations, such as the John Howard Society (discussed below), to operate over 150 halfway houses across the country (Solicitor General of Canada, 2002). The CSC has approximately 16,000 employees, 80 percent of whom work in correctional institutions. The objectives of the CSC are set out in its mission statement and five core values (see Box 1.1).

National Parole Board

A second important federal agency is the **National Parole Board (NPB).** Since 1959 this agency, which is external to the correctional system, has made conditional release decisions. Although institutional staff play a significant role in release decisions by assisting inmates with release plans and assessing their risk of reoffending, the NPB makes the final decision as to when most federal

BOX 1.1

Correctional Service of Canada Mission Statement and Core Values

Mission Statement: The Correctional Service of Canada, as part of the criminal justice system and respecting the rule of law, contributes to the protection of society by actively encouraging and assisting offenders to become law-abiding citizens, while exercising reasonable, safe, secure and humane control.

CORE VALUE 1. We respect the dignity of individuals, the rights of all members of society, and the potential for human growth and development.

CORE VALUE 2. We recognize that the offender has the potential to live as a law-abiding citizen.

CORE VALUE 3. We believe that our strength and our major resource in achieving our objectives is our staff and that human relationships are the cornerstone of our endeavour.

CORE VALUE 4. We believe that the sharing of ideas, knowledge, values and experience, nationally and internationally, is essential to the achievement of our mission.

CORE VALUE 5. We believe in managing the Service with openness and integrity and we are accountable to the Solicitor General.

Source: Correctional Service of Canada (www.csc-scc.gc.ca).

offenders will be released from custody. The decision making as to the NPB will be examined in Chapter 9.

Office of the Correctional Investigator

The **Office of the Correctional Investigator** (www.oci-bec.gc.ca) was established in 1973 under the federal Inquiries Act and was formalized in 1992 under provisions of the Corrections and Conditional Release Act. Situated in Ottawa, this independent agency—which comprises a director of investigations, five investigators, and support staff—has a mandate to investigate the complaints of federal offenders (in institutions and under supervision in the community) and to determine whether the CSC is meeting its obligations as set out in its mission statement and five core values.

Most often, inmates' complaints relate to conditions in correctional institutions. The Correctional Investigator investigates and attempts to resolve not only the specific complaint, but also the larger institution or system-wide factors that may have created the condition or issue raised in the complaint. The Office of the Correctional Investigator's annual reports and recommendations are designed to improve the delivery of correctional services in the CSC, although the recommendations are not binding.

In 2001–02, the Office of the Correctional Investigator received approximately 8,500 inmate complaints (up from 4,000 in 1999–2000) and reviewed over 500 videotapes of incidents involving Institutional Emergency Response Teams. The Auditor General of Canada has recommended that the Correctional Investigator develop strategies to better manage the large caseloads and to inform inmates about the role and activities of the office, as well as other avenues for resolving their grievances.

PROVINCIAL/TERRITORIAL CORRECTIONAL SYSTEMS

Traditionally in Canada, it has been the federal system of corrections, including the offenders and the prisons, that has captured the attention of politicians, commissions of inquiry, the media, and academic researchers. This is true even though most offenders fall under the jurisdiction of provincial/territorial correctional authorities by being sentenced to probation or to a sentence of confinement for less than two years. (See Table 1.1 for a list of provincial/territorial correctional ministries.) The wide diversity of programs and services that provincial/territorial corrections offer, the relatively short periods

Table 1.1   Provincial/Territorial Ministries Responsible for Corrections

Alberta	Ministry of Solicitor General, Correctional Services Division www4.gov.ab.ca/just/dept/deptsolgen.html
British Columbia	Ministry of Public Safety and Solicitor General, Corrections Branch www.gov.bc.ca/pssg
Manitoba	Manitoba Justice, Corrections Division www.gov.mb.ca/justice/index.shtml
New Brunswick	Department of Public Safety, Community and Correctional Services www.gnb.ca/0276/index-e.asp
Newfoundland and Labrador	Department of Justice, Adult Corrections Division www.gov.nf.ca/just
Northwest Territories	Department of Justice, Corrections Services Division www.justice.gov.nt.ca
Nova Scotia	Department of Justice, Correctional Services Division http://gov.ns.ca/just/correcservices.htm
Nunavut	Department of Justice, Corrections and Community Justice www.gov.nu.ca/Nunavut/English/departments/Jus
Ontario	Ministry of Public Safety and Security, Correctional Services www.mpss.jus.gov.on.ca
Prince Edward Island	Attorney General, Community and Correctional Services www.gov.pe.ca/oag/cacs-info/index.php3
Quebec	Sécurité publique Québec www.msp.gouv.qc.ca/index_en.asp
Saskatchewan	Department of Corrections and Public Safety www.cps.gov.sk.ca
Yukon Territory	Department of Justice, Community and Correctional Services www.justice.gov.yk.ca

that provincial offenders remain in confinement, and the assumption that provincial/territorial offenders represent a less serious threat in terms of their criminal behaviour have all conspired to keep the provincial/territorial correctional systems in relative obscurity.

In recent years, however, incidents such as the devastating riot that took place at the Headingley Correctional Institution in Manitoba in 1996 have highlighted the importance of examining the issues in provincial/territorial systems of corrections. They include increasing concern about the conditions in many provincial jails, such as overcrowding, high rates of communicable diseases (including HIV, tuberculosis, and hepatitis C), a lack of inmate safety, and a poor working environment for staff. These issues will be considered in Chapter 5.

Many innovative practices are unique to provincial/territorial correctional systems, such as the use of electronic monitoring as an alternative to confinement or as an early release option. Examining provincial/territorial correctional systems reveals the diversity in practice across the country and provides insights into how correctional personnel attempt to accommodate the specific demands of their jurisdictions. For example, as described in Chapter 5, the Baffin Correctional Centre is the only jail in the world that allows inmates—in the context of supervised hunting expeditions—to handle loaded firearms.

Provincial/Territorial Noncarceral and Carceral Corrections

All of the provinces/territories operate a variety of noncarceral programs and services, including probation, bail supervision, fine options, community service, and diversion programs. Other programs and services include electronic monitoring, most often used as a condition of probation or with temporary absences; house arrest; intensive supervision probation; attendance centres; temporary absences; accelerated temporary absence programs; and parole. The majority of offenders involved in provincial/territorial correctional systems are on probation.

The provincial/territorial governments operate approximately 150 facilities across the country. In addition, provincial/territorial correctional systems are responsible for housing accused persons who are on **remand.** These are persons who have been charged with an offence and ordered by the court to be held in custody while awaiting trial, or persons who are awaiting sentencing after having been found guilty at trial.

Three provinces—Quebec, Ontario, and British Columbia—operate their own provincial parole boards, while provincial probation officers supervise offenders released on parole. In the remaining provinces, the NPB handles the release of some offenders, and parole officers of the CSC supervise offenders.

Provincial Ombudsman

The provincial counterpart of the federal Office of the Correctional Investigator is generally the **provincial ombudsman.** These provincial offices have the authority to investigate citizen complaints against the decisions and actions of provincial government agencies and employees. These complaints include those made by offenders under the supervision and control of provincial correctional systems. See Chapter 7 for more information on the role of the provincial ombudsman.

FEDERAL/PROVINCIAL EXCHANGE OF SERVICE AGREEMENTS

The federal and provincial/territorial correctional systems often enter into agreements to facilitate the delivery of correctional services. The most common are **exchange of service agreements,** under which a federal offender is allowed to complete a sentence of incarceration in a provincial/territorial facility. For example, the federal government and the government of New Brunswick have an agreement under which nonviolent federal offenders are incarcerated in provincial correctional institutions, while higher-risk provincial offenders are confined in federal correctional facilities.

THE PRIVATE, NONPROFIT SECTOR

In Canada, there is a long history of involvement of private, nonprofit organizations in the delivery of correctional services and programs. These include the John Howard Society, the Elizabeth Fry Society, the Salvation Army, and the St. Leonard's Society. In recent years, these four organizations have been joined by a wide range of other nonprofit organizations, including several Aboriginal organizations. The programs and services of these and others are highlighted throughout the text. Here, several of the more well-known organizations are briefly described.

John Howard Society (www.johnhoward.ca)

The John Howard Society is named after John Howard, an English penal reformer who, during the late 1700s, played a key role in prison reform in England. The John Howard Society is active in all of the provinces and territories, with the exception of Yukon Territory, and, through individual branches, operates a variety of programs, including bail supervision, community assessment and parole supervision, residential halfway houses, victim assistance and victim–offender mediation, and public and legal education. In

Calgary, for example, the John Howard Society operates a substance abuse program; a community conferencing program based on the principles of restorative justice; counselling, advocacy, referral, and pre-release planning programs for offenders in correctional institutions; and a halfway house for special-needs offenders.

Elizabeth Fry Society (www.elizabethfrysociety.com)

Elizabeth Fry (Gurney) was born in England in 1780. A Quaker who advocated the equality of women, she worked tirelessly for the humane treatment of prisoners and for prison reform, no small task given the conditions of jails in England and other countries at the time. The first Canadian chapter of the Elizabeth Fry Society was formed in Vancouver in 1939, and there are a number of member societies across the country. Among the goals of the society are to encourage reform at all levels of the criminal justice system, with a particular focus on women in conflict with the law. The society is active in advocating for reform in correctional policies and in developing and operating programs and services for women offenders.

The branches of the society deliver a variety of programs and services, sometimes under contract with the government, but also supported by fundraising and the United Way. These services include community service order programs for probationers, institutional visiting programs, counselling, and pre-release programs to assist women as they reintegrate into the community.

Salvation Army (www.salvationarmy.ca)

The Salvation Army, which has been involved in Canadian corrections since the late 1880s, provides a variety of services and programs, including community service orders, family group conferencing, substance abuse counselling, and supervision of offenders in the community.

St. Leonard's Society of Canada (www.stleonards.ca)

The first St. Leonard's Society was established in 1962 in Windsor, Ontario. The name, first used in Chicago in the 1950s, comes from the patron saint of prisoners, a monk in 6th-century France who took in released inmates with such good results that the king eventually sanctioned the enterprise. Today, there are 14 societies affiliated with the St. Leonard's Society of Canada. Most of the societies are located in Ontario, with one in Nova Scotia and one in British Columbia. For example, the St. Leonard's Society of Brant, in

Brantford, Ontario, offers a broad range of community-based and residential programming, including a house for federal male parolees, three custody facilities for young offenders, a vocational/employment program for offenders, and substance abuse counselling.

Native Counselling Services of Alberta (www.ncsa.ca)

In recent years, there has been an exponential growth in the involvement of Aboriginal organizations in the development and delivery of services and programs designed to assist Aboriginal persons in conflict with the law and to reduce the overrepresentation of Aboriginal peoples in the justice system. The Native Counselling Services of Alberta (NCSA) is the oldest of the Aboriginal organizations involved in providing justice-related programs and services for Aboriginal peoples.

Founded in 1963, the NCSA delivers a wide variety of institutional and community-based correctional programs and services for Aboriginal offenders, many under contract with the Correctional Service of Canada. Among NCSA services are the following:

- adult and youth criminal court workers' program
- the Stan Daniels Healing Centre, a 75-bed community residential centre in Edmonton
- Kochee Mena (Cree for "Try Again") open custody centre in Edmonton
- prison liaison services
- parole supervision

These and other programs and services are designed to fulfill the mission statement of the NCSA, which is "to contribute to the holistic development and wellness of the Aboriginal individual, family, and community by working in partnerships to provide culturally sensitive programs and services and by promoting the fair and equitable treatment of Aboriginal people."

CHALLENGES FOR CORRECTIONS

Corrections has always been the stepchild of the justice family, never having its role clearly defined, the resources to carry out its multitudinous functions, or a constituency to support its efforts. Over the years, corrections' history has been a series of ideas and errors operated within an extremely diverse amalgam of facilities, theories, techniques, and programs.... Little progress has been made in relating correctional programs to the prevention of recidivism, and perhaps even less progress has been made in the establishment of public policy in corrections based on principles that must inherently be a part of a democratic society.

—Breed, 1998:9

Correctional systems share many of the difficulties that other components of the criminal justice system encounter, including policies and programs that are of undetermined effectiveness, structures that are costly to maintain, and a reactive rather than proactive, preventive approach to crime and social disorder. However, correctional systems have a number of additional attributes that set them apart from the police, Crown counsel, and members of the judiciary and that make us appreciate even more the difficulties that correctional personnel face in developing and implementing effective policies and programs. These issues are explored in greater detail throughout the book, but it is important to begin thinking about them now. Here are some of the challenges that confront systems of corrections.

Providing Programs and Services for Offenders, Often for Lengthy Periods

The police and the criminal courts spend very little time with individual offenders during the criminal justice process. It falls to corrections to provide programs and services over the long term, whether in the community or in institutional settings. The costs of providing these services are high, and rising. Other concerns include the aging of the offender population and the high rates of HIV/AIDS in prison populations.

Serving a Diverse Clientele

An array of people become involved in the criminal justice system, including men and women; offenders of various ethnicities; specific categories of offenders, such as white-collar, violent, mentally disordered, long-term, and sex offenders; and, increasingly, elderly offenders. Contributing to this complexity are the diversity of needs of the people within each of these groups and the fact that correctional systems have no control over the number and types of offenders who are placed under their control. In British Columbia, for example, more than one-half of the resources of provincial community corrections are devoted to the management of sex offenders and offenders convicted of spousal assault.

Serving a Marginal Population

For many offenders, criminal behaviour is only a symptom of other difficulties in their personal lives. They may have other functional problems in their families, peer groups, and workplaces. Many offenders were raised in dysfunctional homes marked by alcoholism and violence and were victims of child abuse (physical, sexual, or psychological) or neglect. As adults, many offenders have severe alcohol and/or drug addictions, low levels of formal education, few marketable skills, and low self-esteem. This marginality is even more pronounced among Aboriginal inmates, who report higher levels of alcohol abuse and lower levels of education and employment than non-Aboriginal offenders.

A high percentage of female offenders have been the victims of physical and sexual abuse and exhibit high rates of eating disorders, depression, and sleep disorders. Self-injury among incarcerated women is also quite common.

There is a much higher prevalence of mental-health disorders such as schizophrenia, major depression, and bipolar disorder among carceral and noncarceral populations than among the general population. Among institutional populations, communicable diseases such as HIV/AIDS, tuberculosis, and hepatitis B and C are rampant.

Pursuing Conflicting Goals

Correctional systems and the other components of the criminal justice system have as their primary mandate the protection of society. There is often disagreement, however, regarding how this goal is best accomplished. Many observers argue that the protection of society is best assured by more severe sanctions—more arrests, more convictions, and longer periods of incarceration. Others, however, argue that this "get tough" approach has been unsuccessful in the past, so the criminal justice system should focus on addressing *why* offenders commit crimes, rather than merely reacting to criminal behaviour. This approach would mean focusing on the specific treatment needs of offenders in an attempt to reduce or eliminate future criminal behaviour. The persistence of these two views of the goals of corrections—punishment for the protection of society versus treatment of the offender—is the basis of the **split personality of corrections.**

The Absence of a Knowledge Base

Corrections lacks a well-developed body of empirical knowledge upon which to base the formulation of policies and the operation of programs. Though the amount of research on various types of criminality and on various interventions has increased, the findings of these studies are often contradictory. Further, research often has too little influence on correctional policies, programs, and services, which are affected by a variety of factors, including political considerations and public opinion. As well, research is often prematurely adopted as the basis for policies and programs without additional studies to validate findings.

Contributing to the problem is the lack of experimental research and rigorous evaluation of correctional policies and programs. The CSC maintains a strong research department that produces internationally recognized studies, but many of the studies fall short of the standards for causal research. Moreover, most institutional and community-based programs are operated by provincial/territorial correctional systems and by nonprofit agencies, and these are rarely subjected to evaluation. This makes it difficult to determine whether the policies and programs are effective in achieving their stated objectives.

The Plague of Disinformation

For the majority of Canadians, the criminal justice system is largely a mystery, and their perceptions of the police, courts, and corrections are strongly influenced by the media. Crime dramas and news programs tend to focus on the sensational, albeit rare, crimes. News items are more likely to highlight crimes of a few parolees rather than the fact that the majority of offenders successfully complete their period of parole supervision following release from institutions. Riots, drug overdoses, hostage-takings, and lockdowns tend to receive more media attention than positive initiatives that prison inmates have taken, such as running sports day programs for developmentally challenged youths in the institution, raising money for the fight against AIDS through annual walks within the institution, fighting forest fires, building trails and campgrounds, or completing community service projects.

Although news reporting that focuses on the sensational is not erroneous, it does result in disinformation, since it is not balanced. The bias of the media toward sensational crimes, the tendency of the media to simplify issues related to crime and justice, and the tendency of the public to generalize from specific events all contribute to an uninformed and misinformed public (Roberts, 2001). Systems of corrections have so far been unsuccessful in countering and correcting the images that the media present to the public.

Corrections as a Human Enterprise

Despite the increasing use of technology such as electronic monitoring, the development of sophisticated computer information and tracking systems, and the use of aggregate models of risk assessment, corrections remains first and foremost a human enterprise. The sanctions that judges impose in the criminal court, the pains of imprisonment that inmates confined in correctional institutions experience, and the decisions that members of the parole board make reflect the full range of human emotions, both in their experience and in their consequences.

The Tense Relationship with the Public

Correctional systems do not enjoy the same levels of public support as other components of the criminal justice system. Whereas most Canadians view police services positively, they view corrections with a degree of suspicion and distrust. Only in recent years have systems of corrections become more proactive in disseminating information about correctional programs and services to the media and to the public. Still, the heinous crimes of a very few offenders often overshadow the positive accomplishments of program and treatment staff and of inmates themselves.

Corrections in a Multicultural Society

Multiculturalism is a defining characteristic of Canada. The primary source of this diversity is immigration, which has had a significant impact on Canadian society since Europeans first colonized the country. Visible minorities, the majority of whom live in the major urban areas of the country, now make up just over 10 percent of the population. There is no evidence that immigrants have higher rates of criminality than people born in Canada; in fact, the rate of offending for immigrants is lower. However, cultural diversity poses challenges to the criminal justice system and, more specifically, to systems of corrections. Many new immigrants speak neither English nor French and come from countries where there is widespread distrust of the criminal justice system.

Adding to the cultural diversity of Canada are Aboriginal peoples, who make up approximately 4 percent of the population. Among Aboriginal peoples, there is a great diversity of cultures and communities. Though most Aboriginal people reside in rural and remote areas of the country, many live in urban centres, particularly Vancouver, Winnipeg, Toronto, and Montreal. Aboriginal peoples are overrepresented at all stages of the criminal justice process, from arrest to incarceration.

Although studies have increasingly focused on the issues surrounding the overrepresentation of Aboriginal peoples in the criminal justice and correctional systems in Canada, there is little information on offenders from other cultural and ethnic groups. Similarly, although provincial and federal correctional systems have employment equity guidelines, it has been difficult to attract qualified candidates from the various cultural and ethnic groups in order to match the diversity of Canadian society.

The Paper Burden of Accountability

As correctional agencies develop operational protocols that enhance accountability and reduce exposure to civil liability, the front-line worker is becoming buried under onerous recording tasks that reduce the time available for face-to-face interaction with offenders. Ironically, as staff spend more time sitting in front of a computer inputting information into centralized databases, they have less time to read all of the available material on offenders, let alone to integrate it into appropriate intervention strategies. Consequently, correctional interventions increasingly consist of surveillance and monitoring tasks, such as urinalysis. Concern over two related issues—the staff's paper burden and the delay in admitting inmates into treatment programs owing to delays in completing assessments—led the CSC to implement initiatives, such as Operation Bypass (see Box 8.3 on page 296), to reduce duplication in reports and to hasten the development of programs soon after the inmate is admitted.

TRENDS IN CORRECTIONS

A list of several trends in systems of corrections concludes this introductory discussion. Underlying many of these trends is the fiscal crises of governments, which have resulted in cutbacks to resources for all components of the criminal justice system, including correctional systems. This decrease in funds has prompted correctional agencies, as well as their counterparts in policing and prosecution, to be more innovative and efficient.

The "Americanization" of Canadian Corrections

A recent development in Canadian corrections has been the emergence of an American-style approach to correctional policy and practice—an approach that puts a premium on public safety and security. This approach is reflected in the treatment of serious violence in the Youth Criminal Justice Act (which replaced the Young Offenders Act in April 2003), and in the "tough on crime" initiatives adopted by Ontario and other provinces in recent years. This emerging model of corrections is discussed further in Chapter 2.

Increasing Accountability and Concern with the Rule of Law

In April 1994, in the aftermath of a violent physical confrontation between inmates and correctional officers at the now-closed Kingston Prison for Women, eight inmates were removed from their cells and strip-searched by an Institutional Emergency Response Team. The incident, which is discussed at length in Chapter 5, became the subject of a judicial inquiry after excerpts from a leaked videotape showing the cell extractions and strip searches aired on national television. The inquiry's report (Arbour, 1996) was highly critical of the CSC and led to the resignation of the CSC commissioner. Concerns that correctional administrators were ignoring the legal rights of convicted offenders prompted the CSC to add the phrase "and respecting the rule of law" to its mission statement.

Court decisions have also extended the rights of prison inmates. In a controversial decision, the Supreme Court of Canada recently struck down a federal law that prohibited federal prison inmates from voting, citing the fundamental right to vote of "every citizen" in a democracy (*Sauvé v. Canada, Chief Electoral Officer*, 2002 SCC 68, available at www.lexum.umontreal.ca/csc-scc/en/rec/html/sauve2.en.html).

Focusing on Offender Risk/Needs Assessment and Risk Management

Risk assessment and risk management are the mantras of contemporary corrections. Personnel at all stages of the correctional process, from institutional staff to parole board members to parole officers, have access to theoretically or empirically based assessment instruments and tools. These assessment and management instruments not only provide correctional workers with information from which to develop effective management and treatment plans, but they also reduce the liability and culpability of personnel should the offender commit serious crimes in the community. The increased concern with offender risk has affected decision making throughout systems of corrections. A recent government report on the Corrections and Conditional Release Act declared, "Public protection or community safety is the paramount consideration in all decisions made at all stages of the corrections and conditional release system" (Standing Committee, 2000:4).

Paying Attention to the Rights of Victims

The Corrections and Conditional Release Act and provincial/territorial legislation have established a number of victims' rights in the correctional process.

Crime victims can attend parole hearings, submit written victim impact statements to parole boards, and, upon request, be advised of the parole eligibility dates and release status of offenders. Federal and provincial/territorial systems of corrections have also implemented specific initiatives designed to improve communication with crime victims. Crime victims in Ontario, for example, can call the province's toll-free Victim Support Line to access a wide range of information, including the status and scheduled release dates of provincially sentenced offenders.

Creating Alternatives to Incarceration

Correctional systems are increasingly focusing on intermediate sanctions and on programs based on the principles of restorative justice. Most provinces and territories have in place policies that encourage the development of initiatives such as conflict resolution, community mediations and panels, Aboriginal Elders panels, and community accountability panels. Communities, religious organizations, and nonprofit agencies are playing a major role in the development of alternatives to incarceration.

Reducing the Costs of Corrections

Government cutbacks, particularly at the provincial/territorial level, have affected all levels of correctional systems, resulting in reductions in institutional programming and limits on the development of community-based initiatives. Several provinces have downsized their correctional operations, closing some facilities and consolidating inmate populations into larger facilities. The first jurisdiction to move to "big box" institutional corrections was Ontario, which has built a number of "superjails"; British Columbia has followed suit, closing several correctional camps and medium-security facilities.

The decrease in resources has also affected the recruitment and training of correctional personnel. Many provincial correctional services have adopted pre-employment training models, under which prospective candidates must complete a course of study, at their expense, prior to applying for positions. To assist in offsetting costs, systems of corrections are considering charging offenders a user fee for community supervision and for room and board in correctional institutions.

Developing Policies and Programs for Female Offenders

Although female offenders make up only a small percentage of correctional populations, there has been a concerted attempt to develop correctional policies and programs specific to their needs, through a woman-centred philosophy that empowers women to make changes in their lives. The federal government has constructed a series of small, regional facilities for federal female offenders, including one designed specifically for Aboriginal women.

Focusing on Human Resources

In recent years, it has been recognized that correctional systems can become more efficient and effective only with highly motivated, trained, and skilled employees. The CSC has an extensive program for in-service training and career management, delivering learning programs online as well as in five regional training centres and a management learning centre. Provincial/territorial systems of corrections, however, have been much slower to develop large-scale staff training programs, often because of budgetary restrictions.

Systems of corrections are also giving increased attention to issues of harassment. Anti-harassment coordinators help managers, supervisors, and employees understand the harassment policy and the mechanisms that exist to address cases that arise.

Developing Public–Private Partnerships

Efforts to find more cost-effective ways of providing services have led to a re-examination of the potential of private-sector involvement, not only in program and service delivery, but also in the construction and operation of correctional facilities. The expansion of public–private partnerships (also known as P3s or PPPs) builds upon a long tradition of private-sector involvement in institutional and community corrections. For example, the CSC contracts out for the provision of medical services, technical services, education, and some treatment programs in prisons, and for offender programs in the community.

For-profit treatment services for offenders on probation and parole have emerged. Canada's first privately operated correctional facility opened in Ontario in 2002, the same year in which the province entered into a public–private partnership to expand the Electronic Surveillance Program.

Expanding Aboriginal Corrections

In recent years, Aboriginal communities and organizations have become increasingly involved in designing and delivering correctional services in community and institutional settings. Aboriginal communities are involved in institutional programs through Native liaison workers, activities sponsored by

Aboriginal organizations, and the participation of Elders in providing treatment. Communities and the justice system also collaborate in programs, many of which incorporate elements of traditional Aboriginal spirituality and principles of restorative justice. These programs include sentencing circles, community mediation, and various sentencing advisory committees. Aboriginal communities also create and control their own programs, some of which are geared toward Aboriginal women.

Section 81 of the Corrections and Conditional Release Act authorizes the federal government to enter into agreements with Aboriginal communities to provide correctional services to Aboriginal offenders, while section 84 sets out provisions for Aboriginal communities to be involved in supervising offenders on release in the community. In addition, provincial/territorial governments have expanded programs in Aboriginal corrections; in many jurisdictions, programs are operated in collaboration with Aboriginal bands and organizations. Other initiatives include Aboriginal healing lodges, Native community correctional workers, Native program coordinators within institutions, and Native cultural training for correctional staff.

The Increasing Role of Information Technology and the Rise of Technocorrections

In their drive to become more efficient, systems of corrections are making increasing use of information technology. Many provinces are working to integrate their information systems across components of the justice system and, potentially, with the federal government. Ontario's Integrated Justice Project, for example, is designed to link police, court, and correctional databases to ensure that all decision makers have access to complete information on offenders. The federal government has undertaken a number of Integrated Justice Information initiatives (see the Integrated Justice Information page on the Solicitor General Canada website at www.sgc.gc.ca).

Federal corrections and most provincial/territorial systems of corrections have created offender management systems that make offender case file information available to more than those who possess the actual case file. Electronic monitoring programs allow offenders to serve their sentence in the community. Video-conferencing technology is used for remand, bail hearings, and adjournment hearings to reduce transportation costs and the risks of assault among inmates during trips to court.

As systems of corrections come under pressure to manage their operations in a cost-effective manner without compromising public safety, they are turning their attention to a field known as "technocorrections." Electronic tracking and location systems designed to supervise offenders in the community, the use of drugs to control behaviour in correctional and community settings, and genetic and neurobiological risk assessments that focus on genetic predispositions to violent or criminal behaviour are just three of the emerging areas in technocorrections. As of 2003, the provinces of Ontario and Alberta were considering the use of the satellite-based Global Positioning System (GPS) to track and monitor high-risk offenders (more on monitoring systems in Chapter 4). Although these strategies hold considerable promise, the potential threats they pose are bound to attract controversy in the coming years (Fabelo, 2000).

QUESTIONS FOR REVIEW

1. Identify the "who" of noncarceral and carceral corrections.
2. Identify the components of the "what" of corrections.
3. Define corrections.
4. What federal legislation composes the framework for corrections?
5. Identify the unique characteristics of provincial/territorial correctional systems.
6. What role do private, nonprofit agencies play in the delivery of correctional services?
7. What is meant by the "plague of disinformation" and how does it affect corrections?
8. What attributes distinguish corrections from other components of the criminal justice system?
9. Identify and discuss three challenges in Canadian corrections.
10. Identify and discuss three trends in Canadian corrections.

REFERENCES

Arbour, The Honourable L. (Commissioner). 1996. *Commission of Inquiry into Certain Events at the Prison for Women in Kingston.* Ottawa: Public Works and Government Services Canada.

Breed, A.F. 1998. "Corrections: A Victim of Situational Ethics." *Crime and Delinquency* 44(1):9–18.

Fabelo, T. 2000. "'Technocorrections': The Promises, the Uncertain Threats." *Sentencing and Corrections: Issues for the 21st Century.* No. 5. Washington, D.C.: Office of Justice Programs, U.S. Department of Justice.

Ouimet, R. (Chairman). 1969. *Toward Unity: Criminal Justice and Corrections. Report of the Canadian Committee on Corrections*. Ottawa: Information Canada.

Roberts, J.V. 2001. *Fear of Crime and Attitudes to Criminal Justice in Canada: A Review of Recent Trends*. Ottawa: Solicitor General Canada.

Solicitor General of Canada. 2002. *Correctional Service of Canada. 2002–2003 Estimates. Part III—Report on Plans and Priorities*. Ottawa.

Standing Committee on Justice and Human Rights. 2000. *A Work in Progress: The Corrections and Conditional Release Act*. Ottawa: Public Works and Government Services Canada.

CHAPTER 2
THE EVOLUTION OF PUNISHMENT AND CORRECTIONS

CHAPTER OBJECTIVES

- *Discuss the process of correctional change.*
- *Consider the various perspectives on punishment and corrections.*
- *Document the shifts in the perceptions of crime and the response to criminal offenders over the past several centuries.*
- *Trace the emergence of punishment and corrections in Canada over the past 150 years.*
- *Examine the emergence of new models of correctional practice in the early 21st century.*

KEY TERMS

Conservative (correctional ideology)
Liberal (correctional ideology)
Radical (correctional ideology)
Classical school
Positivist school
Bloody Code
Transportation
Banishment

Hulks
Pillory
Stocks
Pennsylvania model
Auburn model
Moral architecture
Medical model of corrections

Traditionally, Canadians have studied the evolution of punishment and corrections by examining materials from other countries. It is often assumed that the emergence of systems of corrections in this country closely mirrored events in the United States and England. Although there were influences from these countries, Canada has a unique correctional history.

This chapter traces the emergence of punishment and corrections from the early days of settlement to the present, highlighting the legislation, events, and personalities that determined the response to criminal offenders and provided the foundation for contemporary corrections. The discussion will highlight a critical point: systems of corrections exist within, rather than apart from, the larger societal context. There is an interrelationship among social relations, politics, the economy, and religious beliefs that exist in society; the identification of persons and acts as criminal and deviant; the sanctions that are imposed on those persons convicted of criminal or deviant acts; and the objectives of the sanctions.

This historical review also reveals that the difficulties associated with incarcerating offenders in prison have been extensively documented and many reforms have been recommended, but it has proved more difficult for the federal and provincial/territorial governments to effectively address the identified problems. Indeed, many of the issues that confront corrections today first arose almost 200 years ago, indicating the challenges that confront those who seek to implement reforms in corrections.

THE PROCESS OF CORRECTIONAL CHANGE

Correctional change can be said to have occurred when one or more of the following occurs: (1) the severity of punishment of convicted offenders is modified, (2) explanations of criminal behaviour change, (3) new structural arrangements, such as the penitentiary, are created for punishing offenders, and (4) the number or proportion of offenders involved in the correctional process changes (Shover, 1979).

Why do such changes occur? And why were prisons invented in the 18th century? Scholars of penal history study correctional change from a number of perspectives. While some have focused on early reformers' humanitarian ideals, others have argued that prisons were designed primarily to control people who were perceived as threats to the emerging capitalist system of industrialized Europe. The prison, rather than a humane alternative to the death penalty and corporal punishment, was an instrument of isolation and punishment.

The different perspectives on correctional history are best illustrated by the various explanations that scholars have offered for why, during the 18th century, there was a gradual shift away from extensive use of the death penalty and corporal punishment, which were most often inflicted in public, toward confinement for the purposes of punishment and reformation. Was this change due to the philanthropy of well-intentioned people, or was it an attempt to exert even greater control over what was perceived as a rising criminal class that threatened the social order? Following are the views of several notable scholars:

- *David Rothman:* Rothman, author of *The Discovery of the Asylum* (1990), argues that the building of the first penitentiary in America in the late 1700s was due to a change in how crime was viewed. Originally, crime and other social problems were felt to be a natural part of society and not a threat to the social order, which was maintained by strong communities, religious faith, and the family. For a variety of reasons, crime and other forms of deviance came to be viewed as threats to the social order. In response, Americans built prisons, houses for the poor, and asylums for the mentally disordered, hoping that these institutions would cure social ills.
- *Michel Foucault:* Foucault, author of *Discipline and Punish: The Birth of the Prison* (1979), examined the use of imprisonment by the French monarchy. The prison, he argued, was designed to improve, rather than reduce, punishment by removing it from public view and shifting the focus of the punishment from the body of the offender to his mind. The prison was used as an instrument of punishment not only to maintain order, but also to strengthen the power of the monarchy.
- *Michael Ignatieff:* Ignatieff, author of *A Just Measure of Pain: The Penitentiary in the Industrial Revolution—1750–1850* (1978), focuses on the transformations caused by the Industrial Revolution in Europe and argues that prisons were built in an attempt to combat growing social disorder. Through isolation, punishment, and penitence, members of the lower classes would be reformed and become productive members of the new industrial society.

Notably, all of these observers ascribe the transformation in punishment, at least in part, to a desire to maintain social order, often at the expense of the lower classes of society. This motivation explains why the use of imprisonment continued to expand even though there was evidence, very early on, that it was ineffective in reducing criminal behaviour. There is evidence to suggest that during the 1700s the public became disenchanted with the spectacle of gruesome public punishments and supported the rise of what were purported to be humane alternatives, such as the prison. Although no single explanation fully accounts for the transformation that resulted in imprisonment becoming an integral part of the punishment process, the various perspectives do highlight the importance of considering the larger context within which systems of corrections develop and operate.

Cohen (1985) has identified four historical developments in the response to crime and deviance:

1. the increasing centralization of the response to crime and criminals and the concurrent development of bureaucratic institutions to carry out this task
2. the classification of criminals and deviants through the use of experts' "scientific knowledge"
3. the construction of prisons and asylums as places in which to reform criminals and deviants
4. the lessening of the severity of physical punishment and an increased focus on the mind of the criminal/deviant

A review of the history of systems of punishment and correction reveals the following trends:

- an increasing centralization and professionalization of punishment and correction, with formal agents of control assuming responsibility for the identification of, response to, and punishment of offenders
- the diminishing role of the community in the punishment and correction of offenders
- a concern with the effectiveness of the punishment response in protecting society and in reducing the likelihood that offenders will commit further offences

PERSPECTIVES ON PUNISHMENT AND CORRECTIONS

The discussion of the history of punishment and systems of corrections in this chapter will reveal that the explanation of crime and the response to criminal offenders have always been significantly influenced by social, political, religious, economic, and demographic factors in societies. What acts are defined as criminal, the explanations for criminal behaviour, the types of sanctions imposed on offenders, and the objectives of these sanctions are ever changing. There are many competing perspectives on crime and criminal offenders and on what the objectives of corrections should be. Generally, these correctional ideologies can be categorized as **conservative, liberal,** and **radical** (see Box 2.1).

The conservative and liberal perspectives are firmly grounded in the **classical school** and the **positivist school** (of criminological thought) respectively.

BOX 2.1

Correctional Ideologies

Issues	Conservative	Liberal	Radical
1. View of capitalism and the Canadian political system	• Principles fundamentally sound	• Principles need improvement; need greater economic and social equality	• Principles fundamentally unsound and exploitive; need to change to socialism
2. Reason for crime	• Social disorder—lack of discipline in society • Traditional institutions and values have broken down • Lenient criminal justice system—"crime pays"	• Poverty, racism, and other social injustices • Society is not meeting the human needs of people, and crime is a manifestation of this inadequacy in our system	• Capitalist exploitation: the rich exploit the poor and the poor prey on one another
3. Ways to stop crime	• Re-establish social order and discipline • Re-assert traditional values that made Canada great • Increase the costs of crime by stiffer punishments	• Make a better social order through reform • Establish social programs to meet the needs of the disadvantaged • Establish a more humane and just criminal justice system • Focus on rehabilitation of the offender	• Eliminate the capitalist system and establish a new social order

BOX 2.1, continued

Issues	Conservative	Liberal	Radical
4. Focus of corrections	• On the victim of crime and on innocent citizens • Offender commits crime through free will	• On the criminal—help the disadvantaged criminal and prevent future victimization of society • Crime is a result of adverse social conditions, although, increasingly, the attention is on the individual offender, who is easier to change than underlying social conditions	• On the inherent inhumanity of the system • Crime is a result of the way society is structured; any attempt to reduce crime must focus on the system rather than on individual offenders • Criminal justice system is used to repress lower classes
5. Source of crime problem	• Street crime	• Street and white-collar crime	• The crime of capitalism and the rich
6. Prime values	• Social order—"law and order"	• Protection of individual rights and humane treatment of the less advantaged—"doing justice" and "doing good"	• Total economic and social equality—"no classes and no exploitation"
7. Historical influences	• The classical and neo-classical schools of criminology • The notion of deterrence	• The positivist school of criminology	• The writings of Karl Marx

8. Strengths of the perspective	• Focuses on efforts to maintain social order as a determinant of correctional strategies • Emphasizes the role of free will in criminal behaviour	• Considers the role of environmental factors in crime • Attempts to treat and rehabilitate offenders by giving them skills to manage their lives	• Highlights the roles of economics and politics in the development and operation of justice systems • Considers the role of race and class in crime and administration of justice
9. Weaknesses of the perspective	• Fails to consider any external causes of crime • Ignores role of such societal conditions as poverty, race, and discrimination as contributors to criminal behaviour • Relies on reason alone to explain and respond to crime	• Fails to consider role of free will in crime • Ignores potential role of psychological and biological factors in crime	• Few empirical studies • Socialist agenda ignores broad public support for most laws • Gives little attention to victims

These three perspectives often overlap. People with a conservative view may support treatment programs for offenders, and adherents to all three perspectives generally support efforts to reduce unemployment as a way to prevent and reduce crime (Welch, 1996).

QUESTION:

1. After reviewing these three correctional ideologies, which is closest to your views of crime and justice?

Sources: Adapted from Cullen and Gilbert, 1981:41; Welch, 1996:82–118.

The following are the basic tenets of the classical school, as set out in the writings of Cesare Beccaria and Jeremy Bentham in the 1700s:

- The offender exercises free will and engages in criminal behaviour as a result of a rational choice; offenders are responsible for their crimes.
- Criminal behaviour is not influenced by external societal factors or deterministic forces internal to the offender.
- The primary goal of the criminal justice system should be deterrence, not revenge.
- Offenders, like all people, engage in a hedonistic calculus in which they attempt to maximize pleasure and minimize pain; therefore, the costs of crime must outweigh any benefits (i.e., crime must not pay).
- Punishment, to be effective, must be certain and must fit the crime.

The basic principles of the positivist school, as set out in the writings of Cesare Lombroso, Enrico Ferri, and Raffaelo Garafalo in the 1800s, include the following:

- Criminal behaviour is determined by biological, psychological, physiological, and/or sociological factors.
- The scientific method should be used to study criminal behaviour and identify criminal types.
- Criminal offenders are fundamentally different from others in society.
- Explanations for crime centre on the individual, rather than on society.
- Sanctions should focus on treatment and be individualized to the specific needs of the offender.

THE EVOLUTION OF PUNISHMENT: THE BRITISH LEGACY

How societies and groups have chosen to respond to those who violate norms, mores, and laws has varied over the centuries. Personal retaliation was the primary response prior to the creation of the state and the development of formal written laws. This practice was later augmented by the "blood feud," in which the victim's family or tribe avenged themselves on the family or tribe of the offender. During the period prior to the Middle Ages (before A.D. 500), the predominant philosophy underlying the response to criminal offenders was punishment. The death penalty was carried out by hanging, burying alive, stoning, boiling alive, crucifying, or drowning.

Corporal punishment was used, as well as exile and fines. The use of imprisonment as punishment for convicted persons was rare, confinement being employed primarily for those awaiting trial, execution, or corporal punishment or as a means to force payment of fines. In fact, correctional historians have noted that although severe punishments were used up until the beginning of the 17th century, it was economic sanctions, including fines, confiscation, and restitution, that were most commonly imposed (Newman, 1978). With all of these sanctions, the goal was retribution, and there was no attempt to rehabilitate the offender.

It is generally agreed that, with a few exceptions, imprisonment as a form of punishment was not used to any great extent until the 1500s in England and the early 1600s in Continental Europe. One exception was during the Inquisition, in the 1200s, when accused persons were often held for months or years. The first house of correction in England opened in a former royal palace in Bridewell, London, in 1557. This facility operated on the principle that subjecting offenders to hard labour was the best solution to the increasing population of criminals. Private businesspeople under contract with the local government operated the first Bridewell, as they became known, and soon Bridewells were opened throughout the country. The conditions in the houses of correction soon deteriorated and mirrored those of the local jails.

The 1700s marked the beginning of industrialization in England and the breakdown of the feudal, rural-centred society. Courts increasingly used the death penalty in an attempt to stem the rise of what the emerging middle class saw as the "dangerous classes." By 1780, under what had become known as the **Bloody Code,** legislation rendered over 350 offences punishable by death.

England disposed of a large number of offenders through **transportation,** a form of **banishment** that had been used as a sanction (often resulting in death) for centuries. Between 1579 and 1776, England sent as many as 2,000 offenders a year to her American colonies. These convicts were often used to clear and settle the land as indentured slaves. After the American War of Independence in 1776, over 135,000 felons were sent to Australia, until the practice was discontinued in 1875. Convicts were also confined in **hulks,** decommissioned sailing vessels that had been converted into floating prisons, anchored in rivers and harbours. At its peak, the hulk prison system comprised 11 ships holding over 3,000 prisoners.

The Age of Reason

During the 18th century, later known as the Age of Reason or the Enlightenment, a number of ideas emerged that would significantly influence Western society's perception of and response to criminal offenders. During this time, a transition occurred from corporal punishment to imprisonment as a frequently used form of punishment. This change was due in large measure to the writings of philosophers such as Montesquieu, Voltaire, Cesare

Beccaria, and Jeremy Bentham. Reacting to the arbitrary and corrupt systems of criminal justice in England and Europe at the time, the writings of these philosophers embodied a spirit of humanitarianism and a radically different view of human behaviour. Writers of the era saw crime as a choice, as an exercise of free will by a rational man. The person could be dissuaded from choosing to commit a crime by the spectre of a certain, swift, and measured consequence (Radzinowicz, 1966).

In his major work, *Essay on Crime and Punishment*, published in 1764, Beccaria argued that the gravity of the offence should be measured by the injury done to society and that certainty of punishment was the most effective deterrent against criminal behaviour. Punishments that were too severe served only to embitter offenders and perpetuate criminal conduct.

The writings of Jeremy Bentham, who is considered the leading reformer of English criminal law during the 18th century, also had a significant influence on the response to offenders. Bentham posited a *hedonistic calculus*, which held that the main objective of intelligent human beings was to achieve the most pleasure while receiving the least amount of pain. According to Bentham, sanctions should be applied to ensure that the pain resulting from the punishment would outweigh any pleasure derived from the commission of the offence, but punishment should be no greater than necessary to deter the potential offender. For Bentham, imprisonment was a more precise measure of punishment than corporal punishment: the more heinous the crime, the longer the period of confinement.

In retrospect, Beccaria, Bentham, and their contemporaries were somewhat successful in mitigating the severity of punishments imposed on offenders. The increasing use of imprisonment as punishment, however, created an entirely new set of difficulties and controversies, many of which continue today.

John Howard and Elizabeth Fry: Pioneers in Prison Reform

John Howard was a pioneer in efforts to reform the conditions of English prisons during the late 1700s. In his classic work, *The State of Prisons in England and Wales*, published in 1777, Howard proposed a number of reforms relating to the use of confinement, including providing single sleeping rooms for convicts, segregating women and young offenders from men, building facilities for bathing, and employing honest and well-trained prison administrators. Although well intentioned, some of Howard's proposals, such as placing offenders in solitary confinement to protect them from the corrupting influences of other convicts and to provide the proper solitude for moral reflection, contributed to the deprivations convicts experienced. John Howard's humanitarian ideals live on in Canada through the work of the John Howard Society.

Elizabeth Fry was one of the first volunteers to work with female convicts in early 19th-century England, and she gave particular attention to convict mothers. For nearly two decades, she read scriptures and conducted prison ministries. The work of the Elizabeth Fry Society in Canada reflects her legacy.

CRIME AND PUNISHMENT IN EARLY CANADA (1600s–1800s)

The historical record provides key insights into the ways by which offenders were punished in early Canada (see Appendix A for a chronology of important events in Canadian corrections). The punishment of criminal behaviour in early Canada was patterned on the systems of England and France. The sanctions imposed on convicted offenders were harsh, particularly when compared with today's standards. The death penalty was applied to offenders convicted of murder, grand larceny, sodomy, and rape, and a variety of sanctions were available for less serious offences, including branding, transportation, banishment, fines, and whipping.

Reflecting the English system, punishment was progressive: "Murderers were hung while thieves were branded with the letter 'T' on first conviction and hung for a second offence. The lash and stocks served as punishment for less serious crimes" (Coles, 1979:1). In general, sanctions were designed to deter both the individual offender and the general public.

Public Punishments

Public shaming and humiliation were the cornerstones of many of the corporal punishments that were employed. The **pillory** was used in Lower Canada until 1842. This was a solid wooden frame with holes through which the head and hands of the offender were placed. When it was closed, the openings fit around the neck and wrists, holding the offender secure. The pillory was mounted on a pivot so that the person being punished could be made to face in any direction. In Upper Canada, offenders were often put into **stocks,** wooden structures with holes for arms and legs in which offenders were seated. This practice continued until 1872. Both of these structures allowed for public punishments, and often citizens in the community showered the offenders with eggs and other refuse.

Illustrative of the types of sanctions imposed on offenders during the early 1700s is the sentence imposed on Robert Nichols in the community of

The stocks

Annapolis, in what is now the province of Nova Scotia. Nichols had been convicted of assaulting his master. In the words of the presiding judge:

> *The punishment therefore inflicted on thee is to sit upon a gallows three days, half an hour each day, with a rope about thy neck and a paper upon your breast whereon shall be writ in capital letters AUDACIOUS VILLAIN and afterwards thou art to be whipped at a carts tail from the prison house up to the uppermost house of the cape and from thence back again to the prison receiving each hundred paces five stripes upon your bare back with a cat of nine tails. (cited in Coles, 1979:1)*

In Halifax in the mid-1750s, men were hanged for petty crimes. A woman who had stolen two saucepans, a copper pot, a quart and a pint pewter pot, and two brass candlesticks, with a total value of five shillings, was spared hanging only by intervention of local clergy. As punishment, she was branded in the hand with the letter "T" and sent to jail for two months (Raddall,

1988:41). Also in Nova Scotia, an offender convicted of counterfeiting was placed in the pillory for one hour, with one of his ears nailed to the pillory, and then whipped in public. Both men and women were branded, a sanction carried out in open court by the jailer (Baehre, 1990:165). As late as the 1830s in Nova Scotia, nearly 100 offences were punishable by death.

In New France, prior to the adoption of the English system, punishment was often inflicted on the offender at the location where he or she had committed the offence. In 1692, for example, a Montreal judge condemned an offender to have his right hand cut off and his limbs broken before being placed on the rack to die—all of this to be carried out in front of the house of the merchant he had killed (Morel, 1963).

The historical record from Lower Canada reveals that men and women appear to have been treated equally in being sentenced to capital punishment and less severe sanctions such as public humiliation. However, in cases between the two extremes, there was differential treatment. For example, whereas men were banished or sent to the galleys, women received terms of confinement in the Hôpital Général (Morel, 1975).

Banishment

In the early 1800s, justice officials began to banish convicted persons, the offender being ordered "to depart the province at his or her own expense and peril." In Newfoundland, offenders were placed on boats and set adrift, ultimately landing (much to the consternation of those living downwind) in New York State or Prince Edward Island. This practice continued until the early 1900s. Dissatisfaction with banishment as a sanction was one of the factors that precipitated the building of the first penitentiary in the 1830s. In 1831, the Select Committee on the Expediency of Erecting a Penitentiary wrote, "It is no punishment to a rogue to order him to live on the right bank of the Niagara River instead of the left and it is cruelly unjust to our neighbours to send among them thieves, robbers, and burglars" (cited in Beattie, 1977:82). Banishment appears to have fallen out of favour largely owing to the diminishing number of places to send offenders as settlements spread and the population grew.

Transportation

Laws in both Upper and Lower Canada contained provisions for transporting convicts. In Upper Canada, the legal basis for sentences of transportation was provided for in the Act of Legislation of Upper Canada, passed in 1838. This Act authorized judges to grant conditional pardons, even to persons who had been sentenced to death, "upon condition that they be respectively trans-ported as convicts to her Majesty's Colony of Van Diemen's Land" (present-day Tasmania). The length of the banishment could range from seven years to life. Some convicts from Canada were transported to England and confined in hulks, but the majority were sent to Australia and Tasmania, with a smaller number being sent to Bermuda. For example, the men convicted in the rebellions of 1837 and 1838 were transported to Australia (Boissey, 1996).

Transportation as a sanction officially ended in 1853, but it was seriously reconsidered in 1871 when the colonial government attempted to persuade England to establish a penal colony in Hudson Bay Territory to which convicts could be transported (Edmison, 1976).

Workhouses

Although the use of incarceration for punishment was not widespread, there were several attempts during the 1700s to confine persons convicted of certain illegal activities. In 1754, the first workhouse was constructed in Nova Scotia. This facility held a wide variety of individuals in addition to criminal offenders, including vagrants, beggars, prostitutes, fortunetellers, runaways, gamblers, drunks, and orphans (Coles, 1979:1). This workhouse was patterned on the Bridewells that had been constructed in England in the late 1500s to provide employment and shelter for London's riffraff while instilling in them the ethic of hard work.

By 1818, imprisonment in workhouses had become the primary mode of punishment in Nova Scotia. Its use, however, was not without controversy. In 1818, a new workhouse was completed in Halifax, and the prisoners were employed cutting granite and laying roadbed. This employment in prisons pre-cipitated debate (which continues today) as to whether convict labour unfairly competed with outside, or "free," labour. Workhouse authorities had no desire to have convict labour compete with free labour, but neither did they want the con-victs to remain idle. The solution? A proposal to build a human treadmill, or "stepping mill," an "'unproductive dispiriting device upon which prisoners would walk thereby moving sand back and forth or 'grinding the wind'" (Coles, 1979:2). A bill to create stepping mills was introduced in the legislature but defeated by one vote. As discussed below, the conflict between prison labour and free labour would resurface years later at the newly constructed penitentiary in Kingston.

The Local Jails

During the 1700s, with the exception of the workhouses that were built in some areas, there was no use of confinement for the purposes of punishment.

Rather, jails (or local lockups) held people who were either awaiting trial or who had been found guilty at trial and were yet to be punished. Toward the end of the 1700s, however, jails were constructed in Upper and Lower Canada. In 1792, the first Parliament of Upper Canada passed an Act providing for the construction of a courthouse and a jail in each district in the region, and it passed additional legislation in 1810 that established jails as houses of correction in which were to be confined "all and every idle and disorderly person, and rogues and vagabonds, and incorrigible rogues" (Strong, 1969:24). Similar legislation was passed in Lower Canada in 1799.

Records from Upper Canada reveal that, in 1828, the majority of admissions to provincial jails were for debt, although in the following years the percentage of debtors in jail populations declined, their numbers being replaced by persons convicted of more serious crimes (Talbot, 1983:153). Interestingly, there was little use of imprisonment for debt in Lower Canada (Kolish, 1987).

In 1838, the Gaol Construction Act passed in Upper Canada. This legislation created a Board of Gaol Commissioners whose primary function was to oversee the construction of new jails and to improve the conditions for prisoners. For a large percentage of the prisoners, their only crime was poverty. As Talbot has noted, "Complaints about the conditions of district jails began almost as soon as a new jail opened" (1983:283). Upper Canadians, however, appear to have been largely unconcerned about the poor conditions in which many convicts were confined.

CORRECTIONS ON THE FRONTIER

If communities in the more populated areas were slow to develop local jails and other alternatives for punishing convicted people, this was even more evident in the vast land areas in the western portion of the country once known as Rupert's Land. Authorities and settlers in the Prairie regions attempted to replicate the systems of punishment found in Upper and Lower Canada and in England. Until the early 1800s, people charged with more serious offences were sent to England for trial. When this system became too costly, the government in England passed legislation that provided that cases arising from Rupert's Land were to be heard in the courts of Upper or Lower Canada and that any sentences imposed were to be served there.

One of the more unusual aspects of the administration of justice on the early frontier was the role played by the Hudson's Bay Company (HBC). In 1670, the English monarchy gave the HBC exclusive control over a tract of land that covered most of the western region of the country, along with the authority to enact laws and other regulations to control its thousands of employees. The company operated courts until the federal government purchased Rupert's Land in 1869, and, as late as 1861, the presiding judicial officer of the HBC served as sheriff, jailer, chief medical officer, and coroner (Smandych and Linden, 1996).

THE CREATION OF THE CANADIAN PENITENTIARY

The period between 1830 and Confederation in 1867 is one of the most important eras in Canadian corrections. The major development during this time was the building of the first Canadian penitentiary in Kingston, Ontario, in 1835. Equally important was the reformatory movement and the spread of middle-range reformatories. A hierarchy of institutions developed, with the penitentiary at the top. During this relatively short period, several key events and personalities were to shape the course of correctional history. For a variety of reasons, the laissez-faire attitude toward building jails and addressing the sordid conditions of the existing local jails changed. So, too, did the attitudes of communities, particularly in terms of their views on crime and criminals.

Examining the circumstances that led to the building of the penitentiary in Kingston provides insight into the factors that influence systems of punishment and corrections. At the outset, it is important to note that scholars disagree about the specific influences that resulted in the decision to build the penitentiary. Among the more likely reasons for the decision were influences from the United States and changes that occurred in the economic structure of Upper Canada, as well as in how communities viewed crime and criminality. It is important to keep in mind that, historically (as in contemporary times), the majority of people who were convicted of crimes were not sent to local jails or prisons.

The Penitentiary in America

One development that influenced the building of the first Canadian penitentiary was the decision by authorities in several U.S. states during the late 1700s to make more use of imprisonment as punishment. Although England and a number of other European countries had already developed workhouses and houses of correction by the late 1700s, it was in the United States that the widespread use of imprisonment as a form of punishment emerged in its modern form.

During the period 1790–1830, profound shifts occurred in the perceptions of crime and the explanations for criminal behaviour. This was a consequence of the influence of philosophical thought of the time as well as demographic, social, and economic changes in colonial society. Crime came to be viewed as a consequence of community disorder and family instability, rather than as the manifestation of individual afflictions.

Americans sought to create a setting in which the criminal could be transformed into a useful citizen. The setting was to be the penitentiary, so named because inmates could reflect on the error of their ways through religious contemplation and hard work. In 1790, amidst unbridled optimism, the Walnut Street Jail opened in Philadelphia, Pennsylvania. It was followed by the spread of penitentiaries across the eastern United States, which operated on either the **Pennsylvania model** or the **Auburn model.** The Pennsylvania system was a "separate and silent" system, in which prisoners were completely isolated from one another and even kept out of eyesight of one another. Inmates ate, worked, and slept in separate cells. The Auburn system, first applied in a penitentiary in Auburn, New York, allowed prisoners to work and eat together during the day and provided housing in individual cells at night. A system of strict silence, which forbade prisoners from communicating or even gesturing to one another, was enforced at all times. The Pennsylvania system became the model for prisons in Europe, South America, and Asia, whereas the Auburn system was the model upon which most prisons in the United States and Canada were patterned.

Changes in Upper Canadian Society

Some historians contend that an increase in the rates of crime in the 1830s, coupled with overcrowding in the local jails, precipitated the construction of the penitentiary (Bellomo, 1972). Others have argued that serious crime was not an issue and that the primary influence was a changing of Canadians' attitudes toward criminal behaviour. From this perspective, criminality came to be viewed as symptomatic of much deeper social evils that threatened the moral and social fabric of Upper Canadian society; recently arrived immigrants, in particular, were seen as a threat because their values and work ethics were considered suspect (Beattie, 1977:2–3).

Canadian criminologist Russell Smandych (1991) has made an important contribution to the discussion of the events surrounding the building of the Kingston prison. Smandych focuses on the Upper Canadian Tory government of the time and its "paternalistic sensibilities," a key factor in the movement for penal reform. From this perspective, it was the Tory governing elite that was the driving force behind reforms in the penal system. The initiative to build the penitentiary was part of the government's much larger effort to bring about a "'moral uplifting' of the population through education and religious instruction," the prison being "another control mechanism that could be employed to maintain a 'well-ordered' society" (Smandych, 1991:137).

KINGSTON PENITENTIARY

J.C. Thomson, editor of the *Upper Canadian Herald* in Kingston, Ontario, first presented a proposal to construct a penitentiary to the 1826–27 House of Assembly of Upper Canada. In 1831, Thomson was appointed to chair a select committee that was to investigate the potential for building the prison, and in February of that year, he visited Bridewell Prison in Glasgow, Scotland. He later travelled to Auburn, New York, to view the state prison that had been constructed there using the new ideas about penitentiary punishment. Thomson then prepared a report severely criticizing the existing penal system in Canada and set out a number of reasons that a penitentiary should be constructed. These reasons included (1) the levying of fines was unjust owing to the different ability of convicted offenders to pay; (2) capital punishment was rarely being used to punish offenders; (3) confinement in the local jails was no longer a practical alternative because of overcrowding and the lack of proper classification of offenders; (4) corporal punishment was improper and degrading; and (5) banishment as a sanction was no longer practical or effective (Baehre, 1977).

Goals of the Penitentiary

Thomson's recommendations were accepted by the House of Assembly and formally embodied in the Penitentiary Act of 1834. The House of Assembly emphasized the use of the penitentiary both as a general deterrent and as a mechanism for reforming criminals through hard labour. The penitentiary would provide a setting for the moral re-education of convicts. It made religion a focal point of the punishment/reformation process, providing an important role for chaplains, the first noncustodial personnel to work inside on a regular basis. This was the beginning of the involvement of the chaplaincy in penitentiaries (James, 1990).

Upon completion in 1835, the new penitentiary was the largest public building in Upper Canada. It symbolized a **moral architecture,** which reflected the themes of order and morality: "The penitentiary was an ideal society ... much more than a system of dealing with transgression of the law, it became a projection of the world as it should be" (Taylor, 1979:407). Kingston Penitentiary was to be a model for those confined in it, as well as for society, removing what was widely perceived to be the underlying causes of crime: intemperance, laziness, and a lack of moral values.

The Early Years of Kingston Penitentiary

In design, the new penitentiary differed considerably from the district jails. The prison separated offenders by gender and type of offence and allowed the prisoners to have their own bedding, clothing, and food. Design, however, did not translate into practice, and the conditions in which prisoners were kept soon deteriorated:

> *Inmates were kept in absolute seclusion from society and were detained in a state of complete inactivity during the non-working hours. The resultant effect was physical atrophy and mental stagnation. Rules of strict silence prevailed. Prisoners were mixed together young with old, sane with insane. As cells were too small to allow for free movement, inmates were forced to lie down for twelve to sixteen hours a day. (cited in MacGuigan, 1977:11)*

A central feature of life inside Kingston Penitentiary was the silent system. This system presented challenges to the inmates, the guards, and the administration. Prison regulations required convicts to:

- yield perfect obedience and submission to the keepers
- labour diligently and preserve unbroken silence
- not exchange a word or otherwise communicate with one another
- not exchange looks, winks, laugh, nod, gesticulate to each other
- not sing, dance, whistle, run, jump
- not carelessly or willfully injure their work tools, wearing apparel, bedding or any other thing belonging to or about the prison (cited in Talbot, 1983:295)

Male inmates who violated prison regulations were generally whipped, whereas female convicts were placed in solitary confinement. The same punishments were applied to children, some as young as eight years old. Strict silence was maintained at all times, the inmates walked in lockstep, and the constant ringing of bells controlled the convict's day. Convict life was centred on hard work, much of it performed in a stone quarry outside the institution. Breaches of prison regulations brought swift and harsh punishment, including flogging, leg irons, solitary confinement, and rations of bread and water (see Box 2.2). For a fascinating account of life in Kingston Penitentiary and in the community surrounding it, see Simonds (1996).

Labour groups in the Kingston area raised concerns that teaching trades to inmates in the penitentiary would threaten tradespeople's economic well-being. Having failed to halt construction of the prison, the tradespeople filed a petition with the Upper Canada Parliament in 1836 that called for convict labour to be restricted to "breaking stones, pumping water, and working at efforts that would not injure the interests of tradesmen" (Palmer, 1980:16).

By 1840, only five years after its completion, there was growing concern over whether the prison was effectively punishing and reforming offenders

BOX 2.2

Entries from *The Punishment Book of the Prison* (1843)

Offence	Punishment
Laughing and talking	6 lashes; cat-o'-nine-tails
Talking in wash-house	6 lashes; rawhide
Threatening to knock convicts' brains out	24 lashes; cat-o'-nine-tails
Talking to Keepers on matters not relating to their work	6 lashes; cat-o'-nine-tails
Finding fault with rations when desired by guard to sit down	6 lashes; rawhide, and bread and water
Staring about and inattentive at breakfast table	bread and water
Leaving work and going to privy when other convict there	36 hours in dark cell, and bread and water

Source: Shoom, 1966:216. Copyright © 1966 Canadian Criminal Justice Association. Reprinted by permission.

and over the extensive use of corporal punishment inside the facility. Critics pointed to the high rate of recidivism among offenders released from the prison. Oblivious to these difficulties, the English novelist Charles Dickens wrote of his visit to Kingston in 1842: "There is an admirable jail here, well and wisely governed, and excellently regulated, in every respect" (cited in Edmison, 1965:255). Dickens's visit occurred just a month after a 12-year-old girl named Eliza Breen had received six lashes (the sixth occasion on which records indicate she had been whipped).

The Brown Commission: 1848–1849

Public concern with the treatment of prisoners in Kingston Penitentiary culminated in the appointment of a Royal Commission of Inquiry in 1848, chaired by George Brown, editor of the Toronto *Globe* newspaper. The mandate of the commission was to investigate charges of corruption in the institution, specifically charges of mismanagement, theft, and mistreatment of the convicts. In its investigation, the commission found that the warden, Henry Smith, had indeed mismanaged the institution and that there was excessive use

Kingston Penitentiary

of corporal punishment, including the flogging of men, women, and children, some as young as 11 years old.

The Brown commission issued two reports. The first condemned the extensive use of corporal punishment and recommended the removal of Warden Smith for failing to fulfill the objectives of the institution to impose order and discipline and to reform the inmates. The second report, released in 1849, attempted to set future directions. The primary purpose of the penitentiary, the commissioners stated, was the prevention of crime and the rehabilitation of offenders, using the least amount of force necessary. In addition, elements of the Pennsylvania system were to be incorporated in the prison regimen. New inmates would be kept in solitary confinement for a period of six months. This would ensure the submission of new inmates by isolating them for a period while retaining the congregate system that would instill work habits and provide economic benefits for the institution (Beattie, 1977:31–32).

Although the work of the Brown commission was the first systematic inquiry into the operation of Kingston Penitentiary, the impact of its reports on prison reform is unclear. Many of the commission's recommendations were embodied in the Penitentiary Act of 1851, which provided for the construction of cells for solitary confinement of new inmates, established specific guidelines for the use of corporal punishment in the institution, and reduced the practice of allowing citizens to buy admittance to the facility to view the prisoners. This legislation also provided that mentally ill offenders be removed to the Lunatic Asylum of Upper Canada and appointed two inspectors who would oversee the operation of this facility. The Prison Inspection Act, which was passed in 1857, provided for the construction of a separate facility for insane convicts and the building of a reformatory for young offenders, as well as for a system of inspection for the penitentiary, the asylums, and the district jails.

In spite of these changes, corporal punishment, the silent system, and hard labour remained key features of prison life. In retrospect, the Brown commission can perhaps best be viewed as a missed opportunity for Canadians to reconsider the use of imprisonment and to explore other potentially more effective ways to prevent crime and reform offenders.

DEVELOPING SYSTEMS OF CORRECTIONS: 1850 TO THE EARLY 1900s

In 1867, there were prisons located in Kingston, Ontario; in Saint John, New Brunswick; and in Halifax, Nova Scotia. The prisons were at the top of the hierarchy of penal facilities that included small lockups and jails. At Confederation, in 1867, all three institutions came under the authority of the new Parliament of Canada. At this point, the two-year rule came into effect. Under the Penitentiary Act of 1868, the structure of the federal penitentiary system was created, including the Department of Justice, which was to oversee the administration of all justice matters not within the purview of the provinces. During the 1870s, a major expansion of the federal penitentiary system occurred, with prisons being constructed in Montreal, Quebec (1873), Stony Mountain, Manitoba (1876), and New Westminster, British Columbia (1878), as the Canadian Confederation expanded (Zubrycki, 1980). In 1880, a new penitentiary was opened in Dorchester, New Brunswick, and the prisons in Saint John and Halifax were closed.

All the new penitentiaries were patterned on the Auburn model (although there were elements of the Pennsylvania system): "Rows of lightless, airless cubicles were arranged back-to-back in tiers connected by steel walkways overlooking a central rotunda ... the workshop, the chapel and the prison yard were the only common areas. Inmates ate their meals from trays in their cells" (Blanchfield, 1985a:7). Life inside these prisons centred on discipline and hard labour. The bell was the symbol of discipline and controlled the convict's day (the daily schedule of the Manitoba Penitentiary in

Interior of an early prison

1879 is presented in Box 2.3). The food in the penitentiaries left much to be desired. The "coarse diet" was considered part of the punishment for convicts. Kitchen keepers often bought the cheapest foods available. The typical coarse diet for convicts confined during the 1880s is presented in Box 2.4.

The conditions for the guards in these early penitentiaries were often only marginally better than those of the convicts. The guards were required to follow a strict regimen and were not permitted to exercise personal judgment. Salaries were low ($500 per year for guards at Kingston Penitentiary in the 1890s), and job security and pensions were nonexistent. In an attempt to address the deficiencies of the guards, the 1888 Penitentiary Regulations included the provision that "no person shall be employed as an officer of the prison who is not able to read and write with facility, or who cannot readily apply the rules of arithmetic" (cited in Dixon, 1947:3).

BOX 2.3

Symbol of Discipline: The Bell

5:50 a.m. Bell. Prisoners rise, wash, dress, make beds.

6:00 a.m. Officers parade. Keys issued, slops collected. Cells, walls, halls and passages swept. Lamps collected and cleaned. Prisoners unlocked and escorted to work. Names of the sick taken. Night tubs [chamber pots] cleaned and placed outside the prison. Fuel distributed and ashes emptied. Random search of cells. Water pumped into tank.

7:30 a.m. Bell. Prisoners marched to dining halls in groups of three.

7:40 a.m. Bell. Breakfast over. Prisoners marched back to their cells and locked in. Guards have breakfast.

8:30 a.m. Bell. Officers parade. Outside gangs unlocked and escorted outside. Inside workers escorted to their jobs. Surgeon attends the sick.

10:00 a.m. Office hours. Convicts on report are taken to the warden.

12:15 p.m. Bell. Prisoners marched back to their cells and locked up.

12:20 p.m. Bell. Prisoners unlocked and marched to the dining room for lunch.

12:45 p.m. Bell. Prisoners marched back to cells and locked up. Officers have lunch.

12:50 p.m. Eligible prisoners unlocked for school.

1:30 p.m. Bell. Officers parade. Prisoners unlocked and marched off to work. Random search of cells.

5:40 p.m. Night tubs brought back into the prison.

5:50 p.m. Bell. Prisoners marched to cells and locked up. Supper delivered to each cell. Convicts with special requests may use "signal sticks" to summon guards.

6:00 p.m. Bell. Prisoners' clothing collected and placed outside cell door. All cells searched. Prisoners begin their meals. Guards on night shift take over. Keys collected. Chief keeper reads out daily orders.

7:00 p.m. Patrol guards supply water to convicts who signal for it. Kitchen and dining hall locked up.

9:00 p.m. Lights in cells turned down.

10:00 p.m. Lights in passages turned down. Dampers of heating stoves closed. Lights out in officers' room.

(The bell, which was centrally located in the prison, was so hated by the inmates that it was destroyed during the 1971 riot at Kingston.)

Source: Blanchfield, 1985b:5.

BOX 2.4

A Typical Daily Menu for Penitentiary Inmates in the 1880s

Breakfast	1 pint	pease coffee (sweetened with 1/2 oz. brown sugar)
	1/2 lb.	brown bread
	1/2 lb.	white bread or 1/2 lb. potatoes
	1/4 lb.	beef or pork (with beets and vinegar twice a week)
Dinner	1-1/2 pint	soup
	1/2 lb.	white bread or 3/4 lb. potatoes
	1/2 lb.	brown bread
	1/2 lb.	beef, mutton, or pork
Supper	10 oz.	white or brown bread
	1 pint	coffee (with 1/2 oz. brown sugar)

The food allowance for female inmates was generally smaller due to their lighter workload.

Source: Blanchfield 1985c:5.

Local Jails and Provincial Prisons

Meanwhile, conditions in the local jails and provincial institutions continued to deteriorate. The attempt by the province of Nova Scotia to create a system of workhouses at the local level had failed. In 1834, a grand jury report called the facilities unfit for human beings. To keep costs down, prisoners were required to pay for their meals, liquor, and rent and, upon release, the jailer's fee for his services. Those inmates unable to pay the fee were often confined for additional periods or allowed to panhandle in the streets to raise the necessary funds (Coles, 1979:8). A review of historical records indicates that many of the prisoners in Halifax's local jails during the late 1800s were recidivists; from 1864 to 1873, 5 percent of the offenders were responsible for 32 percent of the committals (Fingard, 1984:84). Many of these persons were destitute and when not in jail were in the poorhouse.

The majority of female offenders confined in the jails had been sentenced for morals offences rather than for more serious crimes against person and property. These offences included prostitution, vagrancy, and larceny. On the whole, these women were young and from the powerless segment of society (Price, 1990). For a detailed examination of Canadian women and punishment during the years 1754–1953, see Greenwood and Boissery (2000).

In 1844, a new provincial penitentiary was opened in Nova Scotia, to which the majority of convicted offenders were sent. However, as the following description reveals, conditions in this institution soon deteriorated as well:

> *Within five years, prison life had tumbled to the lowest common denominator. Singing, whistling, smoking, cursing, drunkenness, and sloth became the order of the day. Gaol keepers fraternized with the prisoners and often came to work drunk and disorderly. The Prison's Governor, Thomas Carpenter, spent weeks at a time drunk in his quarters, and in 1849, in a rum-soaked stupor, Carpenter actually aided prisoners in an escape. (Coles, 1979:3–4)*

Similar problems also existed at the local level in Ontario. In 1890, the province of Ontario established a commission of inquiry under the direction of J.W. Langmuir to examine the operation of houses of correction and asylums. In his investigation, Langmuir found that municipalities failed to provide sufficient funds for the operation of the facilities, proper classification of inmates was either nonexistent or inadequate, and half of the admissions were for vagrancy and drunkenness. The majority of offenders were poor and destitute. In Toronto, for example, nearly 60 percent of the population of the Central Prison during the period 1874–1900 were noted as being either "unskilled" or "semi-skilled" (Oliver, 1998). In the west, conditions in the jails were much the same.

The Penitentiary Act of 1886 provided for the appointment of federal prison inspectors and outlined their powers and duties; addressed the need for the separate confinement of female offenders, mentally disordered inmates, and young offenders; and provided for the use of solitary confinement in federal penitentiaries. The Act Respecting Public and Reformatory Prisons (1886) included the following provisions for the operation of provincial correctional facilities:

- the mandatory separation of youthful and older offenders
- procedures for agreements to transfer offenders from federal to provincial institutions
- powers for provincial legislatures to establish regulations for the custody, treatment, discipline, training, and employment of prisoners
- authority for the provinces to establish prisons and to identify facilities to which offenders were sent
- the earning of remission, or "good time," by offenders confined in provincial institutions
- the creation of temporary leaves of absence from provincial institutions for medical, humanitarian, or rehabilitative purposes

This legislation established much of the framework within which contemporary Canadian corrections operates and was the forerunner of the Prisons and Reformatories Act.

The Huron Jail in Goderich, Ontario, served as the county jail from its opening in 1842 until 1972.

THE EARLY 1900s

In 1906, a new Penitentiary Act was passed. This legislation repealed all previous federal legislation relating to the penitentiaries and included:

- provisions for the administration of the federal penitentiary system
- the conditions under which prison inmates could earn remission ("good time")
- the powers and duties of the federal penitentiary inspectors
- the removal of youthful inmates and the mentally disordered from general penitentiary populations

Despite this legislation, there was little change in the philosophy of corrections or in how prisons were operated. In many institutions, the quality of administration and staff was poor. Punitive practices documented by the Brown commission nearly half a century earlier continued. Inmates were subjected to a variety of disciplinary sanctions, many of which continued in use until the 1930s. These punishments included being hosed by a powerful stream of cold water; wearing a ball and chain during work; being handcuffed to bars for hours at a time; and, as a "cure" for offenders with mental disorders, being immersed in a trough of ice and slush (MacGuigan, 1977:12).

The structure and operation of institutions at the provincial and local levels changed little during the first decades of the 20th century. Although the provinces passed legislation providing for the administration of the jails under their jurisdiction, they made no major reforms, and the primary objectives of imprisonment remained deterrence and retribution.

THE BEGINNINGS OF MODERN REFORM: 1930–1970

During the 1930s, there were some initial signs, particularly at the federal level, that the harsh regimen of the penitentiary was changing, albeit slowly. Prisoners displaying good conduct were given lighting in their cells in order to read, were permitted to write one letter every three months to their families, and were allowed half-hour visits by relatives once a month (MacGuigan, 1977:12). A major change was the modification of the strict rule of silence. Under the new regulations, prisoners were permitted to converse prior to work in the morning, during lunch breaks, and until 7:00 p.m. Inmates also began to be paid for work performed in the institution, at a rate of five cents per day. Federal penitentiaries also attempted to improve their medical facilities.

Contributing to the shift in penal philosophy was the report of the Royal Commission on the Penal System of Canada (Archambault, 1938), which concluded that the goal of prisons should be not only to protect society by incarcerating offenders, but also to reform and rehabilitate offenders. More specifically, the report recommended that there be improvements in vocational training and education programs, as well as in the classification of offenders. The Archambault report also found the quality of medical services for inmates lacking, particularly in many of the penitentiaries in the eastern regions of the country.

This increasing focus on the treatment of offenders was to provide the basis for the postwar era in Canadian corrections, which witnessed the development and expansion of vocational and education training programs, the introduction of various treatment modalities, and the creation of community correctional programs.

POST–WORLD WAR II CORRECTIONS: THE MOVE TOWARD TREATMENT

Following World War II, there was a shift toward a treatment model of corrections. The federal prison system introduced vocational training, education, and therapeutic intervention techniques, such as group counselling and individual therapy. Concurrent with these developments was an increase in the numbers of psychologists and psychiatrists on prison staffs. In 1948, Kingston Penitentiary opened the first prison psychiatric hospital and applied electroshock therapy. The philosophy of corrections at this time is best illustrated by comments in the *Annual Report of the Commissioner of Penitentiaries, 1957*:

> *The asocial and antisocial type of individuals who are sentenced by the courts to the penal system have failed through unfortunate circumstances and the vicissitudes of their past life to develop mentally as the average person does.... Reformation, which is the ultimate aim of incarceration, stands to succeed best when the deficiencies and needs of the inmate are known. (1958:47)*

The emerging rehabilitation model of corrections received additional support from the findings of a committee of inquiry (Fauteux, 1956), which argued that the basic principles of Canadian corrections should include:

- a high degree of integration among all parts of the correctional system
- a well-developed and extensive system of adult probation
- a concentration of effort on treatment by way of training, rather than the mere imposition of punishment
- specialization of institutions and methods of treatment
- the development of small, open, minimum-security institutions
- a planned policy of recruitment and training of professional staff

This and other reports highlighted the shift toward rehabilitation under what became known as the **medical model of corrections.** In brief, the medical model held that the offender was ill, physically, mentally, and/or socially. Criminal behaviour was a symptom of illness. As in medicine, diagnosis and treatment would ensure the effective rehabilitation of the offender. Concurrent with this development were the increasing involvement of psychologists and psychiatrists in institutional programs and the development of specialized institutions to meet the needs of offenders.

The decade of the 1960s was the height of the treatment model in Canadian corrections. A number of new medium- and minimum-security facilities were constructed across the country, all of which were designed to hold small populations of offenders. Prisons expanded visiting privileges, as well as education and training opportunities, and included prison physicians as part of the treatment team in an attempt to address the offender's criminal behaviour. This involvement extended to conducting medical experiments on offenders. Throughout the 1960s and 1970s, prison inmates were used as subjects in a variety of experiments that drug companies, federal government agencies, and universities conducted. Psychiatrists also assumed an increasing role in institutional treatment programs, and their techniques included electroshock and drug therapies, which for many years could be administered without an inmate's consent.

The medical studies included trials of new pharmaceuticals, research on sensory deprivation, and pain studies, which used electric shocks. In one set of experiments, doctors gave female inmates at the Kingston Prison for Women the hallucinogenic drug LSD as part of a psychology experiment. Included in the subject sample was a 17-year-old woman who was in solitary confinement at the time. Although the sponsors of the research experiments noted that the inmates had volunteered to participate in the experiments, critics argue that the practice raises serious ethical questions, including whether captive persons can give informed consent.

Provincial correctional systems also moved to adopt the medical model, and terms such as *scientific treatment* began to appear in provincial correctional Acts. A wide range of interventions, including plastic surgery (designed to correct disabilities that may have contributed to criminality), aversion therapy, group therapy, behaviour modification, and electroshock therapy and other psychological treatments were utilized beginning in the early 1950s. Behavioural science professionals became increasingly involved in correctional programming. By the late 1960s, however, critics were raising concerns about the effectiveness of rehabilitation programs in reducing or eliminating criminal behaviour and were calling for a return to a punishment model.

The Shift in Correctional Policy

In 1969, the Canadian Committee on Corrections addressed the problems that were being encountered in attempting to rehabilitate offenders inside correctional institutions and suggested that treatment might more effectively be pursued within a community setting (Ouimet, 1969). This report provided the basis for the expansion of community-based correctional facilities and programs operated by federal and provincial agencies, as well as by private, non-profit organizations such as the John Howard Society, the Elizabeth Fry Society, and the St. Leonard's Society. In 1975, a report by the Law Reform Commission argued that prisons should not be used for rehabilitation, and a number of other federal reports and task forces made the same recommendation during the late 1970s. Interestingly, although many of these reports documented the difficulties of implementing treatment in institutional settings, they gave little or no consideration to modifying the environments of correctional institutions to create environments more amenable to rehabilitation.

The 1970s was a decade of unrest and violence in the federal penitentiaries. In 1975–76 alone, there were 65 major incidents, including strikes, riots, murders, and hostage-takings. This unrest precipitated the appointment of the Sub-Committee on the Penitentiary System in Canada, chaired by Mark MacGuigan. The final report of the sub-committee contained 65 recommendations for improving life inside correctional institutions for both the correctional officers and inmates.

There were further developments in the late 1970s, including a change of name of the Canadian Penitentiary Service to the Correctional Service of Canada (CSC); a recognition that the rule of law must apply in prisons; an expansion of community correctional facilities; the creation of special handling units for violent, dangerous offenders; and the discarding of the medical model, which presupposed that correctional officials could diagnose and treat criminal behaviour. The CSC also opened several regional psychiatric centres (now called regional health centres) across the country for inmates with specialized treatment needs.

1990 TO THE PRESENT: COMPETING MODELS OF CORRECTIONAL PRACTICE

A significant development in Canadian correctional history is the split that has emerged between the federal model of correctional practice and some provincial models. This development can be traced, in part, to the election of Conservative governments in several provinces.

At the federal level, correctional policy and practice is still firmly entrenched in the liberal European model of corrections, which places a high value on proactive intervention in the lives of offenders and the involvement of social and justice agencies in responding to crime. This philosophy is reflected in the closing of the Kingston Prison for Women in 2000, the ongoing construction of small regional facilities for federally sentenced women, the development of Aboriginal healing lodges in partnership with First Nations, and plans to increase the number of federal offenders under community supervision to 50 percent of the total federal offender population. The adoption of the liberal European model of corrections was initially facilitated by Ole Ingstrup, commissioner of the Correctional Service of Canada (CSC) from 1988 to 1992 and again from 1996 to 2000. Ingstrup, who had served as a senior correctional administrator in Denmark before immigrating to Canada, was instrumental in developing the CSC's mission statement and in shifting the focus of correctional policy to one of active intervention in the lives of inmates.

At the provincial level, correctional policy more closely mirrors the punishment-oriented American approach to corrections. Ontario in particular has embraced a no-frills, get-tough approach to crime that puts a premium on community safety (see Box 2.5). In sharp contrast to federal correctional policy, which is based on the dictum that "[m]en come to prison as a punishment, not for punishment" (cited in Gardner, 2002b), is the following statement made by former Ontario corrections minister Rob Sampson:

> *Jails should be punishment.... Just taking away a prisoner's liberty is not enough; convicts must also be subjected to a harsher environment.... People don't expect us to be locking inmates up in the Waldorf-Astoria." (cited in Gardner, 2002b)*

Sampson also attacked the federal prison system for its "glorified country clubs," with their "golf courses, horse stables, and eat-in kitchens" (cited in Gardner, 2002b).

While Alberta and British Columbia are following Ontario's lead in their approach to corrections, the government of Quebec has continued to pursue a correctional policy that attempts to "strik[e] a better balance between the use of harsh measures and the involvement of key social players and the community" (Sécurité publique Québec, 2000:2). The Quebec model of corrections is further characterized by:

- an emphasis on prevention and alternative measures
- public and community involvement in conflict resolution and responses to social problems
- the use of extrajudicial proceedings to keep cases out of court

- the use of incarceration as a last resort
- an emphasis on interagency teamwork (Sécurité publique Québec, 2000)

The federal Liberal government has attempted to straddle, rather than resolve, the two competing models of correctional practice: "On one side it has introduced, or allowed to continue, elements of the European model. But

BOX 2.5

Ontario Provincial Corrections: The Americanization of Canadian Correctional Policy?

The government of Ontario has implemented a number of reforms in the correctional system that, in the view of many observers, have been directly influenced by the American approach to corrections. These include:

- the replacement of 31 correctional facilities with a much smaller number of "superjails" (including Maplehurst, the largest correctional facility in Canada, with beds for nearly 1,500 inmates)
- the development of performance standards for jails that include tracking the number of escapes, disturbances, and suicides at each institution
- a policy of zero tolerance for inmate acts of violence toward correctional staff in prisons and in the community
- changes in parole regulations that have tightened up the criteria for release, accompanied by a 50 percent reduction in the parole grant rate
- the creation of a Prisoner Work Program in which offenders wearing orange coveralls do work in the community
- the introduction of an eight-hour workday for inmates
- the creation of provisions under the Corrections Accountability Act that end the automatic credit of remission and require offenders to earn the privilege of early release by actively participating in programs and demonstrating positive behaviour
- the creation of "strict discipline" facilities for young offenders, modelled on U.S. "boot camps"
- the development of a "strict discipline" model for community corrections that includes frequent and intense monitoring of offenders serving time in the community

Sources: Gardner, 2002b; Ontario Ministry of Public Safety and Security (www.mpss.jus.gov.on.ca).

at the same time ... it has [in the words of criminologist Julian Roberts] 'tried to sort of look tough and act tough' on a few high-profile issues. And sometimes, it has simply split the difference" (Gardner, 2002a). The competing philosophies of the more liberal European model of corrections and the U.S. tough-on-crime approach are also reflected in the correctional institutions operated by the Correctional Service of Canada. For example, Bath Institution, a medium-security facility west of Kingston, features "lawn chairs and razor wire, barbecues and armed guards"—a dichotomy that "sums up the Canadian struggle to choose between U.S.-style hard time and European-style rehab" (Gardner, 2002a).

It is important to note that the American-style approach to corrections has been counterbalanced in the past decade by the emergence of innovative alternatives to incarceration. These initiatives will be examined in Chapter 4.

THE LEGACY OF COMMUNITY CORRECTIONS: PROBATION AND PAROLE

Although the federal and provincial governments failed to pursue with any vigour the reform of correctional institutions in the late 1890s, the foundation was being set for the increased use of noncarceral sanctions. In the 20th century, probation and parole became the cornerstones of what became known as *community corrections*, an ill-defined term that describes any program or initiative for offenders that is not delivered in an institution.

The state of Massachusetts shares with England the distinction of having pioneered the use of probation. Probation evolved in that state from the activities of one John Augustus, a Boston shoemaker who, in 1841, appeared in court and requested that he be permitted to stand as bail for a man charged with being a common drunkard. When the man returned to court three weeks later showing obvious signs of reformation, he was given a nominal fine of one cent for an offence that normally resulted in imprisonment. Spurred on by this success, Augustus "bailed on probation" nearly 2,000 people in the 18 years preceding his death in 1859.

In Canada, the practice of releasing offenders on their own recognizance rather than imposing a sentence was given legal authority in 1889 by the Act to Permit the Conditional Release of First Offenders in Certain Cases. This legislation permitted judges to suspend the imposition of a sentence in the criminal court and, instead, place the offender on "probation of good conduct." In 1892, probation was mentioned in the Criminal Code, and by 1921, changes to the Criminal Code required the offender to report to an officer of the court. The growth of probation, however, was slow and uneven and remained relatively undeveloped until after World War II. This pattern of development was a consequence of probation being under the jurisdiction of provincial/ territorial governments and of geography, since rural and remote areas of the country had no facilities for supervising offenders (Hamai et al., 1995).

The practice of releasing offenders prior to the end of their sentences— today called *conditional release*—originated in the days when English convicts were transported to penal colonies in Australia. For centuries, the only avenue for early release had been to petition the king or queen for a Royal Prerogative of Mercy, which included pardons and remission of prison sentences granted for humanitarian reasons or because the severity of the sentence far exceeded the severity of the crime. The work of 19th-century penal reformers such as Alexander Maconochie was rooted in the observation that the harsh and bru- talizing conditions in prisons did little to encourage convicts to be good cit- izens and, in fact, did much to ensure that they would become hardened criminals. Maconochie was superintendent of Norfolk Isalnd (off the coast of Australia), a penal colony where those offenders thought to be incorrigible and irredeemable were sent. He developed a "mark system" whereby a day's labour earned the offender 10 marks, and 10 marks shortened the sentence by one day. A day's rations and supplies cost between three and five marks, so inmates could earn one day toward early release for every two days of work (Barry, 1973).

In the 1890s, Canada adopted in isolated pockets the indeterminate sen- tence and the mark system, which were first used by Maconochie, for use with juvenile offenders. For adults, the reformatory movement found expression in the concept of "ticket of leave." The Act to Provide for the Conditional Liberation of Penitentiary Convicts, known as the Ticket of Leave Act, was passed in 1899. This legislation allowed federal convicts to be released from prison under specified conditions.

The Prison Gate Section of the Salvation Army undertook to assist those on tickets of leave, there being no equivalents to the modern-day parole offi- cers to supervise and assist reintegrating offenders. The first dominion parole officer was appointed in 1905, a brigadier in the Salvation Army, establishing early on the role of private agencies in this stage of the correctional process. The parole officer made recommendations to the Chief of the Remission Service in Ottawa, as it came to be called. Acting on behalf of the Minister of Justice, the Remission Service made the final decision. But the parole officer was one man in a big country; thus, tickets of leave were limited, and the prac- tice spread slowly. All staff of the Remission Service worked out of Ottawa until 1949, when one-man regional offices were established in Vancouver and Montreal. About this time, officers started to supervise parolees on tickets of leave and, in some cases, write social history reports to accompany applications.

An enormous change to the system of parole occurred after the formation of a committee of inquiry in the mid-1950s (Fauteux, 1956). The commission wanted an independent body affiliated with neither the penal system nor the government to make release decisions. In their view, when an officer of the government makes the final decision about parole, such as the Chief of the Remission Service, political factors could take precedence over a fair examination of the case on its merits. The committee recommended the creation of the National Parole Board (NPB), made up of five full-time members and located in Ottawa. The NPB came into being with the passage of the Parole Act in 1959, while the Ontario Parole Commission was established in 1910.

PARTING THOUGHTS

Although there have been innumerable attempts to reform systems of corrections, particularly the handling and confinement of offenders, many of the challenges that confront systems of corrections at the beginning of the 21st century were first identified early in the 18th century. These challenges include the need for accountability on the part of systems of corrections, community involvement in the prevention of and response to crime and offenders, adequate classification of offenders, humane and safe conditions inside institutions, and effective treatment and training programs. The ways in which Canadian systems of corrections are attempting to meet these ongoing challenges are discussed throughout this text. The major commissions and inquiries that have examined corrections in Canada are profiled in Box 2.6.

BOX 2.6

Commissions and Inquiries into Systems of Corrections

Year	Commission/Inquiry	Focus/Impact
1848	Royal Commission of Inquiry (Brown)	Investigated charges of corruption and mismanagement at Kingston Penitentiary; first report (1848) condemned use of corporal punishment and recommended that the warden be fired; second report (1849) identified crime prevention

Year	Commission/Inquiry	Focus/Impact
		and the rehabilitation of offenders as primary purpose of penitentiaries; impact of prison reform uncertain; most accurately viewed as a missed opportunity to rethink the concept of the penitentiary
1891	Report of the Commission Appointed to Enquire into the Prison and Reformatory System of the Province of Ontario	Documented problems with classification, poor physical facilities, and inadequate management of provincial and local institutions; contributed to early reforms in the Ontario correctional system
1936	Royal Commission on the Penal System of Canada (Archambault)	Appointed to investigate federal prisons; report (1938) concluded that the goal of prisons should be not only to protect society by incarcerating offenders, but also to reform and rehabilitate offenders; gave impetus to an increasing focus on the development and expansion of vocational and educational training programs
1956	Report of a Committee Appointed to Inquire into the Principles and Practices Followed in the Remission Service of the Department of Justice of Canada (Fauteux)	Recommended adoption of a correctional philosophy centred on treatment, the expansion of probation, and recruitment and training of professional staff
1969	Canadian Committee on Corrections (Ouimet)	Examined problems of attempting to rehabilitate offenders in correctional institutions and suggested most effective in community settings; recommendations provided the basis for expansion of community-based facilities and programs

BOX 2.6, continued

Year	Commission/Inquiry	Focus/Impact
1973	Task Force on the Release of Inmates (Hugessen)	Examined the procedures for the release of offenders from institutions prior to the completion of their sentence; recommended the creation of five regional parole boards at the federal level and the appointment of part-time board members
1977	Report of the Parliamentary Sub-Committee on the Penitentiary System in Canada (MacGuigan)	Prompted by riots and disturbances in federal prisons, the final report contained 65 recommendations for improving life inside correctional institutions for inmates and staff; the majority of the recommendations are accepted by the federal government
1990	Task Force on Federally Sentenced Women (Creating Choices)	Examined issues surrounding correctional policy and programs for federal women offenders; recommended that the Kingston Prison for Women be closed and that small regional facilities for female offenders be created, along with a healing lodge for Aboriginal women offenders; recommendations were accepted by the federal government
1996	Commission of Inquiry into Certain Events at the Prison for Women in Kingston (Arbour)	In-depth examination of a critical incident at the Prison for Women, during which women offenders were stripped of clothing by male members of the Institutional

Year	Commission/Inquiry	Focus/Impact
		Emergency Response Team; contained 14 primary recommendations, addressing, among other issues, women's corrections, cross-gender staffing in correctional institutions for women, the use of force and Institutional Emergency Response Teams, the needs of Aboriginal women, the operation of segregation units, ways of ensuring the accountability of correctional personnel and adherence to the rule of law, and procedures for handling inmate complaints and grievances

QUESTIONS FOR REVIEW

1. According to Cohen (1985), what are the four features of the historical development of the response to crime and deviance?

2. What is the relationship between social, political, and demographic changes in society and its response to criminal offenders?

3. What influence did the Age of Reason have on the perception of and response to criminal offenders?

4. Describe the response to criminal offenders in early Canada (1600s–1800s).

5. Discuss the different perspectives that have been offered as to why Kingston Penitentiary was constructed in 1835.

6. What is meant by the term *moral architecture*, and why is this concept important to our understanding of corrections?

7. What lessons should have been learned from the events that occurred inside Kingston Penitentiary during the early years of its operation?

8. What was the medical model of corrections?

9. Compare and contrast the strengths and weaknesses of the conservative, liberal, and radical perspectives on crime and corrections.

10. Describe the emerging model of corrections in Canada in the early 21st century.

REFERENCES

Annual Report of the Commissioner of Penitentiaries, 1957. 1958. Ottawa: Queen's Printer.

Archambault, J. (Chairman). 1938. *Report of the Royal Commission to Investigate the Penal System of Canada.* Ottawa: King's Printer.

Baehre, R. 1977. "Origins of the Penitentiary System in Upper Canada." *Ontario History* 69(3):185–207.

———. 1990. "From Bridewell to Federal Penitentiary: Prisons and Punishment in Nova Scotia Before 1880." In P. Girard and J. Phillips (eds.), *Essays in the History of Canadian Law* (163–99). Vol. III: Nova Scotia. Toronto: University of Toronto Press.

Barry, J.V. 1973. "Alexander Maconochie." In H. Mannheim (ed.), *Pioneers in Criminology* (84–106). Montclair, N.J: Patterson Smith.

Beattie, J.M. 1977. *Attitudes towards Crime and Punishment in Upper Canada, 1830–1850: A Documentary Study.* Toronto: Centre of Criminology, University of Toronto.

Bellomo, J.J. 1972. "Upper Canadian Attitudes towards Crime and Punishment (1832–1851)." *Ontario History* 64(1):11–26.

Blanchfield, C. 1985a. "A New Kind of Punishment: Imprisonment." *Crime and Punishment: A Pictorial History* 10(8). Part II. *Let's Talk.* Special Report. Ottawa: Correctional Service of Canada.

———. 1985b. "Symbol of Discipline: The Bell." *Crime and Punishment: A Pictorial History* 10(11). Part III. *Let's Talk.* Special Report. Ottawa: Correctional Service of Canada.

———. 1985c. "The Monotonous Round: Coarse Diet." *Crime and Punishment: A Pictorial History* 10(11). Part III. *Let's Talk.* Special Report. Ottawa: Correctional Service of Canada.

Boissey, B. 1996. *A Deep Sense of Wrong: The Treason, Trials, and Transportation to New South Wales of Lower Canadian Rebels after the 1838 Rebellion.* Toronto: Dundurn Press.

Cohen, S. 1985. *Visions of Social Control.* Cambridge, U.K.: Polity.

Coles, D. 1979. *Nova Scotia Corrections: An Historical Perspective.* Halifax: Corrections Services Division, Province of Nova Scotia.

Cullen, F.T., and K. Gilbert. 1981. *Reaffirming Rehabilitation.* Cincinnati, Ohio: Anderson Publishing.

Dixon, W.G. 1947. *A Bibliography Relating to the History of the Canadian Penitentiary System and the United States Bureau of Prisons*. Chicago: School of Social Service Administration, University of Chicago.

Edmison, J.A. 1965. "Kingston Penitentiary and Charles Dickens." *Chitty's Law Journal* 13(9):255–57.

———. 1976. "Some Aspects of Nineteenth-Century Canadian Prisons." In W.T. McGrath (ed.), *Crime and Its Treatment in Canada* (347–69). 2nd ed. Toronto: Gage.

Fauteux, G. (Chairman). 1956. *Report of a Committee Appointed to Inquire into the Principles and Procedures Followed in the Remission Service of the Department of Justice of Canada*. Ottawa: Queen's Printer.

Fingard, J. 1984. "Jailbirds in Mid-Victorian Halifax." *Dalhousie Law Journal* 8(3):81–102.

Foucault, M. 1979. *Discipline and Punish: The Birth of the Prison*. New York: Vintage.

Gardner, D. 2002a. "Rooms with a View." *Ottawa Citizen*. March 23. Retrieved from www.canada.com/ottawa/ottawacitizen/specials/crimeandpunishment.

———. 2002b. "Hard Time in Ontario, American-Style." *Ottawa Citizen*. March 24. Retrieved from www.canada.com/ottawa/ottawacitizen/specials/crimeandpunishment.

Greenwood, F.M., and B. Boissery. 2000. *Uncertain Justice: Canadian Women and Punishment, 1754–1953*. Toronto: Dundurn Press.

Hamai, K., R. Ville, R. Harris, M. Hough, and U. Zvekic. 1995. *Probation Round the World: A Comparative Study*. London and New York: Routledge.

Ignatieff, M. 1978. *A Just Measure of Pain: The Penitentiary in the Industrial Revolution—1750–1850*. New York: Columbia University Press.

James, J.T.L. 1990. *A Living Tradition: Penitentiary Chaplaincy*. Ottawa: Chaplaincy Division, Correctional Service of Canada.

Kolish, E. 1987. "Imprisonment for Debt in Lower Canada, 1791–1840." *McGill Law Journal* 32(3):603–35.

MacGuigan. M. 1977. *Report to Parliament by the Sub-Committee on the Penitentiary System in Canada*. Ottawa: Supply and Services Canada.

Morel, A. 1963. "La Justice criminelle en Nouvelle-France." *Cité Libre* 14 (January):26–30.

———. 1975. "Réflexions sur la justice criminelle Canadienne au 18e siècle." *Revue d'histoire de L'Amérique française* 29(2):241–53.

Newman, G. 1978. *The Punishment Response*. New York: J.B. Lippincott.

Oliver, P.N. 1998. "*Terror to Evil-Doers*": *Prisons and Punishments in Nineteenth-Century Ontario*. Toronto: University of Toronto Press.

Ouimet, R. (Chairman). 1969. *Toward Unity: Criminal Justice and Corrections. Report of the Canadian Committee on Corrections*. Ottawa: Queen's Printer.

Palmer, B.D. 1980. "Kingston Mechanics and the Rise of the Penitentiary, 1833–1836." *Social History* 13(25):7–32.

Price, B.J. 1990. "'Raised in Rockhead. Died in the Poor House': Female Petty Criminals in Halifax, 1864–1890." In P. Girard and J. Phillips (eds.), *Essays in the History of Canadian Law* (200–31).Vol. III: Nova Scotia. Toronto: University of Toronto Press.

Raddall, T.H. 1988. *Halifax—Warden of the North*. Toronto: McClelland and Stewart.

Radzinowicz, L. 1966. *Ideology and Crime: A Study of Crime in Its Social and Historical Context*. London: Heinemann Educational.

Rothman, D.J. 1990. *The Discovery of the Asylum: Social Order and Disorder in the New Republic*. 2nd ed. Boston: Little, Brown.

Sécurité publique Québec. 2000. "Correctional Reform: Towards the Moderate Use of Penal and Correctional Measures." Retrieved from www.msp.gouv.qc.ca.

Shoom, S. 1966. "Kingston Penitentiary: The Early Decades." *Canadian Journal of Corrections* 8(3):215–20.

Shover, N. 1979. *A Sociology of American Corrections*. Homewood, Ill.: Dorsey Press.

Simonds, M. 1996. *The Convict Lover*. Toronto: Macfarlane, Walter, and Ross.

Smandych, R.C. 1991. "Beware of the 'Evil American Monster': Upper Canadian Views on the Need for a Penitentiary, 1830–1834." *Canadian Journal of Criminology* 33(2):125–47.

Smandych, R., and R. Linden. 1996. "Administering Justice Without the State: A Study of the Private Justice System of the Hudson's Bay Company to 1800." *Canadian Journal of Law and Society* 11(1):21–61.

Strong, M.K. 1969. *Social Welfare Administration in Canada*. Montclair, N.J.: Patterson-Smith.

Talbot, C.K. 1983. *Justice in Early Ontario, 1791–1840*. Ottawa: Crimcare.

Taylor, C.J. 1979. "The Kingston, Ontario, Penitentiary and Moral Architecture." *Social History* 12(24):385–408.

Welch, M. 1996. *Corrections: A Critical Approach*. New York: McGraw-Hill.

Zubrycki, R.M. 1980. *The Establishment of Canada's Penitentiary System: Federal Correctional Policy, 1867–1900*. Toronto: Faculty of Social Work, University of Toronto.

CHAPTER 3
CRIME, CRIMINAL JUSTICE, AND CORRECTIONS

CHAPTER OBJECTIVES

- *Describe systems of corrections as a component of the criminal justice system.*
- *Discuss the relationship between the community and systems of corrections.*
- *Discuss sentencing as a component of the correctional process.*
- *Examine the continuing debate over the death penalty.*

KEY TERMS

General deterrence

Specific deterrence

Rehabilitation

Incapacitation

Denunciation

Retribution

Restorative/community justice

Dangerous offenders (DOs)

Long-term offenders

Indeterminate sentence

Determinate sentence

Judicial determination

Sentencing disparity

State-raised offenders

Judicial review

NIMBY (Not In My Back Yard) syndrome

CORRECTIONS IN THE CRIMINAL JUSTICE SYSTEM

As noted in the opening pages of the text, corrections is a subsystem of the criminal justice system. The public and the police serve as the "gatekeepers" of the criminal justice system, with the public determining the types of offences that are initially reported and the police deciding whether the complaint will be responded to formally. Situated at the end of the criminal justice process, correctional personnel, agencies, and institutions are affected by the decisions of the public, the police, Crown counsel, and judges in the criminal courts. Through their decision making, for example, criminal court judges determine the number of offenders placed on probation or sent to correctional institutions. The decisions of the judges, in turn, are affected by changes in public and political views on crime and criminal offenders, as well as by legal factors, personal biases, and legal precedent. Public pressure on the judiciary to deal more harshly with offenders or a change in legislation, such as a mandatory sentence, has a direct impact on systems of corrections. Throughout the criminal justice process, a number of key decision-making points will affect the likelihood of an offender's ending up under the supervision of a correctional authority. These key points are illustrated in Figure 3.1.

When systems of corrections are unable to keep up with the shifts in sentencing practices of the criminal courts, overcrowding may occur in institutions. Similarly, an increase in the number of offenders that criminal court judges place on probation may result in higher caseloads for probation officers and may strain resources and personnel.

The way in which cases flow through the criminal justice process has been characterized as a sieve or a funnel, meaning that the further into the process, the smaller the number of cases becomes. Only a small percentage (less than 5 percent) of the incidents that are reported to the police ultimately result in a prison sentence (see Figure 3.2).

CRIME AND CORRECTIONS

As noted in Chapter 2, perceptions of crime have always had a significant impact on both the type and the severity of sanctions imposed on criminal offenders. Unfortunately, the sensational and selective reporting of crime in the media precludes the general public from understanding the facts about crime. Citizens consistently overestimate the levels and seriousness of crime, as well as their risks of being victimized. For example, although crime rates in Canada have stabilized or, in some instances, have fallen, the perception is that crime is increasing. An Ontario study found, for example, that more than two-thirds of a sample of residents thought that the crime rate generally, and the murder rate in particular, were rising, even though neither is (cited in Carey, 1998).

Figure 3.1

The Criminal Justice Process

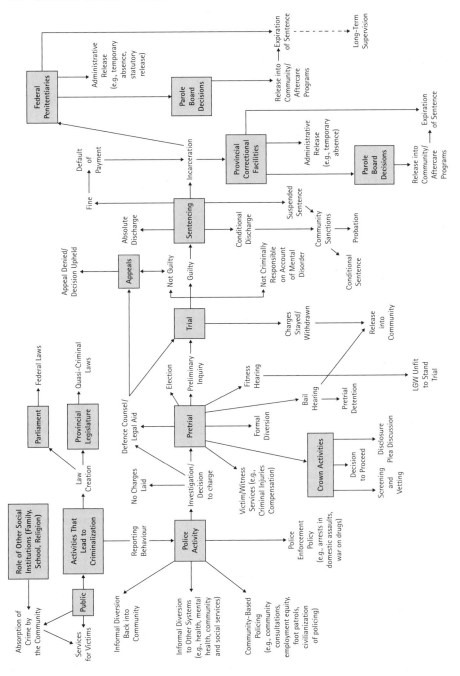

Source: Griffiths and Hatch Cunningham, 2003:11.

Figure 3.2

The Criminal Justice Funnel

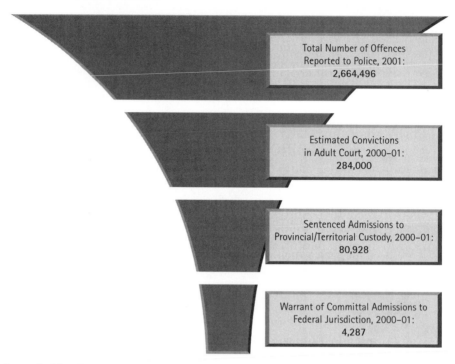

Total Number of Offences
Reported to Police, 2001:
2,664,496

Estimated Convictions
in Adult Court, 2000–01:
284,000

Sentenced Admissions to
Provincial/Territorial Custody, 2000–01:
80,928

Warrant of Committal Admissions to
Federal Jurisdiction, 2000–01:
4,287

Source: Solicitor General Portfolio, 2002:17.

An overview of Canadian crime patterns is provided in Figure 3.3, which reveals the following:

- After declining for nearly a decade, the police-reported crime rate (total offences) for both adult and youth populations increased slightly in 2000–01.
- The property crime rate for both adult and youth populations has been declining steadily since 1991.
- In 2001–01, the most frequent charges in adult criminal court (12.1 percent) were administration of justice charges (which include such offences as failure to appear in court and failure to comply with a probation order), followed by impaired driving (11.4 percent), common assault (7.7 percent), and fraud (7.3 percent).

See Figure 3.4 for the number and type of Criminal Code offences reported to the police.

Figure 3.3

Canadian Crime Patterns

Police-Reported Crime Rate per 100,000 Population, 1991–2001

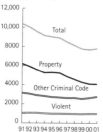

Source: Solicitor General Portfolio, 2002:1.

Property Crime, Canada and the Provinces, 2001

Source: Savoie, 2002:8.

Rates of Youth Charged per 100,000 Youth Population, 1991–2001

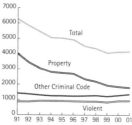

Source: Solicitor General Portfolio, 2002:19.

Violent Crime, Canada and the Provinces, 2001

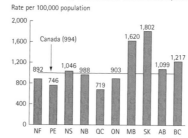

Source: Savoie, 2002:6.

Charges in Adult Court, Percentage of All Federal Statute Charges, 2000–01

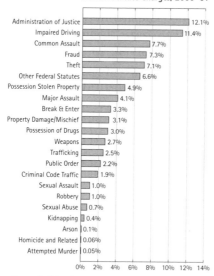

Source: Solicitor General Portfolio, 2002: 9.

Charges in Youth Court, Percentage of All Youth Court Cases by Principal Charge, 2000–01

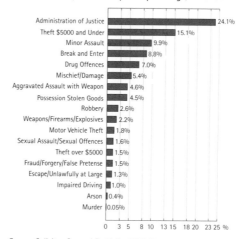

Source: Solicitor General Portfolio, 2002:21

Figure 3.4

Number of Criminal Code Incidents (Excluding Traffic) Reported to the Police by Crime Type, 2000

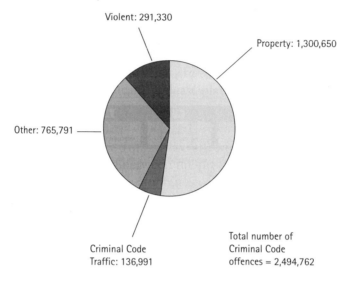

Violent: 291,330

Property: 1,300,650

Other: 765,791

Criminal Code Traffic: 136,991

Total number of Criminal Code offences = 2,494,762

Source: Corrections Statistics Committee, 2000:4.

SENTENCING IN THE CRIMINAL COURTS: BEGINNING THE CORRECTIONAL PROCESS

Although the Canadian judiciary is an independent component of the criminal justice system, the criminal courts can be identified as the beginning of the correctional process. It is here that judgments are passed on offenders and specific sanctions are imposed through sentencing. The decisions that criminal court judges make will not only determine which system of corrections (federal or provincial/territorial) the offender will enter, but also whether the offender will be under supervision and control in the community or be incarcerated. For offenders who are sentenced to a period of confinement, the length of the sentence will have a significant impact not only on the offender, but also on the systems of corrections.

The Objectives of Sentencing

The purpose and principles of sentencing are contained in section 718 of the Criminal Code:

The fundamental purpose of sentencing is to contribute, along with crime prevention initiatives, to respect for the law and the maintenance of a just, peaceful and safe society by imposing just sanctions that have one or more of the following objectives:

(a) to denounce the unlawful conduct;

(b) to deter the offender and other persons from committing offences;

(c) to separate offenders from society, where necessary;

(d) to assist in rehabilitating offenders;

(e) to provide reparations for harm done to victims or to the community; and

(f) to promote a sense of responsibility in offenders, and acknowledgment of the harm done to victims and to the community.

There are three primary goals of sentencing in the criminal courts: utilitarian, retributive, and restorative (Griffiths and Hatch Cunningham, 2003:184).

Utilitarian Goals

The focus here is on the future conduct of the offender, and the sentence is designed to protect the public from future crimes. This is achieved in several ways:

- **general deterrence:** Societal protection is achieved by making public examples of punished offenders to prevent the future crimes of potential offenders.
- **specific deterrence:** The sentence is designed to prevent the offender from engaging in future criminal behaviour.
- **rehabilitation:** There is an attempt through sentencing to identify and address the underlying causes of the individual's criminal behaviour to reduce the likelihood of it recurring.
- **incapacitation:** Incarceration is used to prevent crimes that the offender would likely have committed if out of custody. The most extreme examples of this are the three-strikes laws that were enacted in many U.S. states in an attempt to "get tough" on criminal offenders, particularly those with long histories of serious and violent behaviour. Offenders sentenced under three-strikes legislation are generally confined in prison for life, with no possibility of parole. Research studies have found, however, that not only are three-strikes laws expensive to implement, but these laws have little or no impact on the overall crime rates or on violent-crime rates (Greenwood et al., 1994; Turner et al., 1995).

Retributive Goals

The past, rather than the future, is the focus of these goals of sentencing. Retributive goals include:

- **denunciation:** The sentence is issued to express societal disapproval of the offender's behaviour and is most often severe.
- **retribution:** Based on the ancient "eye for an eye" philosophy of punishment, the sentence is imposed to make the offender "pay" for the criminal behaviour in equal proportion to the harm done.

Restorative Goals

Over the past decade, a variety of sentencing approaches have emerged that can be generally grouped under the term **restorative/community justice.** These approaches include victim–offender reconciliation programs, circle sentencing, family group conferencing, and a number of other innovative strategies that are designed to avoid the more detrimental aspects of the traditional adversarial court process.

Restorative/community justice is based on the principle that criminal behaviour injures not only the victim, but communities and offenders as well. Any attempt to resolve the problems that the criminal behaviour has created should, therefore, involve all three parties. A key feature of restorative/community justice approaches is the attempt to not only address the specific criminal behaviour, but also to broaden the focus to consider the needs of the victims, the community, and the offender in a more holistic framework. Restorative/community justice will be examined in greater detail in Chapter 4.

SENTENCING OPTIONS

Among the sentencing options that judges can select from are the following:

- *absolute discharge:* The offender is found guilty, but is technically not convicted and is set free with no criminal record.
- *conditional discharge:* The offender is released upon condition that he or she comply with certain conditions. If the offender fails to meet the conditions, he or she may be returned to court to be sentenced on the original charge.
- *fine:* The offender must pay a specific amount of money within a specified time or face the prospect of imprisonment for fine default.
- *suspended sentence:* The offender is convicted of the offence, but the imposition of the sentence is suspended pending successful completion of a period of probation.
- *probation:* The offender is placed under supervision in the community for a specified period (maximum three years), must fulfill general con-

ditions, and may be required to adhere to or complete specific conditions (e.g., a number of community service hours).

- *conditional sentence:* The offender receives a term of confinement (less than two years) and is allowed to serve it in the community under the supervision of a probation officer provided he or she meets certain specified conditions (although the offender is not on probation and may be imprisoned for violation of conditions).
- *imprisonment:* The offender is sentenced to a period of confinement.

Some of these options may be mixed and matched; for example, the courts may grant probation in conjunction with a sentence of two years less a day for offenders in provincial/territorial systems and may impose fines along with probation or a period of confinement. Most of these sentencing options will be considered in greater detail in Chapter 4.

Sentences imposed in court may be concurrent, consecutive, or intermittent:

- *Concurrent sentences* are merged into one sentence and served simultaneously. For example, an offender sentenced to 2 terms of 9 months each would serve a 9-month sentence rather than an 18-month sentence.
- *Consecutive sentences* are served separately, with one beginning after the other has expired. An offender sentenced to 2 terms of 9 months each would therefore serve 18 months.
- *Intermittent sentences* are served on a part-time basis, generally on weekends and for no longer than 90 days.

Under the Criminal Code, all sentences are to be concurrent unless the trial judge specifies that they are to be consecutive. Under the Provincial Offences Act, the reverse is true: all sentences are consecutive unless the sentencing judge specifies that they run concurrently. Figure 3.5 presents a breakdown of the adult correctional population.

Dangerous Offender and Long-Term Offender Designations

Sections 752 and 753 of the Criminal Code set out the procedures and criteria for designating certain offenders as either **dangerous offenders (DOs)** or **long-term offenders.** Upon application by Crown counsel, judges may designate as dangerous offenders those persons convicted of committing a serious personal injury offence (except murder)—or exhibiting a pattern of serious violent offences—who are deemed to present a danger to society and are highly likely to put the community at risk if not imprisoned. The application to designate an offender as dangerous must be made at the time of sentencing.

Figure 3.5

Composition of the Adult Correctional Population, 2000–01

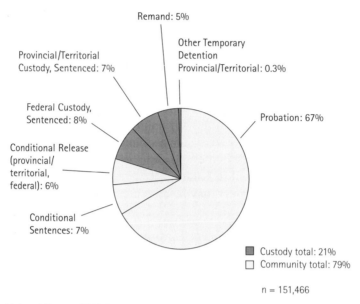

Remand: 5%

Other Temporary Detention Provincial/Territorial: 0.3%

Provincial/Territorial Custody, Sentenced: 7%

Federal Custody, Sentenced: 8%

Conditional Release (provincial/territorial, federal): 6%

Conditional Sentences: 7%

Probation: 67%

■ Custody total: 21%
□ Community total: 79%

n = 151,466

Source: Hendrick and Farmer, 2002:3.

A judge who makes a dangerous offender designation will order that the person serve an **indeterminate sentence.** These offenders are eligible for a hearing before the National Parole Board every two years after serving seven years from the day they were taken into custody.

Features of the DO population include the following:

- Among the 313 active DOs in 2002, 300 have indeterminate sentences and 13 have **determinate sentences.**
- Approximately 83 percent of all DOs have been convicted of at least one sex offence.
- The majority of DOs have been designated in the provinces of British Columbia and Ontario.
- There are no female dangerous offenders.
- Nineteen percent of DOs are Aboriginal. (Solicitor General Portfolio, 2002:91)

The record indicates that very few dangerous offenders are ever released.

The long-term offender designation, which was designed to deal with specific sexual offences, is another option for Crown counsel, particularly in cases in which the Crown falls short of the rigid requirements or level of evidence to file a dangerous offender application. As with dangerous offenders, there must be evidence to indicate that the offender presents a substantial risk of reoffending by committing a serious personal offence. However, there is also risk assessment evidence that the offender may be effectively managed in the community with appropriate supervision and treatment.

The long-term offender designation is available only for those offenders who have received a sentence of more than two years. At sentencing, the judge sets the length of the long-term supervision order. This means that after the sentence ends (which includes confinement and post-release supervision), the long-term supervision order comes into effect. This order requires that the offender be supervised by a parole officer for the remaining period of the order, which may be up to 10 years. The National Parole Board sets the conditions under which the offender will be supervised following the expiration of his or her sentence.

As of mid-2002, the courts had imposed 154 long-term supervision orders, with just over one-third specifying a supervision period of 10 years. Only two of these offenders are women (Solicitor General Canada, 2001; Solicitor General Portfolio, 2002:93).

Judicial Determination

Section 743.6 of the Criminal Code gives sentencing judges the authority to impose on some offenders receiving a sentence of imprisonment of two years or more the requirement that the offender serve one-half of the sentence prior to being eligible for parole, instead of the typical one-third. The primary objectives of this provision are protection of the public and specific and general deterrence.

Offenders who are subject to **judicial determination** are those who have been convicted of one or more Schedule I (specified crimes against the person) and Schedule II (specified drug offences as listed in the Corrections and Conditional Release Act) offences. Research on the sentencing decisions of provincial court judges has revealed the following:

- Most judges make limited use of judicial determination, imposing it on less than 5 percent of those offenders who qualify for it.
- The use of judicial determination is declining.
- Aboriginal offenders are overrepresented in the group of offenders receiving judicial determination.
- Offenders receiving judicial determination are more likely than other offenders to serve their entire sentence in confinement. (Solicitor General Canada, 1998)

SENTENCING DISPARITY

Although some offences, upon conviction, carry mandatory prison sentences, in most cases judges have broad discretion in deciding upon a penalty. Therefore, **sentencing disparity** may result—situations in which similar offenders who commit similar offences receive sentences of different severity. There is also considerable variation among major urban areas across the country in the extent to which incarceration is used as a sanction (see Figure 3.6).

Criminal court judges are granted by statute and precedence considerable latitude in selecting sanctions for convicted offenders. With a few exceptions in which mandatory sentences are required upon conviction, most

Figure 3.6

Percentage of Convicted Cases Sentenced to Prison for the Most Serious Offence in the Case, Eight Provinces and Territories in Canada, 2000–01

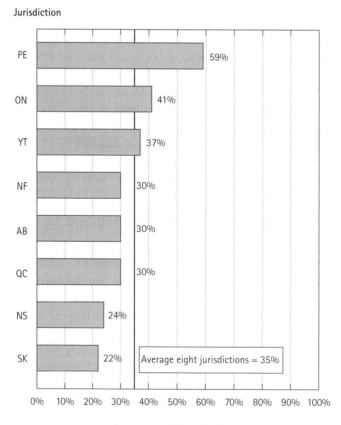

Percentage of Convicted Cases

Source: Thomas, 2002:10.

offences have only a maximum penalty; thus, judges have considerable discretion in deciding both the objective of the sentence and the specific penalty. This latitude also allows judges to consider a broad range of factors specific to the case and the offender, rather than being forced to take into account only information related to prior offences and the current crime. For an in-depth examination of the critical issues surrounding sentencing, see Roberts and Cole (1999).

THE EFFECTIVENESS OF SENTENCING

Beyond the controversies over leniency in sentencing and the high-profile media cases, it is, in fact, very difficult to determine the effectiveness of sentencing and the extent to which it fulfills the various objectives discussed earlier. There are a number of reasons for this:

- Although judges may include recommendations for treatment in their sentencing order, once the offender is convicted, he or she becomes the responsibility of systems of corrections. Judicial recommendations for placement and treatment programming are not binding on correctional decision makers. A wide variety of factors beyond the control of the court, including waiting lists for treatment, overcrowding in correctional institutions, and high caseloads of probation and parole officers, may undermine the objectives of the sentence envisioned by the judge who passed it.
- Matching specific sentencing options with the needs and risks of offenders is, at best, an inexact science. As previously mentioned, one of the challenges of corrections, which also applies to sentencing, is that there is no body of scientific knowledge that would assist judges in reliably selecting sanctions that will have a maximum positive impact on the offender.
- Research on whether sanctions imposed by the criminal courts are effective in specific or general deterrence is inconclusive; that is, regardless of the specific objectives of a sentence, it is not certain that the sanction will have the intended effect.

THE USE AND EFFECTIVENESS OF INCARCERATION

Prisons have failed to reduce crime, don't hold offenders accountable to repay their victims, and do nothing to give communities confidence in their criminal justice system.

—Mennonite Central Committee, 1997:11

If you take a tomato and put it in a box, it comes out rotten.

—inmate in provincial institution, cited in Shephard, 1997:F1

The rate of incarceration in Canada is 116 per 100,000 population. This rate places Canada quite high in the use of confinement when compared with other countries, although it pales in comparison with the U.S. rate of 700 per 100,000 population (see Figure 3.7). To put the U.S. incarceration rate in per-

Figure 3.7

Rates of Incarceration in 15 Countries

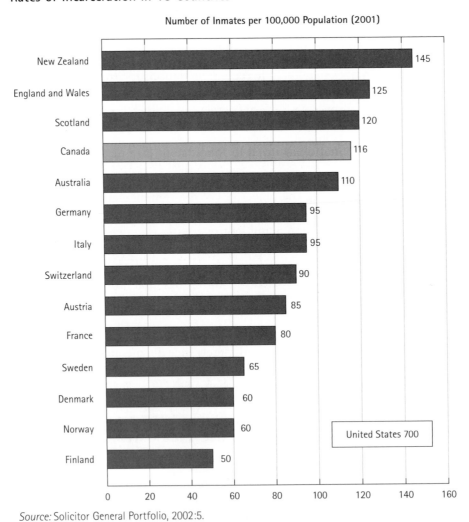

Number of Inmates per 100,000 Population (2001)

Source: Solicitor General Portfolio, 2002:5.

spective, consider the fact that the state of California, with a population just slightly larger than Canada's, has more offenders in prison than Canada, Germany, and Italy *combined*. With only 5 percent of the world's population, the United States is home to 25 percent of its prisoners (Gardner, 2002).

Systems of corrections in the United States have been on a prison-building binge in recent years. In contrast, the Correctional Service of Canada (CSC), motivated in large part by the immense costs of confinement, has attempted to limit construction of new prisons and to explore alternatives to incarceration. However, research suggests that the development of alternatives to confinement alone will not reduce institutional populations; rather, it will be necessary to reduce the length of sentences and the amount of time that offenders serve in confinement (Sprott and Doob, 1998). The majority of provincial/territorial and federal prison sentences are for periods of one month or less (see Figure 3.8).

How effective is incarceration as a general and specific deterrent to crime? This is a question that is very difficult to answer, although there is some evidence that the use of confinement does not have a significant impact on the rate of crime (see Box 3.1). In other words, there is most likely no relationship between crime rates and the number of people that are kept in confinement in a jurisdiction:

- Although Saskatchewan has a much higher rate of imprisonment (256 per 100,000 adults) than Manitoba (186 per 100,000 adults), their crime rates are virtually identical.
- Although Nova Scotia and Saskatchewan are similar in the size and distribution of their populations, resident per capita income, and rates of violent crime, these two provinces differ in the amount of money they spend on corrections and in the rate of incarceration. Saskatchewan spends more on its criminal justice system and has a rate of confinement that is twice that of Nova Scotia, yet its citizens are not any safer than Nova Scotians. (Mennonite Central Committee, 1997:7)

With the exception of confining violent offenders who are likely to reoffend if released into the community (the sentencing goal of incapacitation mentioned earlier), imprisonment appears to play a limited role in crime prevention. In fact, as later chapters will reveal, offenders who are sent to correctional institutions may return more removed from mainstream society and at higher risk for recidivism following release than when they entered confinement.

Incarceration as Opportunity and "Home"

Other factors may limit the effectiveness of incarceration. In their study of crime and criminal justice in the Baffin Region (now part of the territory of

Figure 3.8

Length of Provincial/Territorial and Federal Prison Sentences for Men and Women, 2000–01

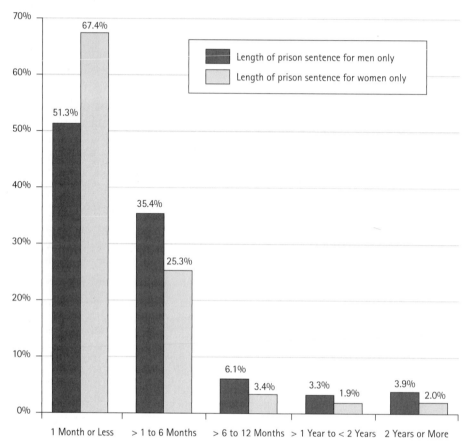

Source: Solicitor General Portfolio, 2002:15.

Nunavut), Griffiths and his colleagues (1995) found that sending Inuit offenders from the villages in the region to the Baffin Correctional Centre in Iqaluit had little impact on their criminal behaviour. Many of these offenders viewed confinement as a welcome break from the monotony of life in an isolated village. In the words of one social worker, "The bulk of offenders are under the age of 25 and their trip to jail is their only chance to get out of here" (cited in Griffiths et al., 1995:164).

The correctional institution may also mark a significant improvement over the quality of life in the offender's community and home environment.

BOX 3.1

Research Summary: The Effectiveness of Incarceration

Research studies on the use of incarceration have revealed the following:

- *With the exception of violent, high-risk offenders, incarceration is ineffective as a specific deterrent.* There are nearly identical rates of reoffending for offenders sentenced to probation supervision and those sent to prison. Offenders who have spent large portions of their youth and adult lives in institutions and have few family ties or other ties to the community may be more comfortable in prison than in the community.
- *It is unlikely that incarceration is effective as a general deterrent.* Rather, the evidence suggests that the likelihood of being caught and punished is the most effective general deterrent.
- *Incarceration, to be effective, must be used selectively.* However, it is difficult to determine which offenders should be incarcerated and for how long in order for imprisonment to be effective. A large portion of the resources currently consumed by the costs of incarceration could be more effectively used to develop alternative sanctions.
- *Increasing the length of incarceration is ineffective.* There is no evidence that increasing the length of carceral sentences either reduces the overall crime rate or the likelihood that an offender will recidivate once released from an institution. In fact, an analysis of recidivism studies conducted by Gendreau, Goggin, and Cullen (1999) found that offenders who served longer sentences had a 3 percent increase in recidivism.
- *There is no relationship between the type or severity of sanctions and punishment in criminal justice and recidivism rates.* There is conclusive research evidence that treatment approaches are more effective than punishment in reducing reoffending. As well, community-based programs have higher overall rates of success than institutional programs.
- *It should not be assumed that incarceration is the most severe punishment that can be inflicted on offenders.* Research on the perceptions of sanctions held by inmates in several U.S. prisons found that, for many, prison was preferable to probation (Crouch, 1993). Two-thirds of the inmates indicated that they would choose one year in prison over 10 years on probation. Nearly one-half of the sample expressed a preference for prison when the probationary period was reduced to five years, and one-third would still opt for confinement instead of three years on probation. In addition, incarcerated offenders may waive their right to a parole hearing, preferring to serve the remainder of their sentence in confinement rather than being subjected to parole supervision.

Sources: Andrews, 1995; Champion, 1994; Crouch, 1993; Gendreau, Goggin, and Cullen, 1999; National Crime Prevention Council, 1997.

Offenders who are unemployed, drug addicted, or living with a medical condition such as HIV/AIDS or hepatitis C may see confinement as a way to get their own bed, three meals a day, a paid job, and plenty of rest. In the words of one inmate incarcerated in a provincial correctional facility: "A lot of the guys who come in here are drug sick. They had served their sentence, or been granted parole, went back out on the street, and got right back into the drug life. They come back, get well, put on a few pounds, and they are ready to go out and start it all over again" (personal communication with C.T. Griffiths).

The world of corrections is replete with stories of offenders who, with winter approaching, deliberately violate the conditions of their conditional release or commit a new offence so as to be sent to a correctional institution. Offenders who have spent most of their youth and adult lives confined in correctional institutions may experience a return to prison as a "coming home" to well-established routines and friendships. For these **state-raised offenders,** surviving in the outside, free community often poses a far greater challenge than doing time in prison (more on state-raised offenders in Chapter 7).

The Costs of Incarceration

The fact that Canada is spending more than four times the amount per prisoner than it is per university student per year is alarming ... the cost of warehousing one offender for one year would more than pay for an entire university degree!

—Mennonite Central Committee, 1997:9

Federal and provincial/territorial systems of corrections spend a large portion of the $2.5-billion budget on incarcerating offenders. The annual costs of incarcerating federal offenders are set out in Box 3.2. These figures illustrate not only that systems of corrections are expensive to operate, but also that the costs of confining an offender are more than if the person were housed in a first-class hotel! The federal and most provincial/territorial governments spend over 80 percent of their correctional budgets on custodial expenses. This despite the fact that less than 5 percent of sentenced offenders are sent to prison. Conversely, though the majority of offenders are under some form of supervision in the community, less than 20 percent of federal and provincial (with the exception of Nova Scotia) corrections budgets are spent on noncustodial programs and services.

BOX 3.2

Incarcerating Offenders: An Expensive Proposition

Confining offenders in correctional institutions consumes a large portion of the CSC budget. The average annual cost per federal male inmate is:

- maximum-security institution: $108,277
- medium-security institution: $71,894
- minimum-security institution: $69,178

The annual cost for a female inmate is $155,589, which is nearly twice that for a male inmate in a medium-security institution. These costs are due, in part, to the small number of female offenders (approximately 375) and the high cost of operating the regional correctional facilities for women.

The average annual cost of supervising an offender in the community is $18,678, about one-third the cost of confining an inmate in a minimum-security institution.

Source: Solicitor General Portfolio, 2002:30.

THE DEATH PENALTY: THE ULTIMATE SANCTION

The most severe sanction that any state can impose on convicted offenders is the death penalty. Although many countries have abolished the death penalty, it has been revived and used with increasing frequency in many jurisdictions in the United States (approximately two-thirds of the states have provisions for the use of capital punishment). Worldwide, China leads all nations in the use of the death penalty, with more executions than all other countries combined.

Capital punishment was abolished in Canada by a free vote in Parliament in 1976, and subsequent attempts to reintroduce this most severe of penalties have failed. Public support for the death penalty has been declining in recent years. A public-opinion poll conducted in 2001 found that 52 percent of Canadians surveyed supported the reinstatement of capital punishment (Cobb, 2001). The declining support for the death penalty has been attributed, in part, to the widely publicized cases of several persons who were wrongfully convicted of crimes.

Inflicting Death

Historically, convicted offenders were put to death by a wide variety of techniques, limited only by the imagination of the authorities. In the United States today, the primary method of execution is lethal injection, although electrocution, hanging, and death by firing squad remain options in several states. Although the death penalty in Canada and the United States was, at one time, carried out in public, it is now done in the United States behind prison walls. There is an audience of invited witnesses that often includes the family of the victim and the offender's family, as well as various representatives from the media.

Arguments against the Death Penalty

- *Innocent people would be put to death.* In Canada, it is likely that David Milgaard, Donald Marshall, and Guy Paul Morin, all of whom were convicted of first-degree murder and sentenced to life imprisonment but subsequently proven innocent, would have been put to death had the death penalty still been in force in Canada. In the United States, a number of death-row inmates have been exonerated by DNA evidence in recent years—a trend that has strengthened the belief among death penalty opponents that innocent people have been executed in the past. In 2003, Illinois Governor George Ryan commuted the sentences of the 167 death-row inmates in that state, commenting: "Because the Illinois death penalty system is arbitrary and capricious, and therefore immoral, I shall no longer tinker with the machinery of death" (http://weekly.ahram.org.eg/2003/622/in6.htm). Information on the case of Guy Paul Morin and other wrongfully convicted persons is available on the website of the Toronto-based Association in Defence of the Wrongfully Convicted (www.aidwyc.org).
- *The death penalty is used disproportionately for minority offenders.* Figures from the United States indicate that a disproportionate number of offenders put to death are black. In fact, the victim's race was found to affect the likelihood of an offender being charged with capital murder or receiving the death penalty in 80 percent of the studies reviewed. More specifically, cases in which the offender was black and the victim was white were more likely to result in the death penalty being imposed (U.S. General Accounting Office, 1990). Since use of the death penalty resumed in the United States in the mid-1970s, 40 percent of those executed have been black.

- *There is no empirical evidence that the death penalty serves as a general deterrent to crime.* There is no consistent research evidence from the United States that the death penalty has any impact on the rates of serious crime (Decker and Kohfeld, 1990; Peterson and Bailey, 1991). The average time from conviction to imposition of the death penalty on offenders in that country is over 10 years. A survey of U.S. criminologists found consensus that the death penalty did not serve as a general deterrent (Radelet and Akers, 1997).
- *Premeditated killing is immoral.* A question frequently heard from death penalty opponents is why do we kill people to show that killing people is wrong? Not only is the deliberate taking of another's life viewed as immoral, but the techniques used have raised concerns (Hanks, 1997; Reitan, 1993). Many state courts have declared the electric chair cruel and unusual punishment, although lethal injection has also been criticized as sanitizing death.
- *Use of the death penalty in the United States has failed to reduce the public's fear of crime.*
- *The death penalty does not save taxpayers' money.* The long legal process associated with death penalty appeals generally results in higher costs than if the offender had been incarcerated for life in a correctional institution.

Arguments for the Death Penalty

- *There is widespread support for the death penalty.* Public-opinion polls indicate that 52 percent of Canadians favour reinstatement of the death penalty for some serious offences, although the specific levels of support vary over time.
- *The death penalty is the ultimate specific deterrent.* The offender will never again commit crimes.
- *The death penalty reaffirms society's right to respond severely to severe violence.* Whether capital punishment serves as a general deterrent is not the primary issue; rather, it is that society and communities have the right to respond severely to violent criminal behaviour that transcends, morally and legally, the boundaries of acceptable behaviour.
- *The absence of the death penalty hinders general deterrence.* The failure to impose severe sanctions on violent criminal behaviour lessens the potential deterrent value of the criminal law.
- *The death penalty provides closure for the families of victims.* In the absence of the death penalty, the families of crime victims are re-victimized by

publicity surrounding the offender and by the offender's subsequent efforts to seek release.

The Death Penalty versus Long-Term Confinement

Under the Criminal Code, persons convicted of murder are subject to life imprisonment. This means that the offender is under sentence for life, although he or she may serve this sentence both in prison and upon release on parole in the community. The Criminal Code sets out the minimum number of years that an offender must serve in prison before being eligible to apply for release on parole. The key word is *apply*—there is no guarantee that the parole board will grant a release.

There are several situations in which life sentences can be imposed:

- as a mandatory sentence for first-degree murder with no eligibility for parole for 25 years (although section 745 of the Criminal Code provides for **judicial review** for some offenders after 15 years)
- as a mandatory sentence for second-degree murder with no eligibility for parole for 10 to 25 years, a period set by the sentencing judge
- as an optional sentence for other offences, including manslaughter, with parole eligibility set at seven years
- as an indeterminate sentence imposed on those persons designated as dangerous offenders

Since the abolition of the death penalty in Canada in 1976, the use of life imprisonment has become the focus of debate and controversy.

PUBLIC ATTITUDES TOWARD THE CRIMINAL JUSTICE SYSTEM

Most people believe the criminal justice system is good in theory but flawed in practice.

—Adams, 1990:13

A lack of substantive information about the criminal justice system and the manner in which the mass media report issues related to crime and criminal justice are the major determinants of the attitudes that the public has toward offenders and the criminal justice system. Public-opinion surveys indicate that crime is far down the list of concerns of Canadians, lagging far behind health care, child poverty, education, the environment, and homelessness (Roberts, 2001). The public, however, is concerned about the criminal justice system and its ability to ensure the safety of citizens.

Foremost in the minds of citizens surveyed about their perceptions of the justice system are the sentencing decisions of criminal court judges. Controversy often erupts when judges hand down sentences that crime victims, politicians, and the public perceive as too lenient and as failing to match the punishment to the crime. In fact, a public-opinion poll conducted in 2002 found that 63 percent of Canadians thought sentences were not severe enough; another poll revealed that the public viewed judges as the weakest link in the justice system when compared with defence lawyers, prosecutors, and police (Aubry, 2002).

Canadians are even more disenchanted with the prison and parole systems, which have, according to one survey, approval ratings of just over 25 percent and 15 percent respectively (Tufts, 2000). Public attitudes toward correctional institutions are undoubtedly shaped, in part, by media commentary like the following: "Hogwash to touchy-feely prisons: Corrections Canada wants to take the pen out of penitentiary so the incarcerated, bless their misunderstood hearts, won't know they're doing time" (*Calgary Herald*, December 21, 1999, A23). Another likely influence on public opinion—the media-savvy Canadian Police Association—is profiled in Box 3.3.

BOX 3.3

The Canadian Police Association: A Vocal Critic of Corrections

The Canadian Police Association (CPA) has been a longtime critic of systems of corrections, particularly the federal system. William Head Institution, a minimum-security facility in British Columbia that features a golf course, townhouse residences, and a panoramic ocean view, inspired the CPA's B.C. representative to comment:

> *It's unbelievable for the public to accept that some of the benefits that the inmates have are necessary to facilitate their rehabilitation....The inmates enjoy a luxury that many people who work for a living aren't able to afford. Who has a golf course in their backyard? (cited in Hatherly, 2002:B1, B2)*

Under pressure from criticisms of a similar nature, the Correctional Service of Canada announced that a golf course at another B.C. facility, the minimum-security Ferndale Institution, would be turned over to a nonprofit community group to operate for the public. A CSC spokesman stated: "We had finally concluded that the

BOX 3.3, continued

kind of attention the golf course attracted was, overall, negative from a correctional point of view. We've got a jail to run" (cited in Bailey, 2002). Ferndale Institution had been the subject of unwelcome media attention once before when a high-profile inmate convicted of murder attempted to have his horse transported to the facility from his Saskatchewan ranch.

The CPA lobbies the federal government on an ongoing basis to make legislative and policy changes, including:

- requiring offenders convicted of first-degree murder to spend a minimum of 25 years in prison—as opposed to the current 15-year minimum—before being eligible for parole
- using an offender's criminal history and current offence as the primary factors in determining the security level at which the offender will serve his or her sentence
- creating an independent public inquiry into the sentencing, corrections, and parole systems, with the objective of identifying ways to reduce the risk to the community
- providing the victims of crime with the opportunity to have more input into sentencing, prison classification, and release decisions (Griffin, 2002)

VICTIMS AND SYSTEMS OF CORRECTIONS

The visibility of victims has been increased by several high-profile incidents, including some in which victims have chosen to shed their anonymity and speak out against their perpetrators (see Box 3.4).

Increasingly, provincial correctional systems are following the federal lead by involving or notifying crime victims about the system's decisions on inmates' applications for temporary absences and paroles, as well as the conditions of release (see Box 3.5). In Ontario, the Victim Empowerment Act (2002) gives victims of crime the right to attend parole hearings and speak to the parole board about the impact of the crime and the continuing effects of their victimization.

Increasing Accountability of Corrections

Systems of corrections are held legislatively accountable to the Canadian Charter of Rights and Freedoms, the provisions of the Corrections and

BOX 3.4

Assault Victim Strikes Back

On May 31, 1997, Tammy Crawford of Oshawa, Ontario, was brutally attacked, terrorized, and sexually assaulted by David Walker. Mr. Walker had served 17 years in a psychiatric prison and was on a day pass when he attacked Ms. Crawford at her parents' store. Rather than suffering in silence and anonymity, Ms. Crawford encouraged the media to print her name and photo, stating, "I want people out there to know what happened to a real person.... He is the criminal, not me. I have done nothing to be ashamed of, but he must not—must never be—allowed to do this to anyone again. People must know what happened or else there will never be a change." In addition to speaking out publicly against her attacker, Ms. Crawford filed a $1 million lawsuit against him and the psychiatric hospital.

Source: Mascoll, 1998:B3.

BOX 3.5

Victims' Right to Information in Manitoba

Under the Victims' Bill of Rights, victims of crime in Manitoba have a right to information about the following:

- the offender's name, the offence that resulted in the charge or conviction, and the court that dealt with the matter
- whether a pre-sentence or a pre-disposition report has been prepared and the name, address, and telephone number of the agency in charge of preparing the report
- whether an offender is under supervision in the community and the name of the office or agency responsible for the supervision
- any terms or conditions of a supervision order, including the date the order begins or the date any conditions end
- whether the offender is in custody, and if so, the name and location of the custodial facility

BOX 3.5, continued

- any relevant dates relating to the status of the offender, including the estimated date of release from custody, dates of temporary absences, or any other type of release
- any terms or conditions of the offender's release or temporary absence and their general destination if known
- notification if an offender is about to be released from a provincial custodial facility; escapes from custody or is unlawfully at large; breaches any terms or conditions of a supervision order; or dies

In addition, crime victims have the right to express their opinions about any release decisions.

Source: Manitoba Justice (www.gov.mb.ca/justice/victims/victimsindex.html).

Conditional Release Act, the federal Office of the Correctional Investigator, correctional ombudsmen at the provincial level, the courts, and commissions and task forces that are created to examine specific incidents or actions of correctional personnel. Commissions of inquiry have played a major role in correctional reform historically and during contemporary times. Box 3.6 lists the internal and external mechanisms of accountability to which the provincial system of corrections in Ontario is subject.

Systems of corrections are coming under increasing political scrutiny (see Box 3.7). Victims of crime and the families of crime victims are also increasingly holding systems of corrections accountable. In recent years, correctional authorities have been the target of an increasing number of civil suits launched by the victims of crime:

- The widow of a restaurant owner killed in a robbery filed suit against her husband's killers and the CSC, alleging that correctional officials had failed to ensure the safety of her and her late husband. One of the offenders, who had over 60 prior criminal convictions (including 15 convictions for escaping custody or being unlawfully at large), had been released from custody on mandatory supervision just 11 days before the murder (Canadian Press, 2001).
- The mother of a female offender who died in the Edmonton Institution for Women filed a lawsuit against the warden, whom she blamed for the

death of her daughter. The daughter had been found hanging in her cell after being transferred to the institution from a federal psychiatric facility. The suit claimed that the warden and prison officials failed to take the necessary security precautions to prevent the death and that the supervision and security of inmates in the facility were inadequate (Barrett, 1997:B1). For more information on this case, see Box 5.9 on page 193.

- A woman who had been raped at knifepoint by a career criminal with 63 prior convictions sued the CSC. The offender, who had been on statutory release and residing in a minimum-security institution, was in the community on a 12-hour day pass at the time of the attack. The suit was settled out of court in 2001 for $215,000 (Hall, 2001:A1, A4).

BOX 3.6

Accountability Mechanisms for Ontario Correctional Services

Internal Monitoring and Evaluation Mechanisms

- operational reviews, security reviews, audits, central and local employee relations committees, and Joint Health and Safety Committees under the Occupational Health and Safety Act

External Agencies

- Ombudsman Ontario
- Office of the Provincial Auditor
- Ontario Human Rights Commission
- Information and Privacy Commissioner
- building inspectors, public health officials, and occupational health and safety inspectors from the Ministry of Labour
- inspectors from local fire departments
- volunteers from special interest agencies, including the John Howard Society and the Elizabeth Fry Society
- local boards of monitors

Source: Ontario Ministry of Solicitor General and Correctional Services, 1996:1.

BOX 3.7

Pizza and Porn Night in the Saskatchewan Penitentiary

On New Year's Eve, 2001, inmates at the Saskatchewan Penitentiary (including more than 100 sex offenders) were shown pornographic movies and served pizzas in an attempt by staff to avoid the kind of disturbances that typically occur on that date. Canadian Alliance MP Randy White commented: "Corrections Canada is a disgrace today. It really is. They tell the people one thing about rehabilitation and then they go and show them sex videos and allow them to use drugs. They're so hypocritical."

Source: O'Neill, 2002:48.

Correctional authorities have also been the targets of civil suits filed by inmates. In 1998, inmates who were brutally attacked during a riot at the Headingley provincial jail in Manitoba filed lawsuits against the institution and the province for failing to provide a safe and secure environment (more on the Headingley riot in Chapter 5).

THE COMMUNITY AND CORRECTIONS

The role of the community in the corrections process has always been somewhat ambiguous. As the discussion in Chapter 2 revealed, historically, offenders were generally punished in public, and community residents not only were able to witness the infliction of the sanction, including hangings, but could often participate in showing their disapproval of the culprit by hurling insults, as well as the occasional rotten vegetable, at offenders. With the advent of jails and penitentiaries, however, punishment became more private, and the role of community residents in the correctional process diminished. This change was accompanied by the development of formal justice and correctional agencies and the increasing professionalization of correctional personnel.

Community Interest Groups and the NIMBY Syndrome

With a few notable exceptions, such as the involvement of community residents as volunteers in correctional institutions and in community programs, the role of the public is primarily reactive. Community sentiment is often expressed through interest groups such as the recently disbanded CAVEAT (Canadians Against Violence Everywhere Advocating its Termination). Most often, interest groups lobby for more severe sanctions for criminal offenders, longer periods of incarceration, and more stringent requirements for release. The extent to which these interest groups represent the views of the public is hard to determine; however, there is little doubt that these groups have been successful in exerting pressure on politicians, legislatures, and correctional personnel, including parole boards, and have significantly affected their decision making.

Because of public opposition, correctional systems have often had a great deal of difficulty in securing community participation in programs and services. A major obstacle to correctional programming in the community is the **NIMBY (Not In My Back Yard) syndrome.** This term describes the resistance that communities exhibit in response to correctional systems' efforts to locate programming and residences for offenders in their neighbourhoods. Among the reasons for community resistance are fear of crime, attitudes toward crime and offenders that are based largely on media accounts, and concerns that property values will be negatively affected (Benzvy-Miller, 1990). Correctional systems have thus far devised very few effective strategies for proactively addressing and counteracting the NIMBY syndrome. Too often, a correctional agency will attempt to locate a facility or program in an area, only to retreat when their intentions are discovered and publicized.

Although correctional authorities often find themselves under siege from the public and must often contend with the NIMBY syndrome when planning programs and facilities, it would be inaccurate to describe the public as being unsupportive of efforts to rehabilitate offenders. Research studies of citizens' attitudes toward crime have found that, in addition to supporting punishment that includes the use of imprisonment for general and specific deterrence, there is general support for efforts to address the underlying causes of criminal behaviour (McCorkle, 1993).

Public Information and Public Support

Corrections has been less successful than other criminal justice agencies, such as police services, in developing partnerships with communities and involving community residents in assisting and supporting criminal offenders. Far too often, correctional personnel find themselves in the position of reactive crisis management—responding to the accusations of citizen interest groups or attempting to reassure a nervous public following an escape or the commission of a serious crime by an offender on parole. Corrections is unique in that it does not have any natural basis of support in the community. Though police

Citizen protest

services may draw upon the interest of community residents in addressing problems of crime and disorder in their neighbourhoods, there are few advocates for convicted persons. This issue is revisited in the discussion of the re-entry of offenders from institutions into the community in Chapter 10.

Interestingly, although the public is often critical of the criminal justice system and particularly the criminal courts for being too lenient with offenders, if given the choice, the public's preference is for developing alternative sanctions rather than building more prisons. An Ontario poll conducted in 1998 found, for example, that 85 percent of adults queried supported spending money for crime prevention rather than building more prisons and 66 percent preferred spending money on developing alternatives to imprisonment (cited in Carey, 1998:A2).

The key to expanding the perspectives of the public beyond merely increasing the severity of punishments is information. Several studies have found, for example, that when citizens are given additional information on various sentencing alternatives, the number of offenders they would "sentence" to prison declines (Roberts, 1992). Therefore, there is a need to provide the public with information about alternatives to confinement, and the media are most likely not the best sources for this knowledge. There is sufficient evidence to suggest that the public will support various correctional programs and services in the community if provided with sufficient information about initiatives that may be more effective than imprisonment.

There is also some evidence to suggest that community residents are now less resistant to having prisons located near their communities and, in fact, competition often occurs among communities when a new prison is being sited. This is due in large measure to the economic benefits, including jobs and increased business for merchants and tradespeople, that are associated with the building and operation of a new correctional facility (Young, 1998). Gravenhurst, Ontario, for example, is well on the way to having the highest per capita prison population of any city in Canada, owing in large measure to proactive lobbying for federal and provincial facilities by the city government (Finlay, 1997:A23).

VOLUNTEERS AND CITIZEN ADVOCATES FOR CORRECTIONAL REFORM

The difficulties that correctional systems have in securing the interest and involvement of community residents in delivering programs and services for offenders should not obscure the fact that, across Canada, thousands of people of all ages volunteer to work with offenders in a variety of institutional and community settings. This volunteer work includes regular visits to institutions by religious groups, service clubs, and sports teams, as well as one-on-one mentoring in literacy programs and pre-release planning. Citizens also volunteer as community sponsors for offenders on parole. And citizens are becoming increasingly involved in various restorative/community justice initiatives (to be discussed in Chapter 4). These activities and contributions of volunteers and community organizations often do not receive the publicity of more sensational events, such as escapes and prison disturbances, yet they are a vital component of systems of corrections.

There have been attempts at both the federal and provincial levels to increase community participation in corrections. Acting as a liaison between federal correctional institutions and the community are Citizens' Advisory Committees (see Box 3.8). In Ontario, a similar function is served by local boards of monitors whose role is to strengthen the link between the province's correctional institutions and communities that host them.

BOX 3.8

Citizens' Advisory Committees

Citizens' Advisory Committees (CACs) are autonomous committees composed of local citizens who "represent various social, cultural, and demographic backgrounds and occupations, and usually reside in proximity to the correctional facility for which the committee serves." The first CAC was established in 1965, and CACs now operate in all federal correctional institutions and district parole offices.

The goals of CACs include promoting public knowledge and understanding of corrections, contributing to the development of correctional facilities and programs, increasing public participation in the correctional process, and serving as impartial observers of the day-to-day operations of the CSC. In carrying out their mandate, CACs provide advice to CSC managers, meet regularly with correctional staff and management, and act as a liaison between correctional institutions and the community.

Source: Correctional Service of Canada (www.csc-scc.gc.ca/text/partenair/partne04_e.shtml).

QUESTIONS FOR REVIEW

1. Summarize the key features of Canadian crime rates.

2. Identify and discuss the objectives of sentencing.

3. What is judicial determination, and how is it used in Canadian criminal justice?

4. What have been the results of the three-strikes laws in the United States?

5. What do research studies indicate about the effectiveness of incarceration as a sanction for convicted offenders?

6. What are some factors that may limit incarceration's effectiveness as a sanction?

7. Summarize the key arguments that are offered by the proponents and opponents of the death penalty.

8. Discuss what is meant by the NIMBY syndrome. What exceptions appear to exist with respect to this syndrome, and why?

9. What opinions and attitudes does the general public hold toward the criminal justice system and corrections?

10. Identify and discuss strategies that could be used by systems of corrections to solicit and secure community support for and participation in correctional programming.

REFERENCES

Adams, M. 1990. "Canadian Attitudes toward Crime and Justice." *Forum on Corrections Research* 2(1):10–13.

Andrews, D. 1995. "The Psychology of Criminal Conduct and Effective Treatment." In J. McGuire (ed.), *What Works: Reducing Reoffending. Guidelines from Research and Practice* (35–62). Chichester, U.K.: John Wiley and Sons.

Aubry, J. 2002. "Our Courts Aren't Tough Enough: Poll." *Ottawa Citizen*. August 11.

Bailey, I. 2002. "B.C. Prisoners Could Lose Golf Privileges." *National Post* (December 11):A1, A8.

Barrett, T. 1997. "Mother of Slain Inmate Sues Prison Warden." *The Edmonton Journal* (October 23):B1.

Benzvy-Miller, S. 1990. "Community Corrections and the NIMBY Syndrome." *Forum on Corrections Research* 2(2):18–22.

Canadian Press. 2001. "Vancouver Widow Sues Corrections Canada over Husband's Stabbing Death." March 14.

Carey, E. 1998. "Crime Myths Prevail: Study People Think Murder Rate Is Rising, but It Isn't." *The Toronto Star* (May 22):A2.

Champion, D. 1994. *Measuring Offender Risk*. Westport, Conn.: Greenwood Press.

Cobb, C. 2001. "Canadians Prefer Prevention over Prisons." *The Vancouver Sun* (March 12):A3.

Corrections Statistics Committee. 2000. *Corrections and Conditional Release: Statistical Overview*. Ottawa: Solicitor General Canada.

Crouch, B.M. 1993. "Is Incarceration Really Worse? Analysis of Offenders' Preferences for Prison over Probation." *Justice Quarterly* 10(1):67–88.

Decker, S.H., and C.W. Kohfeld. 1990. "The Deterrent Effect of Capital Punishment in the Five Most Active Execution States: A Time Series Analysis." *Criminal Justice Review* 15(2):173–91.

Finlay, J.R. 1997. "Town's Lust to Host Jails Is Desperate." *The Toronto Star* (August 20):A23.

Gardner, D. 2002. "Bars and Stripes." *Ottawa Citizen* (March 16):B1.

Gendreau, P., C. Goggin, and F.T. Cullen. 1999. *The Effects of Prison Sentences on Recidivism*. Ottawa: Solicitor General Canada.

Greenwood, P.W., C.P. Rydell, A.F. Abrahamse, J.P. Caulkins, J.R. Chiesa, K.E. Model, and S.P. Klein. 1994. *Three Strikes and You're Out: Estimated Benefits of California's New Mandatory-Sentencing Law*. Palo Alto, Calif.: Rand Corporation.

Griffin, D. 2002. "Prisons: Canada's National Disgrace." *The Canadian Police Association Express* 56 (fall):4–5.

Griffiths, C.T., and A. Hatch Cunningham. 2003. *Canadian Criminal Justice: A Primer*. 2nd ed. Toronto: Nelson.

Griffiths, C.T., E. Zellerer, D.S. Wood, and G. Saville. 1995. *Crime, Law, and Justice among Inuit in the Baffin Region, N.W.T., Canada*. Burnaby, B.C.: Criminology Research Centre, Simon Fraser University.

Hall, N. 2001. "Woman Raped by Parolee Gets $215,000 from Government." *The Vancouver Sun* (January 9):A1, A4.

Hanks, G.C. 1997. *Against the Death Penalty: Christian and Secular Arguments against Capital Punishment*. Scottsdale, Pa.: Herald Press.

Hatherly, J. 2002. "Golf Courses, Ocean Views Do Not a Prison Make." *National Post* (September 30):B1.

Hendrick, D., and L. Farmer. 2002. "Adult Correctional Services in Canada, 2000–01." *Juristat* 22(10). Cat. no. 85-002-XPE. Ottawa: Canadian Centre for Justice Statistics, Statistics Canada.

Mascoll, P. 1998. "Assault Victim Fights Back: Indefinite Jail Term Sought for Sex Attacker." *The Toronto Star* (April 17):B3.

McCorkle, R.C. 1993. "Research Note: Punish or Rehabilitate? Public Attitudes toward Six Common Crimes." *Crime and Delinquency* 39(2):240–52.

Mennonite Central Committee Canada. 1997. *Justice in Crisis: A Report on Canada's Criminal Justice System*. Winnipeg: Mennonite Central Committee Canada.

National Crime Prevention Council. 1997. *Incarceration in Canada*. Ottawa: National Crime Prevention Council.

O'Neill, T. 2002. "Sask Pen's Porn and Pizza Party: Corrections Canada Is Under the Gun after Staff Threw Prisoners a Scandalous New Year's Eve Bash." *Report Magazine* 29(3):48.

Ontario Ministry of Solicitor General and Correctional Services. 1996. *MSGCS Information Paper: Accountability Mechanisms*. Toronto: Correctional Services Division.

Peterson, R.D., and W.C. Bailey. 1991. "Felony Murder and Capital Punishment: An Examination of the Deterrence Question." *Criminology* 29(3):367–98.

Radelet, M.L., and R.L. Akers. 1997. "Deterrence and the Death Penalty: The Views of the Experts." Unpublished paper. Retrieved from www.corrections.com.

Reitan, E. 1993. "Why the Deterrence Argument for Capital Punishment Fails." *Criminal Justice Ethics* 12(1):26–33.

Roberts, J.V. 1992. "Public Opinion, Crime, and Criminal Justice." In M. Tonry (ed.), *Crime and Justice: A Review of Research* (99–180). Vol. 16. Chicago: University of Chicago Press.

———. 2001. *Fear of Crime and Attitudes to Criminal Justice in Canada: A Review of Recent Trends, 2001–02*. Ottawa: Solicitor General Canada.

Roberts, J V., and D.P. Cole. 1999. *Making Sense of Sentencing*. Toronto: University of Toronto Press.

Savoie, J. 2002. "Crime Statistics in Canada, 2001." *Juristat* 22(6). Cat. no. 85-002-XPE. Ottawa: Canadian Centre for Justice Statistics, Statistics Canada.

Shephard, M. 1997. "'Imagine the Worst': Inmates Soon Learn That to Be Sent to a Canadian Prison Is to Be Condemned to a Term of Fear, Pain, Even Torture." *The Toronto Star* (August 31):F1.

Solicitor General Canada. 1998. *CCRA 5 Year Review: Judicial Determination*. Ottawa.

———. 2001. *High Risk Offenders: A Handbook for Criminal Justice Professionals*. Ottawa.

Solicitor General Portfolio Corrections Statistics Committee. 2002. *Corrections and Conditional Release: Statistical Overview*. Ottawa: Public Works and Government Services Canada.

Sprott, J.B., and A.N. Doob. 1998. "Understanding Provincial Variation in Incarceration Rates." *Canadian Journal of Criminology* 40(3):305–22.

Thomas, M. 2002. "Adult Criminal Court Statistics, 2000/01." *Juristat* 22(2). Cat. no. 85-XPE-002. Ottawa: Canadian Centre for Justice Statistics, Statistics Canada.

Tufts, J. 2000. "Public Attitudes toward the Criminal Justice System." *Juristat* 20 (12). Cat. no. 85-002-XPE. Ottawa: Canadian Centre for Justice Statistics, Statistics Canada.

Turner, M.G., J.L. Sundt, B.K. Applegate, and F.T. Cullen. 1995. "'Three Strikes and You're Out' Legislation: A National Assessment." *Federal Probation* 59(3):16–35.

U.S. General Accounting Office. 1990. *Death Penalty Sentencing*. Washington, D.C.: Government Printing Office.

Young, M.G. 1998. "Rethinking Community Resistance to Prison Siting: Results from a Community Impact Assessment." *Canadian Journal of Criminology* 40(3):323–27.

CHAPTER 4
ALTERNATIVES TO CONFINEMENT

CHAPTER OBJECTIVES

- *Identify and discuss traditional alternatives to incarceration.*
- *Discuss probation and the role and responsibilities of probation officers.*
- *Identify and discuss innovative intermediate sanctions.*
- *Consider the effectiveness of intermediate sanctions.*
- *Discuss initiatives in restorative/community justice.*

KEY TERMS

Community corrections
Diversion programs
Net-widening
Mandatory conditions
Additional conditions
Pre-sentence report (PSR)
Differential supervision
Intermediate sanctions/alternative
  sanctions/community sanctions

Intensive supervision probation
  (ISP)
Rigorous custody programs
Electronic monitoring (EM)
Victim–offender mediation (VOM)
Circle sentencing
Community holistic healing
Family group conferences

This chapter examines a broad range of programs and strategies that are used by the criminal justice and correctional systems as alternatives to confinement. These strategies include the more traditional practices of diversion and probation, as well as a variety of intermediate sanctions (or alternative/community sanctions) and restorative/community justice initiatives. Recall from Chapter 3 that the vast majority of offenders who receive a sentence of supervision remain in the community (see Figure 3.5 on page 78). In fact, alternative sanctions are being increasingly used for offenders charged with or convicted of serious offences, including sex offences and spousal assault.

The search for alternative measures has been driven by the escalating costs of confining offenders in correctional institutions and by research evidence that calls into question the effectiveness of incarceration as a general and specific deterrent (see Chapter 3). In addition, the use of alternatives to confinement for less serious offenders allows more resources to be directed toward those offenders who constitute a greater risk to society and who require specialized intervention in the controlled setting of the prison.

A WORD ABOUT COMMUNITY CORRECTIONS

At the outset, it is important to consider the term **community corrections.** Most texts on corrections have at least one chapter on community corrections, which generally appears in the latter part of the book. Into this chapter are grouped such disparate correctional strategies as bail supervision, fine option programs, probation, intermediate sanctions, and electronic monitoring, as well as parole and various programs for offenders who have served a period of confinement. Needless to say, the differences among these very different correctional strategies are often obscured, resulting in considerable confusion.

In this text, there is a deliberate separation of probation, intermediate sanctions, and restorative/community justice (to be discussed in this chapter) from parole and re-entry, which are discussed in Chapters 9 and 10 respectively. This separation is designed to highlight the substantial differences between true alternatives to confinement and those strategies that are applied to the offenders who have served a period of time in confinement and are then released by a parole board or after having served their sentence, minus time earned for good behaviour and/or positive performance in the institution.

The decision not to use "community corrections" as a chapter title was also intentional. This term is surrounded by so many misconceptions and has been overused to the point that it is of limited use in the study of systems of corrections. For example, any program with the term *community* in it implies that there is significant participation in and support of the particular strategy by community residents. Yet, community residents are notable by their general absence of involvement in community-based correctional programs and may even be hostile toward systems of corrections. As used in this text, the term community corrections refers to correctional programs and the supervision of offenders that take place in the community, rather than in institutional settings.

THE COMMUNITY AND ALTERNATIVE SANCTIONS

It has been previously noted that correctional systems have experienced difficulty in countering the disinformation on crime and criminal justice presented by the media and in securing the support and participation of community residents in correctional programs and services offered in the community. There is research evidence to suggest, however, that the public is not opposed to alternative sanctions under which the offender is closely supervised in the community rather than incarcerated. Community residents are generally willing to support community correctional alternatives if they are provided with information on specific programs, the levels of supervision, and the types of offenders in the program. As well, community residents actively participate in many restorative/community justice initiatives, several of which will be discussed later in the chapter. These initiatives provide an opportunity for the public to become directly involved in the response to offenders as well as to participate in addressing the larger issues that may have contributed to the offending behaviour.

DIVERSION

Diversion programs have been a feature of Canadian criminal justice for the past 30 years. Offenders can be diverted from the formal criminal justice process at several stages; there are pre-charge police diversion programs, post-charge diversion programs, and post-sentencing diversion programs, all of which allow offenders to avoid incarceration. The objective of all diversion programs is to keep offenders from being processed further into the formal criminal justice system, although more specific objectives of diversion programs include the following:

- avoidance of negative labelling and stigmatization
- reduction of unnecessary social control and coercion
- reduction of recidivism

- provision of services (assistance)
- reduction of justice system costs

These competing objectives often function to limit the potential effectiveness of diversion programs.

Diversion programs tend to target first-time, low-risk offenders, raising the concern of **net-widening**—that is, involving offenders who would otherwise have been released outright by the police or not charged by Crown counsel. There are, however, diversion programs that are directed toward specific offender groups and more serious offences. Some examples of diversion programs in operation across the country are profiled in Box 4.1. Note that these and other diversion programs may also accommodate other offenders, including probationers, unless they are exclusively identified as a post-charge, pre-trial diversion option.

Most diversion programs require that offenders acknowledge responsibility for their behaviour and agree to fulfill certain conditions within a specified period of time. These conditions might include paying restitution to the victim or completing a number of community service hours. Box 4.2 presents a case study that illustrates how diversion works.

BOX 4.1

Selected Diversion Programs

Mid-Island Diversion Program (Nanaimo, B.C.): Operated by the John Howard Society, this program is for minor, first-time adult offenders who have acknowledged responsibility for their actions. The objectives of the program include holding offenders accountable for their behaviour, reducing the costs of criminal justice, and ensuring victim involvement. Available programs include anger management, employment and education programs, and victim–offender mediation.

Community Sex Offender Program (Canim Lake, B.C.): Operated by a First Nations community, this program for sex offenders and victims of sexual abuse is designed to address the needs of the offender and the victim within a family and community context and to provide a more effective response than the formal, adversarial justice system. Services include education and prevention programming, an "amnesty" period in which undetected offenders can disclose their offences and receive treatment without being subject to criminal charges, and interventions that combine modern treatment techniques and traditional healing practices.

BOX 4.1, continued

Regina Alternative Measures Program (RAMP) (Regina): RAMP provides a variety of culturally sensitive pre- and post-charge diversion programs for adult and youth offenders, including mediation, family group conferencing, and healing circles. The program also offers a Narcotic Education Intervention Program that is designed to address the needs of violent and repeat offenders. Further information on RAMP is available online at www.saskjustice.gov.sk.ca/Comm_Services/justice_programs/regina.shtml.

Macadam (Chicoutimi, Que.): Funded by the government of Quebec and the Canadian Mental Health Association, this program provides assistance to people with mental-health problems who are in conflict with the law. In addition to offering assistance in locating housing and accessing medical and social services, program staff provide anger management counselling, education and work programs, and intensive supervision services. Referrals are made to the program at either the pre- or post-charge stage.

Community Council Program (Toronto): This program is directed toward urban Aboriginal offenders and is designed to return a greater degree of responsibility to the Aboriginal community, to reduce recidivism, and to instill in offenders responsibility and accountability for their behaviour. The offender is an active participant in discussions about the offence and lifestyle issues. The council, composed of Aboriginal people from the community, has at its disposal a number of sanctions that it can impose to reintegrate the offender into the community and to begin the healing process. Available options include fines, the payment of restitution to the victim, completion of a number of community service hours, and referral to treatment resources.

Adult Diversion Program (Dartmouth, N.S.): This is a post-charge, pre-trial option program for offenders who have committed nonviolent offences. Staffed by probation officers, the program includes community service, supervision of restitution to the victim, and the option of no additional intervention.

Drug Treatment Court (Toronto/Vancouver): Cases are diverted to these courts by Crown counsel, who determine eligibility—most often, persons charged with minor drug-related offences (those charged with violent offences are not eligible). Offenders avoid incarceration by agreeing to abide by specified conditions, including participation in drug abuse treatment programs and regular drug testing. Although total abstinence from drugs is not mandatory, offenders must report relapses to program staff and demonstrate progress toward a reduction in their level of drug dependency. Upon successful completion of the program, those persons who have been charged with less serious offences may have the charges stayed or withdrawn, while more serious offenders may receive a period of probation. Failure to abide by the conditions of the program results in the offender being processed through the regular court system.

Sources: Chiodo, 2001; Creechan and Grekul, 1998.

PROBATION

Section 731 of the Criminal Code provides that, in those cases in which there is no minimum penalty prescribed, the sentencing judge may place the offender on probation. Although probation is generally used as an alternative to confinement, it may be used in conjunction with a period of incarceration,

BOX 4.2

A Case from the Nova Scotia Adult Diversion Project

The offender is a 38-year-old divorced mother of two children who was receiving social assistance. She is accused of defrauding social assistance of $14,000. The victim and the offender agreed that restitution would be an acceptable resolution. The charge was laid (sworn) by the police but not placed on the court docket. The police made the referral directly to the program staff, established contact with the victim to determine their wishes/concerns, and interviewed the offender to determine her interest in participating in the diversion option. Following an assessment interview with the diversion (probation) officer regarding the offence and the proposed resolution, the client signed a written agreement outlining her obligation to make monthly payments of $100 directly to the social assistance office.

The offender had a part-time job but is highly motivated to acquire a better job and hopes to repay the restitution more quickly. If she fails to abide by the condition of the diversion agreement, the matter will be referred to the police for processing through court.

Source: Church Council on Justice and Corrections, 1996:89.

including intermittent sentences, which are generally served in provincial/territorial facilities on weekends. The maximum length of time that a probation order can be in effect is three years for adults and two years for young offenders.

Once ordered, probation falls under the authority of the provincial/territorial correctional systems and may be used alone or following a period of confinement. Probation is not available for federal offenders, except in those cases in which the offender is sentenced to exactly two years in confinement; in this instance, the judge may attach a probation order for up to three years.

Statistics on the use of probation in 2000–01 indicate the following:

- The use of probation continues to increase.
- There is considerable variation among the provinces/territories in the use of probation.
- Probation is the most frequently imposed sanction, accounting for 44 percent of convicted cases.
- Probation is most often imposed in cases involving crimes against the person.
- Probation often follows a period in custody.
- Nearly one-half of probation orders are for periods of six months to a year.
- The average length of an adult probation order is one year.
- There are, proportionately, more female offenders on probation than males, primarily because women tend to commit less serious offences.
- Aboriginal offenders represent about 12 percent of probationers nationwide. (Thomas, 2002)

Probation is the most common disposition in youth courts; it may either be a stand-alone disposition or follow a period of confinement in a youth detention facility. An adult offender can be on probation in one of five ways: (1) as part of a conditional discharge, (2) as a condition of a suspended sentence, (3) as part of an intermittent sentence, (4) as a sentence on its own (the most common), or (5) following a prison term of less than two years.

Probation may be used in conjunction with any of the following dispositions:

- fine
- imprisonment for a term of up to two years less a day
- intermittent sentence
- conditional sentence

Offenders who receive a conditional discharge, suspended sentence, or intermittent sentence *must* be placed on probation. Those receiving a fine, incarceration, or conditional sentence *may* be placed on probation. In those cases in which probation follows a term of confinement, probation supervision begins either at release or at the expiration of parole.

The Conditions of Probation

Each adult probationer must comply with three **mandatory conditions:**

- Keep the peace and be of good behaviour.
- Appear before the court when required to do so by the court.
- Notify the court or the probation officer of any change of name, address, or occupation.

As well, the sentencing judge may impose **additional conditions,** which are tailored to meet the specific needs of the offender. Following are the more common additional conditions of probation:

- Report as required to a probation officer.
- Abstain from drugs and/or alcohol.
- Abstain from owning, possessing, or carrying a weapon.
- Provide for the support and care of dependents.
- Perform up to 240 hours of community service work over a period not to exceed 18 months.
- With the offender's agreement, participate in a treatment program.
- Avoid contact with specified persons (e.g., co-accused or victims).
- Comply with any other conditions set out by the court.
- Pay restitution to the victim.
- Participate in a victim–offender reconciliation program.
- Observe an imposed curfew or area and travel restrictions.
- Be placed under home confinement and/or be electronically monitored for compliance.

For young offenders, additional conditions may include attending school, seeking and maintaining employment, or living with parents or other adults deemed appropriate by the court.

Probation conditions must be reasonable and, ideally, designed with an eye to preventing the offender from committing additional crimes. During the period of supervision, the probation officer may request that the sentencing judge increase or decrease the number of additional conditions, eliminate all additional conditions, or reduce (but not lengthen) the total period of the probation order. An adult probationer who without reasonable excuse fails or refuses to comply with a condition, or who commits a new offence, may be charged with breach of probation. A breach of probation is an elective (or hybrid) offence that can carry a maximum penalty of two years if proceeded with by indictment. Young offenders on probation may be charged with breach of probation for failing to adhere to the conditions of their probation order. A copy of a probation order, with all key identifiers removed, is presented in Appendix 4.1 on page 141.

Recruitment and Training of Probation Officers

As noted earlier in this chapter, probation falls under the authority of the provinces/territories. Each jurisdiction has developed its own procedures and standards for recruiting and training probation officers. In recent years, there has been a shift toward a pre-employment training model wherein potential applicants must complete prerequisite courses (often at their own expense) before applying for the position of probation officer. In British Columbia, for example, persons who intend to apply for positions in probation must first complete the following courses:

1. Role and Mandate of the Adult Probation Officer
2. Introduction to the Criminal Justice System (Community)
3. Sentencing and Custody
4. Professional Ethics and Standards of Conduct
   (www.jibc.bc.ca/corrections/programs/public/adultProbation.htm)

In Ontario, the training for probation (and provincial parole) officer recruits consists of an 18-month developmental process and includes an orientation to the local area, the achievement of specific skills, two five-day residential courses, a self-study program, and two oral examinations. The training focuses on developing skills in report-writing, supervision, and enforcement, as well as integrating the theory and practice of probation.

Most jurisdictions offer ongoing in-service training courses that focus on the supervision of special populations (e.g., sex offenders, the mentally disordered) and the use of assessment instruments.

Role and Responsibilities of Probation Officers

The activities of probation officers are centred on assessing clients with respect to their needs and the risk they pose, providing individualized case management with the objective of reducing criminal behaviour, and supervising offenders on probation as well as persons who have been released on bail while awaiting trial.

Preparation of Pre-Sentence Reports

Probation officers are involved in preparing the **pre-sentence report (PSR)** on adult offenders who have been convicted. The PSR contains a wealth of information on the offender's sociobiographical background and offence history, as well as victim impact information and assessments by treatment professionals. Most PSRs conclude with a sentence recommendation, and although judges are not bound by this recommendation, they generally accept it. A completed PSR, with all key identifiers removed, is presented in Appendix 4.2 (page 144). Note the emphasis on the possibility of using traditional Aboriginal approaches to justice.

Probation officers are also responsible for setting bail conditions and providing supervision. A recognizance of bail form, with all key identifiers removed, is presented in Appendix 4.3 on page 151.

Assessment of Offender Risk and Needs

One of the core components of the probation officer's role is completing assessments that are designed to identify the offender's needs, to evaluate risk, and to assist in formulating a plan of supervision. The probation officer completes these assessments at the time the offender is sentenced. The assessments are used not only in the case management process but also by parole boards in determining whether to grant conditional release to offenders in custody (more on this in Chapter 9).

A risk/needs assessment instrument used by probation officers in Ontario is the Level of Service Inventory–Ontario Revision (LSI-OR), which uses offender characteristics to determine the likelihood of reoffending. Probation officers in British Columbia use the Community Risk/Needs Assessment (CRNA); the Spousal Assault Risk Assessment (SARA); and the Static-99, which is replacing the Sex Offender Risk/Needs Assessment (SORA). A CRNA form is reproduced in Appendix 4.4 on page 154. This form is divided into two sections: (1) a Needs Assessment that lists dynamic factors (offender attributes that can be altered through intervention); and (2) a Criminal History Risk Assessment that lists static factors (offender attributes that *cannot* be altered through intervention) (more on dynamic and static factors in Chapter 8).

There are several limitations in the use of assessment instruments, one of which is that there is often a lack of sufficient community resources to meet the identified needs of the probationer. In such situations, risk assessment instruments might more appropriately be viewed as a way for correctional personnel to protect themselves from criticism and civil suits should an offender subsequently commit a serious crime.

Assessment of Offenders Applying for Provincial Parole

In British Columbia, Ontario, and Quebec, the three provinces with provincial parole boards, probation officers serve as parole officers. In this capacity, they prepare community assessments that are used by the parole board to assess the viability of the inmate-applicant's release plan (more on this in Chapter 9).

Probation Supervision

Supervision plays a critical role in the effectiveness of probation. Therefore, the relationship established between the probation officer and the probationer is very important. Among the attributes of a positive relationship are:

- establishing and maintaining a good rapport
- considering the individual needs of the offender
- empowering the probationer to take responsibility and initiative
- maintaining a proper balance between control and assistance
- engaging in **differential supervision,** based on the risk the offender presents

Probation appears to be most successful when the probation officers create relationships in which the offenders can speak openly about their concerns and problems, feel they are being treated as individuals, and view the probation officer as a person who genuinely cares about them. It is also important that probationers understand what is expected of them and that there is consistency in supervision. In intensive supervision programs, which generally involve working with special groups of probationers such as sex offenders, caseloads are smaller, and the probation officer can see clients more often than officers engaged in general probation work can. The probation officers can also do more external supervision, including home visits.

The supervision strategies that a probation officer employs should match the requirements and needs of the offender. For offenders who are less cooperative, an approach based on control may be effective, whereas for offenders who are motivated to change, the probation officer can provide encouragement, support, and assistance. Over the past decade, there has been a decided shift in the role and orientation of probation officers toward control/surveillance. This shift has been due in large measure to increasing caseloads, the focus on risk assessment in order to ensure accountability and reduce liability, and the increasing number of special categories of offenders (such as sex offenders and assaultive male offenders) who are receiving sentences of probation.

The Dual Role of Probation Officers

Probation officers perform a dual role of providing assistance and support to offenders in their caseload while at the same time enforcing the conditions of the probation order. These duties may lead to a conflict in roles. For example, a probationer with a history of drug addiction who falls off the wagon may want to ask his or her probation officer for help in finding a treatment program, but may fear that disclosing the illegal drug use will trigger a charge of breach of probation. On the other hand, failure to disclose the drug relapse may result in the probationer committing further criminal acts to support his or her addiction. A probation officer who discovers that the probationer is not adhering to the conditions of the probation order may have considerable discretion in deciding whether to revoke probation. That decision often turns on the severity of the alleged breach.

Programs for Probationers

Provincial/territorial systems of corrections and nonprofit organizations offer a wide variety of programs and services for probationers. Probation officers are becoming increasingly involved as facilitators of core programs for persons under community supervision. An offender's participation in one of these programs is generally stipulated on his or her probation order. Several examples of programs for probationers are highlighted in Box 4.3. Note that participants in many of these programs may include persons other than probationers.

Obstacles to Effective Probation

The efforts of probation officers have been hindered by a variety of factors, including the following:

- *increasing workloads:* The duties of probation officers have continued to expand and now include providing bail supervision to adult criminal courts; preparing PSRs for the sentencing court; supervising offenders on conditional sentence orders; and liaising with social services, the police, and courts.

BOX 4.3

Selected Programs for Probationers

Family Violence Intervention Program (Kamloops, B.C.): This 20-week, nonresidential program is designed to teach men to take responsibility for and effectively manage their anger, abuse, and violence. It is directed toward offenders convicted of spousal assault and is operated by the John Howard Society.

Family Life Improvement Program (Edmonton): This program is designed to teach family life skills, with a particular focus on urban Aboriginals. Among the services offered are counselling, anger management, education, and community service. The program strongly emphasizes personal responsibility.

Anger Management Program (Winnipeg): This 21-session program for assaultive offenders is centred on cognitive-behavioural modification. It focuses on offenders assuming responsibility for their behaviour, anger, and aggression; on alternative behaviours that will assist in avoiding future aggression; and on problem-solving strategies.

Learning Resource Program (St. John's): Operated by the John Howard Society and staffed by social workers, this provincially funded program is based on a cognitive-behavioural approach that attempts to address the criminogenic needs of offenders. Courses and counselling are offered in a number of areas, including substance abuse, anger management, and cognitive skills.

Thelma and Louise Program (Toronto): Operated by the Elizabeth Fry Society, the Thelma and Louise Program targets women with drug and alcohol problems, many of whom are in conflict with the law. The program revolves around weekly group sessions that focus on harm reduction and on providing support for program participants.

Sexual Deviance Assessment/Treatment Program (Charlottetown): This program is aimed at people who are either at risk of engaging in or who have engaged in deviant sexual behaviour. Services include sex offender treatment interventions, anger management, relapse prevention, and support for the offender's family.

Source: Creechan and Grekul, 1998.

- *increasing caseloads:* The large caseloads of probation officers (as high as 100 cases per officer in some jurisdictions) preclude probation officers from giving adequate time and attention to the individual management and treatment needs of offenders in the community. Owing to time constraints, most case management and supervision is done by telephone rather than in face-to-face encounters.

- *changing profile of probationers:* In recent years, the profile of offenders receiving a period of supervision under probation has changed. Previously, the typical probationer was an offender who was convicted of a nonviolent property offence and had no extensive criminal history. Probation caseloads are now increasingly populated by special categories of offenders, including those convicted of sex offences and spousal assault and who have a history of violence. In British Columbia, for example, men convicted of spousal assault make up 30 percent of the probation caseload. The growth in special categories of offenders has placed additional demands on probation services to develop specialized services and to provide close supervision. To effectively supervise and assist special categories of offenders, probation officers require specialized training courses. Provincial/territorial systems of corrections are increasingly shifting resources to high-risk offender groups.

- *funding cutbacks and lack of resources:* Government cutbacks in funding for community resources mean that there are often inadequate services available to probationers with special needs, such as mentally disordered offenders. Although probationers are routinely assessed, there are often no resources that can be accessed after the assessment stage. And although probation officers in specialized units may be involved in facilitating group sessions with probationers, offenders requiring one-on-one counselling may find it difficult to access services, unless the probationer has the resources to pay for private services.

- *stress and burnout among probation officers:* All of the above factors have made probation services an increasingly stressful occupational field. Officers are at increased risk of emotional exhaustion (often referred to as burnout) and feelings of cynicism directed at their clients in particular and the justice system in general.

The obstacles to providing effective probation services are especially formidable in remote and northern regions (see Box 4.4).

The Effectiveness of Probation

Despite its long history and extensive use in correctional systems, the effectiveness of probation as a correctional strategy continues to be questioned. Research studies suggest that probation is most effective with those offenders

BOX 4.4

Probation in the Remote North

A study (Griffiths et al., 1995) of crime and justice in the Baffin region, in what is now the territory of Nunavut, found that Inuit residents and justice and social service personnel had numerous concerns about the effectiveness of probation. Among the more serious problems with probation in Baffin communities were (1) the overuse and inappropriate use of probation; (2) the ineffectiveness of probation in controlling the offender and protecting the community; (3) the inability of supervisory personnel to enforce the conditions of probation; (4) the absence of community-based programs and services for probationers; (5) the ineffectiveness of existing counselling programs in addressing the needs of offenders; and (6) the questionable effectiveness of program personnel.

Concern about the effectiveness of probation was reflected in the comments of an Inuit woman who had been the victim of violence in one of the communities:

> *He was charged with assault. Then, a few weeks later, he was in JP court and he got six months probation. I thought it was going to be ok because after the JP court he said he would quit beating me up. But after one month he started again. That was against his probation. He'd go see his probation officer every month and when he still had six or eight months to go, he quit going. Nobody said anything and nothing happened. He was still drinking when he was on probation. It's just a lot of words, no action. (Griffiths et al., 1995:159)*

Contributing to the overuse and inappropriate use of probation in remote areas such as Nunavut is the reluctance of circuit court judges to sentence offenders to periods of confinement in correctional institutions, which may be hundreds of kilometres from the offenders' home community.

who are in a stable personal relationship, are employed, have higher levels of education, and do not have an extensive criminal record. However, there is no conclusive evidence that probation is effective in reducing recidivism.

In many jurisdictions, efforts are being made to reinvent probation to make it more effective. Strategies for improving probation include the following:

- *supervising probationers in the community rather than in the office:* It is important that probation officers have firsthand knowledge of the offender's residence, family situation, and the other aspects of the offender's life.

- *introducing 24/7/365 supervision:* Community supervision must be carried out at night, on weekends, and holidays, not just during regular business hours.
- *focusing supervision on high-risk offenders who pose a public safety risk (e.g., sex offenders):* The province of Ontario has implemented a service delivery model that utilizes this strategy.
- *ensuring strict enforcement of probation conditions:* Historically, breaches of probation have often not been taken seriously by either the probationer or the supervising probation officer. Offenders have rarely been convicted for breaching the conditions of their probation order.
- *developing partnerships between probation services and the community:* This would increase citizen awareness in addition to providing offenders with prosocial support networks and greater access to treatment resources.
- *creating performance-based initiatives to assess the effectiveness of probation practice and programs.* (Corbett, 1999)

INTERMEDIATE SANCTIONS

The term **intermediate sanctions,** also often referred to as **alternative sanctions** or **community sanctions,** describes a wide variety of correctional programs that generally fall between traditional probation and incarceration, although specific initiatives may include either of these penalties. Intermediate sanctions include fines, community service, day centres, home detention with or without electronic monitoring, intensive probation supervision, strict discipline camps, and conditional sentence orders. These are intermediate options along a continuum that has imprisonment as the most severe punishment and traditional probation as the least severe. Many of these programs were originally developed to reduce the large numbers of offenders being sent to correctional institutions.

There are two sets of objectives for intermediate sanctions:

- offender-oriented objectives, which include the assurance of real punishment, retribution, and some degree of incapacitation and control of offenders
- system-oriented objectives, which include reducing institutional populations and the costs of corrections, as well as the rates of recidivism (Junger-Tas, 1994:11, 13)

The primary objective of intermediate sanctions is to hold offenders responsible for their behaviour; treatment and rehabilitation are generally secondary. Studies that have queried offenders about their perceptions of the severity of intermediate sanctions as opposed to incarceration confirm that alternatives to incarceration can effectively punish and control (Petersilia and Deschenes, 1994).

Intensive Supervision Probation

Intensive supervision probation (ISP) was originally designed as an intermediate sanction between traditional probation practice, which generally involves minimal supervision, and incarceration. ISP programs include reduced caseloads for probation officers, increased surveillance of probationers, various treatment interventions, and efforts to ensure that offenders are employed. ISP imposes rigorous conditions on the probationer, such as multiple weekly reporting requirements, random drug testing, strict enforcement of the mandatory and additional conditions of the probation order, and the requirement that offenders secure and maintain employment. ISP is more suited for offenders who are classified as posing a greater risk to the community and a greater risk of reoffending.

Over the past two decades, ISP programs have developed in every state in the United States, and a number of programs have been introduced by provincial systems of corrections in Canada. An underlying premise is that the expansion of ISP programs can assist in reducing the number of prison admissions, reduce operational costs, and protect the public, while providing increased supervision of more serious offenders.

Boot Camps/Strict Discipline Programs/Rigorous Custody Programs

These programs, which are used primarily for young offenders, are based on a quasi-military model. Programs are centred on strict discipline, physical training, and manual labour, as well as education and life skills. This intense incarceration experience is then followed by close supervision in the community.

In Manitoba, several facilities for young offenders have been designated as **rigorous custody programs.** These are secure custody programs that emphasize discipline and a highly structured regimen, focusing on behaviour modification, community service, and personal accountability. Youths rise at 6 a.m., and there are no televisions or video games in the facility. The average sentence in custody is 12 months, and there is an intensive post-release supervision program.

In Ontario, a privately run pilot project called Project Turnaround has served as the template for a number of programs that emphasize self-discipline, personal accountability, and life skills development in a highly structured, no-frills environment. Youths are required to participate in education and life skills programs and rigorous physical activities, and they must earn their privileges. The objective is to have dawn-to-dusk programming that keeps the youths active. Intensive supervision in the community is provided following release.

Conditional Sentences

Section 742 of the Criminal Code states that a convicted person who would otherwise be incarcerated for a period of less than two years can be sentenced to a conditional term of imprisonment that is to be served in the community rather than in custody. Under this sentencing option, referred to as a conditional sentence, the offender is required to fulfill certain conditions attached to the conditional release.

The standard, mandatory conditions contained in conditional sentence orders are similar to those contained in probation orders. Additional conditions may also be prescribed. These include:

- abstaining from alcohol or other intoxicants
- abstaining from owning, possessing, or carrying a weapon
- providing for the support or care of dependents
- performing up to 240 hours of community service work
- attending a treatment program

Additional conditions can be added or waived by the court over time (more on mandatory and additional conditions in Chapter 9). A conditional sentence order, with all key identifiers removed, is presented in Appendix 4.5 on page 156.

Failure to comply with the conditions of the conditional release will result in the offender being returned to court. If the judge is satisfied, on a balance of probabilities, that a condition has been breached, there are four options:

1. Take no action.
2. Add or eliminate additional conditions.
3. Suspend the conditional sentence order and incarcerate the offender to serve a portion of the unexpired sentence in custody (in which case, the conditional sentence resumes when the offender is released from confinement).

4. Terminate the conditional sentence order and commit the offender to custody to serve until the release on parole or the discharge-possible date.

There is some evidence to suggest that violations of conditional sentence orders are not uncommon. A Canadian study found that 40 percent of offenders in three jurisdictions breached the conditions of their conditional sentence order (North, 2001).

Although offenders on conditional sentences are supervised in the community by probation officers, they are not technically on probation. In *R. v. Proulx* ([2000] 1 S.C.R. 61), the Canadian Supreme Court clearly defined the differences between conditional sentences and probation. The major difference is that probation is focused on rehabilitation, while conditional sentences rely on the principles of punitive justice and rehabilitation. This means that the conditions attached to a conditional sentence will generally be more onerous and restrictive than those attached to a probation order. The Supreme Court also ruled that no offences, including serious and violent crimes, could be excluded from consideration for a conditional sentence. The Court directed that two primary factors should be taken into account in determining whether a conditional sentence is appropriate: (1) the risk of reoffence posed by the offender, and (2) the amount of harm the offender would cause in the event of a reoffence.

There has been a steady increase in the number of conditional sentences handed down in criminal courts since the introduction of this sentencing option. Research findings indicate the following:

- There is considerable regional variation in the use of conditional sentences, with judges in Quebec, Ontario, and British Columbia using this sanction more than their counterparts in the other jurisdictions.
- Reducing the use of imprisonment is the most frequently cited objective of conditional sentences.
- The highest percentage of conditional sentences are imposed on offenders convicted of property crimes.
- The average length of conditional sentence orders is eight months.
- Judges would like the courts of appeal to provide more guidance on the use of conditional sentences.
- Judges would impose conditional sentences more frequently if there were sufficient community resources.
- Most judges believe that the use of conditional sentences has reduced the number of admissions to correctional institutions.
- There is a widespread perception among judges that the general public does not understand conditional sentences, but that those citizens who

are well informed tend to support their use. (Roberts, Doob, and Marinos, 2000; Roberts and LaPrairie, 2000)

Conditional sentences are a popular sentencing option for judges, but they have also generated considerable controversy. Critics cite numerous cases in which offenders were granted a conditional sentence when a period of incarceration should have been imposed (see Box 4.5). And defence lawyers routinely argue, even in serious cases, that the court should impose a conditional sentence in lieu of incarceration. In a Winnipeg case heard in 2001, for example, the judge rejected the argument of a defence lawyer that his client— a former Anglican priest who had been convicted of fondling three young boys, one of whom was disabled—be given a conditional sentence (Canadian Press, 2001:A9).

The government of Ontario has taken the position that the use of conditional sentences should be severely restricted and, more specifically, that offenders convicted of serious and violent crimes should not be eligible for this sentencing option. Public attitudes toward conditional sentences are mixed. A national survey found that community residents would support the use of conditional sentences even in cases of assault if there were sufficient restrictive conditions attached to the sentence. However, there was almost unanimous agreement among the respondents that conditional sentences should not be

BOX 4.5

Street Racers' Sentences Outrage Victim's Family

In November 2000, a woman walking on a sidewalk died instantly when she was struck by one of two cars that were "street racing"—travelling at speeds up to 140 km per hour on a Vancouver street. At trial, the two drivers were found guilty of criminal negligence causing death. Although the offence carries a maximum life sentence, the presiding judge imposed a two-year conditional sentence on each driver. Among the reasons cited for the sentences was the fact that neither man had a prior criminal record, and neither had abused alcohol or drugs. The judge also indicated that Canada incarcerates too many people.

The victim's sister said she was "appalled" by the decision, while the provincial attorney general stated that it had shaken the public's confidence in the criminal justice system.

Source: Hume, 2003.

used in cases of sexual violence. The same survey revealed a lack of understanding of conditional sentences among the general public: only 43 percent of the respondents were able to identify the correct definition of conditional sentences, while even fewer (38 percent) chose the correct definition of parole (Sanders and Roberts, 2000).

Electronic Monitoring

Originally developed in the United States and now used by several provincial systems of corrections, **electronic monitoring (EM)** programs represent the first large-scale application of high technology to the supervision and control of offenders. EM programs involve placing an offender under house arrest and then using electronic equipment to ensure that he or she fulfills the conditions of confinement. Electronic monitoring equipment generally includes a bracelet that is strapped to the offender's ankle. This bracelet emits radio signals within a range of 45 metres (150 feet). A receiver attached to the offender's telephone receives the signals and relays them to a central monitoring system. Some systems also include a breathalyzer, which detects the use of alcohol and raises an alarm in the central monitoring system. Offenders are generally permitted to be absent from home for specific periods to attend work or school programs. The supervising officer may make random visits to the home or workplace.

EM systems may be either active or passive. Active systems require the offender to answer the telephone and speak to program personnel or to insert the bracelet into a receiver to verify his or her presence at home. Passive systems involve signals emitted by the bracelet. If the offender moves out of range, program personnel are automatically alerted.

Among the primary objectives of EM programs are to provide an alternative to incarceration, to reduce the operating costs for correctional systems, and to allow offenders under supervision and control in the community to remain employed and with their families. Only those offenders convicted of less serious, nonviolent offences and who have a stable residence and a telephone are eligible for participation in EM programs.

EM Programs in Canada

The first EM program was created in British Columbia in 1987. Since then, EM programs have been implemented by most provincial systems of corrections. The CSC currently does not have any EM programs.

There are both front-end EM programs and back-end EM programs, referring to the stage of the correctional process at which the strategy is used.

In Saskatchewan, EM is a front-end sentencing option that the judge may select at the time of sentencing. In Ontario, EM is used as a condition of early release from incarceration and is generally available only to nonviolent offenders who are involved in an approved activity such as school or employment. Offenders with a history of sex offences or domestic abuse are generally not eligible for EM.

A number of criticisms have been directed toward EM programs, including:

- the potential for net-widening, wherein offenders who would otherwise not have been sent to prison are placed on EM
- issues related to the rights of privacy
- the impact of EM on the offender's family

The Effectiveness of EM Programs

A study of EM programs in British Columbia, Saskatchewan, and Newfoundland compared a sample of 262 male offenders under EM supervision with 240 inmates and 30 probationers, matched on key risk factors. Among the findings:

- EM supervision had no significant impact on program completion or on recidivism. Offenders under EM supervision engaged in as much criminal behaviour following program completion as did offenders who were in prison or on probation.
- EM resulted in net-widening. Many of the offenders under EM supervision were low-risk and could have been effectively managed in the community without EM supervision, indicating that EM was not generally being used as a true alternative to confinement.
- There was no clear evidence that EM was more cost-effective than probation or other correctional strategies. (Bonta, Wallace-Capretta, and Rooney, 2000)

These findings raise serious questions as to whether EM programs are more effective than traditional methods of community supervision. A number of jurisdictions have been rethinking these programs in recent years. In British Columbia, for example, EM is no longer a sentencing option, and its use as a condition of release from confinement has been sharply reduced.

Global Positioning System

In the United States, an increasing number of correctional systems are using the satellite-based Global Positioning System (GPS) to monitor high-risk offenders in the community. GPS monitoring is being used both as an alternative to confinement and as a means of supervising and controlling offenders released from custody. In contrast to EM programs, GPS monitoring makes it possible to determine where an offender is at any given time. In addition, it is possible to customize tracking by specifying the boundaries of an offender's movements and setting out locations where the offender is not permitted (e.g., schools or playgrounds in the case of a sex offender). A monitoring program can be created that will alert both the offender and the agency if the offender violates certain area restrictions.

An evaluation of the GPS program in Florida found that:

- sex offenders composed the largest group (37 percent) in the GPS program
- the majority of offenders placed in the GPS program in 2000–01 had been convicted of violent offences
- sex offenders under GPS monitoring had a lower rate of absconding from supervision and of revocation than did offenders in general
- GPS monitoring was nearly four times as expensive as standard probation, but only about one-third the cost of incarceration (Johnson, 2002)

These findings suggest there is considerable potential for utilizing GPS for supervising high-risk offenders in the community.

The government of Ontario has announced plans to introduce GPS and other compliance tools (including voice verification systems and electronic paging) through a public-private partnership, in which private companies will supply the technology to be used in supervising offenders. This development is certain to raise a number of legal and ethical issues in the coming years.

RESTORATIVE/COMMUNITY JUSTICE

Among the nations of the world, Canada has long assumed a lead in the development and implementation of alternative justice policies and programs. Restorative/community justice is based on the fundamental principle that criminal behaviour injures not only the victim but also the community and the offender and that any efforts to address and resolve the problems created by the criminal behaviour should involve all of these parties. The concept of restorative/community justice is best illustrated by comparing it with the principles of retributive justice, upon which the adversarial system of criminal justice is based. The key differences are listed in Table 4.1.

It is important to note that restorative/community justice is not a specific practice, but rather a set of principles that provides the basis for communities

Table 4.1   Principles of Retributive Justice and Restorative/Community Justice

Retributive Justice	Restorative/Community Justice
• Crime violates the state and its laws	• Crime violates people and relationships
• Justice focuses on establishing guilt so that doses of pain can be meted out	• Justice aims to identify needs/ obligations so that things can be made right
• Justice is sought through conflict between adversaries in which the offender is pitted against state rules and intentions outweigh outcomes—one side wins and the other loses	• Justice encourages dialogue and mutual agreement, gives victims and offenders central roles, and is judged by the extent to which responsibilities are assumed, needs are met, and healing (of individuals and relationships) is encouraged

Source: Zehr, 1990.

and the justice system to respond to crime and social disorder. (Figure 4.1 depicts the interrelationships among the various parties that may be involved in a restorative/community justice approach.) The primary objectives of restorative/community justice are:

- to fully address the needs of victims of crime
- to prevent reoffending by reintegrating offenders into the community
- to enable offenders to acknowledge and assume responsibility for their behaviour
- to create a "community" of support and assistance for the victim, the offender, and the long-term interests of the community
- to provide an alternative to the adversarial system of justice (Marshall, 1999:6)

The Dimensions of Restorative/Community Justice

Among the more common restorative/community justice initiatives are **victim–offender mediation (VOM), circle sentencing, community holistic healing,** and **family group conferences.** There are critical differences among the various models of restorative/community justice, including their mandate and relationship to the formal adversarial system, the role of the crime victim and other participants, and the procedures for preparation for the event and for

Figure 4.1

The Relationships of Restorative Justice

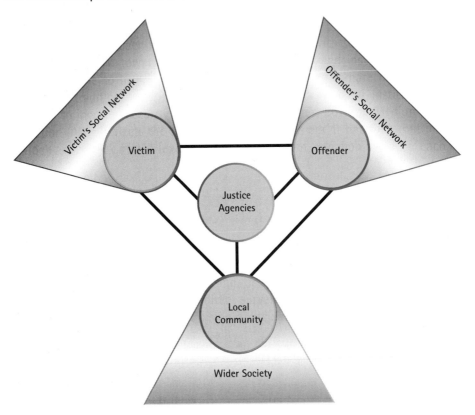

Source: Marshall, 1999:5.

monitoring and enforcing the agreement (Van Ness and Strong, 1997; Bazemore and Schiff, 2001). The models also differ in terms of their objectives, the degree to which the model requires that the justice system share power with community residents, and the extent to which the model is designed to empower the community, as well as address the specific incident and behaviour in question (Bazemore and Griffiths, 1997).

Victim–Offender Mediation

Victim–offender mediation (VOM) programs, sometimes referred to as victim–offender reconciliation programs (VORP), have been operating in Canada since the early 1970s and are widely used across the country. VOM takes a restorative approach, in which the victim and the offender have the opportunity to express their feelings and concerns. With the assistance of a mediator, who is a neutral third party, the offender and the victim are able to resolve the conflict and consequences caused by the offence and, ultimately, to understand each other. See Box 4.6 for an example of a VOM program.

There are generally four phases of a mediation: (1) intake of the case from a referral source, (2) preparation for the mediation, which involves the mediator meeting separately with the victim and the offender, (3) the mediation session, and (4) post-session activities, including ensuring that any agreement reached during the mediation session is fulfilled. In recent years, VOM and VORP have been extended to cases involving crimes of violence and have included incarcerated offenders.

BOX 4.6

Restorative Resolutions Project (Winnipeg)

Restorative Resolutions is an intensive supervision program using victim–offender mediation to achieve restorative justice. The program is an alternative to incarceration for offenders who are willing to take responsibility for their behaviour and to compensate their victims. Among the services provided are counselling, anger management, and intensive supervision. Restorative Resolutions is operated by the John Howard Society of Manitoba and staffed by workers trained in probation practices and restorative justice.

A Case Study

A 32-year-old man with a lengthy youth and adult record of assault and break and enter was charged with four new counts of break and enter and theft. The Crown attorney wanted a period of incarceration. Restorative Resolutions staff prepared an alternative plan recommending that the judge issue a suspended sentence (with supervision of the offender to be carried out by Restorative Resolutions) and that the offender complete the Interpersonal Communication Skills Course, complete the Addictions Foundation of Manitoba assessment, attend AA regularly, complete the conditions outlined in the mediation agreement, and receive literacy training. The judge accepted the plan.

Source: Church Council on Justice and Corrections, 1996:5.

Circle Sentencing

Circle sentencing originally developed in several Yukon communities as a collaboration between community residents and territorial justice personnel, primarily RCMP officers and judges from the Territorial Court of Yukon. In circle sentencing, all of the participants, including the judge, defence lawyer, prosecutor, police officer, victim and family, offender and family, and community residents, sit facing one another in a circle. Through discussions, those in the circle reach a consensus about the best way to dispose of the case, taking into account both the need to protect the community and the rehabilitation and punishment of the offender.

Circle sentencing is based on traditional Aboriginal healing practices and has multifaceted objectives, including addressing the needs of communities, victims, the families of victims, and offenders through a process of reconciliation, restitution, and reparation. A fundamental principle of circle sentencing is that the sentence is less important than the process used to select it. A circle sentencing case from Yukon Territory is presented in Box 4.7.

There are a number of important stages in the circle sentencing process, each of which is critical to its overall success. Circle sentencing is generally only available to offenders who plead guilty. The operation of the circle sen-

Healing circle, Aboriginal Ganootamaage Justice Services (Winnipeg)

BOX 4.7

Circle Sentencing: A Case Study

The victim—the wife of the offender, who had admitted to physically abusing her during two recent drunken episodes—spoke about the pain and embarrassment her husband had caused her and her family. After she had finished, she passed the ceremonial feather (used to signify who would be allowed to speak next) to the next person in the circle, a young man who spoke about the contributions the offender had made to the community, the kindness he had shown toward the Elders by sharing fish and game with them, and his willingness to help others with home repairs. An Elder then took the feather and spoke about the shame the offender's behaviour had caused to his clan, noting that in the old days, the offender would have been required to pay the woman's family substantial compensation.

After hearing this discussion, the judge confirmed that the victim still wanted to try to work it out with her estranged husband and that she was receiving help from her own support group (including a victim's advocate). Summarizing the case by again stressing the seriousness of the offence and repeating the Crown counsel's opening remarks that a jail sentence was required, the judge then proposed that sentencing be delayed for six weeks until the time of the next circuit court hearing. The judge would not impose the jail sentence if, during that time, the offender (1) met the requirements presented earlier by a friend of the offender who had agreed to lead a support group, (2) met with the community justice committee to work out an alcohol and anger management treatment plan, (3) fulfilled the expectations of the victim and her support group, and (4) completed 40 hours of service under the group's supervision. After a prayer, in which the entire group held hands, the circle disbanded, and everyone retreated to the kitchen area of the community centre for refreshments.

Source: Bazemore and Griffiths, 1997. Reprinted by permission.

tencing process is specific to communities, meaning that it may (and should) vary between communities, and the circle sentencing process relies heavily upon community volunteers for its success (Stuart, 1996). Both Aboriginal and non-Aboriginal victims, offenders, and community residents participate in sentencing circles. The majority of offenders who have had their cases disposed of through sentencing circles have been adults, although the number of youth cases has been increasing.

Table 4.2 compares the attributes of the formal, adversarial criminal court with the community-based, restorative approach as exemplified by circle sentencing. The significant differences between the process and principles of circle sentencing and the formal, adversarial system of criminal justice are outlined in Table 4.3. It is important to note that offenders who have their cases heard in a sentencing circle may still be sent for a period of incarceration; however, there are a wide range of other sanctions available, including banishment (generally to a wilderness location), house arrest, and community service.

Circle sentencing is an example of how the principles of restorative/ community justice can be applied within a holistic framework in which justice system personnel share power and authority with community residents. In contrast to the adversarial approach to justice, circle sentencing:

- re-acquaints individuals, families, and communities with problem-solving skills
- rebuilds relationships within communities
- promotes awareness and respect for the values and the lives of others
- addresses the needs and interests of all parties, including the victim
- focuses on the causes, not just the symptoms, of problems
- recognizes existing healing resources and creates new ones
- coordinates the use of local and government resources
- generates preventive measures (Griffiths and Hatch Cunningham, 2003:212–13)

Table 4.2   Comparison of Formal Criminal Court Process with Restorative/Community Justice

	Formal Court Process	Restorative/ Community Justice
People	Experts Nonresidents	Local people
Process	Adversarial State v. offender	Consensus Community v. problem
Issues	Laws broken	Relationship broken
Focus	Guilt	Identify needs of victim, offender, and community
Tools	Punishment/ control	Healing/support
Procedure	Fixed rules	Flexible

Table 4.3   Differences between Criminal Courts and Community Circles

Criminal Courts	Community Circles
• View the conflict as the crime	• View the crime as a small part of a larger conflict
• Hand down sentence to resolve the conflict	• View the sentence as a small part of the solution
• Focus on past conduct	• Focus on present and future conduct
• Take a narrow view of behaviour	• Take a larger, holistic view
• Avoid concern with social conflict	• Focus on social conflict
• Result (i.e., the sentence) is most important	• Result is least important; the process is most important, as the process shapes the relationship among all parties

Source: Griffiths and Hatch Cunningham, 2003:212. Reprinted by permission of Justice Barry D. Stuart.

Circle sentencing has spawned a number of variations, including community sentence advisory committees, sentencing panels, and community mediation panels. There is some evidence that circle sentencing may be very effective in reducing and eliminating criminal and disruptive behaviour, particularly on the part of offenders who have lengthy records in the formal criminal justice system.

Restorative/Community Justice in Aboriginal Communities

Aboriginal communities have become increasingly involved in developing community-based justice services and programs that are designed to address the specific needs of community residents, victims, and offenders. These initiatives have been developed as part of a process of cultural and community revitalization and in conjunction with the increasing movement to reassert their authority over all facets of community life (Griffiths and Hamilton, 1996). Communities have also begun to explore alternatives to confinement in order to decrease the large numbers of Aboriginal offenders incarcerated in provincial/territorial correctional institutions.

These initiatives vary widely in the types of offences and offenders processed; in the procedures for hearing cases, reaching dispositions, and imposing sanctions; and in the extent to which they involve justice system professionals. Restorative/community justice initiatives in Aboriginal communities may be, but are not necessarily, premised on customary law and traditional practices. Many involve Elders and emphasize healing the victim(s), offenders, and, when required, the community. Rather than focusing only on the offender and the offence, the response to criminal behaviour occurs within a broader, holistic framework. This holistic approach facilitates the inclusion of crime victims and their families, the offender's family, and community residents in responding to the behaviour and formulating a sanction that will address the needs of all parties (Green, 1997, 1998).

Another attribute of these initiatives is that the Aboriginal band and/or community maintains a high degree of control over the disposition and sanctioning processes, which are controlled by the community or shared, on a partnership basis, with justice system personnel (as in the case of circle sentencing). Other programs, such as the Community Holistic Circle Healing Program described below, are more autonomous and are controlled by the community.

Community Holistic Circle Healing Program, Hollow Water (Manitoba)

The Community Holistic Circle Healing Program was designed as a community-based response to the high rates of sexual and family abuse that afflicted the community. It includes a 13-phase process, shown in Figure 4.2. Traditional healing practices are used in an attempt to restore peace and harmony to the community, the family, and the individual. The offender signs a healing contract and apologizes publicly to the victims and to the community for the harm done. The circle healing process is designed to consider the needs of all of the parties to the abuse—the victim, the offender, and the community— and is directed beyond merely punishing the offender for a specific behaviour.

Restorative/Community Justice in Urban Centres

In discussions of the potential for developing restorative/community justice initiatives, it is often assumed that programs such as circle sentencing, which involve substantial community participation, are suited only to rural and remote communities with a strong cultural identity and foundation. This assertion is often used to deflect suggestions that justice personnel in suburban and urban areas should explore the potential for restorative/community justice approaches that would better serve the needs of offenders, their victims, and

Figure 4.2

The 13 Phases of the Hollow Water Community Holistic Circle Healing Process

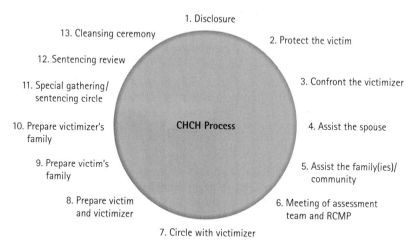

1. Disclosure
2. Protect the victim
3. Confront the victimizer
4. Assist the spouse
5. Assist the family(ies)/ community
6. Meeting of assessment team and RCMP
7. Circle with victimizer
8. Prepare victim and victimizer
9. Prepare victim's family
10. Prepare victimizer's family
11. Special gathering/ sentencing circle
12. Sentencing review
13. Cleansing ceremony

CHCH Process

Source: Lajeunesse and Associates, 1996:33.

the community. In fact, a number of successful restorative/community justice programs are currently operating in urban centres. One such initiative is the Collaborative Justice Project (CJP), discussed below.

The Collaborative Justice Project (Ottawa-Carleton Judicial District)

The Collaborative Justice Project is a post-plea, pre-sentence restorative/ community justice program in the Ottawa-Carleton judicial district. The CJP focuses on cases of serious offending, including robbery, break and enter, assault causing bodily harm, weapons offences, and driving offences causing death or bodily harm. Cases are referred to the CJP by the judiciary; judicial pretrials; Crown or defence counsel; and police, probation, or victim services.

Cases undertaken by the CJP must meet the following criteria:

- The crime is serious and the Crown is seeking a period of custody.
- The accused person displays remorse and is willing to take responsibility for—and work to repair—the harm done.
- There is an identifiable victim who is interested in participating.

See Box 4.8 for an example of a CJP case.

BOX 4.8

Impaired Driving Causing Death: A Case Study from the Collaborative Justice Project

The accused, Robert, was driving the wrong way on a multi-lane, divided highway, entering by the off-ramp. After travelling 2 km in the wrong direction, narrowly missing several vehicles, he collided with the victim's car, killing a 60-year-old man and slightly injuring his wife. Robert had close to three times the legal limit of alcohol in his blood and was charged with impaired driving causing death and criminal negligence causing death.

The CJP caseworker met with Robert, who expressed a willingness to take responsibility for his offence, to work toward some form of reparation, and to meet with the victim's family. Satisfied that Robert met CJP criteria, the caseworker then met with Phillip, the adult son of the victim, and his mother, Claire. Phillip wanted something good to come out of the tragedy. He felt that Robert might speak to people about drinking and driving, or even go with Phillip to speak to groups. However, Phillip believed that Robert would not be willing or able to speak publicly, so he didn't expect his hope could be realized. Phillip wanted to meet with Robert to learn who Robert was and whether he would drink and drive in the future. His mother didn't wish to meet Robert, but needed more information about the accident from the police so that she could move on with her own grieving process.

The caseworker obtained and forwarded the information to Claire, and then met with Robert regularly over the next six months to discuss how he had ended up in this situation, his alcohol problem, the people he had harmed, and what he might do to facilitate the healing process. He was receiving ongoing psychological and addiction counselling. Similarly, the caseworker was meeting with Phillip to support him and his family, to explore what he needed from the process, and to prepare for a possible meeting with Robert. The caseworker conveyed information between Robert and Phillip so that each had a better understanding of the other's situation and needs.

Six months later, Robert and Phillip met in a mediation. They talked to each other in a supportive manner about the impact of the incident on them and their families, and about what they would like to see happen. While Robert had previously indicated that he felt unable to speak publicly about what had occurred, after meeting with Phillip he agreed to do so with him. Robert and Phillip met on four further occasions and together addressed a classroom of high-school class students who were deeply moved by the presentation.

Robert received a sentence of two years less a day in a provincial jail. The Crown attorney's original recommendation of three to five years was mitigated in light of the work done by the accused and the victim's son and their interest in continuing such work. During the following year, there was continuing periodic contact with Robert and Phillip. Arrangements were made for Robert to be released on temporary absence day passes from time to time in order to speak publicly with Phillip about impaired driving and their personal experiences.

Source: Adapted from the Church Council on Justice and Corrections website (www.ccjc.ca/news/casestories.cfm).

Critical Issues in Restorative/Community Justice

The emergence of restorative/community justice in Canada has been spurred by the high cost of incarcerating offenders, by the increasing involvement of communities as partners in the criminal justice system, and by the efforts of Aboriginal communities to reassert control over the response to crime and social disorder (Clairmont, 2000). Despite the success of many restorative/ community initiatives, their expansion in many jurisdictions has been slow. One obstacle has been that many of the key principles of restorative justice are unfamiliar to politicians, policymakers, and criminal justice personnel (including judges). Terms such as *forgiveness, community, empowerment, healing,* and *spirituality* are not found in the Criminal Code of Canada and are foreign to many criminal justice practitioners.

There are a number of other critical issues (discussed below) that must be addressed before restorative/community justice programs become established as alternatives to the adversarial system of criminal justice.

Crime Victims and Restorative/Community Justice

Although crime victims are often marginalized by and excluded from the formal adversarial system of criminal justice, concerns have been expressed that restorative/community justice initiatives may give inadequate attention to the rights and needs of vulnerable groups, specifically women, adolescents, and children. As a consequence, crime victims may be re-victimized by the process of restorative/community justice. Aboriginal women, for example, have voiced concerns about the high rates of sexual and physical abuse in communities and have questioned whether restorative/community justice provides adequate protection for the victims of violence and abuse and whether the sanctions imposed are appropriate (Presser and Van Voorhis, 2002).

The Effectiveness of Restorative/Community Justice

Few evaluations have been conducted on the extent to which restorative/community justice strategies achieve their stated objectives. Despite the widespread publicity accorded circle sentencing, for example, no controlled evaluations of this strategy have been completed (Roberts and LaPrairie, 1997).

Attempts to assess the effectiveness of restorative/community justice programs face a number of challenges. One is that the holistic approach and multifaceted objectives of many restorative/community justice programs require a broader evaluative framework than has been used for traditional crime control initiatives. Program objectives may encompass macro-level dimensions such as cultural and community revitalization and empowerment, as well as community, family, and individual healing.

The Dynamics of Community Justice

The significant role that communities in restorative/community justice initiatives assume requires a close consideration of the strengths, as well as the potential pitfalls, of community justice. Canadian observers have raised a number of concerns and have identified several factors, which, if not addressed, can undermine the efficacy of restorative/community justice initiatives. These include (1) ensuring that the general "health" of the community, including community leaders and those who would assume key roles in any restorative/community justice initiatives, is adequate; (2) acknowledging that there are, within all communities, power and status hierarchies that may undermine consensus-building and place certain residents, be they victims or offenders, in positions of vulnerability; and (3) ensuring that the legal rights of offenders are protected (Griffiths and Hamilton, 1996). For a response to the critics of restorative/community justice, see Morris (2002).

BOX 4.9

Research Summary: The Effectiveness of Alternative Sanctions

Diversion: Few formal evaluations have been conducted. Programs tend to target low-risk, first-time offenders convicted of minor offences. Programs may "widen the net," resulting in offenders being placed under supervision who would have otherwise not been subjected to any sanction. There is no evidence that diversion has any

---

impact on recidivism or on correctional populations. Diversion may increase the justice system's workload and costs (Bonta, 1998; Nuffield, 1997). Preliminary results from the Drug Treatment Court in Toronto suggest that this approach may reduce reoffending among repeat offenders with extensive criminal records (National Crime Prevention Strategy, 2002).

Probation: How supervision is carried out is an important factor in the success of probationers. Few specific programs for probationers have been evaluated. Formal evaluation of the Restorative Resolutions project in Winnipeg (see Box 4.6) indicated that this program is successful in reducing recidivism (Bonta, Wallace-Capretta, and Rooney, 1998).

Intensive Supervision Probation (ISP): There is no evidence that ISP programs reduce prison overcrowding. Close monitoring of offenders may result in higher violation rates. Studies of whether ISP programs result in cost savings are inconclusive. ISPs are effective in providing close supervision of high-risk offenders.

Home Confinement/Electronic Monitoring Programs: There is no evidence that EM programs reduce prison admissions, lower costs for systems of corrections, or reduce the likelihood of future criminal behaviour (Bonta, Wallace-Capretta, and Rooney, 2000).

Rigorous Custody Programs: Evaluations of boot camps in the United States indicate that the programs have no long-term impact on recidivism rates and may not result in cost savings. There have been no formal evaluations of rigorous custody programs in Canada to date.

Conditional Sentence: There is no evidence that conditional sentences have reduced rates of incarceration. Studies of the effectiveness of conditional sentences, as compared to probation or incarceration, have not been conducted.

Restorative/Community Justice: Research findings indicate that restorative/community justice approaches can be more effective than traditional correctional strategies such as probation (Latimer, Dowden, and Muise, 2001). Victim–offender mediation programs receive high marks from victims and offenders in terms of the fairness of the process and the outcome of the mediation session (Umbreit, Coates, and Vos, 2001). An evaluation of the Hollow Water program found that the program has increased community awareness of sexual abuse and family violence and the rates of disclosure by offenders. It has also significantly reduced the rate of alcoholism in the community, improved educational standards, and increased services for at-risk children and youths (Couture et al., 2001).

QUESTIONS FOR REVIEW

1. Discuss the positive features of diversion, as well as the concerns that have been raised about this alternative sanction.

2. Identify and discuss what is meant by mandatory and additional conditions of probation.

3. What are some of the core components of the probation officer's role?

4. What are some of the major sources of stress for probation officers?

5. What does research suggest about the effectiveness of probation as an alternative sanction?

6. What are intermediate sanctions and what objectives do they generally attempt to accomplish? Provide examples.

7. What has been the Canadian experience with electronic monitoring? What do research studies suggest about the effectiveness of this correctional strategy?

8. What is meant by restorative/community justice? Provide examples, and then compare and contrast restorative/community justice with retributive justice.

9. Describe circle sentencing, and then compare it with the approach to sanctioning offenders that occurs in the formal criminal court.

10. Identify and discuss some of the concerns that have been raised about restorative/community justice.

APPENDIX 4.1

Probation Order

Probation Order   Police File No.   Court File No.

(Suspended Sentence) ▮▮▮▮▮▮▮   ▮▮▮▮▮▮

Canada: Province of British Columbia

BRITISH COLUMBIA

☐ Ban

D.O.B.: ▮▮▮▮▮▮▮▮

☐ Interpreter   Proceeded: summarily

Whereas on ▮▮▮▮▮▮▮▮▮ 2001 at ▮▮▮▮ British Columbia,

▮▮▮▮▮▮▮▮▮

was convicted or found guilty, as the case may be, upon the following charge(s) and whereas on December 14, 2001 the Court adjudged that the passing of sentence upon the offender be suspended and that the offender be released upon the conditions hereinafter prescribed:

```
Count 1, on or about ▮▮▮▮▮ 2001, at or near ▮▮▮▮▮▮▮▮▮▮ , B.C.,
did commit an offence of theft $5000 or under, contrary to Section 334(b)
Criminal Code.
SENTENCE: Probation Order: 2 year(s); Suspended Passing of Sentence; Victim
Surcharge: $50.00 Due Date: February 14, 2002.
```

Now, therefore, the said offender shall for the probation period from the date of this order comply with the following conditions, namely, that the said offender shall:
- keep the peace and be of good behaviour,
- appear before the court when required to do so by the court, and
- notify the court or the probation officer in advance of any change of name or address, and promptly notify the court or the probation officer of any change of employment or occupation, and in addition,

```
        See Attachment
```

Dated: December 14, 2001   at ▮▮▮▮▮▮▮   British Columbia

I, the undersigned offender, acknowledge that I have received:
- a copy of the *Probation Order*: an explanation of the substance of the sections dealing with changes to the *Probation Order* and failing to comply with *Probation Order* (Sec 732.2(3) and (5), and Sec 733.1), and
- an explanation of the procedures for applying for changes to the *Probation Order*, and that I understand the terms of this *Probation Order* and the explanations which I have received.

▮▮▮▮▮▮▮	▮▮▮▮▮▮▮
Offender	Clerk of the Court on behalf of Judge ▮▮▮▮

Probation Order (Suspended Sentence)

Notice of Victim Surcharge   Police File No.   Court File No.

███████████   █████████████

Canada: Province of British Columbia

D.O.B.: ████████████

☐ Ban

DL#:

☐ Interpreter

DL Expiry:

Vehicle Plate:

On ███████████ 2001   in the Provincial   Court at ██████████   British Columbia,

█████████████████

Address: ████████████████ Telephone Number: (604) ████████████

was convicted or found guilty, as the case may be, upon the following charge(s), and whereas the Court has imposed a sentence other than a fine, the offender is obliged to pay the following victim surcharge:

Count 1, on or about ██████████ 2001, at or near ██████████, BC, did commit an offence of theft $5000 or under, contrary to Section 334(b) Criminal Code. SENTENCE: Probation Order: 2 Year(s); Suspended Passing of Sentence; Victim Surcharge: $50.00 Due Date: 14, 2002;

For a total of $50.00

Dated ████████████ 2001

at ██████████████████   British Columbia

███████████████████████

Clerk of the Court on behalf of Judge ████████████

I understand the total amount MUST BE PAID by the DUE DATE unless, before the due date, I or someone on my behalf has successfully applied to change the terms of this order, including extending the time to pay. If the amount is not paid by the due date, and I or someone on my behalf has not applied for a change to the order, the court may consider that I HAVE REFUSED TO PAY THE VICTIM SURCHARGE and may commence enforcement proceedings against me, which could include issuing a Warrant of Committal.

I have received a copy of this order and have received an explanation of the substance of Sections 734(3) to (7) and Sections 734.3, 734.5, 734.7 and 734.8, and the procedures for applying for a change in the terms of the order.

PAYMENT MAY BE MADE by cash, cheque or money order payable to Minister of

Finance and Corporate Relations. Payment may be paid in person or mailed to:

Court location address

██████████████

██████████████

YOU MUST SUBMIT THIS NOTICE WHEN MAKING A PAYMENT OR APPLYING FOR AN EXTENSION OF TIME TO PAY.

██████████████████

Signature of Offender

Dated ████████████

at ██████████   British Columbia

████████████████

Signature of Person who provided explanation

Notice of Victim Surcharge

**Probation Order
(Suspended Sentence)
Canada: Province of British Columbia**

British Columbia

Police File No. ███████

Court File No. ███████

☐ Ban

D.O.B.: ███████

Re: ███████

Conditions Attachment

■ CONDITION 1 on count(s) 1: Report immediately in person to a Probation Officer at the ███████ Probation Office, and after that report to the Probation Officer when and as directed by the Probation Officer.

■ CONDITION 2 on count(s) 1: Provide your residential address to your Probation Officer and do not change that address without first obtaining the permission of your Probation Officer.

■ CONDITION 3 on count(s) 1: You are not to attend the ███████ store at ███████ , BC.

■ CONDITION 4 on count(s) 1: Attend for psychological and/or psychiatric assessments or counselling and/or such other counselling or therapy as directed by your Probation Officer.

■ CONDITION 5 on count(s) 1: Attend for and complete alcohol counselling and/or drug counselling, and/or residential treatment or psychological counselling and other counselling as directed by your Probation Officer.

■ CONDITION 6 on count(s) 1: If available, you are to complete the Elizabeth Fry shoplifters program or similar program as directed by your Probation Officer.

I have read and understand the contents of this document and acknowledge that I am the person to whom the statements contained herein refer, and further acknowledge that I have been made aware of the provisions of Section 732.2(3)(5)/733.1 Criminal Code of Canada

Signed: ___███___   Witnessed: ___███___
                                              Probation Officer

Dated: ___███___ at ___███___ B.C.

Dated ___███___ 2001_____ at ███ British Columbia

I, the undersigned offender, acknowledge that I have received:
- a copy of the *Probation Order*
- an explanation of the substance of the sections dealing with changes to the *Probation Order* and failing to comply with *Probation Order* (Sec 732.2(3) and (5), and Sec 733.1), and
- an explanation of the procedures for applying for changes to the *Probation Order*, and that I understand the terms of this *Probation Order* and the explanations which I have received.

███████	███████
Offender	Clerk of the Court on behalf of Judge ███

Probation Order (Suspended Sentence)

APPENDIX 4.2

Pre-Sentence Report for an Aboriginal Offender

Contacts

1. Mr. ███████████████   -Subject of Report
2. Ms. ███████████████   -Mother of Subject
3. Ms. ███████████████   -Sister of Subject
4. Ms. ███████████████   -Sister of Subject
5. Ms. ███████████████   - ████████ Native Justice Worker
6. RCMP File # ███████████████
7. Community Corrections File Review

Family & Social History

Mr. ████████ was born in ████████, British Columbia, and is the fourth youngest child born to Ms. ████████. He has ██ half-sisters, ████████, ████████ and 1 full sister, ████████. His father, Mr. ████████, may have originated from the ████████ Reserve near ████████. The Subject's mother, Ms. ████████ states that ████████ was in and out of jail for most of his adult life and the last time she and the children saw him was in ████████. The family speculates that ████████ may be serving a custodial sentence in the United States.

Mr. ████████ provided a detailed verbal and written account of his childhood. Mr. ████████ explains that as a child, he never lived in one place for very long: his dad was in and out of jail and his mother was always drunk. His first childhood memories are of him crying because he had not seen his mother for days.

Mr. ████████ states that when he was 4–5 years old, his mother moved them to ████████ to their Grandparent's house and she would be away a lot of the time leaving him and his sister ████████ in the care of their cousin, ████████. His mother had lost custody of the three older girls during this time due to her heavy drinking. Mr. ████████ states that ████████ began to sexually abuse him and then threaten him by saying that if he ever told anyone, he would kill him.

Although Ms. ████████ remembers that Mr. ████████'s behaviour had changed somewhat during this time, she states that she was not aware of the abuse. Mr. ████████ states that he tried to tell his mother about the abuse but she did not believe him. His mother states that her memory is blank about certain circumstances due to heavy drinking and blacking out.

During ████████, Mr. ████████'s mother married ████████, and Mr. ████████ states that his son ████████ Junior was sexually abusing his sister. When he told his mother, once again, she did not believe him until finally she caught ████████ Junior in the bathroom with her daughter. Mr. ████████ states that shortly after that incident, they were once again packing their bags and moving. Mr. ████████ describes the house they moved into as having no windows and he also recalls that they slept on the floor. He states that he remembers being very hungry and that his mother would take him and ████████ to a restaurant and order food for them and not eat anything herself. Sometime during this time, Mr. ████████ and ████████ were able to reside with their father. Mr. ████████ does not remember very much about this time other than the fact that when his mother retrieved them, they were very dirty.

Ms. ████████ moved the children to ████████ again and Mr. ████████ states that he was once more left with ████████ who sexually abused him again. This time, instead of just threatening Mr. ████████, ████████ hit him and choked him stating that he would kill him if he told anyone about the abuse. Mr. ████████ states that when ████████ would come to their residence bringing candy for him and his sister, he would usually go to his bedroom to avoid him until one day when he overheard ▆▆▆ telling Ms. ▆▆▆ that he is willing to take Mr. ▆▆▆ and ▆▆▆ to his residence. Mr. ▆▆▆ states that he got scared about this and finally told his mother again. But it was several years later when his mother caught Mr. ▆▆▆ and ▆▆▆ 'playing with themselves' that she sought the assistance from the Ministry of Children and Families. Ms. ▆▆▆ states that it was during this investigation that she realized that ▆▆▆ had been sexually abusing Mr. ▆▆▆ as well as his sister ▆▆▆. Criminal charges were laid; however, Ms. ▆▆▆ states that there was not enough evidence for a conviction.

Mr. ▆▆▆ explains that this was the most difficult thing he had ever done; confront his offender in court when he was so scared of him. Needless to say, Mr. ▆▆▆ was greatly disappointed when ▆▆▆ was not convicted and he states that this is when he lost faith and trust in everyone.

Ms. ▆▆▆ explained that the Ministry for Children and Families offered counselling to the children; however, they were reluctant to accept it as they were not able to trust anyone. Ms. ▆▆▆ explains that Mr. ▆▆▆ began to become involved in negative situations. He would run away for several days at a time as well as becoming very stubborn and non-compliant.

During 1985, Mr. ▆▆▆ moved in with his oldest sister ▆▆▆ and her husband ▆▆▆. Mr. ▆▆▆ describes this as the best time of his life because his sister did not drink, and he was doing well in school and he had just started his first job. Also, ▆▆▆ was like a substitute father for Mr. ▆▆▆ and he was living a stable life while at their residence. However, Mr. ▆▆▆'s mother remarried and brought him back to her house. Her new husband ▆▆▆ was very strict with Mr. ▆▆▆ which resulted in Mr. ▆▆▆ running away for good. Ms. ▆▆▆ states that he would run from one sister's residence to another family member's residence; however, he never came back to reside with her. Ms. ▆▆▆ states that removing Mr. ▆▆▆ from ▆▆▆'s residence was the biggest mistake that she ever made in her life because Mr. ▆▆▆ was very happy while he lived there. Subsequently, Mr. ▆▆▆ passed away during ▆▆▆, and Mr. ▆▆▆ states that "he died in a funny way, I thought he was murdered, and this had a big effect on me."

Currently, Mr. ▆▆▆ has two children from two different relationships: ▆▆▆ (▆ years old) born to ▆▆▆, and ▆▆▆ (▆ years old) born to ▆▆▆. Mr. ▆▆▆ maintains contact with both of his children and quite often, has his daughter ▆▆▆ reside with him.

Mr. ▆▆▆ is currently not involved in an intimate relationship and resides at his sister ▆▆▆'s residence. He maintains contact with his mother; however, they have many unresolved past issues that have formed barriers towards them developing any meaningful type of relationship. ▆▆▆ states that she is very close to her brother and has on a few occasions talked him down from thinking about committing suicide. She is concerned for him and hopes that he finds the support that he needs to recover from his childhood experiences.

Employment & Education

Mr. ▆▆▆ attended ▆▆▆ Elementary School and only completed grade ten before he dropped out of High School.

Mr. ▆▆▆ states that in the past, he has been employed as a prep cook, maintenance worker, painter and salesperson, and most recently, he had been self-employed as a commercial fisherman.

Mr. ▆▆▆ is currently unemployed and circulating his resume in the hope of procuring employment.

Substance Use

Mr. ███████ has struggled with alcohol addiction for several years. He has completed a 29-day residential treatment program at ████████ Alcohol and Drug Treatment Center.

The ████████ denies using drugs for the past three years and claims to have stopped consuming alcohol as of ████████, ████████. His sister advises that neither alcohol nor drugs have been a problem when he has resided with her. He has one Driving While Impaired conviction in ████████; other than that there is nothing on his record that suggests an alcohol or drug abuse problem. However, it should be noted that his Provincial case file does state that alcohol abuse has been a serious problem for the subject. He successfully completed the ████████ Treatment Program while on parole during this summer.

Health

Mr. ████████ reports that he is in good health. As a child, he endured over 50 stitches as a result of a tree branch falling on his head. Mr. ████████ also spent two weeks in the hospital due to a car accident.

According to his mother, Mr. ████████ had been offered therapy as a child in order to help him deal with the trauma he felt by being subjected to sexual abuse from his cousins; however, he refused to participate.

Aboriginal/Native Background

Mr. ████████ is a registered Indian with the ████████ Band of the ████████ .

████████ Nation

The ████████ Nation offers several programs for the native community, namely the ████████ ████████ process which is described in further detail:

████████ Process
████████ is the ████████ word that best describes "justice" according to the ████████ worldview. It reflects a "way of life" that incorporates balance and harmony. It is a way of helping one another to survive and to care and share amongst all people; it is a form of justice that focuses on relationships and the interconnectedness of all living life.

████████ is a means by which the ████████ people are given the opportunity to assert their inherent right to be self-determining and therefore their right to experience "justice" according to ████████ customs and traditions. It is a means by which "justice" is brought back to the people in the sense that they are given an opportunity to play meaningful roles in not only the problem, but also the solution.

████████ is about being responsible. A person who has caused harm is given the opportunity to take responsibility within a forum that focuses on maintaining family ties and community connections.

Most of the work involved with ████████ is done through "circle work" where the elders play a vital role and the family is the center of all activities. All matters brought to the attention of ████████ are dealt within a circle. For the ████████, this forum of relating to others is safe, non-confrontational and provides an equal voice to all participants. It is also inherently spiritual, which often encourages and facilitates healing.

████████ is guided by the following **three principles:**

1. ████████ is driven by the ████████ people,
2. ████████ is supported by ████████ communities,
3. ████████ is based on ████████ culture, customs, and traditions.

Upon receiving a referral to ███████████ the Native Justice Worker or a ███████████ Facilitator must ensure the following criteria are met:

1. The person who has done the damage is taking responsibility for his/her behavior; and
2. All relevant persons, particularly the victim(s), where there is one, are willing to have the matter dealt with by ███████████ .

In more serious cases, the following areas are considered:

1. The remorse (i.e. The level of awareness) of the person who caused the harm;
2. The community's willingness to deal with this person;
3. Resources available to the wrongdoer, the person(s) harmed and family members (i.e., are there enough ███████████ people to help with the situation);
4. Where the wrongdoer is in his/her own journey of healing;
5. The thoughts and opinions of the person(s) who has been harmed;
6. What passive actions the wrongdoer has taken since the incident.

███████████ Circles

The ███████████ circles are available for use in three different stages of the prosecuting process. A circle can be arranged to:

1. replace the trial process: a sentencing circle is comprised with representation from the ███████████, Crown Counsel, Presiding Judge, support people, and victims or their representatives are invited;
2. make a sentencing recommendation; and/or
3. assist with the reintegrating of Aboriginal offenders back into their communities.

Court History

1991–09–25 ████, B.C.	Theft Under $1000 Sec 334 (B) CC (RCMP ███████████)	1 day & Probation 8 mos

1992–05–08
████, B.C.
	1) Assault with a Weapon
	    Sec 267 (1) (A) CC
	2) Theft Over $1000 Sec 334 (A) CC
	3) Assault Sec 266 CC
	(RCMP ███████████)
		1) 8 mos & Probation
		    2 yrs & Firearms
		    Proh 5 yrs
		2) 8 mos & Probation
		    2 yrs
		3) 8 mos conc

1992–10–27 ████, B.C.	At Large/Escape Lawful Custody	JD 7 days
1993–12–01 ████, B.C.	Assault Sec 266 CC (███████████)	7 days

1994–07–26
████, B.C.
	1) Poss of Property Obtained by
	    Crime Over $1000 Sec 355 (A) CC
	(RCMP ███████████)
	2) Driving While Ability Impaired
	    Sec 253 (A) CC
	(███████████)
		1) 30 days & Probation 12 mos
		2) $400 I-D 14 days &
		    Probation 12 mos

1994–08–19 ████, B.C.	At Large/Escape Lawful Custody	JD 30 days

1995–01–11 ▮▮▮, B.C.	Poss of Property Obtained by Crime Over $1000 Sec 355 (A) CC (RCMP ▮▮▮▮)	14 days & Probation 18 mos
1995–07–27 ▮▮▮, B.C	Driving While Disqualified Sec 259 (4) CC (RCMP ▮▮▮▮)	14 days
1995–08–3 ▮▮▮, B.C.	1) Fail to Attend Court Sec 145 (2) (B) CC 2) Att Theft Over $5000 Sec 463 & 334 (A) CC (▮▮▮▮) 3) Use of Credit Card Obtained by Crime Sec 342 (1) (c) CC 4) Poss of Credit Card Obtained by Crime Sec 342 (1) (C) CC (RCMP ▮▮▮▮) 5) Poss of Property Obtained by Crime Over $1000 Sec 355 (A) CC 6) Theft Over $1000 Sec 334 (A) CC 7) Obstruct Peace Officer Sec 129 (A) CC 8) Theft Sec 344 CC 9) Dangerous Operation of Motor Vehicle Sec 249 (1) (A) CC (RCMP ▮▮▮▮)	1) 30 days 2–7) 3 mos on each chg conc 8) 3 mos & Probation 18 mos 9) 30 days & Proh Dri 6 mos
1997–08–11 ▮▮▮, B.C.	Forgery of Credit Card Sec 342 (1) (B) CC (RCMP ▮▮▮▮)	$1500 & Probation 1 yr
1998–10–09 ▮▮▮, B.C.	1) Mischief Under $5000 Sec 430 (4) CC 2) Unlawfully in Dwelling House Sec 349 (1) CC (RCMP ▮▮▮▮)	1–2) 45 days on each chg
1998–08–31 ▮▮▮, B.C.	1) Poss of Stolen Property 2) Breach of Recog	1) JD 30 days - S 2) JD 30 days
2002–02–14 ▮▮▮, B.C.	Break and Enter	JD 9 mos

Prior Community Supervision

Community Corrections in B.C. have supervised ▮▮▮ since he was 14 years old. He has a record of non-compliance with reporting condition of Bail and Probation Orders, now also with

Parole Orders. According to the Provincial Case file, Probation Officers and Bail Supervisors have filed with the Crown Counsel five separate breaches of Bail and two separate breaches of Probation Orders. He also has two escape lawful custody convictions and most recently his Parole was revoked. ███████ was released on Parole on ████████, 2002 and his Parole was suspended on ████████, 2002 for changing his residence without notifying and obtaining permission of his Parole Supervisor. However, subsequently, his Parole was reinstated. ████████ presents well and he has a supportive family but his response to Corrections has been poor.

Attitude Towards Offence

███████ denies stealing the cheques; he claims that he became involved when a fellow that he knew from jail approached him with a scheme to make some easy money. He claims that "the guy" was a big fellow who "packed a gun" and bought native status cards in the bar for $50.00 and then doctored them up for false I.D. cards.

███████ states that he received $50.00 for each cheque he cashed and that in all he received $1200.00 before he moved to get away from "the big fellow". ████████ further states that "the big fellow" had lots of people working for him but that he will not "rat him out" as he fears what would happen to him. The ███████ admits that he fears "the big fellow" more than he fears the RCMP or the Courts.

Victim Impact

The Province lost over $13,000.00 as a result of ███████ involvement in this offence not counting the bureaucratic, police and court costs involved. Furthermore, if ██████ is to be believed, a major offender is still at large.

Technical Suitability

███████ currently resides with his sister, ███████, in a two storey detached house. The residence meets the technical suitability criteria necessary for the electronic monitoring program.

Evaluation & Recommendations

Before the Court stands a 30 year old Native man from the ███████ Band, of the ███████ Nation, who has plead guilty to 1 count of (1)(a) Fraud over $5000 contrary to section 380 CCC, 1 count of (1) Fraud contrary to section 380 CCC, and 8 counts of Possession of Stolen Property contrary to section 355 CCC.

Mr. ███████ has a history of being emotionally and physically neglected, lack of family stability and being the victim of sexual abuse. His family believes that he would benefit from counselling which will be relevant to his past experiences of being sexually abused.

Mr. ███████ has alcohol addiction problems and although he has completed a term of residential treatment, it is to his benefit to seek further support to abstain from alcohol use. Mr. ███████ is also a devoted father to his two children that he maintains close contact with. His sisters, particularly ███████ and ███████ are very supportive of him.

Mr. ██████ belongs to the ███████ Nation, who provide alternative measures such as the ███████████ program. However, Mr. ███████'s performance on community supervision has been poor. He has been involved in the Criminal Justice system since he was 14 years old and continues to be involved in criminal behaviour. Mr. ███████ would not make a good candidate for community supervision.

Mr. ███████ has had many opportunities to seek assistance for his behaviour as well as opportunities to address his past issues, however, he has not taken the initiative to work out his problems.

If the Court is seeking a custodial sentence, Mr. ████████ would benefit from counselling available in an institutional setting.

Respectfully Submitted

████████Probation

APPENDIX 4.3

Recognizance of Bail Form

☐ Amended document   Police File No. ▮▮▮▮   Court File No. ▮▮▮▮

BRITISH COLUMBIA

Recognizance of Bail
Canada: Province of British Columbia

☐ Ban

Receipt No: ▮▮▮▮   D.O.B.: ▮▮▮▮

BEFORE THE HONOURABLE JUDGE ▮▮▮▮ ON DECEMBER 28 2001

Whereas ▮▮▮▮

has been charged that

```
Count 1, on or about November 08, 2001, at or near ▮▮▮▮, BC, did
commit an offence of attempted murder using firearm, contrary to Section
239(a) Criminal Code.

Count 2, on or about November 08, 2001, at or near ▮▮▮▮, BC, did
commit an offence of possessing weapon, imitation weapon, prohibited device,
ammunition or prohibited ammunition for purpose dangerous to public peace or
for purpose of committing an offence, contrary to Section 88(1) Criminal
Code.
```

The following person(s) personally came before a Justice and acknowledged owing the following amount to Her Majesty The Queen:

Name and Occupation	Address	Total Bail Amount	With a Deposit of
▮▮▮▮	▮▮▮▮	$2,000.00	without deposit with 1 or more sureties
Surety ▮▮▮▮	▮▮▮▮	Surety Bail Amount $2,000.00	With a Surety Deposit of

If the accused fails to meet the condition listed below, Her Majesty the Queen may seize any of the person's possessions or the possessions of any sureties equal to this amount, to be used as Her Majesty sees fit.

This recognizance remains in effect until the matters before the Court arising from the above charges are concluded. It then becomes void unless the accused has failed to meet the following conditions:

The person must attend court
on ▮▮▮▮, 2002   at 01:30 PM in the   Provincial Court
at ▮▮▮▮   British Columbia

and continue to attend as the Court requires in order to be dealt with according to law. And further, the accused must:
    See Attachment

Acknowledged before me at ▮▮▮▮   British Columbia

▮▮▮▮	▮▮▮▮	
Signature of Accused	Date	Signature of a Justice of the Peace in and for the Province of British Columbia
▮▮▮▮	▮▮▮▮	
Signature of Surety	Date	Signature of a Justice of the Peace in and for the Province of British Columbia
Signature of Substitute Surety	Date	Signature of a Justice of the Peace in and for the Province of British Columbia

Note: If no contact condition, fax copy to POR. If firearms prohibition, fax copy to Firearms Prohibition Registry.
See Notice of Language Rights at Trial and other important information within.

Recognizance of Bail

Original: Court - Copies: Accused, Surety, Police, SPD

Police File No. ▮▮▮▮▮

Court File No. ▮▮▮▮▮

Recognizance of Bail
Canada: Province of British Columbia

☐ Ban

Re: ▮▮▮▮▮

Conditions Attachment

D.O.B.: ▮▮▮▮▮

CONDITION 1: KEEP THE PEACE AND BE OF GOOD BEHAVIOUR.

CONDITION 2: Report by 4:00 pm to a Bail Supervisor on Monday ▮▮ December ▮▮ at ▮▮▮▮▮ B.C. and thereafter as and when directed.

CONDITION 3: Reside at ▮▮▮▮▮, ▮▮▮▮▮ B.C. and obey all rules and regulations imposed upon you at that residence.

POR CONDITION 4: HAVE NO CONTACT OR COMMUNICATION WHATSOEVER with ▮▮▮▮▮. You are not to attend within 50 metre radius of the place of employment or residence of ▮▮▮▮▮.

CONDITION 5: Undertake and successfully complete substance abuse counselling and treatment as directed by the Bail Supervisor.

CONDITION 6: Abstain completely from the consumption of alcohol and non-prescription drugs.

CONDITION 7: Undergo a breathalyzer test, urinalysis or blood test at the request of a Bail Supervisor or reasonable request of a peace officer.

FPR CONDITION 8: You are prohibited from possessing any firearm, crossbow, prohibited weapon, restricted weapon, prohibited device, ammunition, prohibited ammunition, or explosive substance. If you possess any items mentioned above (as in Section 515.4(1)) you will surrender those items to the ▮▮▮▮▮ R.C.M.P. on ▮▮▮▮▮, B.C. by 7pm today. You will surrender all licenses, authorizations and registration certificates.

FPR CONDITION 9: You are not to possess any WEAPONS as defined by the Criminal Code.

CONDITION 10: You will take reasonable steps to maintain yourself in such condition that: a) your psychiatric disorder will not likely cause you to conduct yourself in a manner dangerous to yourself or anyone else, and b) it is not likely you will commit further offences.

Signature of Accused

Date

Signature of a Justice of the Peace in and for the Province of British Columbia

Original: Court - Copies: Accused, Surety, Police, SPD

Recognizance of Bail

Recognizance of Bail

Canada: Province of British Columbia

Police File No. ▮▮▮▮▮

Court File No. ▮▮▮▮▮

☐ Ban

Re: ▮▮▮▮

| Conditions Attachment |

D.O.B.: ▮▮▮▮

Condition 11: You will thereafter report as directed by the Bail Supervisor from time to time to Dr. ▮▮▮▮▮ (family physician) or a medical professional approved of by the Bail Supervisor, for the purpose of receiving such medical counselling and treatment as may be recommended except that you shall not be required to submit to any treatment or medication to which you do not consent.

Condition 12: If you do not consent to the form of medical treatment or medication which is prescribed or recommended, you shall forthwith report to your Bail supervisor and thereafter report daily in person to your Bail Supervisor.

Condition 13: You shall provide your treating physician as named by your Bail Supervisor with a copy of this order and the name, address and telephone number of your Bail Supervisor. You shall instruct your treating physician that if you fail to take medication as prescribed by the Doctor or fail to keep any appointment made with the Doctor, the Doctor is to advise your Bail Supervisor immediately of any such failures.

I have read and understand the contents of this document and acknowledge that I am the person to whom the statements contained herein refer, and further acknowledge that I have been made aware of the provisions of Section 145, 524 Criminal Code of Canada

Signed: ▮▮▮▮ Witnessed: ▮▮▮▮

Probation Officer

Dated: ▮▮▮ at ▮▮▮ B.C.

▮▮▮▮▮

Signature of Accused

Date

Signature of a Justice of the Peace in and for the Province of British Columbia

Recognizance of Bail

Original: Court - Copies: Accused, Surety, Police, SPD

APPENDIX 4.4

Adult Community Risk/Needs Assessment

BRITISH COLUMBIA	Ministry of Public Safety and Solicitor General Corrections Branch	Adult Community Risk/Needs Assessment

CS#: _____ Surname: _____ Given: _____ Middle: _____ DOB: __/__/__ yr mth day

Gender: _____ Office/Centre: _____ Assessor UserID/Name: _____

Assessment Completion Date: __/__/__ yr mth day

Brief Description of Current Offence (optional) : _____

Needs Assessment (Dynamic Factors)	A	B	C	D
Case Needs Area	Factor Seen as an Asset to Community Adjustment	No Immediate Need For Improvement	Some Need for Improvement	Considerable Need for Improvement
1. Family Relationships	☐ Pattern of stable and supportive relationships	☐ No current difficulties	☐ Occasional instability in relationships	☐ Very unstable pattern of relationships
2. Living Arrangements	☐ Pattern of satisfactory living arrangements	☐ No current difficulties	☐ Occasional changes in residence or temporarily situated	☐ Frequent changes in residence and no permanent address
3. Companion/ Significant Others	☐ Pattern of non-criminal and/or positive associations	☐ Mostly non-criminal and/or positive associations	☐ Some criminal and/or negative associations	☐ Mostly criminal and/or negative associations
4. Academic/Vocational Skills		☐ No current difficulties	☐ Level of skills causing minor interference	☐ Level of skills causing serious interference
5. Employment Pattern	☐ Stable pattern of employment	☐ No current difficulties	☐ Employment situation causing minor adjustment problems	☐ Employment situation causing major adjustment problems
6. Financial Management	☐ Pattern of effective management	☐ No current difficulties	☐ Situational or minor adjustment problems	☐ Severe difficulties
7. Behavioural/Emotional Stability		☐ No current difficulties	☐ Behavioural/emotional problems that indicate some need for assistance	☐ Severe behavioural/ emotional problems that indicate significant need for assistance
8. Substance Abuse		☐ No current usage or difficulties	☐ Some usage causing moderate adjustment problems	☐ Frequent or uncontrolled usage causing serious adjustment problems
9. Attitude	☐ Actively involved and responding consistently well to assistance	☐ Motivated to change, receptive to assistance	☐ Recognizes problem areas but not receptive to assistance	☐ Unable to recognize problem areas and not receptive to assistance

Remarks: _____
_____
_____
_____
_____
_____
_____
_____

NEEDS				Supervision Rating			
R I S K	L	M	H	Overall **NEEDS** Rating:	☐ Low	☐ Medium	☐ High
	L	L	M	Overall **RISK** Rating:	☐ Low	☐ Medium	☐ High
	M	L	M	H	C.M. determined **SUPERVISION** Level:	☐ Low	☐ Medium ☐ High
	H	M	H	H			

CS#: _____ Surname: _____ Given: _____ Middle: _____ DOB: __/__/__

Criminal History Risk Assessment (Static Factors)

	Lesser Risk ← → Greater Risk			
	A	**B**	**C**	**D**
1. Number of Current Convictions		☐ One	☐ Two	☐ 3 or more
2. Number of Prior Court Dispositions	☐ None	☐ One	☐ 2 to 4	☐ 5 or more
3. Number of Prior Supervision Periods	☐ None	☐ One	☐ Two	☐ 3 or more
4. Number of Prior Failures to Comply	☐ None	☐ One	☐ Two	☐ 3 or more
5. Age at First Arrest/Conviction	☐ 25+	☐ 18 to 24	☐ 14 to 17	☐ 13 & under
6. Ever Imprisoned After a Conviction	☐ No			☐ Yes
7. Seriousness of Escape History	☐ None	☐ Low	☐ Medium	☐ High
8. Weapons Use/Threat	☐ No			☐ Yes
9. Frequency of Violence	☐ None	☐ Low	☐ Medium	☐ High
10. Severity of Violence	☐ None	☐ Low	☐ Medium	☐ High

Overall Risk Rating: Enter rating in 'Supervision Rating' box on bottom of page one.

Remarks:

Special Factors

	Yes	**No**
Arson?	☐ yes	☐ no
Sex Offender?	☐ yes	☐ no
Violent Offender?	☐ yes	☐ no
Mentally Disordered?	☐ yes	☐ no
Domestic Violence?	☐ yes	☐ no

Additional Assessment Indicated or Other Factors? (list below)

APPENDIX 4.5

Conditional Sentence Order

Canada: **Province of British Columbia**

BRITISH
COLUMBIA

	Police File No.	Court File No.

☐ Interpreter

Primary Enf. Agency:

☐ Ban

D.O.B.: ▮▮▮▮
Proceeded: ▮▮▮▮

On ▮▮▮▮ , 2002   at   ▮▮▮▮ , British Columbia

▮▮▮▮ was convicted upon the following charge(s) and on ▮▮▮▮ the Court adjudged that the offender be sentenced to a term of imprisonment as follows:

```
Count 1, on or about June 11, 2002, at or near ▮▮▮▮, BC, did commit an
offence of theft $5000 or under, contrary to Section 334(b) Criminal Code.
Sentence: Conditional Sentence: 4 Month(s);
```

and that the serving of the sentence in the community would not endanger the safety of the community.

It is ordered that the offender shall from the date of this order, or where applicable the date of expiration of any other sentence of imprisonment, serve the sentence in the community subject to the offender's compliance with the following conditions:

Namely, the said offender shall:

1. keep the peace and be of good behaviour,
2. appear before the Court when required to do so by the Court,
3. report to a Supervisor Today
   at ▮▮▮▮ , BC
   and thereafter when required by the Supervisor, and in the manner directed by the Supervisor.
4. remain within the Province of British Columbia, unless written permission to go outside of the province is obtained from the Court or the Supervisor.
5. notify the Supervisor in advance of any change of name or address, and promptly notify the Supervisor of any change of employment or occupation.

And in addition,

```
                    See Attachment
```

Dated ▮▮▮▮ 2002   at ▮▮▮▮   British Columbia

I, the undersigned offender, acknowledge that:
* I have received a copy of this order,
* I have received an explanation of the sections dealing with changes to the Conditional Sentence Order (Sec. 742.4) and failing to comply with the Conditional Sentence order (Sec.742.6)
* I understand the Conditional Sentence Order, and the explanations which I have received.

▮▮▮▮

Offender's Signature

Clerk of the Court on behalf of Judge ▮▮▮▮

Offender's address ▮▮▮▮

Offender's phone number ▮▮▮▮

Conditional Sentence Order

Original: Court File - Copies: Offender, Police, Supervisor, Crown, Victim

NEL

Conditional Sentence Order

BRITISH COLUMBIA

Police File No. ▓▓▓▓▓

Court File No. ▓▓▓▓▓

Canada: Province of British Columbia

☐ Interpreter   ☐ Ban

D.O.B.: ▓▓▓▓▓
Proceeded: summarily

Re: ▓▓▓▓▓

Conditions Attachment

CONDITION 1 on count (s) 1: During the first 30 days of the Conditional Sentence order you are to remain continuously in your residence and nowhere else save and except for attending at medical appointments or with written permission of your Conditional Sentence Supervisor.

CONDITION 2 on count (s) 1: Do not attend at the Safeway Store at ▓▓▓▓▓ , ▓▓▓▓▓ BC

Dated: November 4, 2002

at ▓▓▓▓▓

British Columbia

▓▓▓▓▓

Offender's Signature

Offender's address ▓▓▓▓▓

Clerk of the Court on behalf of Judge ▓▓▓▓▓

Offender's phone number ▓▓▓▓▓

Original: Court File - Copies: Offender, Police, Supervisor, Crown, Victim

Conditional Sentence Order

REFERENCES

Bazemore, G., and C.T. Griffiths. 1997. "Conferences, Circles, Boards, and Mediations: The 'New Wave' of Community Justice Decisionmaking." *Federal Probation* 61(2):25–37.

Bazemore, G., and M. Schiff. 2001. *Restorative and Community Justice*. Cincinnati, Ohio: Anderson.

Bonta, J. 1998. "Adult Offender Diversion Programs." *Research Summary: Corrections Research and Development* 3(1). Ottawa: Solicitor General Canada.

Bonta, J., S. Wallace-Capretta, and J. Rooney. 1998. *Restorative Justice: An Evaluation of the Restorative Resolutions Project*. Ottawa: Solicitor General Canada.

———. 2000. "Can Electronic Monitoring Make a Difference? An Evaluation of Three Canadian Programs." *Crime and Delinquency* 46(1):61–75.

Canadian Press. 2001. "Former Priest Sentenced to 2½ Years." *The Globe and Mail* (June 30):A9.

Chiodo, A.L. 2001. "Sentencing Drug-Addicted Offenders and the Toronto Drug Court." *Criminal Law Quarterly* 45(1/2):53–100.

Church Council on Justice and Corrections. 1996. *Satisfying Justice: Safe Community Options That Attempt to Repair Harm from Crime and Reduce the Use or Length of Imprisonment*. Ottawa: Correctional Service of Canada.

Clairmont, D. 2000. "Restorative Justice in Nova Scotia." *Canadian Journal of Policy Research* 1:145–49.

Corbett, R.P. 1999. *Transforming Probation Through Leadership: The "Broken Windows" Model*. New York: Center for Civic Innovation, Manhattan Institute. Retrieved from www.manhattan-institute.org/html/broken_windows.htm.

Couture, J., T. Parker, R. Couture, and P. Laboucane. 2001. *A Cost-Benefit Analysis of Hollow Water's Community Holistic Healing Process*. Ottawa: Solicitor General of Canada and the Aboriginal Healing Foundation.

Creechan, J.H., and J. Grekul. 1998. *Survey and Directory of Non-Custodial Adult Justice Programs*. Edmonton: Population Research Laboratory, University of Alberta.

Green, R.G. 1997. "Aboriginal Community Sentencing and Mediation: Within and Without the Circle." *Manitoba Law Journal* 25(1):77–125.

———. 1998. *Justice in Aboriginal Communities: Sentencing Alternatives*. Saskatoon: Purich Publishing.

Griffiths, C.T., and R. Hamilton. 1996. "Sanctioning and Healing: Restorative Justice in Canadian Aboriginal Communities." In J. Hudson and B. Galaway (eds.), *Restorative Justice: Theory, Practice, and Research* (175–91). Monsey, N.Y.: Criminal Justice Press.

Griffiths, C.T., and A. Hatch Cunningham. 2003. *Canadian Criminal Justice: A Primer*. 2nd ed. Toronto: Nelson.

Griffiths, C.T., E. Zellerer, D.S. Wood, and G. Saville. 1995. *Crime, Law, and Justice Among Inuit in the Baffin Region, N.W.T., Canada*. Burnaby, B.C.: Criminology Research Centre, Simon Fraser University.

Hume, M. 2003. "Street Racers' Sentences Outrage Victim's Family." *National Post* (February 4):A2.

Johnson, K. 2002. "States' Use of GPS Offender Tracking Systems." *The Journal of Offender Monitoring* 15(2):15–26.

Junger-Tas, J. 1994. *Alternatives to Prison Sentences: Experiences and Developments.* New York: Kugler Publications.

Lajeunesse, T., and Associates. 1996. *Evaluation of Community Holistic Circle Healing: Hollow Water First Nation.* Vol. 1. Final Report. Winnipeg: Manitoba Department of Justice.

Latimer, J., C. Dowden, and D. Muise. 2001. *The Effectiveness of Restorative Justice Practices: A Meta-Analysis.* Ottawa: Department of Justice Canada.

Marshall, T.F. 1999. *Restorative Justice: An Overview.* London, U.K.: Research Development and Statistics Directorate, Home Office.

Morris, A. 2002. "Critiquing the Critics: A Brief Response to Critics of Restorative Justice." *British Journal of Criminology* 42(3):596–615.

National Crime Prevention Strategy. 2002. *Drug Treatment Court of Toronto.* Ottawa: Government of Canada. Retrieved from www.prevention.gc.ca.

North, D. 2001. "The Catch-22 of Conditional Sentencing." *Criminal Law Quarterly* 44(3):342–74.

Nuffield, J. 1997. *Diversion Programs for Adults.* Ottawa: Solicitor General Canada.

Petersilia, J., and E.P. Deschenes. 1994. "What Punishes? Inmates Rank the Severity of Prison vs. Intermediate Sanctions." *Federal Probation* 58(1):3–8.

Presser, L., and P. Van Voorhis. 2002. "Values and Evaluation: Assessing Processes and Outcomes of Restorative Justice Programs." *Crime and Delinquency* 48(1):162–88.

Roberts. J.V., A.N. Doob, and V. Marinos. 2000. *Judicial Attitudes To Conditional Terms of Imprisonment: Results of a National Survey.* Ottawa: Department of Justice.

Roberts, J.V., and C. LaPrairie. 1997. "Sentencing Circles: Some Unanswered Questions." *Criminal Law Quarterly* 39(1):69–83.

———. 2000. *Conditional Sentencing in Canada: An Overview of Research Findings.* Ottawa: Research and Statistics Division, Department of Justice.

Sanders, T., and J.V. Roberts. 2000. Public Attitudes Toward Conditional Sentencing: Results of a National Survey. *Canadian Journal of Behavioural Science* 32(4):199–207.

Stuart, B. 1996. "Circle Sentencing in Yukon Territory, Canada: A Partnership of the Community and the Criminal Justice System." *International Journal of Comparative and Applied Criminal Justice* 20(2):291–309.

Thomas, M. 2002. "Adult Criminal Court Statistics, 2000/01." *Juristat* 22(2). Ottawa: Canadian Centre for Justice Statistics, Statistics Canada.

Umbreit, M.S., R.B. Coates, and B. Vos. 2001. "The Impact of Victim–Offender Mediation: Two Decades of Research." *Federal Probation* 65(3):29–35.

Van Ness, D., and K.H. Strong. 1997. *Restoring Justice.* Cincinnati, Ohio: Anderson Publishing.

Zehr, H. 1990. *Changing Lenses: A New Focus for Crime and Justice.* Scottsdale, Pa.: Herald Press.

CHAPTER 5
CORRECTIONAL INSTITUTIONS

CHAPTER OBJECTIVES

- *Identify the types of correctional institutions.*
- *Discuss the structure, operation, and management of institutions.*
- *Identify and discuss the eras of prison architecture.*
- *Discuss the social organization of the prison.*
- *Identify and discuss the challenges of operating and managing correctional institutions.*
- *Examine prison riots through the use of a case study.*
- *Consider the issues surrounding private prisons.*

KEY TERMS

Correctional centres/reformatories/
  établissements/penitentiaries
Jails and detention centres
Remand centres
Correctional camps/farms/day
  detention centres/treatment
  centres/community residences
Minimum-security institutions
Medium-security institutions
Maximum-security institutions
Special Handling Unit
Multi-level institutions
Static security

Dynamic security
Total institution
Continuum of correctional institutions
Unit management system
Institutional parole officers
Unit management team
Commissioner's directives
Regional instructions
Standard operating procedures (also
  known as standing orders)
Post orders
Prison-industrial complex

Although only 5 percent of those who come to the attention of the criminal justice system are ultimately incarcerated for their offences, the prison is one of the most visible and controversial components of corrections and has been the subject of a great deal of study. Federal and provincial/territorial systems of corrections spend the largest proportion of their budgets on institutions. This chapter examines a variety of topics related to correctional institutions, ranging from their structure and operation to the key challenges that confront the senior correctional personnel who manage institutional populations. A case study of a prison riot illustrates what happens when management loses control of a correctional institution.

TYPES OF CORRECTIONAL INSTITUTIONS

There are a wide variety of correctional facilities operated by the federal government and provincial/territorial governments. The designations given to these institutions can be quite confusing. Here are some of the more common terms that are used:

- **correctional centres/reformatories/établissements/penitentiaries:** used to confine sentenced offenders
- **jails and detention centres:** used to house short-term inmates and offenders on remand
- **remand centres:** used to confine offenders awaiting trial on remand
- **correctional camps/farms/day detention centres/treatment centres/community residences:** used to house lower-risk inmates in a minimum-security setting or those on conditional release (Robinson et al., 1998)

Federal Correctional Institutions

Federal correctional facilities are categorized into the following security levels:

- **minimum-security institutions:** These institutions allow unrestricted inmate movement, except during the night, and generally have no perimeter fencing.
- **medium-security institutions:** In these institutions, inmates are surrounded by high-security perimeter fencing but have more freedom of movement than in maximum security.
- **maximum-security institutions:** In these highly controlled institutions, surrounded by high-security perimeter fencing, inmates' movements are strictly controlled and continually monitored by video surveillance cameras.

- **Special Handling Unit:** A high-security institution for inmates who present such a high level of risk to staff and inmates that they cannot be housed in maximum-security facilities. There is a Special Handling Unit at the Regional Reception Centre in Ste-Anne-des-Plaines, Quebec. There are also a number of regional health centres operated by the Correctional Service of Canada (CSC). These facilities house violent offenders and offer treatment programs centred on violence and anger management.
- **multi-level institutions:** These institutions contain one or more of the above security levels in the same facility or on the same grounds. In addition, there may be distinct inmate populations within the same institution that, for security and safety reasons, are not allowed to commingle. For example, Kent Institution, a federal maximum-security institution east of Vancouver, houses three separate populations: close custody, general population, and protective custody.

The CSC operates nearly 50 facilities across the country, ranging from minimum-security work camps to maximum-security prisons. These include a number of small, regional facilities for female offenders (see Box 5.1). Approximately 63 percent of federal offenders are confined in minimum-

BOX 5.1

Institutions for Federally Sentenced Women

- Nova Institution for Women (Truro, N.S.)
- Springhill Institution (Springhill, N.S.)*
- Joliette Institution (Joliette, Que.)
- Grand Valley Institution (Kitchener, Ont.)
- Saskatchewan Penitentiary (Prince Albert, Sask.)*
- Regional Psychiatric Centre (Saskatoon, Sask.)
- Okimaw Ohci Healing Lodge (Maple Creek, Sask.)
- Edmonton Institution for Women (Edmonton, Alta.)
- Burnaby Correctional Centre for Women (Burnaby, B.C.)**

* Institutions for men with on-site facilities for maximum-security women.

** This provincially operated facility is scheduled to close in 2004. The provincially sentenced women will be moved to a refurbished men's facility. The federally sentenced women are to be transferred to the Sumas Community Correctional Centre in Abbotsford, which will be converted to a multi-level security facility.

security institutions. Unbeknownst to many Canadians, the federal government (not the CSC) also operates the Canadian Forces Service Prison and Detention Barracks in Edmonton, Alberta (see Box 5.2).

Provincial/Territorial Institutions

The provinces and territories operate approximately 160 facilities with different levels of security, although there are no uniform designations. Interestingly, in comparison to the federal CSC, the provinces/territories make more extensive use of maximum-security institutions, primarily because of the responsibility for housing persons who are on remand awaiting trial or sentencing. These individuals represent a broad range of security risks and, in the absence of time to assess individual offenders, all are detained in maximum security. Provincial correctional systems also operate treatment facilities for special populations such as sex offenders.

BOX 5.2

There's No Jail Like It: The Canadian Military Prison

Members of the Canadian military can be convicted of offences under the Canadian Criminal Code and the military Code of Conduct. The Canadian Armed Forces have their own justice system, including police, defence lawyers, prosecutors, courts, and prison. Established in 1949, the Canadian Forces Service Prison and Detention Barracks receives male and female members of the military who have been sentenced for periods from 15 days to two years less a day. Offenders with longer sentences are then transferred to a federal correctional facility to serve the remaining portion of their sentence. These offenders are eligible for parole, as are any federal inmates.

The regimen of the military prison is quite different from that of other correctional institutions. Inmates rise at 5:30 a.m. and follow a tightly controlled schedule until 9:00 p.m. The facility operates on strict discipline: both the guards and the inmates move through the day with military precision. Conjugal (overnight) family visits are not permitted. New inmates cannot speak to one another during the first two weeks of confinement. Activities such as watching television and reading are privileges that inmates must earn. Unlike civilian institutions, the military prison has a low incidence of violence, and contraband weapons and drugs are unknown. Less than 5 percent of the inmates are repeat offenders.

Sources: Department of National Defence and Canadian Forces (www.forces.gc.ca); Moon, 1997.

In Ontario, jails and detention centres house offenders who are awaiting trial (or other court proceedings) or serving short sentences. Jails are often small, old buildings, while detention centres tend to be large, modern facilities built to meet the needs of several municipalities. The province also operates correctional centres for offenders typically serving terms of up to two years less a day. One of the more unusual territorial prisons is profiled in Box 5.3. For information on the correctional facilities operated by each of the provincial/territorial systems of corrections, visit the websites listed in Table 1.1, page 11.

FEDERAL/PROVINCIAL JOINT INITIATIVES

The attempt to increase the efficiency and effectiveness of correctional services has led to increased cooperation between federal and provincial correctional authorities in developing programs and services. In Prince Edward Island, the Offender Program Resource Centre provides services to both federal and provincial offenders, and in Newfoundland and Labrador, the Provincial Correctional Centre in Stephenville operates primarily as a provincial institution for federally sentenced offenders. Staff have been certified to deliver federally developed programs in substance abuse and cognitive skills training. Federal and provincial correctional personnel make joint decisions about case management, and provincial probation officers may provide supervision for federal offenders on conditional release. In Nunavut, probation and parole supervision are provided under exchange of service agreements with the federal government.

BOX 5.3

The Baffin Correctional Centre: Where the Inmates Are Armed

The Baffin Correctional Centre, located in the Nunavut town of Iqaluit, is the only correctional facility in the world in which inmates may handle loaded firearms. The Land Program allows inmates to leave the centre under the supervision of an Inuit staff member and hunt for seal, walrus, caribou, whale, or Arctic hare, depending on the season. Most of the game harvest is donated to Elders or to infirm residents in the community. A small portion is prepared by the kitchen staff at the institution.

Aboriginal Healing Centres and Lodges

The federal government has also entered into agreements with First Nations groups across the country to develop and operate healing lodges, including the following:

- Pê Sâkâstêw (Cree for "New Beginning") is a minimum-security facility located near Hobbema, Alberta, in the Samson Cree Nation.
- The Prince Albert (Saskatchewan) Grand Council Spiritual Healing Lodge for male Aboriginal offenders, located in the Wahpeton Dakota First Nation Community, houses 25 provincial offenders and five federal offenders.
- The Okimaw Ohci Healing Lodge, a facility for federally sentenced Aboriginal women situated on the Nekaneet Indian Reserve in Maple Creek, Saskatchewan, houses up to 30 women and 10 children.
- The Ochichakkosipi Healing Lodge in Crane River, Manitoba, is a 24-bed facility with a spiritual centre, four residences, and a family cabin for visitors.
- Waseskun Healing Centre, near Montreal, offers residential therapy for men and women referred from Aboriginal communities and provincial or federal correctional institutions. (Correctional Service of Canada, 2002)

Although healing lodges operate under the auspices of the CSC, they are also accountable to a governing council composed of Elders and other First Nations representatives. The treatment programs offered in healing lodges will be discussed in Chapter 8.

SECURITY AND ESCAPES

All correctional facilities have two types of security:

- **Static security** includes perimeter fencing, video surveillance and alarms, and fixed security posts, such as control rooms and position posts, where officers remain in a defined area.
- **Dynamic security** includes ongoing interaction, beyond observation, between correctional officers and inmates—working with and speaking with inmates, making suggestions, providing information, and, in general, being proactive.

Although prison escapes are a Hollywood staple, they are in fact quite rare. The number of escapes from federal institutions runs (no pun intended) around 200 per year. Most of these involve inmates walking away from minimum-security facilities. At the provincial/territorial level, the majority of "escapees" are offenders who fail to show up to serve weekend, intermittent sentences.

PRISON ARCHITECTURE

One way to trace the changing philosophy of corrections and punishment is by examining the architecture of correctional institutions. As noted in Chapter 2, the first prisons constructed in Canada during the 1800s were designed to reflect both the role of the institutions in Canadian society at that time as well as the objectives of incarceration. The term *moral architecture* was used to indicate that institutions were places where inmates would be taught proper attitudes and values through a strict regimen. Much has changed in the past half-century, and inmates and correctional personnel from earlier years would not recognize many of the correctional institutions that have been constructed in recent years.

The Eras of Prison Architecture

A review of the history of prison architecture in Canada reveals a number of distinct design phases that can be related to shifts in correctional philosophy. These eras are reflected in the federal correctional institutions that have been constructed, beginning with Kingston Penitentiary in 1835 and continuing to the late 1990s. Note that the timeline dates presented in Box 5.4 are general, rather than definite, and only some of the more distinctive attributes of each era have been identified.

BOX 5.4

The Eras of Prison Architecture

Pre-1835

Imprisonment was not used as a sanction, and little consideration was given to the structure in which offenders were housed while awaiting trial or punishment. Institutions had congregate housing with little or no separation of offenders by age, gender, or offence.

1800s–1940s

The first penitentiary in Kingston was built on the Auburn plan, with inmates working and eating together during the day and housed separately in cells at night. A rigid silent system (in effect in some institutions until the early 1950s) was used to prevent moral contamination among inmates. Living conditions improved in some institutions with the installation of plumbing and ventilation. The institutional design usually consisted of tiers (floors) of small, barred, windowless cells built in layers like stacked cages overlooking a tall common space.

Institutions built during this era include Dorchester Penitentiary (N.B., 1880); Kingston Penitentiary (Ont., 1835); Collins Bay Institution (Ont., 1930); and the Prison for Women (Ont., 1934).

1950s

During this era, there was an emphasis on privacy, with smaller tiers and larger cells with a solid door and a view window. Security was static. Institutions incorporating this design include LeClerc Institution (Que.) and Joyceville Institution (Ont.).

1960s

During the 1960s, prison architecture reflected an effort to dilute the prison as a distinct building form. There was an attempt to normalize the institutional environment, and buildings were designed to reduce inmates' isolation and loss of personal dignity. A number of facilities were constructed that incorporated a campus-style layout and included residential-scale buildings for living units. There was an increase in the use of dynamic security, which encouraged positive staff–inmate interaction. Among the institutions incorporating this design were Matsqui Institution (B.C.), Springhill Institution (N.S.), and Drumheller Institution (Alta.).

1970s

Institutional designs continued to reflect an attempt to create physical spaces that would increase interaction between staff and inmates. Designs included living units, each of which housed a number of inmates supervised by a unit management team. There was an emphasis on providing space for rehabilitation programs and efforts were made to create a more relaxed environment. Mission Medium Security Institution (B.C.) is an example of this design approach.

BOX 5.4 continued

1980s

A mixed design approach was evident during this era, with some new institutions reflecting the trend toward creating physical facilities and institutional environments conducive to increased inmate responsibility, staff–inmate interaction, and less use of traditional security barriers. A number of existing institutions were upgraded to increase security and control over inmates. Bowden Medium Security Institution (Alta.) reflects the new designs during this era. It has cells that inmates can lock and unlock at will (except at night) and open, common areas for each cell cluster.

1990s

In this decade, small regional facilities were constructed for federal female offenders; Frontenac Institution (Ont.) and William Head Institution (B.C.) were renovated to create neighbourhood housing, or small, autonomous housing units for five to eight inmates with reduced direct surveillance; and Pê Sâkâstêw Institution for Aboriginal offenders was built, using a circular layout and building design that reflects Aboriginal culture and spirituality.

Sources: Centen, 1991; Correctional Service of Canada, 1991.

Contemporary Prison Design

Prison design in the early 21st century reflects the split between the competing models of correction discussed in Chapter 2: the liberal European model, which has been adopted by the federal government, and the punishment-oriented American approach embraced by provinces such as Ontario. The design of many of the new and renovated federal correctional facilities reflects an emphasis on the reintegration of offenders, as well as on the needs of specific offender groups, including women and Aboriginal offenders. These facilities are designed to promote positive group interaction among small groups of inmates, to promote responsibility, and to prepare inmates for life outside.

- At the Grand Valley Institution for Women, located in Kitchener, Ontario, there are no cells and no uniforms, and the front-line staff are called primary workers, rather than guards or correctional officers.

There are a number of cottages, and each female inmate has her own bedroom, which can be locked from the inside. Some bedrooms have space for baby cribs.

- At Frontenac Institution, a federal minimum-security facility in Ontario, inmates participating in the Phoenix program reside in condominium-like living units consisting of a living room, kitchen, dining room, bathroom, and individual bedrooms. Inmates can lock their own bedrooms, and the units themselves are secured only between midnight and 4 a.m. The inmates in each unit have a monthly budget from which they must buy food, and household responsibilities, including cooking and cleaning, are shared.

- The design of Pê Sâkâstêw reflects efforts to increase inmate responsibility, to reduce institutionality, and to prepare inmates for life in the community. Inmates at Pê Sâkâstêw live in one of eight five-man communal groups and share responsibilities for cooking, cleaning, and house management (see photo).

- William Head, a federal minimum-security institution located near Victoria, B.C., features three units, each containing two "communities." Each community consists of four two-storey duplexes (eight five-man

Pê Sâkâstêw Institution (Alberta)

houses) and a community building that contains unit staff offices, common areas, a boardroom, and a laundry room (see photo and Figures 5.1 and 5.2).

In sharp contrast, the province of Ontario is building no-frills mega-prisons that reflect "the new American school of prison architecture" (Gardner, 2002:2). Within the framework of the Adult Infrastructure Renewal Project, 14 provincial institutions are being closed and replaced with five "superjails." The first of Ontario's new superjails is Maplehurst Correctional Complex (see photo and Box 5.5). It is anticipated that the per diem costs per inmate in these facilities will be reduced by half and will result in other operational savings. The institutions are designed to be austere and to have few amenities. Extensive use will be made of surveillance technology in order to

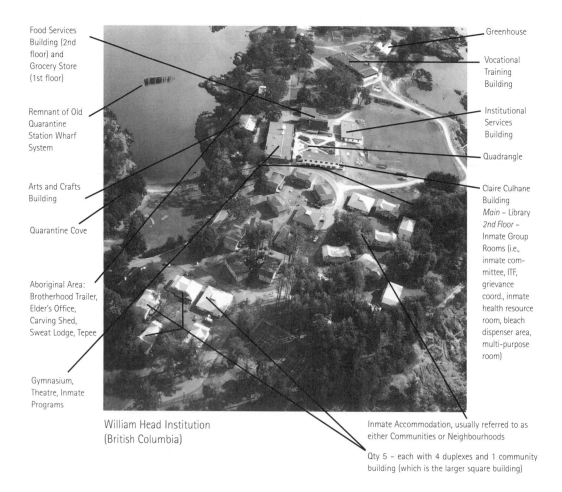

Food Services Building (2nd floor) and Grocery Store (1st floor)

Remnant of Old Quarantine Station Wharf System

Arts and Crafts Building

Quarantine Cove

Aboriginal Area: Brotherhood Trailer, Elder's Office, Carving Shed, Sweat Lodge, Tepee

Gymnasium, Theatre, Inmate Programs

Greenhouse

Vocational Training Building

Institutional Services Building

Quadrangle

Claire Culhane Building
Main – Library
2nd Floor – Inmate Group Rooms (i.e., inmate committee, ITF, grievance coord., inmate health resource room, bleach dispenser area, multi-purpose room)

William Head Institution (British Columbia)

Inmate Accommodation, usually referred to as either Communities or Neighbourhoods

Qty 5 – each with 4 duplexes and 1 community building (which is the larger square building)

Figure 5.1

Typical Layout of Housing Unit, William Head Institution (B.C.)

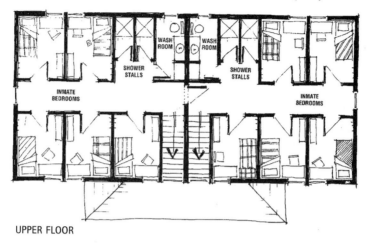

UPPER FLOOR

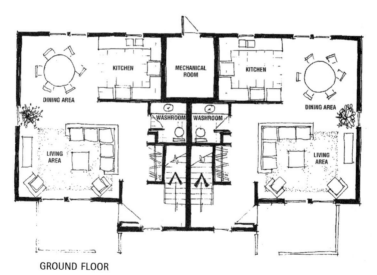

GROUND FLOOR

WAGG AND HAMBLETON ARCHITECTS, VICTORIA, BRITISH COLUMBIA

Source: Johnston, 1991:15. Reproduced with permission of the Correctional Service of Canada.

reduce staffing and security personnel costs. Other provinces, including British Columbia, are following suit, closing minimum-security correctional camps and medium-security prisons, and housing inmate populations in a few large institutions.

Figure 5.2

Typical Layout of Neighbourhood Centre, William Head Institution (B.C.)

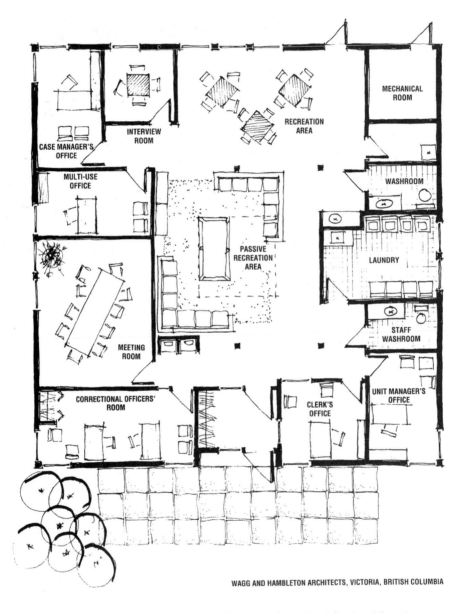

WAGG AND HAMBLETON ARCHITECTS, VICTORIA, BRITISH COLUMBIA

Source: Johnston, 1991:17. Reproduced with permission of the Correctional Service of Canada.

Maplehurst Correctional Complex (Ontario)

BOX 5.5

Maplehurst Correctional Complex: An American-Style Prison in Canada

Maplehurst Correctional Complex in Milton, Ontario, is a 1,500-bed facility that has been called "a symbol of the rise of American-style 'tough-on-crime' policies in this country" (Gardner, 2002:2). At Maplehurst, security and cost control are key objectives. There are 21 different types of security systems and 300 metres of razor wire. Inmates live in self-contained units called pods that "are designed so guards can see directly into each cell from [a central] command post" (Gardner, 2002). Inmate movement is severely restricted by the fact that all activities take place within the pods, each of which is equipped with interview and program rooms, an exercise yard, and a visiting area. Court appearances can be done via video conferencing, reducing the need for trips outside of the institution.

Prison architecture across the country is also being influenced by the expansion of alternatives to confinement (see Chapter 4) and by the emphasis on early release and reintegration (see Chapters 9 and 10), which have altered the composition of inmate populations. Increasingly, inmate populations in federal institutions are composed of violent, high-risk offenders who do not qualify for conditional release programs. In provincial correctional facilities, there has been a corresponding increase in the number of inmates with serious criminal profiles. These trends have limited the ability of systems of corrections to design facilities that provide more freedom of movement and increased responsibility for inmates.

THE ATTRIBUTES OF THE MODERN PRISON

Correctional institutions have a number of unique features that distinguish them from other public- and private-sector agencies and organizations. These features determine the daily challenges that confront correctional managers as well as the patterns of interaction that occur among the various groups who live and work inside correctional facilities. Three of the more significant features include the following.

Prisons Are Asked to Pursue Conflicting Goals

The primary goal of correctional institutions is to protect society by housing offenders who pose a serious risk to the community. However, correctional institutions are also charged with preparing offenders for eventual release into the community as law-abiding and contributing members of society. These goals illustrate the split personality of corrections, and this conflict is reflected in much of the interaction that occurs within the prison, including the relationship between correctional officers and treatment staff (to be discussed in Chapter 6) and the delivery of treatment programs (to be discussed in Chapter 8).

Prisons Are Political and Public Institutions

The role of social, political, and economic forces in the creation and operation of Canadian prisons was illustrated in Chapter 2, and these forces continue to determine the goals of incarceration and the extent to which they are achieved. Politicians, provincial legislatures, and the federal government exercise considerable control over the way in which correctional institutions are operated, the goals they are asked to pursue, and the resources that are made available to correctional personnel. These aspects are part of the external environment (the external and internal environments of a correctional institution are depicted in Figure 5.3).

Interior of a modern prison cell

Figure 5.3

The External and Internal Environments of a Correctional Institution

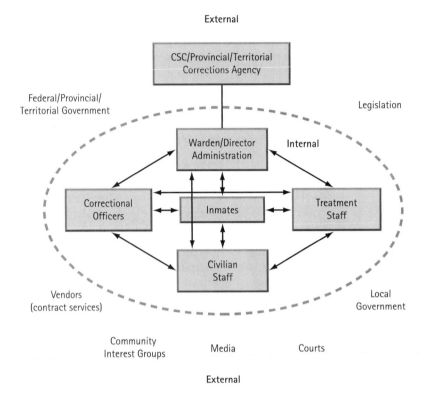

External

CSC/Provincial/Territorial
Corrections Agency

Federal/Provincial/
Territorial Government

Legislation

Warden/Director
Administration

Internal

Correctional
Officers

Inmates

Treatment
Staff

Civilian
Staff

Vendors
(contract services)

Local
Government

Community
Interest Groups

Media

Courts

External

Prisons Are Total Institutions

One of the more significant contributions to the study of corrections was made over 40 years ago by the sociologist Erving Goffman, who introduced the concept of the prison as a **total institution.** According to Goffman (1961:xii), a total institution is "a place of residence and work where a large number of like-situated individuals, cut off from the wider society for an appreciable period of time, together lead an enclosed, formally administered round of life."

In his treatise, Goffman (1961:6) outlined the major attributes of life inside total institutions, among which he included mental hospitals, military installations, and prisons:

- All aspects of life are conducted in the same place under the same single authority.

- Each phase of the patient's daily activity is carried on in the immediate company of a group of others, all of whom are treated alike and required to follow the same regimen.
- All phases of the day's activities are tightly scheduled and controlled by an administrative hierarchy (see Box 5.6).

While all correctional institutions share a common identity as total institutions, some institutions are more "total" than others. Correctional facilities vary in terms of their affiliation (federal/provincial/territorial), security classification, size, management style, characteristics of the inmate population, and other key factors that affect the patterns of activity and interaction that occur within them. To reflect this variability, a rough **continuum of correctional institutions** can be constructed, based on the extent to which the structure and

BOX 5.6

Daily Inmate Routine in an Ontario Prison

Morning

1. Wake-up call at approximately 06:30 hours
2. Inmate stand to count
3. Breakfast
4. Health-care rounds
5. Inmate: releases, transfers, and counts
6. Unit clean-up
7. Work gangs out to their assigned areas (community work, laundry, etc.)
8. Education and recreation periods

Afternoon

1. Lunch
2. Recreation period for inmates on work details
3. Health-care rounds
4. Rehabilitative programming or quiet time
5. Visits
6. Inmate stand to count

BOX 5.6, continued

Evening

1. Supper
2. Unit clean-up
3. Inmate stand to count
4. Visits
5. Evening recreation and/or other programs (e.g., Alcoholics Anonymous)
6. Health-care rounds
7. Showers
8. Televisions off
9. Bedtime/lights out at approximately 23:00 hours

Source: Ministry of Public Safety and Security, Correctional Services, from a page in the website www.mpss.jus.on.ca that was recently deleted.

regimen of a particular prison approximates Goffman's description. At one end of such a continuum could be located minimum-security and community correctional facilities, while at the other would be maximum-security institutions. Needless to say, it would be expected that the dynamics of everyday life inside institutions at either end of the continuum would be considerably different. Even institutions at the same security level can be said to have their own "personalities"—a function of history, the orientation of administrators, specific attributes of the inmate population, and other less tangible factors.

A major feature of the prison as a total institution is a split between the inmates and the institutional staff. Each group may view the other in terms of stereotypes. The interaction between the inmates, who occupy a position of powerlessness and deprivation within the institutional hierarchy, and the correctional officers, who enforce the rules and regulations of the institution at the line level, is a key feature of institutional life. These patterns of interaction will be explored in greater detail in the discussion of correctional officers in Chapter 6.

THE ORGANIZATION OF THE PRISON

Perhaps the best way to understand the influence of the prison's external environment and the dynamics of life inside correctional institutions is to view the prison as a formal organization, with goals, rules, regulations, and a hierarchical structure of authority. Like all organizations, correctional institutions are affected by forces in the external environment as well.

Unit Management System

Federal correctional facilities and many provincial/territorial institutions are structured around the **unit management system.** Among the features of unit management are:

- a decentralized approach to inmate management
- small living units designed to facilitate extensive interaction with inmates
- a single manager who supervises all activities in the unit
- clear lines of authority
- relegation of much of the decision making to the unit level
- an emphasis on staff cooperation
- integration of case management and security activities at the line and administrative levels (Hughes, 1996:13)

Each unit in the institution has a unit manager, who reports to a deputy warden. The unit manager's responsibilities include security, case management, programming, health and safety issues, and administrative duties. In federal institutions, the unit team is composed of **institutional parole officers,** two levels of correctional officers (CO1 and CO2), and correctional supervisors. Each **unit management team** is responsible for up to 120 inmates. See Figure 5.4.

The unit management model is designed to decentralize authority and decision making to the individual unit level and to facilitate direct lines of communication between the various team members as well as between team members and the inmates. In many institutions, however, these objectives have not been fulfilled. The relations of correctional officers, case managers, and the institutional administration will be discussed in Chapter 6.

Legislative and Policy Framework

All correctional institutions operate within a legislative and policy framework. Federal institutions, for example, are subject to:

- the Corrections and Conditional Release Act (CCRA) and other legislation
- **commissioner's directives,** which are rules for the management of service delivery and for carrying out the provisions of the CCRA

Figure 5.4

Organization of Management Services and Operations in a Federal Correctional Institution

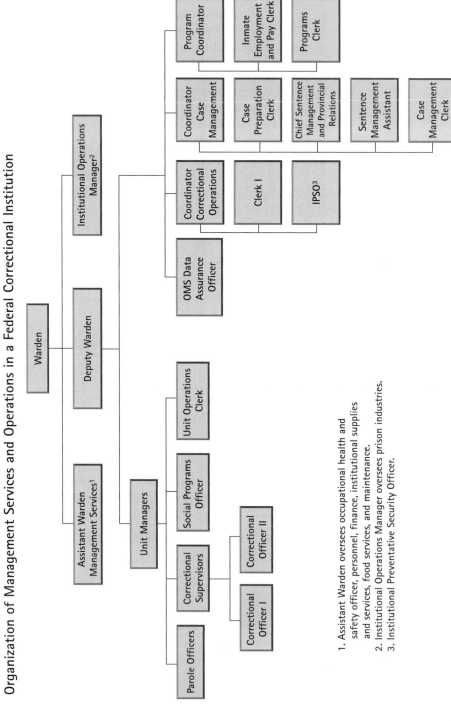

1. Assistant Warden oversees occupational health and
   safety officer, personnel, finance, institutional supplies
   and services, food services, and maintenance.
2. Institutional Operations Manager oversees prison industries.
3. Institutional Preventative Security Officer.

Source: Solicitor General Portfolio, 2002:17.

- **regional instructions,** which are issued by the CSC Regional Headquarters and elaborate on commissioner's directives or address specific regional issues
- **standard operating procedures (also known as standing orders),** which repeat or elaborate on provisions contained in the CCRA commissioner's directives and regional instructions, in addition to providing procedural instructions for specific activities within the institution.
- **post orders,** which provide more in-depth guidelines and outline the responsibilities for staff members who occupy specific positions, or posts, within the facility
- policy manuals on such topics as security, case management, and the conducting of investigations

Despite this myriad of directives, rules, and regulations, the federal system of corrections has experienced difficulty in ensuring that the principles of the rule of law are applied in policy and practice. This difficulty was evident in an incident that occurred at the Kingston Prison for Women in 1996. This incident and the findings of the commission of inquiry (Arbour, 1996) completed in its aftermath have had a significant impact on the operation of federal correctional institutions.

The Incident at the Kingston Prison for Women: A Breakdown in the Rule of Law

On April 22, 1994, a violent physical confrontation occurred between six inmates and several correctional officers at the Kingston Prison for Women. While brief, the incident resulted in the women being placed in segregation and criminally charged (five of the six inmates subsequently pleaded guilty). In the immediate aftermath of the incident, a high level of tension existed in the institution, compounded by the presence of a large number of relatively inexperienced correctional staff and correctional officers who were overworked and overstressed. The lack of administrative leadership from the warden of the institution also contributed to the events that unfolded over the next several days.

Two days later, on April 24, three other inmates who were housed in the segregation unit caused further disruption by slashing, taking a hostage, and attempting suicide. On April 26, correctional officers from the institution demonstrated outside the institution in support of their demand that the inmates involved in the violent altercation on April 22 be transferred to a higher security institution.

On the evening of that same day, the warden of the institution sent an all-male Institutional Emergency Response Team (IERT) to extract eight inmates in the segregation unit from their cells and strip-search them. Six of the eight had been involved in the initial confrontation on April 22. The IERT did not complete the cell extractions until early the following morning, at which time the eight women were left in empty cells in the segregation unit. The women had been stripped (in the presence of male members of the IERT), dressed in paper gowns, and placed in restraints and leg irons. All of the cell extractions and strip searches had been recorded on videotape as per routine procedure. The following evening, seven of the eight inmates were subjected to body cavity searches. Six of the women involved in the original April 22 incident then were placed in segregation for many months.

Although the CSC investigated the incidents, the report that was issued neglected many of the events that had occurred. In February 1995, the report of the Correctional Investigator was tabled in the House of Commons. This report criticized the actions of the CSC, the correctional staff, and the IERT. The pressure on the federal government to take action increased when portions of the videotape, showing the cell extractions and strip searches by the IERT, were shown on national television. An independent judicial inquiry was called for and was subsequently appointed in April 1995. The commissioner of the inquiry was the Honourable Louise Arbour, a highly respected member of the Quebec judiciary and now a member of the Supreme Court of Canada.

The final report of the commission of inquiry (Arbour, 1996) was extremely critical of the actions taken by correctional staff, the members of the IERT, and the warden of the institution. In addition, the report severely criticized the response of senior CSC officials and ultimately resulted in the resignation of the commissioner of corrections.

The inquiry's report documented the violations of the rule of law, policy, and institutional regulations in a number of areas, including the use of segregation, the use of force by the IERT, and the manner in which the women had been strip-searched and subjected to body cavity searches. Serious concerns were raised as to whether the CSC was capable of implementing the necessary reforms to ensure that the rule of law and justice were adhered to without outside intervention and monitoring. The Arbour report also contained 14 primary recommendations relating to cross-gender staffing in correctional institutions for women, the use of force and of IERTs, the operation of segregation units, the needs of Aboriginal women in correctional institutions, ways of ensuring accountability and adherence to the rule of law among correctional personnel, and procedures for handling inmate complaints and grievances.

The CSC responded to the Arbour report with the following initiatives:

- appointed a Deputy Commissioner for Women
- amended the use of force policy to prohibit (1) the use of all-male IERTs as a first response in women's correctional institutions, and (2) the presence of male staff during strip searches of female inmates
- made significant changes to the procedures surrounding the use and monitoring of segregation
- appointed a Cross Gender Monitor to examine the issues surrounding cross-gender staffing in federal women's correctional facilities (discussed further in Chapter 6)
- developed mandatory training programs such as CSC and the Law
- revised the process for prioritizing inmate grievances
- increased efforts to involve Aboriginal communities in the provision of correctional services to Aboriginal women offenders
- closed the Kingston Prison for Women (Vanneste, 2001)

The CSC rejected recommendations in the Arbour report that a healing lodge be constructed in eastern Canada, that there be independent adjudication of decisions to segregate offenders, and that the Deputy Commissioner for Women personally answer all complaints filed by women offenders.

INSTITUTIONAL STAFF

The staff in a correctional institution are the core of the organization and are the most directly involved in supervision and control of inmates, program delivery, and case management. These various staff members can have such different duties and responsibilities that tension and conflict may result.

Among the findings of a survey of staff in federal correctional institutions are the following:

- The lower the security level of the institution, the more favourable are staff's attitudes toward the work environment.
- Correctional personnel who work outside of institutions, such as parole officers, report more positive views of their work environment.
- Correctional officers are the most critical of their work environment of any employee group.
- Institutional personnel have strong reservations about the unit management model and case management scheme.
- Institutional staff are generally satisfied with their jobs. (Price-Waterhouse, 1994:15-1, 15-2)

We will explore the views of correctional officers and personnel involved in case management in Chapters 6 and 8, respectively.

THE INMATES

The number of offenders sentenced to confinement in federal and provincial/territorial correctional facilities has declined in recent years (although the proportion of women admitted to federal custody has risen, as has the number of offenders sentenced to custody for violent crimes). The size of inmate populations at any given time is determined by such key factors as the crime rate and the sentencing decisions of judges. These factors, in turn, are affected by demographics, changes in the Criminal Code, the enforcement practices of the police, public policy, and societal expectations (Federal/Provincial/Territorial Ministers, 2000).

A General Profile of Inmate Populations

Offenders confined in correctional institutions tend to be:

- *male*, with women composing just under 10 percent of provincial/territorial inmate populations and about 4 percent of admissions to federal facilities
- *young*, with the majority of inmates falling into the 20–34 age group
- *single*
- *parents*, with 60 percent of male inmates and nearly 70 percent of female inmates having children or stepchildren
- *marginally skilled*, with inmates more likely to have low levels of education and to be unemployed at the time of conviction
- *disproportionately Aboriginal*, with Aboriginal offenders composing 17 percent of the total inmate population but only 3 percent of the general population
- *disproportionately black*, with black males composing 5 percent and black females 7 percent of federal inmate populations (Griffiths and Hatch Cunningham, 2003:225–26; Solicitor General Portfolio, 2002)

Federal Carceral Populations

Inmates confined in federal correctional institutions have the following attributes:

Offence
- 60 percent have been convicted of a crime of violence
- 17 percent have been convicted of first- or second-degree murder

Aboriginal Offenders
- 17 percent of federal inmates are Aboriginal
- 84 percent have been convicted of crimes of violence or murder
- 38 percent are serving sentences of four years or less
- 23 percent are serving sentences of more than 10 years or life

Female Offenders
- 68 percent are incarcerated for violence or murder
- nearly 50 percent are serving sentences of four years or less
- 24 percent are serving sentences of more than 10 years or life

Sex Offenders
- make up 20 percent of the inmate population (Reed and Roberts, 1998)

As noted earlier in the chapter, the profile of inmates admitted to federal custody has become more serious in recent years. Information from the Pacific region of CSC for the period 1997–2002 reveals the following:

- *security classification:* There was an 86 percent increase in the number of inmates who scored high on the institutional adjustment index.
- *pre-admission behaviour:* There was a 31 percent increase in the number of inmates who had previously been placed in disciplinary segregation, as well as a 22 percent increase in the number of inmates who had a record of previous escapes or being unlawfully at large.
- *offence:* One in four federal inmates is serving a sentence for homicide.
- *need:* Nearly 80 percent of the inmates are abusers of drugs and alcohol.
- *cognitive:* 80 percent of the inmates are identified as having poor problem-solving skills.
- *mental health:* 15 percent of the inmates have a previous mental-health disorder diagnosis.

These federal inmates present challenges to correctional managers, treatment staff, correctional officers, and also may threaten the safety and security of other inmates.

Provincial/Territorial Carceral Populations

The majority of incarcerated offenders fall under the jurisdiction of provincial/territorial systems of correction. The more notable attributes of these inmate populations include the following:

- The number of offenders entering provincial/territorial correctional institutions has been declining over the past decade, having peaked in 1991–94.

- In many jurisdictions, correctional facilities are operating at overcapacity, ranging from 6 percent overcapacity in Ontario to 66 percent in Quebec. (However, as we shall see in Chapter 9, many on-register inmates are serving their sentences on temporary absences.)
- Approximately 50 percent of adult admissions to custody are persons on remand. This includes persons who have been found guilty and are awaiting trial, as well as persons who have been charged with an offence and ordered by the judge to be placed in custody until their next court appearance.
- Many provincial/territorial institutions hold large numbers of Aboriginal persons.
- The majority of offenders have previous criminal convictions and have also served time in custody.
- More than one of every 10 adults sent to provincial/territorial jails have been convicted of impaired driving.
- Most offenders spend only a short time in confinement; 25 percent are there for two weeks or less, over 33 percent for less than one month, and 66 percent are serving sentences of one year or less.
- Just over 20 percent of provincial/territorial admissions to custody are for fine default—that is, failing to pay a fine levied by a sentencing judge. There is considerable variation across the jurisdictions in the number of admissions to custody that are fine defaulters, ranging from Ontario (2 percent), to Alberta (33 percent), to Quebec (57 percent). (Reed and Roberts, 1999)

A profile of the inmate population in Ontario is presented in Box 5.7.

BOX 5.7

Who Goes to Ontario Jails?

Every year, there are 70,000 new admissions to correctional facilities in Ontario. These inmates have the following attributes:

- 94 percent are male
- 60 percent have no high-school diploma
- only 4 percent have some postsecondary education
- 50 percent have been convicted of assault, violation of a court order/escape, or theft/possession of stolen property
- The average stay in custody is 72 days for males and 50 days for females.

Source: www.safejails.ca.

SPECIAL CATEGORIES OF OFFENDERS

Female Inmates

Most women serving sentences in federal and provincial/territorial correctional institutions are from marginalized backgrounds. Their past and current situations are likely to include poverty, histories of abuse, long-term drug and alcohol dependency, responsibilities for primary care of children, limited educational attainment, and few opportunities to obtain adequately paid work. A recent profile of federally sentenced women has revealed an increase in the diversity of their racial and cultural diversity backgrounds (Correctional Service of Canada, 1998). Box 5.8 presents a composite profile of an Aboriginal woman serving time in a federal institution.

BOX 5.8

Profile of a Federally Sentenced Aboriginal Woman

The Aboriginal woman offender is generally 27 years old with a grade nine education and single with two or three children. She has limited education and employment skills and she is usually unemployed at the time of her crime.

Contributing factors that may impact negatively on the life of an Aboriginal female include moving to an urban centre (isolation and loneliness). Alcoholism and violence in the family home. Lack of familial support and supervision. Lack of resources (financial). Lack of opportunities to become involved in positive interaction with others.

Generally the Aboriginal offender has experimented with drugs and alcohol at a young age. Often she has become in conflict with the law as a youth and with lack of intervention continues into the adult system. She is likely to leave school at a young age to associate with friends who are street wise. Her abuse of drugs and alcohol continues to the point where she will become a prostitute to continue her addiction. Under the influence of her associates and a negative lifestyle she commits more serious crimes such as robberies, assaults or murder as she becomes more street wise.

She may leave home because she experienced violence (whether she was abused or she witnessed abuse) and her home life has become unbearable. Or she may live under very rigid conditions that she leaves because she wants to become independent. Or she may be lured away by friends who have a life of drugs, alcohol and partying. She may work the streets because she needs money to live on and she does

BOX 5.8, continued

not have the education, skills and training to get a job. She may be subjected to racism, stereotyping and discrimination because of her race and colour. However, her experience on the streets becomes violent as she continues to experience sexual, emotional and physical abuse. She is likely to become involved in an abusive relationship. There are usually children born from this relationship and the social, emotional and economic struggle continues. The cycle of an unhealthy family continues.

A high percentage of Aboriginal women who come in conflict with the law are convicted of crimes committed while under the influence of drugs and alcohol.

These contributing factors are often related to their history of physical, psychological and emotional abuse where they have not dealt with the effects of this abuse. This harmful way of dealing with the past history of dysfunctional behaviour may continue unless these past abuses and effects are dealt with.

Source: Excerpted from "Profile of an Aboriginal Woman Serving Time in a Federal Institution" by Norma Green. Retrieved from Correctional Service of Canada (www.csc-scc.gc.ca/text/prgrm/correctional/abissues/know/5_e.shtml).

Aboriginal Inmates

Despite a concerted effort over the past two decades to address the specific needs of Aboriginal peoples and to reduce their overrepresentation in the criminal justice system, the incarceration rate of Aboriginal peoples remains high (see Figure 5.5). It is predicted that the number of Aboriginal inmates will double in the coming years and that, by 2010, 20 percent of the carceral population in Canada will be Aboriginal.

Elderly Inmates

There has been a significant increase in the average age of inmates admitted to correctional institutions (although, as a group, inmates are younger than the general Canadian adult population):

- Offenders over the age of 50 now compose about 12 percent of federal and provincial/territorial carceral populations.
- Nearly half of the inmates over 50 are chronic offenders.

Figure 5.5

Aboriginal Adult Admissions to Custody, Provincial/Territorial and Federal Institutions, 1998–99

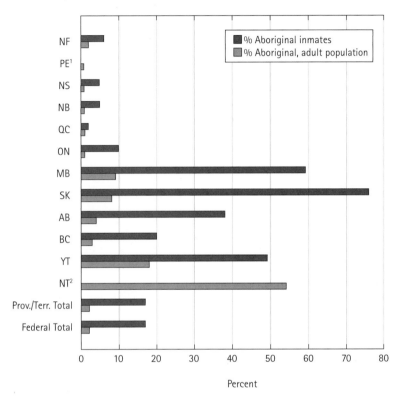

Percent

1. Number too small to be expressed: percentage, Aboriginal inmates.
2. Figure not available: percentage, Aboriginal inmates.

Source: Adapted from Canadian Centre for Justice Statistics, 2001:10.

- The age category of 40+ will represent the greatest increase in federal institution populations over the next 20 years.
- Of the 600+ inmates currently serving life sentences in federal prisons, 40 percent will be over the age of 55 when they become eligible for release on parole.
- Of offenders 50 years and older, 70 percent are serving their first federal prison term.
- Of those inmates 60 years and older, nearly 50 percent have been convicted of a sexual offence. (Uzoaba, 1998)

The "graying" of Canada's prisons is due to a number of factors, including changes in the Criminal Code and increased rates of reporting by crime victims, particularly of sexual offences that may have occurred many years earlier. Older offenders are more likely to have been convicted of more serious violent offences or sexual offences, although in most cases they pose a lower risk to the community than younger offenders do.

The elderly present challenges to systems of correction. Chronic illnesses, disabilities, hearing and vision loss, incontinence, mental disorientation, and Alzheimer's disease require special attention and resources. In addition, older inmates (particularly those serving their first prison term) may have difficulty adjusting to the regimen of the prison and may be vulnerable to manipulation and abuse by younger inmates. As well, the treatment needs of this population may be different from that of younger inmates. Older inmates may require educational upgrading and vocational skills to be successful in the job market upon release (Uzoaba, 1998). In response to these challenges, the CSC has created the Older Offenders Division, which has a mandate to develop policies and programs for this population of offenders.

Violent Offenders

Violent offenders are the focus of media attention, politicians, and community interest groups, especially when parole applications of violent offenders are under review and they are released into the community. There has been a steady increase in the number of offenders sentenced to confinement for the violent offences of homicide, sex crimes, and robbery. Offenders convicted of violent offences:

- are older (average age 34)
- are white, although Aboriginal violent offenders (approximately 20 percent of the violent offender population) are overrepresented
- have prior records involving violence
- tend to receive longer sentences and spend a larger proportion of their time in confinement (Motiuk and Belcourt, 1997)

Sex Offenders

Sex offenders are a high-profile offender group that presents unique challenges to corrections in terms of treatment programming and supervision in both institutional and community settings. While less likely to exhibit the marginal attributes of other inmates, sex offenders have cognitive and behavioural difficulties that must be addressed. Correctional administrators also may have to take steps to ensure their safety and protect them from other inmates.

Long-Term Offenders

Long-term offenders are defined as those inmates serving life terms, indeterminate sentences, or sentences of 10 years or more. About 7,000 offenders—6,668 men and 187 women—were categorized as long-term offenders in 2001 (Motiuk, Boe, and Nafekh, 2002). There has been a slow and steady rise in the number of lifers since the replacement of capital punishment with a mandatory minimum sentence for murder in 1976. Whereas most sentences end at some point, a life sentence lasts as long as the offender, so the members of this group accumulate over time.

THE CHALLENGES OF OPERATING AND MANAGING CORRECTIONAL INSTITUTIONS

Meeting the Requirements of Legislation

The legal framework within which correctional systems operate has become increasingly complex. Senior correctional personnel must not only remain informed about changes in law and policy but also ensure that the operation of the institution and the activities of the institutional staff comply with these requirements. The incident at the Kingston Prison for Women is an example of a warden's failing to ensure that staff followed the rule of law and administrative policies. The findings and recommendations of the commission of inquiry (Arbour, 1996) have had a significant impact on the operation of correctional institutions, particularly in relation to the operation of segregation units and to procedural safeguards for inmates' rights. In some federal institutions, wardens now visit the segregation unit every day to speak with inmates and apprise themselves of each inmate's situation.

Wardens and other correctional officials are also increasingly the targets of legal action initiated by inmates, the families of inmates who have been victimized or who have died in prison, and crime victims and their families. Institutions are also subject to periodic external audits to ensure that they are following proper administrative and fiscal procedures.

Managing with Reduced Resources

Both community-based and institutional correctional systems are being significantly affected by the fiscal crises of governments. Although wardens/directors do not control the budgets, they must ensure that the funds they receive to operate the institution are utilized in the most effective way. This task is even more challenging when additional strategies are developed by senior policymakers and no additional funding is provided.

Overcrowding

Until the 1990s, correctional systems in Canada had largely avoided over-crowding and double-bunking inmates. Changes in judicial sentencing patterns, the increase in the number of long-term inmates, the increasing reluctance of parole boards to release offenders into the community, and the absence of new facilities have all contributed to institutions operating at overcapacity. As of 2002, approximately 25 percent of federal inmates were required to share cell space. Provincial systems of corrections are also experiencing overcrowding; in Ontario, double-bunking is a key component of the province's no-frills custodial policy.

Overcrowding and double-bunking may significantly impact daily prison life by increasing tension among inmates and between inmates and correctional officers, taxing program resources, and compromising security. Overcrowding has been identified as a contributing factor in a number of disturbances in federal and provincial facilities. Federal and most provincial/territorial systems of correction have attempted to reduce overcrowding by focusing on reintegration as a core component of the case management process. The Office of the Correctional Investigator has called on the CSC to end the practice of double-bunking.

Ensuring Inmate Safety

Ensuring the safety of inmates is an onerous task, particularly in federal maximum-security institutions. Although wardens do not determine the numbers and types of inmates that are sent to their facilities, they are responsible for the safety and security of the inmates. In recent years, there have been a number of violent incidents in federal institutions that have put pressure on the CSC to improve operational policies and procedures concerning inmate safety. One such incident occurred in 1996 at the recently opened Edmonton Institution for Women, one of the small regional facilities that had been constructed for federally sentenced women. At that time, minimum-, medium-, and maximum-security inmates were mixed into one population. For an inmate named Denise Fayant, this arrangement had fatal consequences (see Box 5.9).

HIV/AIDS and Infectious Diseases

Perhaps the most critical challenge to correctional authorities is the spread of communicable diseases in inmate populations, including HIV/AIDS, tuberculosis, and hepatitis B and C. In many U.S. prisons, AIDS is the leading cause

BOX 5.9

The Murder of Denise Fayant

Denise Fayant was found strangled in her cell 30 hours after she was transferred from a regional psychiatric centre and placed in the general prison population at the Edmonton Institution for Women. The 21-year-old woman died two days later in hospital. An investigation into her death—originally ruled a suicide—revealed that she had been slain by two inmates, one of whom had been her former lover and against whom she had been scheduled to testify.

A subsequent inquiry conducted by Alberta provincial court judge Albert Chrumka found that Fayant had repeatedly told correctional officials that she feared for her safety if she were transferred to the newly opened institution. In the inquiry report, Chrumka concluded that "callous and cavalier" actions on the part of the CSC led to Fayant's murder: "She was ... a victim of a process intent upon implementing an untested concept to manage federally sentenced female inmates. She was the test. The process failed tragically and inhumanely. Her death was avoidable" (cited in Cowan and Sheremata, 2000).

The Chrumka report was quickly seized on by critics who felt that the CSC had "[removed] the concept of punishment from female corrections policy almost completely" (Bunner, 2000:13). In its first six months of operation, the Edmonton Institution for Women experienced—in addition to Fayant's slaying—numerous inmate assaults on staff, suicide attempts by inmates, and seven escapes. In recent years, the CSC has been implementing the Intensive Intervention Strategy (unveiled in 1999), which called for the modification and expansion of regional facilities to accommodate female inmates classified as maximum-security.

of inmate death, and there are alarmingly high rates of infection in federal and provincial/territorial institutions in Canada.

Although the HIV virus can be transmitted via anal intercourse between inmates, the largest increase in the infection rate is due to intravenous drug use and the sharing of HIV-contaminated needles and syringes. HIV and other blood-borne diseases such as hepatitis B and C are also transmitted by pens, pencils, and wire instruments that inmates use for body piercing and tattooing. In addition, many offenders are infected prior to entering systems of corrections.

A 2002 report provides data, for the year 2000, on HIV/AIDS and hepatitis C (HCV) in federal prisons:

- There were 217 federal inmates with HIV or AIDS, a rate 10 times that of the general Canadian population and a 35 percent increase in known cases since 1996.
- The known cases of HIV infection among women in federal prisons ranged from 0 percent at the Grand Valley Institution (Ont.), to 4.88 percent at the Nova Institution (N.S.), to nearly 12 percent at the Edmonton Prison for Women.
- HCV rates were higher than HIV/AIDS prevalence rates, with approximately 20 percent of all federal offenders and 41 percent of female inmates known to be HCV-positive. At the Edmonton Prison for Women, 75 percent of the inmates were HCV-positive, compared with 0.8 percent of all Canadians. (Lines, 2002)

It is important to note that the above figures are based on *reported* cases. Many inmates may choose not to disclose their medical condition or may not know they are infected.

In Ontario provincial institutions, the prevalence of HIV infection among inmates is at least six times higher than in the general population. Inmates having a history of injected drug use are at a higher risk than offenders with no reported history of injecting drugs. The rates of HIV/AIDS are particularly high among Aboriginal offenders incarcerated in provincial facilities in the three Prairie provinces.

Provincial/territorial and federal systems of corrections face immense challenges in responding to the increasing numbers of inmates with infectious diseases. These challenges include providing short- and long-term health care, providing medication, and developing policies to combat high-risk behaviour in inmate populations. The triple drug therapy, or "cocktail," for AIDS patients, for example, costs about $1,200 per patient each month, while the treatment for hepatitis C costs is also very expensive.

Several inmates have taken legal action against the CSC for failing to protect them against HIV/AIDS and for failing to provide appropriate medical care once they became infected (Lines, 2002).

Prevention Strategies

Systems of correction have developed a number of initiatives in an attempt to prevent and reduce high-risk behaviour among inmates and to reduce the levels of infection. The CSC, for example, provides inmates with condoms, lubricants, dental dams, and bleach kits. In several federal institutions, inmates are trained as peer health counsellors to educate others on how to reduce the risks of infection and the various types of prevention. These programs are based on a pilot project first developed at Dorchester Penitentiary in New Brunswick.

Provincial/territorial systems of corrections have undertaken similar efforts. The challenges are considerable, given the higher turnover of inmates and the short period most offenders are confined. British Columbia provides orally administered methadone maintenance treatment (MMT) for offenders who were in similar programs before entering a provincial institution. In Ontario, condoms are provided but the correctional officers' union has opposed providing inmates with bleach kits and a clean needle exchange. Many provinces, however, do not yet provide condoms to inmates. The dilemma facing correctional administrators is to what extent the government should be involved in harm-reduction initiatives, such as providing condoms and bleach kits, while continuing to enforce institutional regulations against drug use and sexual relationships between inmates (Wolfe, 1998).

In recent years, there have been several high-profile cases in which inmates have taken legal action against the CSC for failing to provide MMT and/or needle exchange or distribution programs in federal correctional facilities. The CSC has responded by expanding access to MMT in federal institutions. Despite this initiative and others, inmates report that the high-risk behaviour continues. In the words of one inmate, "A lot of addicts in any prison share needles. They don't care. They even ask to share with inmates they know are sick" (cited in Brady, 1998:R2). Inmates' estimates of the number who use drugs in prison range as high as 70 percent. Despite the risks, many inmates bring the drug lifestyle from the street into the prison.

In a harm-reduction rating compiled to measure the availability and accessibility of prevention strategies (ranging from condoms to MMT) in federal and provincial/territorial prison systems, British Columbia received the highest mark (B). Next were the federal system (B-) and Newfoundland and Labrador (D). The remaining jurisdictions received a failing grade (Lines, 2002).

Federal and provincial/territorial systems of correction also offer a variety of substance abuse treatment programs, which will be discussed in Chapter 8. The Canadian Aboriginal AIDS Network has developed a peer education model for Aboriginal offenders in federal correctional facilities.

Interdiction Strategies

The general public would be surprised to learn how prevalent illegal drugs are in correctional institutions. The CSC uses a number of proactive strategies in an attempt to reduce the use of illegal drugs and other high-risk behaviours, such as tattooing. These strategies include frequent searches, a urinalysis program, drug dogs, video surveillance, and ion scanners that can detect drug residue on clothing and other objects worn or brought in by visitors and any inmates returning from absences in the community.

The effectiveness of these strategies is uncertain. A survey of correctional staff found that only 21 percent of the correctional officers, as opposed to 64 percent of the managers, felt that the drug strategies were successful (Robinson, Lefaive, and Muirhead, 1997). One concern is that the various drug detection strategies may lead to an increase in hard drug use in institutions because drugs such as marijuana and hashish remain in the blood stream for many days, whereas heroin stays in the body's system for approximately 48 hours. This makes the chances of being caught by a random urinalysis test higher for those inmates who use "soft" drugs.

In 2000, the CSC opened an Intensive Support Unit in each of its five regions. These drug-free units provide a safe environment for inmates who are committed to abstaining from drug use and who wish to avoid the problems associated with inmate drug use.

AT ISSUE

REDUCING THE RISKS

Should Inmates Be Issued Condoms and Bleach Kits?

Currently, all inmates incarcerated in federal correctional facilities have access to free condoms and bleach kits for cleaning needles.

Should There Be a Needle Exchange Inside?

The question of whether to provide inmates with clean needles was under discussion but, as of 2003, no decision had been made by the CSC.

Should Inmates Receive Methadone Maintenance Treatment?

The policy of the CSC is to provide treatment to inmates who are addicted to heroin.

Proponents of these programs contend that:

- condoms, bleach kits, and MMT reflect the reality that drugs will always be available to inmates
- condoms and bleach kits help to reduce the risk of HIV and other infectious diseases
- MMT reduces the use of hard drugs inside and assists inmates in overcoming their addiction
- MMT has not been shown to jeopardize the security of the institution

Opponents counter that:

- providing condoms will encourage inmates to violate institutional regulations prohibiting sexual relations
- condoms do not prevent nonconsensual sex
- providing bleach kits and clean needles will encourage rather than discourage drug use in prison, which not only violates institutional regulations, but is against the law
- inmates could use needles as weapons against correctional staff
- inmates can overcome their addiction to hard drugs by abstaining from drug use inside and by adhering to institutional regulations prohibiting drug use
- methadone is an addictive drug that does little to eliminate drug dependency and may prolong the inmate's involvement in the drug culture

The Research Evidence

Canada is one of the few countries in the world where condoms and bleach kits are made available to inmates (although not to inmates in all provincial/territorial facilities). There are no published research studies on whether providing condoms and bleach kits reduces the risk and levels of infection among inmate populations. Needle exchange programs operate in Swiss, German, Spanish, and Australian prisons and appear to be successful in reducing rates of infection. It is uncertain whether these programs have reduced the levels of hard drug use among inmate populations. Research on methadone maintenance programs in the community has produced mixed results. It is uncertain, for example, whether these programs have reduced the levels of heroin addiction, and there is the added problem that methadone itself is an addictive drug.

QUESTIONS

1. Do you agree with the CSC's policy of providing free condoms and bleach kits to inmates?
2. The CSC is considering providing clean needles to inmates. Would you support the implementation of this policy? Why or why not?
3. Should methadone maintenance programs be expanded to include all inmates in federal and provincial/territorial institutions?
4. What do you see as the most beneficial aspects of these policies for reducing risk in prison populations? What are the most negative aspects?

PRISON RIOTS: THE BREAKDOWN OF ORGANIZATIONAL STABILITY AND CONTROL

Riots and disturbances continue to be a feature of life in federal and provincial institutions. Though every prison riot is the culmination of a unique set of circumstances and events, riots are symptomatic of a breakdown of policy and practice from the most senior administrative levels to the line-level correctional staff. More minor disturbances are often the result of fiscal cutbacks or a change in institutional policy, such as smoking bans. An in-depth examination of the circumstances surrounding the 1996 riot at the Headingley Correctional Institution, a provincial facility in Manitoba, provides an opportunity to explore the circumstances that create the conditions for a major disturbance.

A Case Study: The Riot at Headingley Correctional Institution

Any assumptions that only federal correctional institutions are susceptible to major prison disturbances were erased by the brutal and devastating riot that occurred at the Headingley Correctional Institution, a provincial facility in Manitoba, on April 25–26, 1996. The riot was started by an inmate who was attempting to prevent correctional officers from discovering drugs during a cell search and investigating his involvement in beating another inmate. The attempted search occurred in a section of the jail housing members of two rival Aboriginal street gangs: the Manitoba Warriors and the Indian Posse.

The failure of correctional officers to follow proper procedures in the cell search led to the officers being beaten by the inmates, who seized the officers' keys and went on a drug-fuelled rampage in the institution. The inmates set fires and severely beat inmates in protective custody, mutilating several by cutting off their fingers. One protective custody inmate was the victim of an attempted castration. The riot lasted for 24 hours and caused $3.5 million in damage to the institution. Eight correctional officers and 31 inmates were beaten during the melee. Twelve inmates were subsequently sentenced to between two and eight years for their role in the uprising. Two years after the riot, 25 percent of the correctional staff remained off the job because of stress or physical injuries.

An independent review (Hughes, 1996) of the role and activities of senior provincial correctional officials, the director of the facility, correctional officers, and inmates documented the conditions that existed in the institution at the time of the riot and identified a number of factors that sparked the outbreak. Interviews with correctional staff and inmates revealed that "the institutional atmosphere prevailing at Headingley at the time of the riot was extremely negative, and the staff was a dysfunctional conglomerate torn apart by strife, hatred, bitterness, unpleasantness, and nastiness" (Hughes, 1996:7). Officer morale was described as being "lower than a snake's belly in a wagon rut" (Hughes, 1996:9). There was distrust and ill-will between the correctional officers and the administration. There were also conflicts among the correctional officers. Many of the institutional staff interviewed by the independent

The aftermath of the Headingley riot

investigator mentioned the "Headingley mentality"—a negative, militant approach to work in the institution.

The report of the independent investigator identified several key factors that contributed to the unstable institutional environment at the time of the riot. Several of these factors, which are discussed below, seriously affected the ability of correctional officers and the administration of the facility to respond to the disturbance in an effective manner.

The Adoption, Several Years Earlier, of the Unit Management System

This resulted in a significant change to the management structure of the institution. The position of unit manager was created, and these personnel were responsible for all activities in the living units. Many of these duties were previously the responsibility of shift managers (or duty officers), who continued to work in the units. There was often conflict between these two groups.

Introduction of the unit management system also altered the role of the correctional officers who had previously been responsible only for security and "turning keys." In the unit management system, correctional officers were required to become actively involved in case management and in programs and to have more extensive knowledge of the inmates under their care and control. This was a role that many of the older officers, in particular, were either unable or unwilling to accept.

The Appointment, Several Years Earlier, of an Inexperienced Person as Superintendent of the Institution

The superintendent of the institution at the time of the riot had entered the field of corrections via the private sector, where he had been involved primarily in personnel administration. Prior to coming to Headingley, the superintendent had never worked in a correctional institution that included dangerous inmates in its population, nor did he have the skills and experience to manage the conflicts that existed between the administration and correctional officers.

A Poor Working Relationship among Senior Administrative Personnel in the Institution

Also owing to a lack of experience, the superintendent was unable to facilitate a collaborative and cooperative working relationship among senior staff in the institution. The institutional management team was afflicted by interpersonal conflicts and competition and was, in effect, non-functioning. The ineffectuality of the management team is illustrated by the finding that "during the night of terror, the Deputy Superintendent, the number two person responsible for the entire facility, was at home. He first heard of the riot when his wife brought him the daily newspaper the following morning, which reported the rampage of the night before" (Hughes, 1996:23).

The Lack of Awareness of the Conditions at Headingley among Senior Provincial Correctional Officials

For a variety of reasons, senior correctional personnel in Manitoba appeared to have had little knowledge of the conditions at Headingley. Neither the provincial Minister of Justice nor the Deputy Minister of Justice received any information about the serious conflicts that existed between correctional officers and the administration at the prison and the tense conditions that these conflicts created in the facility.

The Prevalence of Illegal Drugs in the Institution

A key feature of institutional life in Headingley was the presence of large quantities of illegal drugs. The intimidation and extortion among inmates caused by the flow of drugs into the institution and drug use contributed to the unstable environment of the facility. The independent investigator documented the various ways in which illegal drugs entered the institution, including the coercion of weaker inmates into having drugs brought in from the outside.

The Composition of the Inmate Population

There is general agreement that inmate populations in provincial institutions are becoming more violent and defiant. This is due to a variety of factors, including the development of a wide variety of alternatives to confinement (see Chapter 4) and liberal temporary absence programs (see Chapter 9), which result in only the most dangerous and high-risk offenders being incarcerated and remaining inside. The independent investigator found that correctional institutions such as Headingley were not built to accommodate this type of inmate population, which increasingly includes members of rival street gangs. Another feature of the inmate population is the high percentage (approximately 70 percent at Headingley) of Aboriginal inmates, many of whom have extremely dysfunctional backgrounds and special needs. These inmates are particularly susceptible to being recruited by street gangs while in the community and to continue their activities while incarcerated.

The Lessons from Headingley

Senior provincial correctional officials, the prison administration, correctional officers, and inmates all played a significant role in creating the conditions for the riot that occurred at Headingley Institution. Although the inmates in the institution initiated the riot and caused harm to staff, other inmates, and the facility itself, the independent review found that correctional personnel within and outside the institution were also responsible for the riot and its consequences. The Headingley riot also highlights an area of Canadian corrections—provincial correctional institutions—that has remained largely unstudied.

The final report of the independent investigator documented the breakdown of the social organization of the institution and of the collaborative and cooperative relationships that must exist among the administration, correctional officers, and inmates for institutions to operate smoothly and safely. In the next two chapters, we'll consider the role and activities of correctional officers and the world of inmates in greater depth.

In the aftermath of the Headingley riot, correctional authorities in Manitoba took steps to more effectively manage the provincial correctional population. A new medium-security unit was constructed at the Headingley Correctional Institution to house offenders convicted of violent and gang-related offences. A maximum-security unit—the first in the province—was also constructed.

PRIVATE PRISONS: COMING SOON TO A COMMUNITY NEAR YOU?

As noted in Chapter 1, a major trend in corrections is the increasing involvement of the private sector in the delivery of correctional services. Although nonprofit groups such as the Salvation Army have a long tradition of involvement in community-based and residential programs for offenders, the groups are encountering stiff competition from for-profit organizations. This development is due in large measure to the fiscal crises of governments and the search for more cost-effective ways to operate institutions.

The private sector is most extensively involved in the design, construction, and management of prisons in the United States, Puerto Rico, Britain, and Australia. In 2001, the government of Ontario contracted U.S.-based Management and Training Corp. to operate the 1,184-bed Central North Correctional Centre (CNCC), a superjail located in Penetanguishene, Ontario. The performance of CNCC—the country's first privately operated prison—will be compared with that of an identical, provincially operated facility in Lindsay, Ontario, providing the first report card on the privatization of correctional institutions in Canada.

AT ISSUE

SHOULD PRISONS BE PRIVATIZED?

The federal government has been reluctant to consider privatizing correctional facilities. At the provincial level, developments at the Central North Correctional Centre, Ontario's experiment in privatization, will no doubt be watched closely by other provincial systems of corrections. The debate over the privatization of correctional facilities has centred on the issues of cost control, operational efficiency, quality of service, and accountability.

Proponents of private prisons assert that these facilities are:
* more cost-effective than public prisons
* more flexible and able to expand physical capacity and programs more quickly than government-operated facilities
* more accountable to monitoring and review than public prisons
* an important comparative yardstick against which to measure the performance of public prisons

Opponents of privatization express a number of concerns, including:
* private-sector companies that construct and manage prisons and those that manufacture prison "hardware" are components of the *prison-industrial complex,* "a set of bureaucratic, political, and economic interests that encourage increased spending on imprisonment, regardless of the actual need" (Schlosser, 1998:54)
* politicians have used the public's (largely unjustified) fear of crime to promote private-sector involvement in building more prisons, as have communities that benefit economically from institutions built in their locales
* the private sector has little economic incentive to decarcerate offenders: although violent crime rates in the United States have fallen by 20 percent since 1991, prison populations have risen by 50 percent, which has fuelled an explosion in prison construction in a fruitless attempt to reduce overcrowding in institutions
* "punishment for profit" is unethical
* the involvement of the private sector is a costly and ineffective response to crime, and any cost savings recorded by private prisons are due to lower, nonunion wages paid to employees

The Research Evidence

Developing measures of the effectiveness of prisons is, in itself, a difficult task. Attempting to determine whether private prisons are more effective than public prisons is even more challenging, particularly when the ethical and moral dimensions of the debate are factored in. Nevertheless, research studies conducted in the United States and England suggest that private prisons are not more cost-effective and that there are more similarities than differences between private prisons and public prisons when it comes to staffing patterns, levels of work, education and programs for inmates, and rates of prison disturbances. The poor performance of some private prisons in the United States has led governments to consider the development of public–private partnerships in corrections.

QUESTIONS

1. After considering the arguments for and against the private sector's involvement in operating correctional institutions, what is your position on this issue? What would you consider to be the strongest arguments in favour of your position?
2. Would you support allowing private companies to build and manage correctional institutions in Canada? If yes, should the test case be a facility for provincial, territorial, or federal inmates? What is the basis for your position?

Sources: Austin and Coventry, 1999; Thomas, 1998. See also issues of the *Prison Privatisation Report International* (PPRI), available online at www.psiru.org/justice.

THE HIGH–TECH PRISON

The exponential growth in high technology, combined with the needs of governments to reduce the costs of operating correctional institutions, has led to the emergence of the high-tech prison in Canada. These institutions incorporate the latest in electronic security and video surveillance technology, allowing larger numbers of inmates to be housed, monitored, and controlled with fewer staff. The potential applications of technology to correctional populations appear to be limitless.

Although institutions utilizing high technology may be less expensive to operate, high costs may occur as a result of disturbances and riots by inmates and increased rates of recidivism when inmates are released from these facilities. Technology may improve security, but it also reduces contact between the correctional staff and inmates. This lack of contact may have significant implications for the development of effective treatment interventions (see Chapter 8) and the involvement of correctional officers in positive interactions with inmates (see Chapter 6).

QUESTIONS FOR REVIEW

1. Discuss how prison architecture can be used to illustrate changing perspectives on crime and punishment.
2. What is meant by the prison as a total institution and how does this concept assist us in our study of corrections?

3. Discuss what is meant by the prison as a public and political institution and then indicate how this concept assists us in our study of corrections.

4. What was the significance of the incident at the Kingston Prison for Women and what impact did it have on the federal system of corrections?

5. Discuss the challenges to institutional corrections posed by HIV/AIDS and other communicable diseases.

6. Identify and discuss the various interdiction strategies that are used in an attempt to reduce the use of illegal drugs and other high-risk behaviour.

7. Note the major points raised by the proponents and opponents of the various strategies designed to reduce the risk of HIV/AIDS and other infectious diseases in correctional institutions.

8. Describe two of the factors that were identified as contributing to the riot at the Headingley Correctional Institution.

9. Discuss the major points raised by the proponents and opponents of privatizing correctional institutions.

10. What are the benefits and the drawbacks of high-tech prisons?

REFERENCES

Arbour, The Honourable L. (Commissioner). 1996. *Commission of Inquiry into Certain Events at the Prison for Women in Kingston.* Ottawa: Public Works and Government Services Canada.

Austin, J., and G. Coventry. 1999. "Are We Better Off? Comparing Private and Public Prisons in the United States." *Journal of the Institute of Criminology* 11(2):177–201.

Brady, M. 1998. "Pens and Needles: Prison Population Growth Has Cranked Up the Risk of Infectious Disease Transmission." *Financial Post* (May 16):R2.

Bunner, P. 2000. "A Philosophy on Death Row: Corrections Boss Ingstrup May Not Survive the Growing Clamour for Punitive Justice." *Report Magazine* 26(49):12–13.

Canadian Centre for Justice Statistics. 2001. *Aboriginal Peoples in Canada.* Ottawa: Statistics Canada.

Centen, G. 1991. "Architecture, Operations and Change." *Forum on Corrections Research* 3(2):27–30.

Correctional Service of Canada. 1991. "An Historical Overview of the Construction of Canadian Federal Prisons." *Forum on Corrections Research* 3(2):3–5.

———. 1998. *Community Strategy for Women on Conditional Release: Discussion Paper.* Ottawa: Correctional Service of Canada.

————. 2002. *Working Together: Healing Lodges for Aboriginal Federal Offenders*. Retrieved from www.csc-scc.gc.ca/text/prgrm/correctional/abissues/challenge/11_e.shtml.

Cowan, P., and D. Sheremata. 2000. "Death in Experimental Prison Unit—'She Was Helpless.'" *The Edmonton Sun*. February 9.

Federal/Provincial/Territorial Ministers Responsible for Justice. 2000. *Corrections Population Report*. 4th ed. Ottawa: Solicitor General Canada. Retrieved from www.sgc.gc.ca/corrections/publications_e.asp.

Gardner, D. 2002. "Hard Time in Ontario, American-Style." *Ottawa Citizen*. March 24. Retrieved from www.canada.com/ottawa/ottawacitizen/specials/crimeandpunishment.

Goffman, E. 1961. *Asylums: Essays on the Social Situation of Mental Patients and Other Inmates*. Garden City, N.Y.: Doubleday.

Griffiths, C.T., and A. Hatch Cunningham. 2003. *Canadian Criminal Justice: A Primer*. 2nd ed. Toronto: Nelson.

Hughes, The Hon. E.N. (Ted). (Chair). 1996. *Report of the Independent Review of the Circumstances Surrounding the April 25–26, 1996, Riot at the Headingley Correctional Institution*. Winnipeg: Ministry of Justice, Province of Manitoba.

Johnston, J.C. 1991. "A Psychological Perspective on the New Design Concepts for William Head Institution (British Columbia)." *Forum on Corrections Research* 3(2):14–21.

Lines, R. 2002. *Action on HIV/AIDS in Prisons: Too Little, Too Late—A Report Card*. Montreal: Canadian HIV/AIDS Legal Network.

Moon, P. 1997. "Life Moves Smartly at Military Prison." *The Globe and Mail* (February 3):A1, A4.

Motiuk, L., and R. Belcourt. 1997. "Profiling Federal Offenders with Violence Offences." *Forum on Corrections Research* 9(2):8–13.

Motiuk, L., R. Boe, and M. Nafekh. 2002. *The Safe Return of Offenders to the Community*. Ottawa: Correctional Service of Canada.

Price-Waterhouse. 1994. *CSC All Staff Survey. Final Report*. Ottawa: Correctional Service of Canada.

Reed, M., and J.V. Roberts. 1998. "Adult Correctional Services in Canada, 1996–97." *Juristat* 18(3). Cat. no. 85-002-XPE. Ottawa: Canadian Centre for Justice Statistic s, Statistics Canada.

————. 1999. "Adult Correctional Services in Canada, 1997–98." *Juristat* 19(4). Cat. no. 85-002-XPE. Ottawa: Canadian Centre for Justice Statistics, Statistics Canada.

Robinson, D., P. Lefaive, and M. Muirhead. 1997. *Results of the 1996 CSC Staff Survey: A Synopsis*. Ottawa: Research Branch, Correctional Service of Canada.

Robinson, D., W.A. Millson, S. Trevethan, and B. MacKillop. 1998. "A One-Day Snapshot of Inmates in Canada's Adult Correctional Facilities." *Juristat* 18(8). Cat. no. 85-002-XPE. Ottawa: Canadian Centre for Justice Statistics, Statistics Canada.

Schlosser, E. 1998. "The Prison-Industrial Complex." *The Atlantic Monthly* 282(6):51–77.

Solicitor General Portfolio Corrections Statistics Committee. 2002. *Corrections and Conditional Release Statistical Overview.* Ottawa: Public Works and Government Services Canada.

Thomas, C.W. 1998. "Issues and Evidence from the United States." In S.T. Easton (ed.), *Privatizing Correctional Services* (15–61). Vancouver: Fraser Institute.

Uzoaba, J.H.E. 1998. *Managing Older Offenders: Where Do We Stand?* Ottawa: Research Branch, Correctional Service of Canada.

Vanneste, H. 2001. "The Arbour Report Five Years Later." *Let's Talk.* Ottawa: Correctional Service of Canada. Retrieved from www.csc-scc.gc.ca/text/pblct/letstalk/2001/no1/13_e.shtml.

Wolfe, J. 1998. Aboriginal People and HIV in Prison." In B. Warhaft (ed.), *Aboriginal People and HIV in Prison—The Report.* Burnaby, B.C.: Public Policy Programs, Simon Fraser University.

CHAPTER 6
CORRECTIONAL OFFICERS

CHAPTER OBJECTIVES

- *Discuss role and responsibilities of correctional officers.*
- *Discuss the recruitment and training of correctional officers.*
- *Identify and discuss the orientations and attitudes of correctional officers.*
- *Discuss the relationships among correctional officers.*
- *Examine the relationships between correctional officers and inmates.*
- *Discuss the relationships between correctional officers and treatment staff and administration.*
- *Identify and discuss the sources of stress for correctional officers.*
- *Consider the issues surrounding female correctional officers.*
- *Consider the issues surrounding cross-gender staffing in women's correctional facilities.*

KEY TERMS

Correctional Training Program
Basic Case Management Program
Staff Application, Recruitment, and Training (START)
Career Management Program
Occupational subculture

Post-traumatic stress disorder (PTSD)
Critical incident stress
Critical incident stress debriefing
Cross-gender staffing

This chapter considers the activities of correctional officers, including the patterns of interaction that develop among the officers themselves and the relationships with the prison administration, treatment staff, and inmates. Given the extensive interaction that officers have with inmates, the discussion focuses particular attention on the orientations and attitudes of correctional officers.

The examination of correctional officers is hindered by a lack of Canadian research. Most of the published materials are from the United States, although some research has been conducted on federal correctional officers in this country. Studies of correctional officers in provincial/territorial institutions are virtually nonexistent, even though the majority of incarcerated offenders in Canada are under provincial jurisdiction.

ROLE AND RESPONSIBILITIES

Correctional officers play a pivotal role in correctional institutions. On a daily basis, it is correctional officers who have the most contact with the inmates. Although systems of corrections make extensive use of high technology, such as video surveillance and various warning devices (static security), it is correctional officers who are the primary mechanism by which institutional policies and regulations are implemented and the inmates are controlled (dynamic security). Correctional officers are also a key part of efforts to rehabilitate offenders.

The role and responsibilities of correctional officers have become more complex and challenging in recent years. The duties of correctional officers centre on providing static and dynamic security and include carrying out motorized and foot patrols, staffing control posts, counting and escorting offenders, searching for contraband, enforcing institutional regulations, and providing emergency response. Officers mediate conflicts, control inmate movement within the facility, admit and process new arrivals, and serve as an information and referral source for inmates. In many institutions, correctional officers play an active role in case management; in some provincial institutions, they assist in the provision of core programming to inmates. Hemmens and Stohr (2000:327) sum up the activities of correctional officers as follows:

> *Correctional staff are engaged in guiding, mentoring, facilitating, developing, and watching inmates. If an inmate needs assistance with a job, getting along with others, programming, interacting with staff, or obtaining privileges, then correctional officers are their more likely resource, given their proximity and frequency of contact.*

In the federal system of corrections, there are two levels of correctional officers: CX1 and CX2. Both groups are responsible for the care, custody, and control of offenders. CX2s also have case management responsibilities that include the following:

- meeting regularly with offenders to assess their progress and needs
- consulting with other professionals in the institution about offender needs, criminal risk, and correctional and release plans
- making recommendations regarding offender discipline
- producing regular reports, including Correctional Plan Progress Reports (Joint Committee, 2000:42)

Despite the critical role played by correctional officers, it has only been in the past two decades that the federal and provincial/territorial systems of correction have made a concerted effort to professionalize the occupation of correctional officer, a continuous process reflected in the development of standards for recruitment and increased attention to in-service training. Even so, it is not uncommon for correctional officers to feel alienated from the organizations in which they work. Many hold negative or cynical attitudes toward inmates, treatment staff, and their co-workers, and experience considerable stress associated with working inside institutions on a daily basis.

RECRUITMENT AND TRAINING

In referring to the criteria that were used to hire correctional officers until the 1960s, one correctional administrator stated to C.T. Griffiths, "About the only qualification was that the potential applicant had to be able to walk around the top of the wall (of the prison) without falling off." The low pay and lack of training reflected the low status of correctional officers. As late as the 1980s, one observer noted that the only requirements for security personnel assigned to guard towers were "20/20 vision, the IQ of an imbecile, a high threshold for boredom, and a basement position in Maslow's hierarchy" (Toch, 1978:87). Today, working inside a correctional institution requires much more than the ability to turn a key. Officers must have good communication and interpersonal skills, exercise common sense and good judgment, be aware of legal and procedural issues, and be adaptable to the changes in correctional philosophy and policy.

There have been changes in the demographic profile of correctional officer recruits in recent years. More Aboriginal people and other visible minorities are being selected for training, a measure of the success of efforts to promote diversity in Canadian corrections. At the same time, there has been a decrease in the numbers of women recruits and recruits who have a college or university degree; the findings with respect to gender and education require further study (Tellier et al., 2001).

CSC's Correctional Training Program

The Correctional Service of Canada (CSC) operates five training facilities, called regional staff colleges, across the country. These facilities are used for training correctional officer recruits, as well as for in-service staff training and development. Potential recruits must successfully complete the Bona Fide Occupational Requirements for correctional officers and a set of medical and physical standards, including the Correctional Officer Physical Abilities Test.

The **Correctional Training Program** is a 12-week course that combines classroom instruction with self-directed learning. The topics covered in the training program include the mission statement and core values, interpersonal and communication skills, security procedures and strategies, and self-defence. The regional staff colleges also offer the **Basic Case Management Program** for personnel who have been appointed as institutional or community-based case management officers.

In addition, there is within the CSC a special process for selecting and training staff to work in institutions for federally sentenced women. Specific criteria are used to identify personnel who are sensitive to women's issues, their life histories, and their unique needs. In addition to the training provided to all new correctional officers, staff selected to work in women's facilities must complete a "women-centred training" course. This course consists of a number of modules covering areas such as women's criminality and the links to personal history, self-injury and suicide, same-sex relationships, cultural sensitivity, and dealing effectively with lifers (Lajeunesse et al., 2000).

Provincial Training Programs

There are no nationwide standards for recruiting and training correctional officers for employment in provincial systems of corrections. Each province has established its own procedures, standards, and training courses. In most provinces, new recruits are trained with some combination of initial and on-the-job training programs. Increasingly, potential recruits are required to assume the costs of their own training. In some jurisdictions, pre-employment courses are offered through community colleges. The correctional officer **Staff Application, Recruitment, and Training (START)** program in Ontario is highlighted in Box 6.1.

BOX 6.1

START Program (Ontario)

Candidates for employment in Ontario provincial corrections must complete, at their own expense, the START program, which includes the following components:

The Admission Process

There are three stages in the admission process:

Stage 1: Mandatory Qualifications
Applicants must:

- be eligible to work in Canada
- have Ontario grade 12 graduation diploma or formal equivalency
- have current Emergency First Aid and CPR Heartsaver certificates

Stage 2: Information, Testing, and Evaluation
Several times a year, information, testing, and evaluation sessions are presented at various locations throughout the province. Candidates are provided with information on the activities and duties of correctional officers and also complete a testing and evaluation process, which includes:

- the Canadian Achievement Survey Test for judgment and comprehension, competency in arithmetic, and written expression
- a video-based judgment test
- a video and written observation skills test
- a personality inventory

Stage 3: Personal Interview and Testing

Personal interviews and testing, centred on core competencies required of correctional officers, are conducted. Those candidates who successfully complete this stage are then required to undergo a medical exam, physical abilities test, and a background check.

Pre-employment Training

Candidates who successfully complete the admissions process are invited to enroll in the six-week pre-employment training program with a focus on either adult or youth offenders. Vacancies in correctional facilities are filled from a list of those persons who have successfully completed the pre-employment training program and have met the medical and security requirements.

Candidates are required to pay tuition fees as well as room and board costs while at the training centre.

Institutional Orientation

Each institution in the provincial correctional system offers a one- to three-week orientation for new correctional officers when they are hired. This orientation provides the new officer with information on the rules and operating procedures of the institution, programs and services, case management, and other features of daily institutional life.

Source: Ministry of Public Safety and Security, Correctional Services (www.mpss.jus.gov.on.ca/english/corr_serv/careers_corr_admission.html).

In British Columbia, the various stages of recruitment and training are similar to those in Ontario. Qualified applicants are invited to enroll (at their own expense) in the Adult Correctional Officer Employment Readiness Program, a six-week training course taught at the Corrections Academy at the Justice Institute of British Columbia and at other locations throughout the province. Among the nearly 40 topical areas covered in the program are Aboriginal awareness, case management, crisis intervention, interpersonal communication skills, stress management, and use of force. An online version of the program is also available.

In-Service Training

The **Career Management Program** in the CSC allows in-service correctional officers the opportunity to upgrade their knowledge and skills through training courses and self-guided instruction (see Box 6.2). A self-learning program is made available via computer and includes a series of modules on a variety of topics, including report writing, interviewing techniques, and case management. These materials can be accessed by correctional officers at the

C01 and C02 levels to prepare for the examination for promotion to the position of institutional parole officer. The promotion examination also includes role-playing scenarios and interviews. The self-learning program is a good illustration of how systems of corrections use high technology.

Recent reductions in funding have hindered the development of comprehensive in-service training programs for provincial/territorial correctional officers. In-service training at these levels tends to be issue-focused and is designed to ensure that staff have the skills and specific knowledge required by legislation. Training courses include CPR/first aid; suicide intervention; behaviour management; workplace harassment and cultural sensitivity; training required under legislation, such as provincial occupational health and safety Acts; and training for the Institutional Emergency Response Teams. In Ontario, in-service correctional officers are required to attend advanced training every five years. In Prince Edward Island, in-service training courses

BOX 6.2

CSC's Career Management Program

Central to the human resources policies of the CSC is the Career Management Program, which is designed to support the development of a motivated, qualified workforce by defining career paths and making available a variety of activities for professional development. The program is initiated by the employees, who complete a career plan based on a self-assessment of their interests, areas of competency, and career objectives. Management personnel assist in the development of the plan, which is then used as the basis for periodical reviews of the employee's progress.

The four components of the Career Management Program, which apply to all operational levels of the CSC, are:

- human resource planning
- performance evaluation and review
- staff development
- the rating of merit (Solicitor General Canada, 1998:8)

To implement the Career Management Program, the CSC has developed and implemented a competency-based staffing procedure, which includes standardized qualifications and assessment instruments, a clearly defined selection process to fill positions, and performance evaluation reports, which are used in the selection process.

are offered under an agreement between the Justice Institute of Canada and provincial correctional authorities.

An additional factor that hinders the development of comprehensive training packages and programs is the relatively small number of staff at individual correctional centres. The ability to "backfill" positions (provide staff coverage) to free up staff time for training is limited when staff numbers are small. The CSC, on the other hand, can develop in-service training programs for staff across the country.

Provincial governments are often unable to offer continuing education and upgrading courses to staff in correctional institutions that are situated in the northern and more remote areas of the provinces.

GOING INSIDE: THE SOCIALIZATION OF NEW CORRECTIONAL OFFICERS

There are a number of challenges that confront new correctional officers, not the least of which is the lack of knowledge of what it will be like working inside a prison:

> *Unless one has either worked in or served time in a prison, one's ability to experience the tasks and atmosphere of prison work is usually limited to movies, paperback novels or the frequently sensational accounts of prison violence that appear in the popular press. Personal experience directly related to prisons is something no one has until one finds himself within the walls. (Lombardo, 1981:22)*

In learning to exercise discretion and carry out their tasks effectively, new correctional officers must learn the subtle nonverbal cues that will assist them in "reading" individual inmates and become familiar with the various intricacies of the inmate social system, the methods used to distribute and use contraband goods and drugs, and other activities such as gambling, strong-arming, and debt collection. During the initial stages of employment, correctional officers will also be "tested" by the inmates to determine how they will exercise their discretion and authority. These processes of adaptation and learning and the development of strategies to cope with the pressures and demands of everyday life in the prison are similar to that experienced by new inmates.

Another challenge confronting new correctional officers is to gain acceptance from co-workers. Through their actions, the new officers must demonstrate their solidarity to their co-workers, and there is often a "probationary" period during which the neophytes must prove that they can be trusted and have the abilities to perform the requirements of the job.

Patterns of Relationships among Correctional Officers

It has long been assumed that correctional officers, similar to their police counterparts, constitute an **occupational subculture** with definable attributes. The tenets that are said to provide the foundation for a normative code among correctional officers include the following:

- Always assist another officer who is in real or potential danger.
- Do not become overly friendly with the inmates.
- Do not abuse your authority with inmates.
- Always back your colleagues in decisions and actions; don't backstab.
- Do your job and don't leave work for other officers to do.
- Defer to the experience of veteran officers. (Farkas, 1997; Kauffman, 1988)

Among the factors that have been identified as contributing to the development of solidarity among correctional officers are the ever-present potential for injury on the job; the hostility directed toward correctional officers by inmates; the often conflicting demands made on correctional officers, largely as a consequence of shifting correctional philosophies; a work environment where rewards and recognition are few and far between; and the reliance of officers upon one another (Grossi and Berg, 1991). This code of behaviour provides a mechanism for correctional officers to cope with the demands of both inmates and the prison administration.

Upon closer examination, however, the subculture of correctional officers does not appear to be a monolithic entity. The extent to which correctional officers exhibit solidarity depends on a number of factors, including the security level of the institution; the age, gender, and experiential backgrounds of the officers; the relations that exist between the officers and the administration; and other factors that are less tangible, including the extent to which the correctional officers in any one institution perceive they are threatened by the inmates or administrative policies. It is likely, for example, that in high-security institutions, where the daily regimen is more controlled and the threat (real or perceived) of injury is greater, solidarity among officers may be more evident. Similarly, there may be greater solidarity among officers working in institutions where the administration provides neither clear guidelines for officer activities nor support for the decision making of officers.

Correctional officers as a work group may be as fragmented as the inmates are. Line-level security personnel group into friendship networks, which may be gender-based or centred on a shared experience, such as having completed a university degree. One potential source of friction between correctional officers is education. Increasingly, new officers hired by the CSC are required to have at least two years of postsecondary education, and many new officers have university degrees. Tension may exist between these officers and those hired when the minimum education standards were lower. University graduates may be viewed by these officers as having little or no experience in the real world and as being naive, lacking in common sense, and susceptible to manipulation by inmates.

In fact, for many correctional officers, it is relations with their colleagues, rather than with inmates, that is the primary source of job-related stress. Gossip among officers, correctional officers who share information with inmates, and colleagues who are perceived to be too authoritarian in their approach are potential sources of stress for line-level personnel. Conflict may also arise when certain officers are viewed as "slackers," for example, because of sleeping during graveyard shifts and not making their rounds at the appointed times.

ORIENTATIONS AND ATTITUDES

As the one group of institutional personnel who staff the prison 24 hours a day, correctional officers have the most extensive contact with inmates. For this reason alone, it is important to examine and understand the orientations and attitudes of officers. Even though officers may not be directly involved in the delivery of treatment programs or in the case management process, there is the potential for officers to be change agents and to facilitate positive attitudes and behaviours among inmates.

A Typology of Correctional Officers

There have been attempts to categorize correctional officers based on their orientation and attitudes toward their co-workers, the inmates, their occupation, and the institutional environment. Although such efforts are fraught with difficulty, as it is unlikely that any one officer will exhibit all of the attitudinal and behavioural features of one particular type, it does sensitize us to the fact that not all correctional officers think and act the same. Box 6.3 presents a typology developed from a study of correctional officers in several prisons in the United States.

Attitudes toward Inmates

Researchers have attempted to determine the variables that are associated with the attitudes and orientations that correctional officers have toward inmates. A

BOX 6.3

A Typology of Correctional Officers

To develop her typology, Mary Ann Farkas surveyed a sample of officers and classi-fied their responses according to their orientation toward:

- rule enforcement (RE)
- negotiation or exchange in working with inmates (NE)
- norms of mutual obligation toward colleagues (MO)
- desire or interest in human service delivery (HS)

	RE	NE	MO	HS
Rule Enforcer	rule-bound, inflexible in discipline; mandate is custody and control; rules enforced to maintain order and teach discipline	unwilling to negotiate or exchange to secure inmate compliance	norms of mutual obligation with other officers strong	no interest in human service; avoid contact with inmates
Hard Liner	subtype of the rule enforcer; hard, inflexible with rules; power-hungry; rules enforced to punish and show authority	at times, abusive and aggressive toward inmates; extremely negative attitudes toward inmates	identify strongly with officers who share their negative views of inmates	resent having to provide services to inmates
People Worker	older, more experienced; rely on verbal skills and common sense	comfortable style in working with inmates; flexible in rule enforcement; secure inmate compliance with interpersonal communication and personalized relations; problem-solvers	more focused on conflict resolution than on maintaining authority of fellow officers	enjoy challenge of working with inmates

	RE	NE	MO	HS
Synthetic Officer	synthesis of rule enforcer and people worker; follow rules closely, but attempt to consider the circumstances in dealing with inmates	response to inmates highly situational; firm but fair	support other officers	attempt to treat inmates fairly while not being taken advantage of
Loner	strict enforcement of rules to avoid being criticized; prevalent among minority and female officers	conform strictly to rules and regulations to provide validation to inmates and fellow officers and to avoid making a mistake; unwilling to negotiate for inmate compliance	feel need to continually "prove" themselves to co-workers and management; alienated from other officers	wary of inmates; mistrust; prefer to work posts away from inmates (and other officers)

Source: Adapted from Farkas, 2000.

number of studies have reported that correctional officers hold negative attitudes toward inmates, including the view that inmates are manipulative and that the likelihood of rehabilitation is slight (Whitehead and Lindquist, 1989). In addition, correctional officers may believe that inmates have too much power and control, which, in turn, places the officers at an increased risk of injury or even death. Correctional officers often attribute this risk to weak administrators who, often inadvertently, impose policies that undermine the authority of correctional officers and upset the routine and regimen of daily prison life. In comparison with administrators and treatment staff, correctional officers may exhibit attitudes that are more punitive, less empathetic, and less supportive of rehabilitation (Larivière, 2002; Larivière and Robinson, 1996).

A number of factors appear to influence the attitudes that correctional officers have toward inmates, including the following:

- *Institutional setting:* Correctional officers working in minimum-security correctional facilities tend to hold more favourable attitudes toward offenders than those in medium- and maximum-security institutions (Jurik, 1985; Larivière and Robinson, 1996).
- *Age and experience:* There is some evidence to suggest that more positive attitudes toward inmates are held by older correctional officers with multiple years of experience on the job. This is most likely a consequence of officers adjusting to the realities of their workplace and developing strategies for coping with inmates and the variety of stressors that they experience in carrying out their tasks (Larivière and Robinson, 1996; Plecas and Maxim, 1987).
- *Region of the country:* Findings from Canadian research on federal correctional officers suggest that there are regional variations in correctional officers' attitudes. Officers working in federal institutions in the Pacific region of the CSC, for example, held attitudes that were more empathetic and less punitive toward offenders, whereas officers working in federal institutions in Quebec were less empathetic and the most punitive of any region. Additional research is required to explore and identify the sources of these regional differences.

Job Satisfaction and Commitment to the Organization

Studies have attempted to determine the impact of race, gender, age, level of education, and length of service on the perceptions that officers have of their work environment and on levels of job satisfaction. Among the more significant findings:

- Female officers and those officers with more years of experience are more satisfied with their work.
- Correctional officers who are empathetic, non-punitive, and supportive of rehabilitation programs are more committed to their jobs, are more satisfied with the work they perform, and experience less stress on the job.
- As with attitudes toward inmates, correctional officers' attitudes are found to vary by the length of time in service; there is evidence of a "mellowing effect," whereby officers who are older and who have more years on the job are more positive in their attitudes.

- In comparison to other institutional staff, correctional officers often score lowest on perceptions of staff empowerment, staff recognition, fair treatment of employees, and overall job satisfaction.
- Contrary to expectations, there may be an inverse relationship between level of education and job satisfaction. (Morgan, Van Haveren, and Pearson, 2002)

The extent to which level of job satisfaction among correctional officers is affected by the personalities and background experiences of individual officers, as well as by the work itself, remains to be explored by future research.

A prerequisite for correctional staff to be effective is commitment to the institution in which they work. A study of staff commitment to the CSC found the following:

- Correctional officers and case managers showed less commitment than persons in supervisory and administrative positions.
- New staff had higher levels of commitment than officers who had been in the service for a number of years.
- Female staff tended to be more committed than their male counterparts.
- Neither education nor age was related to level of commitment. (Robinson, Porporino, and Simourd, 1992)

CORRECTIONAL OFFICER–INMATE RELATIONSHIPS AND PATTERNS OF ACCOMMODATION

The unique features of daily life inside institutions create pressures for correctional officers and inmates to develop accommodative relationships, which, for inmates, help to reduce the pains of imprisonment, and, for the officers, ensure daily stability and order. Relations with inmates are generally not a source of stress for correctional officers, although officers realize that they are outnumbered by the inmates and that peace and order in the institution require the cooperation of the inmates.

The specific patterns of interaction that develop between correctional officers and the inmates will depend on a variety of factors, including the individual correctional officer, the size of the inmate population, the security level of the facility, and the policies and management style of senior administration. Generally, inmates serving life sentences (25-year minimum) are the easiest group to deal with, whereas younger offenders, many of whom have a "get high today, the hell with tomorrow" attitude, are often a source of instability in the institution.

Ironically, even as the conditions within correctional institutions have improved, life has become more unpredictable for correctional officers and staff. In the words of a correctional officer at Kingston Penitentiary:

> *There is no "routine." You've got at KP some pretty nasty people ... sitting locked up or out in their own little society. You've got all sorts of things going on. Like drug deals, or I don't like the way this guy cuts his hair, or I don't like the colour of this guy's skin, or this guy comes from the East Coast and I don't like downeasters, or comes from out west. (cited in Harris, 2002:46)*

Instability and lack of routine in correctional institutions may be due, in part, to an erosion of the traditional "inmate code" (to be discussed in Chapter 7) that has brought about changes in how inmates relate to one another. In the past, some inmates functioned as "elder statesmen," maintaining control in the units and helping to establish peace and stability in the institution as a whole. But today, in the words of one correctional officer, "it's all intimidation, and brute force, and who has the most drugs to sell" (cited in Harris, 2002:48).

The Custodial Agenda of Correctional Officers

The public, or custodial, agenda of correctional officers is constructed around the image of the officer as a "mindless and brutal custodian" (Johnson, 1996:197). The historical record of correctional institutions is replete with documented cases of the arbitrary and excessive use of force by correctional officers. Today, however, correctional officers are not only better trained, but are supervised and held accountable for their actions. Although there are occasional well-publicized incidents involving the abuse of authority by correctional officers, it would be inaccurate to portray officers as predisposed to violence or as systematically misusing and abusing their authority.

The extent to which the environment of the prison itself, with its total institutional features, contributes to many of the problems that arise must also be considered. As one researcher has observed:

> *Officers and inmates are the chief antagonists in prison conflict. As such, they are typically blamed for problems that plague prisons. Just as prisons are regarded as deviant environments, those who live and work in them are dismissed as possessing deviant characters and interests.... The intractable problems posed by prisons are not rooted in the identities and characters of officers or inmates. The problems are much more fundamental. They are rooted in the nature of the goals prisons are erected to serve. (Kauffman, 1988:264–65)*

The Correctional Agenda of Correctional Officers

If correctional officers cannot build relationships with inmates that are based on trust, they are not precluded from engaging in activities that are helpful to the inmates. This duty is part of the private "correctional" agenda and involves the correctional officer functioning as a change agent: "It is by helping prisoners—by promoting secure and, ideally, responsive prison regimes—that some officers rise above the limitations of their formal custodial role" (Johnson:1996:223).

While maintaining an appropriate social distance from inmates, officers can help inmates deal with the institutional bureaucracy, provide information, and, to a lesser extent, assist with inmates' personal problems. There are a number of specific human service activities that correctional officers can provide to inmates, including:

- ensuring that the inmates receive basic goods and services, such as food, clothing, medication, and sundry items, in a timely manner, thereby lessening tensions
- acting as a referral agent and advocate for inmates, often serving as an intermediary between the inmate and the institutional bureaucracy
- assisting inmates in solving problems related to their incarceration, including the management of personal crises (Johnson, 1996:229–41)

Those officers who develop a rapport with inmates beyond the basic "keeper and the kept" level are generally more effective in maintaining order in the units. A positive relationship with inmates may increase the amount of information that "snitches" or "information providers" pass along to officers and may also allow inmates to inform officers of problems that develop in the unit. Generally speaking, it appears that the majority of inmates "get along" with correctional officers.

Exercising Authority: Correctional Officer Discretion and Decision Making

The central dilemma faced by guards is that they can neither expect inmate cooperation nor govern without it.... To achieve a smoothly running tour, a guard has to gain inmate acquiescence with the carrot rather than the stick. The best reward a guard can offer is to ignore certain offenses when they are committed or to make sure that s/he is not around when a rule is being broken.

—Hewitt, Poole, and Regoli, 1984:446

Correctional officers have a high degree of discretion in carrying out their daily activities and in determining when and how they will enforce the rules and regulations of the institution. Officers are well aware that full enforcement of all institutional regulations at all times would make life unbearable for both themselves and the inmates. As one correctional officer commented, "Read the book, but don't throw the book. Do not go prescriptively into any situation" (Yates, 1993:115). The discretion that officers have allows considerable flexibility in the application of many of the more minor institutional regulations. Within the context of the accommodative relationships that develop between officers and inmates, minor and in some instances major transgressions may be ignored or not responded to in a formal manner, depending on the circumstances and the inmate(s) and correctional officer(s) involved.

Styles of Decision Making

Some officers are pretty stiff and enforce the rules and regulations. Some people are pretty lax, although some of the staff over the years have adopted the attitude, "Well, if I don't bother the cons, they're not going to bother me."

—federal correctional officer, cited in Harris, 2002:45–46

Correctional officers can be located on a continuum, based on how they exercise their discretionary authority, from those who are rigid and attempt to enforce all the rules at all times, to officers who do little or no rule enforcement. This latter group may include officers who are close to retirement. In the middle are officers who are consistent in their decision making and straightforward with inmates, do not make arbitrary decisions, and temper their exercise of authority with common sense and a respect for the rule of law. These officers have good judgment, have the ability to mediate potentially explosive behavioural situations, and are good judges of character. Recall the various "types" of correctional officers identified in Box 6.3.

Commenting on decision making and the role of experience, one former correctional officer noted:

If you are not a shrewd assessor of human character, then you had better learn to be one fast. Some people are inside because they never had a break in their lives and some are in because they were "born to lose." You give the former the benefit of the doubt and you bend the rules for the latter only when it suits your purpose. In certain circumstances, you think of the inmate as an individual, a fellow human being. In others, you must first think of the good of the institution in general. It's a matter of making judgment calls, and it can't be taught except through experience. (Yates, 1993:115)

Abuse of Authority and Misuse of Force by Correctional Officers

The low visibility of daily life inside correctional institutions, combined with the broad discretion exercised by correctional officers, may create situations in which officers abuse their authority and, in certain instances, violate the law. Research conducted in five Ontario provincial institutions raised the issue of whether correctional officers systematically abused their discretionary powers in dealing with black inmates (Gittens and Cole, 1995). The perception was widespread among black inmates that they were punished more frequently and more severely, for less cause, than white inmates. Black inmates also felt more vulnerable to physical violence by correctional officers. Support for these views was provided by some of the correctional officers interviewed for the study.

An examination of correctional officers' disciplinary practices revealed that black inmates were more likely to be charged with misconduct that involved interpretation of behaviour, including those involving an assessment of "attitude," whereas white inmates were more likely to be disciplined for incidents where the discretion of the correctional officers was more limited, such as discovering an inmate with contraband. There was also evidence that black and white inmates were treated differently in the imposition of a penalty for misconduct, with black inmates being overrepresented in the punishment category of closed confinement (or segregation).

Determining the extent to which correctional officers abuse authority and discretion is made difficult by a number of factors, including the low visibility of the decisions that officers make every day inside institutions; the culture of silence among officers, which results in officers protecting one another (see Box 6.4); and the relatively short periods for which provincial inmates are incarcerated. Increasingly, correctional officers are being held accountable and civilly liable for their actions, and correctional officers have been fired from their jobs following riots or inmate deaths. Ironically, this increased accountability may reinforce the code of silence among officers.

BOX 6.4

Death of an Inmate

In 1995, two correctional officers from Kingston Penitentiary were charged with killing Robert Gentles, a black inmate, during a cell extraction. This was the first instance in Canada in which correctional officers had been prosecuted over the death of an inmate. A justice of the peace ruled that the inmate's mother could privately prosecute the correctional officers and their supervisor for manslaughter. The prosecution was taken over by the Attorney General's office, but all the charges were eventually dropped.

During a coroner's inquest into the death, the lawyer for Gentles' family accused an officer of covering up the actions of other officers, suggesting that the officer "didn't see anything" because correctional officers who expose misconduct by other guards put their jobs—and even their lives—at risk. The coroner's jury subsequently ruled the death accidental. At the same time, it presented the CSC with a list of 74 recommendations relating to the development of policies and procedures for extracting noncompliant inmates from their cells. Included were the recommendations that all alternatives be considered before a cell extraction is ordered and that all cell extractions be videotaped.

Sources: Correctional Service of Canada (www.csc-scc.gc.ca/text/pblct/gentles/index_e.shtml); Tyler, 1998a, 1998b.

RELATIONSHIPS WITH THE PRISON ADMINISTRATION

Research on the orientation and attitudes of correctional officers, discussed above, revealed that a primary source of stress and alienation is the relationships between officers and the senior prison administration. Officers may view administrators with a mixture of distrust and cynicism and may see them as being quite distant from the everyday realities of the prison. Officers are particularly critical of administrators who fail to provide clear and consistent operational policies. The prison administration may be viewed as being concerned with fiscal and administrative issues that have little relevance to correctional officers at the line level. In the words of one former correctional officer, "There is a high wall between line screws and all corrections personnel about them. It becomes a situation of guards and cons against the system. The inmate code of silence and the guard culture are distorted mirror images of one another" (Yates, 1993:60). You will recall from Chapter 5 that the severely troubled relations between correctional officers and senior administration were a major factor in the riot that occurred in the Headingley Correctional Institution.

RELATIONSHIPS WITH TREATMENT STAFF

Many correctional officers hold a rather dim view of treatment programs. Just over 50 percent of the federal correctional officers surveyed in a Price-Waterhouse (1994) study felt that rehabilitation programs were a waste of money, a view that was supported in part by a report of the Auditor General of Canada (1996), which found little evidence that inmate needs were being matched with treatment programs. Officers may also be suspicious of positive statistics on recidivism generated by the systems of correction, perceiving that such figures are used to justify expenditures on treatment programs.

Another study found that only 50 percent of a sample of correctional officers felt that inmates could be rehabilitated (Weekes, Pelletier, and Beautette, 1995); the percentage of officers who felt that sex offenders could be effectively treated was even lower (20 percent). The view of correctional officers that very few inmates have the ability, capability, resources, and interest to make significant changes in their attitudes and behaviours may limit the potential of correctional officers to be effective change agents in the institution.

A common view among correctional officers is that programs should be offered only for inmates who indicate an interest in taking them. There is often the perception that programs are delivered for the wrong reasons—to achieve administrative objectives and the goals of case managers, rather than those of offenders. Currently, much of the impetus for inmate participation in treatment programs comes from the plan prepared by the inmate's case management officer. Some support for this view is provided by a survey of federal inmates that found that one in four inmates admitted they signed up for treatment programs only to please their case managers (Makin, 1996:A5). There is also the perception that many inmates become involved in treatment programs primarily to improve their chances of release on parole, rather than for self-improvement.

Whereas federal correctional officers at the CX2 level are involved in case management, the majority of provincial/territorial correctional officers may have little input into the case management process and often find themselves at odds with case managers. This conflict is, in part, a consequence of the different roles that correctional officers and case management officers play in the institution: the primary role of many correctional officers is security, whereas case managers are charged with developing, implementing, and monitoring the offender's plan of treatment. For example, correctional officers who charge offenders for violations of institutional rules may be asked or coerced by case managers to remove this information from the offender's file, if such information is seen as jeopardizing the plan for the inmate, such as transfer to a lower-security facility. Tension may result, as line-level security personnel may perceive that case managers are not fully aware of the inmate's conduct in the institution.

As one correctional officer remarked to C.T. Griffiths: "The inmates are on their best behaviour from 9 to 4 during the week. It's after hours and on the weekends that we have to deal with disruptive behaviour. The treatment staff and case management officers don't see this." Correctional officers may assign more responsibility to inmates for their behaviour than do case management officers and other treatment staff. Case management officers may have few opportunities to interact with correctional officers who spend the majority of their time in the units or on the tiers.

SOURCES OF STRESS FOR CORRECTIONAL OFFICERS

As they carry out their role and responsibilities, correctional officers can experience high levels of stress. Some common sources of this occupational stress are discussed below.

Threats to Personal Security

Concerns about personal security are a leading cause of stress among correctional officers (Millson, 2002). Many correctional officers feel that institutional policies and procedures are not adequate to ensure their personal security. The threat of violence is a primary concern. The slayings of two provincial correctional officers in Quebec in 1997 highlighted the risks that correctional officers face on the job (see Box 6.5).

Among the safety concerns of correctional officers is the potential hazard of being exposed to inmates who are infected with HIV/AIDS, hepatitis, and tuberculosis. There is no mandatory testing of inmates for HIV/AIDS and, as a matter of policy, correctional officers are not informed of which inmates are HIV-positive. Therefore, officers are required to be trained in universal precautions—that is, to assume that every inmate with whom they have contact may be infected with a communicable disease.

BOX 6.5

Death on the Job

In 1997, two Quebec correctional officers were killed by ambush. Diane Lavigne was killed in June as she was driving home from her job at Bordeaux jail, and Pierre Rondeau was ambushed in September as he drove a bus to pick up prisoners from a provincial jail. The gangland-style attacks were carried out by a biker gang, the Nomads, who are affiliated with the Hell's Angels. Two members of the gang were subsequently charged and convicted of the slayings and sentenced to life imprisonment with no possibility of parole for 25 years.

The killings of the correctional officers were part of a series of violent incidents, growing out of an ongoing war between two Montreal biker gangs—the Hell's Angels and the Rock Machine—to control the illicit drug trade. The killings were likely intended to intimidate authorities who have mounted a crackdown on the gangs in recent years. Pressure from the correctional officers' union resulted in the provincial government's allowing correctional officers who are transporting prisoners to be armed and to wear bulletproof vests.

Source: Fitterman and Gatehouse, 1998.

Lack of Support and Respect

There is a widespread feeling among correctional officers that senior managers, the media, and the general public neither understand nor respect their profession. This view is reflected in the words of two correctional officers:

> *We are the only group of people whose job it is to keep the cons inside the walls. Everyone else is working to get them out of jail. For this, we are the prison doormat.... I dream of the day when the officers will be treated at least as good as the inmates. (cited in Harris, 2002:253)*

> *We are asked to work in an environment that imposes a heavy personal toll on us, and we get no recognition for it. We do not feel valued by management, and we certainly are not valued by either the inmates or the general public. We're the only ones who understand the difficult environment. (cited in Joint Committee, 2000:54)*

A related source of frustration for correctional officers is the absence of communication with and support from management and the fact that policies are often developed without input from front-line workers.

The Increasing Emphasis on Inmate Rights

Recall from Chapter 1 that a key trend in corrections has been an increasing focus on accountability, the rule of law, and the rights of inmates under the Canadian Charter of Rights and Freedoms. Decisions by Canadian courts concerning inmate rights have had a significant impact on the operation of systems of correction. Many correctional officers feel that the new emphasis on inmate rights has come at the expense of their own rights. There is even a widespread perception among correctional officers that it is the inmates who are running the institutions. In the words of one officer: "No two ways about it, we can do nothing to them now. Absolutely nothing. At one point, at least we had the threat of being able to lock them up and charge them, or some type of control. Now you tell them you are going to charge them—they laugh at you" (cited in Harris, 2002:49).

Multiple Tasks

The duties of federal correctional officers may include not only patrolling, conducting searches, and intervening in inmate disturbances, but also issuing permits and passes, performing casework and reclassification, transferring and processing inmates, and answering the telephone. In short, in addition to the security requirements of the job, correctional officers are called upon to play the multiple roles of "nurse, psychologist, parole officer, administrator, police, criminologist, fireman, and teacher" (Environics Research Group, 2000:7).

A source of considerable stress is the conflicting demands of casework and security. In the words of a correctional officer at Kingston Penitentiary: "A difficulty is handling the two philosophies of corrections right now, which is security and rehabilitation. Having a caseload and security. The caseload … it's hard to be a guard and hug him in the morning and them mace him in the afternoon because he's been a bad person" (cited in Environics Research Group, 2000:7)

Inadequate Training

A common complaint among correctional officers is that the duration and content of training is insufficient for the variety of tasks they are asked to perform. As a consequence, a considerable amount of learning occurs "on the job." A review of training for federal correctional officers found that training needs and requirements have not kept pace with the increased knowledge and skills required of correctional officers (Joint Committee, 2000:84).

The Impact on Personal Life

Many correctional officers find it difficult to separate their work life from their personal life. At the same time, many officers are unwilling or unable to talk about their work experiences with people outside the profession. Relations with family and friends can suffer as a result. In the words of one correctional officer: "[The job] screws up your relationships. You limit the friends that you've got. How many people are you going to talk to about, other than a cop or an ambulance driver, what kind of mayhem you went through that day ... it's indescribable" (cited in Environics Research Group, 2000:15).

Shift Work

Correctional officers generally work rotating shifts. For federal officers in the CSC, the most common schedule is seven days on one shift, followed by three days off, then another seven days on another shift, followed by four days off. The most common starting times for shifts are 7 a.m., 3 p.m., and 11 p.m. There is considerable variation in the shifts that individual officers work, depending on their seniority and on the staffing requirements of the institution.

Shift work often results in loss of sleep and a disruption of the circadian rhythm (or biological clock) that controls the sleep, wake, and arousal periods of the human body. Disruptions of the circadian rhythm result in a feeling similar to jet lag: fatigue, nausea, irritability, and loss of appetite. Shift workers may be more prone to poor performance, accidents, and health problems.

Shift work can also affect the correctional officer's private life and make the management of family and other personal relationships more difficult, as well as limit opportunities to interact with children during non-school hours and participate in community activities. A survey of federal correctional officers, which included officers at the CO1 and CO2 levels, found that over 70 percent of officers at each level felt that shift work had a negative or very negative impact on their family life. In addition, the level of job satisfaction was lower (and stress higher) among those reporting very negative impacts of shift work on family relations (Grant, 1995). A study of Ontario correctional officers found that officers who switched from an eight-hour workday to a 12-hour day and compressed workweek had higher levels of absenteeism than other officers (Venne, 1997).

The Institutional Environment

There is some evidence to suggest that levels of stress among correctional officers are related to the specific correctional environment in which the officer is working. Maximum-security institutions, as well as more "secure" medium-security facilities, may have more tension and a greater potential for violence both between inmates and directed toward officers. Problems with co-workers are another source of stress (Hughes and Zamble, 1993).

Contributing to the stress experienced by correctional officers are the conflicting expectations of them by the different groups in the institution:

> *Each of the officer's audiences within the prison demands something different: administrators look to officers to lead inmates rather than relate to them or otherwise deal with them in interpersonally skillful ways; inmates value interpersonal skills in officers, especially as these relate to problem-solving in everyday prison life, and are suspicious of efforts to lead them. (Johnson, 1996:206)*

The Impact of Critical Incidents

During the course of their careers, correctional officers may be exposed to a wide range of critical incidents, including disturbances and riots, hostage takings, inmate murder, inmate self-mutilation and suicide, threats to the officer's safety, and injury to the officer. These incidents may result in symptoms generally associated with **post-traumatic stress disorder (PTSD)**, an extreme form of **critical incident stress,** which include nightmares, hypervigilance, intrusive thoughts, and other forms of psychological distress (Rosine, 1995). In its most extreme forms, such as that found among veterans of combat, sufferers experience flashbacks in which they relive the trauma as if they were there.

A study of a sample of federal correctional officers in the Ontario region found the following:

- During their career, the officers had been exposed to an average of 27.9 critical incidents.
- 61 percent of the officers had been injured at work, with a majority requiring leave time.
- 17 percent of the officers who had experienced severe critical incident stress were ultimately diagnosed as having PTSD.
- For the majority of officers, the symptoms disappeared within three years.

- The most common symptoms experienced by officers were sleep disturbances, nightmares, and exaggerated startle response (i.e., hypervigilance).
- Nearly 95 percent of the officers rated the impact of these symptoms on their personal life as severe.
- Nearly 50 percent indicated that their exposure to critical incidents had an impact on their family and family relations.
- Only 40 percent of the officers sought professional assistance for their problems. (Rosine, 1992)

The results of this survey highlight the need for systems of correction to develop policies for critical incident stress management centred on **critical incident stress debriefing.** This technique involves on-scene debriefing of the officer by a trained intervenor after a critical incident has occurred; defusing by a mental-health professional or trained peer, during which the symptoms of stress are identified and strategies for stress management are provided to the officer; a formal critical incident stress debriefing; and, if required, a follow-up critical incident stress debriefing. The primary objective of critical incident stress debriefing is to provide protection and support for the correctional officer, while imparting information and strategies that will assist the officer in effectively coping with any symptoms of critical incident stress that might arise.

In addition, correctional officers have access to federal or provincial/territorial employee assistance programs, which provide financial and legal support as well as assistance with a wide range of issues (family, work, mental and physical health, etc.).

Coping with Stress

Although correctional officers experience a considerable amount of stress working inside institutions, the evidence suggests that most officers have developed effective coping mechanisms and are generally satisfied with their occupation. For many officers, interpersonal relationships (having someone to speak to about problems on the job) are an important source of support in coping with the stresses of the job.

In contrast to the stereotype of correctional officers that has developed largely from studies in the United States, the sample of Canadian officers surveyed by Hughes and Zamble (1993) did not drink to excess, spent a large portion of their off-duty time with their families, and did not limit their socializing to activities with other officers. A further reflection of the adequacy of the coping skills of most correctional officers is that officers, as a group, report relatively the same alcohol consumption patterns as the general population (Holden et al., 1995).

FEMALE CORRECTIONAL OFFICERS

Historically, women were confined to clerical and noncustodial positions in correctional facilities. Considerable resistance was encountered as women were hired as correctional officers. Women were (and often still are) perceived by male co-workers and supervisors as lacking the mental or physical toughness to survive the rigours of institutional life, to control inmates when required, and to back up male officers in crisis situations. In addition, male correctional officers may believe that women are more prone to victimization and manipulation by the inmates (Lawrence and Mahan, 1998). There is also the issue of the privacy of male inmates, particularly in relation to frisks and strip searches. In the case of *Conway v. Canada* ([1993] 2 S.C.R. 872), however, the Supreme Court of Canada reaffirmed the right of women to be employed as correctional officers in male institutions.

Research studies have found that the resistance and hostility of male officers tend to diminish as women demonstrate their abilities as correctional officers. Further, there is no evidence to indicate that female correctional officers are assaulted more frequently or are more easily manipulated by inmates than their male counterparts. Research on the experiences of female correctional officers in the United States has revealed that female officers have a positive impact on the management of inmates in maximum-security institutions, are less likely than their male counterparts to be assaulted by inmates, and are less confrontational and often more able to defuse potentially explosive situations (Rowan, 1996).

Sexual Harassment

Although systems of correction have made concerted efforts to recruit qualified female applicants and women are employed as correctional officers in all types of institutions, problems remain. Several internal surveys conducted by the CSC found a high incidence of sexual harassment, discrimination, and abuse of authority in many federal institutions. Over 50 percent of female employees in Ontario and the Prairie regions indicated that they had been subjected to harassment or abuse, and in one federal institution 62 percent of the female staff stated that they had been harassed by a co-worker. At this particular institution, female correctional officers were openly called "100-pound weaklings," along with more vulgar names. Female correctional officers in Ontario cited instances in which threatening notes had been left on the windshields of their cars and in which they had been harassed and embarrassed by male co-workers in the presence of inmates. The report concluded that senior management was responsible for harassment being an integral part of the daily life in many institutions (cited in Canadian Press, 1995; Price-Waterhouse, 1994).

CROSS-GENDER STAFFING IN FEMALE INSTITUTIONS

The incidents at the Kingston Prison for Women in April 1994 (discussed in Chapter 5), which involved an all-male Institutional Emergency Response Team extracting female inmates from their cells and stripping them of their clothing, rekindled the debate over male staff in women's correctional facilities. Men work at all levels in federal and provincial/territorial women's institutions, from senior management positions to the line level. This has not always been the case, however. At the now-closed federal Kingston Prison for Women, for example, male staff were restricted from supervising women in the living units until 1989. When male unit managers did enter the living units, it was mandatory that their presence be announced and that they be accompanied by a female correctional officer. The position of correctional supervisor in the prison was limited to women, as this job involved many activities in the living units. The Public Service Commission changed this policy in 1989.

In 1998, the CSC appointed a Cross Gender Monitor to provide an independent review of the policy and operational impact of **cross-gender staffing** in federal women's correctional facilities. The final report of the Cross Gender Monitoring Project included the recommendation that male correctional officers working in women's facilities not be permitted to (1) carry out security functions in living and segregation units or (2) serve as members of cell extraction teams (Lajeunesse et al., 2000).

AT ISSUE

SHOULD MALE CORRECTIONAL OFFICERS WORK IN FEMALE INSTITUTIONS?

Proponents of cross-gender staffing argue that:

- the presence of male correctional officers helps to normalize daily institutional life
- male employees should be treated fairly and equally, rather than excluded from job competitions, deployments, and other staffing procedures on the basis of gender

- for female inmates who have never had a positive relationship with a respectful, non-discriminatory male, there is rehabilitation and reintegration value in having men work in front-line positions
- there is a divergence of opinion among female inmates as to whether men should be employed in women's facilities

Opponents of cross-gender staffing contend that:
- the presence of male correctional officers and treatment staff has a negative impact on female inmates who have histories of abuse by men
- the unique power imbalances in correctional officer–inmate relationships require measures that do not replicate standard employment practices
- the presence of men as front-line correctional workers increases the risk of privacy violations and sexual misconduct
- female inmates who have been abused by men in positions of authority will require that only women serve as front-line workers

Questions

1. What is your position on cross-gender staffing in women's correctional facilities?
2. Which of the above arguments do you find most persuasive? Least persuasive?
3. If men are prohibited from being front-line workers in women's institutions, should the same restriction apply to women working in male institutions? Why or why not?

Sources: Arbour, 1996; Lajeunesse et al., 2000.

QUESTIONS FOR REVIEW

1. What are the main features of Ontario's START program?
2. Compare and contrast in-service training programs for correctional officers in federal and provincial/territorial systems of correction.
3. What is meant by the occupational subculture of correctional officers? What are some of the tenets of the normative code among correctional officers?
4. Discuss the influence of the following on correctional officer attitudes toward inmates: (a) gender of the officer, (b) institutional setting, (c) age, (d) experience, and (e) region of the country.
5. Describe the "helping and human" relationships that may exist between correctional officers and inmates.
6. What were the main findings of the investigation into the relationship and patterns of interaction between correctional officers and black inmates in Ontario provincial institutions?

7. Identify and describe two sources of stress for correctional officers.

8. What is critical incident stress and what impact does it have on correctional officers?

9. What do research studies indicate about the performance of female correctional officers in institutions for male offenders?

10. What have research studies and internal staff surveys indicated about the nature and extent of sexual harassment of female correctional officers?

REFERENCES

Arbour, The Honourable L. (Commissioner). 1996. *Commission of Inquiry into Certain Events at the Prison for Women in Kingston*. Ottawa: Public Works and Government Services Canada.

Auditor General of Canada. 1996. "Correctional Service Canada—Rehabilitation Programs for Offenders." *Annual Report, Chapter 10*. Ottawa: Minister of Public Works and Government Services Canada.

Canadian Press. 1995. "Female Guards Complain of Harassment." *The Globe and Mail* (January 9):A4.

Environics Research Group. 2000. *Focus Group Report to the Joint Committee of the Public Service Alliance of Canada, Treasury Board and Correctional Service Canada on the Jobs and Working Environment of Federal Correctional Officers and RCMP Officers*. Ottawa: Public Service Alliance of Canada, Treasury Board, and the Correctional Service of Canada.

Farkas, M.A. 1997. "The Normative Code among Correctional Officers: An Exploration of Components and Functions." *Journal of Crime and Justice* 20(1):23–36.

———. 2000. "A Typology of Correctional Officers." *International Journal of Offender Therapy and Comparative Criminology* 44(4):431–49.

Fitterman, L., and J. Gatehouse. 1998. "Biker Boss's Murder Trial Delayed—Another Hell's Angel-Turned-Witness Pleads Guilty in the Slaying of Prison Guard." *The Gazette (Montreal)* (March 20):A5.

Gittens, M. (Co-Chair), and D. Cole (Co-Chair). 1995. *Report of the Commission on Systemic Racism in the Ontario Criminal Justice System: A Community Summary*. Toronto: Queen's Printer for Ontario.

Grant, B. 1995. "The Impact of Working Rotating Shifts on the Family Life of Correctional Staff." *Forum on Corrections Research* 7(2):40–42.

Grossi, E.L., and B.L. Berg. 1991. "Stress and Job Dissatisfaction among Correctional Officers: An Unexpected Finding." *International Journal of Offender Therapy and Comparative Criminology* 35(1):73–81.

Harris, M. 2002. *Con Game: The Truth about Canada's Prisons*. Toronto: McClelland and Stewart.

Hemmens, C., and M.K. Stohr. 2000. "The Two Faces of the Correctional Role: An Exploration of the Value of the Correctional Role Instrument." *International Journal of Offender Therapy and Comparative Criminology* 44(3):326–49.

Hewitt, J.D., E.D. Poole, and R.M. Regoli. 1984. "Self-Reported and Observed Rule-Breaking in Prison: A Look at Disciplinary Response." *Justice Quarterly* 1(4):437–47.

Holden, R.W., L.W. Swenson, G.K. Jarvis, R.L. Campbell, D.R. Lagace, and B.J. Backs. 1995. "A Survey of Drinking Behaviors of Canadian Correctional Officers." *Psychological Reports* 76:651–55.

Hughes, G.V., and E. Zamble. 1993. "A Profile of Canadian Correctional Workers." *International Journal of Offender Therapy and Comparative Criminology* 37(2):99–113.

Johnson, R. 1996. *Hard Time: Understanding and Reforming the Prison*. Belmont, Calif.: Wadsworth.

Joint Committee on Federal Correctional Officers. 2000. *A Comparison of the Duties, Working Conditions and Compensation Levels of Federal Correctional Officers, Uniformed RCMP Officers and Selected Provincial Correctional Officers*. Ottawa: Public Service Alliance of Canada, Treasury Board Secretariat, and the Correctional Service of Canada.

Jurik, N.C. 1985. "Individual and Organizational Determinants of Correctional Officer Attitudes toward Inmates." *Criminology* 23(3):523–39.

Kauffman, K. 1988. *Prison Officers and Their World*. Cambridge, Mass.: Harvard University Press.

Lajeunesse, T., C. Jefferson, J. Nuffield, and D. Majury. 2000. *The Cross Gender Monitoring Project: Third and Final Report*. Ottawa: Correctional Service of Canada. Retrieved from www.csc-scc.gc.ca/text/prgrm/fsw/gender3/toc_e.shtml.

Larivière, M. 2002. "Antecedents and Outcomes of Correctional Officers' Attitudes toward Federal Inmates: An Exploration of Person–Organization Fit." *Forum on Corrections Research* 14(1):19–23.

Larivière, M., and D. Robinson. 1996. *Attitudes of Federal Correctional Officers Towards Offenders*. Ottawa: Research Division, Correctional Service of Canada.

Lawrence, R., and S. Mahan. 1998. "Women Corrections Officers in Men's Prisons: Acceptance and Perceived Job Performance." *Women and Criminal Justice* 9(3):63–86.

Lombardo, L.X. 1981. *Guards Imprisoned: Correctional Officers at Work*. New York: Elsevier.

Makin, K. 1996. "Inmates Fear Attacks; Drug Use Common." *The Globe and Mail* (June 7):A1, A5.

Millson, W. 2002. "Predictors of Work Stress among Correctional Officers." *Forum on Corrections Research* 14(1):45–47.

Morgan, R.D., R.A. Van Haveren, and C.A. Pearson. 2002. "Correctional Officer Burnout: Further Analyses." *Criminal Justice and Behavior* 29(2):144–60.

Plecas, D.B., and P.S. Maxim. 1987. *CSC Correctional Officer Development Study: Recruit Survey*. Ottawa: Correctional Service of Canada.

Price-Waterhouse. 1994. *CSC All Staff Survey: Final Report.* Ottawa: Correctional Service of Canada.

Robinson, D., F.J. Porporino, and L. Simourd. 1992. *Staff Commitment in the Correctional Service of Canada.* Research and Statistics Branch, Correctional Service of Canada.

Rosine, L. 1992. "Exposure to Critical Incidents: What Are the Effects on Canadian Correctional Officers?" *Forum on Corrections Research* 4(1):31–37.

———. 1995. "Critical Incident Stress and Its Management in Corrections." In T.A. Leis, L.L. Motiuk, and J.R.P. Ogloff (eds.), *Forensic Psychology: Policy and Practice in Corrections* (213–26). Ottawa: Correctional Service of Canada.

Rowan, J.R.. 1996. "Who Is Safer in Male Maximum Security Prisons?" *The Keepers' Voice.* Retrieved from www.acsp.uic.edu.

Solicitor General Canada. 1998. *CCRA 5-Year Review: Human Resources.* Ottawa.

Tellier, C., J.A. Mileto, C. Dowden, and B. Vuong. 2001. *Profile of Correctional Officer Recruits.* Ottawa: Research Branch, Correctional Service Canada.

Toch, H. 1978. "Is a 'Correctional Officer' by Any Other Name a 'Screw'?" *Criminal Justice Review* 3(2):19–35.

Tyler, T. 1998a. "Probe of Inmate's Death Puts Spotlight on Guards." *The Toronto Star* (May 3):A1.

———. 1998b. "Penitentiary Guard Couldn't See Who Restrained Inmate: Jury Told Officers Who Tell on Others at Risk, Lawyer Suggests." *The Toronto Star* (May 12):A6.

Venne, R.A. 1997. "The Impact of the Compressed Work Week on Absenteeism: The Case of Ontario Prison Guards on a Twelve-Hour Shift." *Industrial Relations* 52(2):382–400.

Weekes, J., G. Pelletier, and D. Beautette. 1995. "Correctional Officers: How Do They Perceive Sex Offenders?" *International Journal of Offender Therapy and Comparative Criminology* 39(1):55–61.

Whitehead, J.T., and C.A. Lindquist. 1989. "Determinants of Correctional Officers' Professional Orientation." *Justice Quarterly* 6(1):69–87.

Yates, J.M. 1993. *Line Screw: My Twelve Riotous Years Working Behind Bars in Some of Canada's Toughest Jails.* Toronto: McClelland and Stewart.

CHAPTER 7
DOING TIME: THE INMATES

CHAPTER OBJECTIVES

- *Discuss the experience of inmates entering and living inside correctional institutions.*
- *Discuss the inmate social system.*
- *Consider inmate strategies for coping with confinement.*
- *Discuss the patterns of violence and exploitation among inmates.*
- *Consider the issues surrounding the inmate family.*
- *Discuss inmate suicide.*

KEY TERMS

Mortification
Status degradation ceremonies
Pains of imprisonment
Inmate subculture
Deprivation theory
Importation theory
Prisonization
Institutionalized
Inmate code

Niches
Social (or argot) roles
Mature coping
Expressive violence
Instrumental violence
Passive precautions
Aggressive precautions
Private family visits

GOING INSIDE

I remember the day that I came in; the first time I went to the cafeteria and I could feel a hundred sets of eyes on me. I could see everybody wondering who you are, what you're in for, how long you're doing.

—lifer, cited in Murphy and Johnsen, 1997:41

Upon entering the prison, offenders undergo a process of **mortification,** during which they are transformed from free citizens into inmates (Goffman, 1961:18–20). This psychological and material stripping of the individual, which involves a series of **status degradation ceremonies,** includes the issuing of prison clothing, the assignment of an identification number, the loss of most personal possessions, and the end of unhindered communication with the outside community (Cloward, 1969). These procedures are the mechanism by which the offender is moved from residency in the community, with its attendant freedoms, to the world of the prison, with its rules, regulations, informal economy, and social system. As discussed in Chapter 5, prisons are *total institutions:* inmates are isolated from the community, and their activities are tightly scheduled and controlled 24 hours a day.

Unfortunately, although systems of corrections have perfected the mechanisms for transforming citizens into inmates, there are no *status restoration ceremonies* at the end of the inmate's confinement that would function to convert the inmate back into citizen. The consequences of this absence of mechanisms for reintegration will be explored in Chapter 10.

The specific impact that entry into the prison has on individual offenders will vary, depending on a variety of factors, including their personality, offence history, and previous incarcerations. While first-time offenders may experience severe cultural shock, offenders with extensive criminal histories and previous confinements are likely to be relatively unaffected. For these inmates, the process and procedures related to entry into the institution and confinement are well known, as are many of the correctional officers and inmates in the facility. Returning to the prison may be more of a homecoming than a banishment. For the uninitiated inmate, however, adjusting to the regimen of prison life can be a stressful and frightening experience. Although all incoming inmates are provided with copies of the institutional regulations and an orientation, each inmate is left to his or her own devices (and wits) to adjust to life inside and to develop strategies and techniques of coping and survival.

LIVING INSIDE

> *The cells are filthy. The walls are pocked with the carcasses of dead flies. During the day, the roaches visit, at night the mice. The door and door frames to the cells are solid steel, and every time they close, steel against steel, the sound is deafening. It seems as if there is a contest among the guards to determine who can make the doors bang loudest on closing. A constant reminder, if you need one, of where you are and the role you have to play.*
>
> —inmate's description of life in the reception centre at Millhaven Institution, cited in Ault, 1997:A14

The Pains of Imprisonment

> *Surely the inability to return home is punishment enough without locking people up in small cells, counting them at every move, restricting their movement and otherwise dehumanizing them. Those treated as untrustworthy can hardly learn to trust. Those treated as subhuman can hardly be expected to develop good habits of human conduct.*
>
> —Hamilton and Sinclair, 1991:432

A key concept in understanding the carceral experience is the **pains of imprisonment.** In his classic study of a maximum-security prison, presented in the book *Society of Captives*, Gresham Sykes (1958) identified a number of deprivations experienced by inmates. These include the loss of:

- liberty
- access to goods and services
- access to heterosexual relationships
- personal autonomy
- personal security

Of all of the pains of imprisonment, the loss of liberty is perhaps the most devastating for the majority of offenders, particularly in a society that places a high premium on the rights and freedoms of its citizens. In prison, inmates must find ways to cope with the loneliness, boredom, and hopelessness that are associated with the loss of freedom. Although federal and provincial/territorial systems of corrections operate family visiting programs, many inmates are not visited by anyone. An inmate may go for years without receiving a letter, much less a personal visit. The pains of imprisonment may be particularly acute for

Aboriginal and Inuit inmates, who are often incarcerated in institutions hundreds or even thousands of kilometres from their home communities.

It also appears that the pains of confinement may be much more severe for female offenders. This is due to a number of factors, including the fact that many federally sentenced women are housed in facilities that are far from their home communities; many inmates are mothers who have been separated from their children; and confinement can have a strong impact upon women who have experienced physical and emotional abuse during their childhood and adult years.

THE INMATE SOCIAL SYSTEM

Inmates are an insular minority vulnerable to oppression and discrimination, not only from the "outside" but from the strict rules and values of the inmate power structure and its own codes of silence and loyalty.

—John Howard Society of Alberta, 1992:3

A universal attribute of correctional institutions is the existence of an inmate social system, often referred to as the **inmate subculture.** Over the past 50 years, criminologists have attempted to determine the origins, components, and functions of the inmate social system, and these efforts have provided insights into prison life and the experience of incarceration.

From his study of life inside a maximum-security prison, Sykes (1958) concluded that the inmate social system developed as a result of inmates' attempts to mitigate the pains of imprisonment. Through participation in this social system, inmates could gain access to goods and services (albeit illicit), attain some measure of personal security and autonomy, and have access to consensual sexual relations. The social system also provided inmates with friendship networks, which assisted in reducing loneliness and boredom and created a sense of solidarity. By banding together, inmates could present a united front against correctional officers and the administration. This view came to be known as the **deprivation theory** of the inmate social system.

Several years later, the criminologists John Irwin and Donald Cressey (1962) proposed an alternative explanation—the **importation theory**—for the origins of the inmate social system. These observers argued that rather than being a response to the pains of imprisonment, the attitudes and behaviours that characterized the inmate social system were "imported" into the institution by offenders who had criminal careers on the outside. Research studies have found that both theories are useful in understanding the origins of the inmate social system.

In the classic work *The Prison Community*, Donald Clemmer (1940) used the term **prisonization** to describe the process by which inmates become socialized into the norms, values, and culture of the prison. This process includes becoming immersed in the inmate social system and adopting the behavioural tenets of the inmate code. Prisonization is not a uniform process, however. Those inmates with extensive carceral experiences are likely to already have developed antisocial, criminally oriented attitudes and behaviours. These offenders have considerable difficulty adapting to a law-abiding life in the community once released from a correctional institution. Prisonization also appears to be a function of the degree to which the inmate feels powerless and the extent to which the inmate relies on fellow inmates for information and support (Lawson, Segrin, and Ward, 1996). Offenders are said to be **institutionalized** when they have become prisonized to such a degree that they are unable to function in the outside, free community.

Inmates without an extensive criminal history or record of confinement may be highly susceptible to becoming prisonized, depending on their personality, the level of support they receive from family and friends while confined, and the length of their incarceration. The longer an inmate is confined, the more difficult it may be to retain prosocial attitudes and behaviours, particularly when the inmate is confined with offenders with more criminal orientations.

A major challenge confronting systems of correction is preventing offenders from becoming so immersed in the culture of the prison that staff's efforts to promote positive values and behaviours cannot be effective. There is also the challenge of how to "unprisonize" inmates as they move closer to their release date. This step would be part of a process of status restoration, which currently does not exist. Unfortunately, many of the attitudes and values that exist within the inmate social system are antithetical to those of the outside, law-abiding community.

The Inmate Code

A key component of the inmate social system is the **inmate code,** first identified over 40 years ago by Gresham Sykes and Sheldon Messinger (1960). The inmate code is a set of behavioural rules that govern interaction among the inmates and with institutional staff. The basic tenets of the code in its ideal form are outlined in Box 7.1.

It appears that the inmate code as a behavioural guideline for inmates has changed over the years. In a survey of inmates in several federal institutions, Cooley (1992) identified a set of informal rules of social control, which provide cohesion among inmates while also dividing them. The rule sets include the following:

- *Do your own time:* Don't rat on other inmates; stay out of other inmates' business (see Box 7.2).
- *Avoid the prison economy:* Avoid debt, which can result in psychological intimidation and victimization.
- *Don't trust anyone:* Don't offer information—the less other inmates know about you, the less likely you are to be snitched on.
- *Show respect:* Don't be a "goof"—don't act out, interrupt, or cause disruptions.

However, unlike the traditional inmate code, which was purported to increase inmate solidarity and provide a united oppositional front against correctional officers and the prison administration, each of these sets of informal

BOX 7.1

The Inmate Code

1. Don't interfere with inmate interests:
   - never rat on a con
   - don't be nosy
   - be loyal to your class—the cons

2. Don't lose your head:
   - play it cool and do your own time

3. Don't exploit inmates:
   - don't break your word
   - don't steal from cons
   - don't sell favors
   - don't be a racketeer
   - don't welch on debts

4. Don't weaken:
   - don't whine
   - don't cop out (or cry guilty)
   - don't suck around
   - be tough; be a man

5. Don't be a sucker:
   - don't accept the guards' view of the world
   - be sharp

Source: Welch, 1996:150.

BOX 7.2

"Do Your Own Time"

Thompson (2002:15–16) provides the following characterization of "do your own time," based on extensive correspondence with inmates in Canada and the United States:

> It means keep yourself separate from everything and everybody. Don't comment, interfere, or accept favours. Understand that you are "fresh meat" and need to learn the way of the joint. You have to deal with the "Vikings" (slobs, applied to both guards and cons), "booty bandits" (someone looking for ass to fuck), and the "boss," "hook," "grey suit," or "cookie" (all terms for prisons officials of various ranks) without "jeffing" (sucking up) to the staff. You have to deal with other cons who want you as a "punk" or a "fuck boy." Anybody can be carrying a "shank" [homemade knife] made out of a toothbrush and a razor blade or a piece of sharpened steel. Probably the more innocent someone looks, the more you have to worry.

A new arrival at Millhaven, a maximum-security federal correctional facility, received this advice from a fellow inmate:

> Drugs and alcohol are everywhere and I urge you to avoid that trip. Ninety percent of all killings revolve around the dope scene.... Don't accept anything from anyone, because you don't want to put yourself in a position where you'll have to repay the favor. Nothing is free.... It's in your best interest to avoid cliques. You'll be spending a lot of time on your own—it's much safer that way.... Don't encourage conversation with anyone. Be brief and polite.... Don't promise anyone anything.... Stay quiet and mind your own business. (cited in Dube, 2002:238–39)

rules can either increase cohesion among the inmate population or separate and divide them. For example, the rule that inmates should do their own time and not interfere with other inmates encourages stability and cohesion among inmates; on the other hand, it can isolate inmates from one another, as individuals attempt to avoid becoming involved in activities that may place them at risk of being victimized.

These informal rules of social control create institutional environments that are, in Cooley's words, "'partially unstable': the prison is neither in a constant state of turmoil nor in accord" (1992:34). Contributing to the lack of loyalty and solidarity among inmates is the rat (or snitch) system, by which inmates may improve their own position and prospects with correctional officers and the administration, often at the expense of fellow inmates. In the final analysis, the mere existence of an inmate code does not alter the fact that an inmate's greatest source of danger is other inmates.

Status and Power among Inmates

Although the days in which one inmate "boss" controlled an entire population in an institution are over, there is still a hierarchy of status and power among inmates. Some inmates wield considerable influence in the prison. High status is generally accorded to inmates who are serving life sentences, inmates who possess intelligence and are able to articulate the concerns and issues of the inmate population, and inmates whose pre-prison status and activities are well known and admired. Other inmates exercise power based on their ability to control illicit goods and services within the institution, including drugs and gambling, and on their sheer physical strength (Faulkner and Faulkner, 1997).

On the other hand, there are inmates who, because of their personality, offence, or lack of size, have little or no power and influence. Inmates confined for sexual offences, particularly against children, have low status in most institutional populations. The power and status an inmate has may be directly related to his or her risk of being victimized. In U.S. prisons, status and power are often associated with membership in prison gangs, which may be based on ethnicity or race. In Canada, membership in outlaw motorcycle gangs, such as the Hell's Angels and Rock Machine in federal prisons in Quebec, and in Aboriginal gangs in provincial institutions in the Prairie provinces, may provide the basis for status and power. As of November 1, 2001, 7.6 percent of federal inmates were members of criminal organizations, and there were 48 gangs or gang types—the most prevalent of which were bikers, Aboriginal criminal gangs, and street gangs—in federal institutions (Correctional Service of Canada, 2002:6, 7). Gang members and their associates are involved in a disproportionate number of disruptive incidents in many facilities (Saskatchewan Ombudsman, 2002).

A defining feature of life in contemporary correctional institutions is that inmates tend to group themselves into **niches,** or friendship networks. These networks may be based on associations formed during previous incarcerations or in the outside community; on shared ethnicity or culture; or on length of sentence (for example, lifers may group together). It is this friendship group, rather than the inmate population as a whole, that provides the individual inmate with security and support and that is the recipient of the inmate's loyalty. These groups create an inmate population that is characterized by pluralism, rather than uniformity of thought and action.

Inmate Social Roles

There are a number of **social (or argot) roles** that are associated with the inmate social system. These roles are based on the inmate's friendship networks, sentence length, current and previous offences, degree of at least verbal support to the inmate code, and participation in illegal activities such as gambling and drug distribution. Though the specific names may vary, several of the more common roles include the following:

- *square-john:* exhibits prosocial attitudes and behaviours; not involved in the inmate social system; positive toward staff and administration
- *right guy:* antisocial; heavily involved in the inmate social system; opposed to staff and administration
- *rat* (also known as *squealers* or *snitches*): provides information on inmates, illegal activities, and plans to correctional officers; despised by inmates; at high risk of physical injury if detected; may be placed in protective custody for safety
- *tough* (also known as *outlaws*): violent, aggressive, and often unpredictable; willing to use violence to intimidate and secure goods and services; often feared by both inmates and correctional officers; disruptive to the daily routine of the institution and to the accommodative relationships that exist between correctional officers and inmates
- *wolf, fag, and punk:* sexual roles in the prison—the wolf actively seeks out other inmates to have sexual relations with; the fag voluntarily assumes a passive role in sexual relations; and the punk is coerced or bribed into a passive role in sexual encounters
- *merchant* (also known as a *peddler*): extensively involved in importing and distributing contraband, including drugs and money; prospers at the expense of other inmates (Welch, 1996:150)

That these types of roles exist among inmate populations provides strong evidence that the inmate code is not the defining feature of inmate behaviour. In fact, inmate relations are characterized by considerable intimidation, fear, violence, and manipulation, depending on the particular correctional institution and the offenders housed in it.

A related feature of inmate society is a specialized vocabulary. Examples of prison slang—a constantly changing vocabulary—are provided in Box 7.3.

BOX 7.3

The Inmate Vocabulary

Term	Meaning
beef	type of crime (e.g., murder beef, sex beef)
bit	sentence (e.g., five-year bit)
book	life sentence (e.g., doing book)
bug juice	any drug used to calm an inmate
bugs	inmates others see as annoying or crazy
date	sentence warrant expiry date
deuce less	sentence of less than two years
fish	new inmate
goof	inmate who acts inappropriately
hole	segregation unit (generally 23-hour lockup)
house	prison cell
kite	illegal letter or note
piped	hit on the head with a metal pipe
rats	informers
shakedown	the searching of an area within the prison
shank	homemade knife
short	inmate who is close to release
skinner	sex offender
waterhead	see *goof*
yard	recreation area

Sources: Murphy and Johnsen, 1997:xvii–xix; National Parole Board, n.d.

Parting Thoughts on the Inmate Social System

The early research on inmate social systems provided invaluable insights into the dynamics of life inside correctional institutions. The question is to what extent the findings from these studies apply to the modern prison and, more specifically, to Canadian correctional institutions. Although the absence of Canadian research limits our ability to answer this question conclusively, we can update the discussion on inmate social systems by piecing together the findings of Canadian and U.S. studies. Unfortunately, the lack of research on life inside correctional institutions for women makes it difficult to include more than passing comment on this important area of Canadian corrections.

Although contemporary prisons share many features of their earlier counterparts and are total institutions, in many respects the contemporary prison is less "total" than its predecessors. Increasingly, prison administrators and correctional staff are being held accountable to the rule of law, and inmates have recourse through grievance procedures and the courts for perceived injustices. The living conditions of inmates have improved dramatically. New regional facilities have been constructed for federal female offenders; facilities incorporating elements of Aboriginal culture and spirituality have been established for Aboriginal offenders; and new architectural designs allow inmates to live in apartment-like residences in several minimum- and medium-security facilities.

It is likely that inmate social systems are the most highly developed in federal correctional facilities, which house offenders with more extensive criminal records for longer periods. The relatively rapid turnover of inmates in provincial/territorial institutions would seem to mitigate against the development of an inmate social system. On the other hand, many provincial/territorial inmates have been incarcerated on previous occasions and may be well schooled in the various facets of doing time. There have been no studies of inmate social systems in provincial/territorial facilities to date. While it can be assumed that some type of social system exists among the inmates, the specific forms that these systems take, the extent to which there is an inmate code, and whether social roles exist have yet to be determined.

Despite the improvement in correctional institutions, incarceration is still a painful experience. The pains of imprisonment ensure that the inmate social system will remain a key feature of institutional life. That said, it is important not to mythologize "the good old days" in prisons. It is unlikely that inmates ever constituted a united front against the guards and administration. Certainly, institutional life during these times was not free from violence and exploitation among inmates and not all inmates had equal power and status.

COPING WITH CONFINEMENT

Few are so fearless and beyond pain that they are incapable of experiencing uncertainty, fear, and a sense that they are in a deplorable situation. Nevertheless, such normal feelings can never be openly expressed.

—Terry, 1997:38

While incarcerated, inmates spend considerable energy attempting to reduce the pains of imprisonment. Inmates often become involved in obtaining, distributing, and/or using illicit goods and services, including drugs and other contraband. Consensual sexual relationships may also be entered into. Participation in the underground economy is not without risk. Inmates who incur gambling debts, for example, may be in jeopardy of being physically harmed or may be pressured to have family members smuggle drugs and contraband into the prison. To protect themselves, these inmates may have to request placement in a protective custody unit, where their freedom of movement within the institution and access to programs are severely curtailed.

Drugs and Contraband

Illicit drugs and alcohol are the central driving force in the lives of inmates: they not only supply ways of escaping the deadening routine of doing time but also confer currency, collateral, and power on their dealers. Just as on the street, substance abuse in prison leads to violence and further crime.

—Harris, 2002:185

In most federal and provincial/territorial correctional facilities, drugs are as freely available as they are on the street. Inmates use drugs or alcohol to cope with their environment, to forget their problems, or just to relax (Chubaty, 2002; Plourde, 2002). Many offenders become addicted to drugs while in confinement.

The smuggling networks are extensive and sophisticated. Organized gangs play a major role in the importation and distribution of drugs, particularly in federal institutions. As the warden of Fenbrook, a federal medium-security institution in Ontario, observed: "Biker gangs actually compete with one another to see who will get a prison's business. I would guess that 40 percent of our population uses drugs, maybe more. Eighty percent of the drugs come in the front door and 20 percent through the back door" (cited in Harris, 2002:67–68). Drug distribution and usage are commonly associated with intimidation, extortion, and staff corruption. In addition, violence and victimization among inmates is often the result of non-payment for illicit drugs.

At first glance, the problem of illicit drugs and contraband inside prisons might be surprising, given the strict regimen of correctional institutions, the various static and dynamic security arrangements, and drug interdiction strategies. (These include non-intrusive searches of all visitors, metal detectors, ion scanners, drug-sniffing dogs, cell searches, physical searches of inmates, and, at the federal level, a national random urinalysis program that tests the urine samples of 5 percent of the inmate population each month.) In reality, however, it is virtually impossible for correctional staff to adequately monitor or eliminate the flow of drugs and contraband. More than 40 percent of federal inmates in a recent survey indicated that they had used drugs since arriving in the institution. Within a one-year period, 15 percent of the inmates in one federal correctional facility were hospitalized after ingesting alcohol or drugs (Harris, 2002:186). There is some evidence to suggest that correctional officers are more tolerant of "soft" drugs than of alcohol or hard drugs (Plourde, 2002).

The widespread availability of drugs and contraband is due, in some measure, to the fact that prisons are not as "total" as in previous decades. Inmates have extensive contact with outside visitors, the number of offenders who leave institutions on temporary absences and day paroles has increased, and inmate labour is used in a variety of non-institutional settings, including community service and firefighting. While alcohol is generally brewed on the premises, illicit drugs flow into prison through several channels, including (1) family members (including children) and friends on visiting days, (2) inmate work crews that were deployed to various areas outside the institution, and (3) drop-offs on prison property by family members or friends. The most common way that drugs are moved into institutions is through rectal or vaginal insertions.

In Box 7.4, a correctional officer at a provincial facility in Manitoba describes how drugs were moved into the prison, transferred to an inmate, and taken into the living unit. In this case, a family member had placed the contraband in a condom and inserted it into a body cavity on visiting day and then removed it in the washroom in the visitors' area. The description picks up at that point.

Sexual Gratification

Inmates also attempt to cope with the deprivation of heterosexual relationships and to secure sexual gratification. Masturbation and consensual sexual relations with another inmate are the two most common types of sexual activity in correctional institutions. Consensual sex, while technically homosexual, is an adaptation to a unique circumstance and inmates revert to het-

BOX 7.4

Condoms, Coke Machines, and Contraband

One of the tricks they used—we have a Coke machine in there, did at that time, a pop machine. A girl would go up and buy a drink. She would put the money in and she would deposit the drugs in the little opening where the pop would come out. She'd put the condom of drugs in there. She'd buy a drink, take the drink and leave. The person who was now going to get the drugs, it's usually a kid, first timer, we'd never suspect he was a drug carrier. He would go and buy a drink, along with the condom of drugs and he'd take them back to the location. He would do that for fear of being badly beaten if he didn't agree to it....

The only people really chosen at random for a strip search at the end of visiting are known drug users, guys who are really bad characters, guys who are giving staff a lot of problems. We would strip search them. A young kid, that's the first time into the building, that's the guy the inmates would get to carry their drugs back, because we wouldn't suspect him.... He would insert the drugs in his rectum. Quite often we'd search and we'd find the rear of their pants would be sliced and their underwear would be sliced and they would be sitting right at the table. As rude and crude as that sounds, that's the culture we're dealing with. And this may be a well educated, blond hair, blue eyed kid. But he was going to do it or he was going to get a terrible licking when he got back to his range. So, he took the risk and did it.

Source: Hughes, 1996:49.

erosexual sexual activity upon release. Little is known about how gay inmates adapt to confinement and how their attempts at sexual gratification are viewed and responded to by heterosexual inmates. A less common means of sexual release, which is also a manifestation of power and control in the inmate social system, is the rape of an inmate victim; this will be discussed in greater detail below.

Humour

Another way in which inmates cope with the deprivations of confinement is through humour, an under-researched feature of doing time. Inmates often relate to fellow inmates sad tales about their experience with the justice system, particularly the sentence they received, in a humorous way. Inmates also often mock the rules and regimen of the prison in subtle and not so subtle ways. Following is a researcher's description of "insubordinate farting" by inmates in a jail:

> *A standing rule exists stating all inmates must be silent until count is cleared. Violation of this requirement can result in a loss of privileges for all inmates, regardless of who breaks the rule. During count the men sit or lie on their three-tier high bunks in silence while a guard walks up and down the dorm counting the bodies on the beds. With an expression that can be seen as nothing less than defiance, inmates will, once the guard has passed their bed area and is a safe enough distance away to insure their anonymity, fart loudly. The resulting laughter obviously mocks the guard. It also, in a safe way, attacks the system, or, in this case, the people responsible for creating the rule that all must be silent during count. It also allows the inmates to break the rules and reaffirm, at least for themselves, their own power. (Terry, 1997:32)*

Mature Coping

> *One of the ironies of prison is that the thing you lose is the very thing you gain. I am talking about time. Time in prison is different from time in the outside world. In the outside world time is a flash flood, a whirling blur of forces and temptations and choices and consequences. In prison, time stops. Maybe that is part of the idea—that you suddenly have time to face who you are.*

> —Hubbell, 1997:2

Although there are many opportunities to participate in illegal activities during their confinement, inmates may choose to mitigate the pains of imprisonment through more constructive means. **Mature coping** is a positive approach to adapting to life inside.

There are three components of mature coping that inmates must learn:

- dealing with problems in a straightforward way rather than engaging in denial and manipulation
- avoiding the use of deception and violence in addressing problems
- making an effort to care for oneself and others—being altruistic (Johnson, 1996)

Inmates engage in mature coping when they take a proactive approach toward problems, plan specific courses of action, and abstain from reacting to events until carefully considering the nature of the problem. Through positive coping actions, inmates develop self-esteem and maturity, learn to manage failure, and use the incarceration experience for positive growth. Positive coping, in turn, increases the likelihood that the inmate will benefit from participation in rehabilitation programs and be successful upon release from the institution.

There are obstacles to the practice of mature coping. First, the ability of individual inmates to fulfill the behavioural requirements of mature coping may be seriously affected by the regimen and dynamics of prison life. In many respects, the features of the prison as a total institution are antithetical to inmates taking responsibility for their actions and exercising independent judgment. Inmates who lack power and status in the inmate social system are hardly in a position to be altruistic, lest they become even more vulnerable to victimization.

Second, it is difficult to predict how individual offenders will respond to confinement and how the various dynamics of life inside correctional institutions interact with personal attributes of the inmate to determine the strategies he or she will adopt to survive the carceral experience. Needless to say, if inmates are required to expend considerable energy on developing strategies to survive in the prison and to cope with the pains of imprisonment, their receptiveness to programs designed to promote prosocial values and behaviours may be limited.

Finally, there are the abilities of individual inmates. As noted in Chapter 1, many people confined in correctional institutions are marginal in terms of their backgrounds, skill levels, and offence histories. A history of substance abuse, exposure to physical and emotional abuse as children, mental illness, and a long history of confinement in youth and adult facilities may diminish the inmate's ability to adopt mature coping as a response to incarceration and to benefit from treatment intervention. For self-change to occur, an inmate must not only be committed to altering attitudes, values, and behaviours, but must also have the capacity to pursue such a course of action (more on this in the discussion of correctional treatment in Chapter 8).

DOING LIFE

Picture yourself falling into a tunnel, totally dark, and it's going to take you twenty-five years to walk out ... one step at a time.

—lifer, cited in Murphy and Johnsen, 1997:43

As noted in Chapter 3, Canada abolished the death penalty in 1976 and replaced it with mandatory penalties of long-term confinement. That change has resulted in an increasing number of inmates serving minimum sentences of 10 to 25 years before becoming eligible for a parole hearing. Concerns have been raised about the morality and effectiveness of long-term sentences.

Coping with Long-Term Confinement

As one lifer interviewed by Murphy and Johnsen (1997:30) observed:

> *I've been in for two and a half years, just about going on three years. Seems like forever already. It's hard to remember what it's like out there. So many things can happen in three years. It's a terrible transition period; it's a terrible thing to go through. Especially when you don't see a light at the end of the tunnel anywhere. You're just stuck here and you're herded into your cell every few hours for a count. You feel like cattle. You get a feeling like you're helpless. Herd you in, lock the door. They count you like diamonds and treat you like shit.*

Long-term sentences present challenges not only for systems of corrections in terms of housing and programming, but also for the individual inmate. How lifers cope with confinement and their views on doing long sentences are important because one day nearly all will be released back into the community. The Correctional Service of Canada (CSC) operates a program called Life Line In-Reach, which is designed to assist lifers in effectively managing their time and program opportunities during confinement and to assist them in preparing for judicial review and/or release on parole (more on this in Chapter 10).

Despite the commonality of sentence length, there are considerable differences among long-term offenders in terms of their attitudes and how they adjust to confinement. These differences are reflected in a survey of long-term federal offenders, which found the following:

- Life-sentence offenders are at a high risk to commit suicide or homicide.
- The extent of a prior criminal career is the most significant predictor of how an offender will adjust to confinement.
- First-term lifers are at greater risk of being victimized during the early years of their confinement, rather than later in their sentence, when they avoid conflict and confrontations and "do their own time." (Porporino, 1991)

Aside from losing their freedom, the loss of relationships and contact with family, friends, and children is perhaps the most serious pain of imprisonment for the long-term offender. Whereas some inmates cope with this deprivation by severing all ties with family members, others attempt to maintain contact, which may inadvertently add to their frustration and anxiety. Realistically, it is highly unlikely that most long-term offenders will be able to sustain their pre-prison relationships, particularly if relations with a spouse and/or children were unstable. As one lifer stated, "If I come out at fifty-six, as a thirty-one-year old, after twenty-five years in prison, I'll be the same mental age as my children. How do you deal with that?" (cited in Murphy and Johnsen, 1997:79).

The loss of family is a primary catalyst for the bonds that develop between inmates doing life. In the words of one lifer, "Once you get over the initial hurdle of being separated from your family ... the lifers become your comrades. They become the guys you really become close to. I've got twenty years in, so I really don't feel that close to the short-timers that are coming in, because they're just like shadows" (cited in Murphy and Johnsen, 1997:197).

The Impact of Long-Term Confinement

Despite these pains of imprisonment, there is no empirical evidence that long-term confinement leads to mental and physical deterioration in inmates or to an impairment in coping abilities. More specifically, the duration of confinement is unrelated to changes in attitude or personality among inmates, to feelings of bitterness and demoralization, or to a loss of perceptual-motor or cognitive functioning (Paulus and Dzindolet, 1992; Zamble and Porporino, 1988). Over time, most inmates appear to adapt to confinement by becoming involved in work, sports, and other activities. These findings, while not conclusive (many of the studies did not consider the age of the inmate or prior prison experiences), are nevertheless quite surprising given the many negative features of life inside correctional institutions.

It is important to note, however, that though long-term confinement may not produce the predicted negative impacts on inmates, neither does it promote positive changes. Although most inmates appear to ultimately adjust to life in prison, this may make it more difficult for them to survive in the outside, free community upon release.

PRISON AS "HOME": THE STATE-RAISED OFFENDER

There are offenders who have spent the majority of their youth and adult lives confined in correctional institutions. These state-raised offenders have experienced only limited periods of freedom in the community and may have neither the social skills nor the ability to function outside the total institutional world of the prison. Many have become institutionalized and are frightened by the prospect of having to cope with the fast pace of modern life. For the state-raised offender, the prison provides security, friends, room and board, and a predictable routine, none of which is guaranteed in the outside community. The prison, rather than the community, is home.

You will recall from the discussion of the effectiveness of incarceration in Chapter 3 that some inmates preferred prison over probation. Further analysis of these data revealed that the attributes of the inmate were related to how he or she viewed prison and probation. Those offenders who had few ties to the community and those who were older, unmarried, and "in the life" had little to lose from confinement. For these offenders, prison provided a structured environment with routine, predictability, and friendships. Offenders who pre-ferred probation over prison, on the other hand, were more highly educated and had family and friendships in the community that would be severely dis-rupted by confinement. In short, these offenders had a stake in the outside, free community and, therefore, had more to lose by being sent to prison (Crouch, 1993). These same variables may also be related to the success or failure of inmates in the community following release from a correctional institution (more on this in Chapter 10).

VIOLENCE AND EXPLOITATION AMONG INMATES

Male inmates in Canadian federal institutions have a higher likelihood of being murdered than males in the outside, free community. This risk, along with violence in institutions generally, has increased in recent years. Toughness is a central feature of inmate identity, and inmates may use extreme violence for self-protection, to achieve and maintain power and status, and to retaliate against snitches. An inmate in the Don Jail, a provincial facility in Toronto, stated: "It's always scary and you fear for your life. But the scarier part after awhile is, you get used to what goes on. You get desensitized and don't know any other way of living" (cited in Shephard, 1997:F1). Although there are instances in which correctional officers are the source of brutality inflicted on inmates, other inmates present the greatest danger to inmates' safety. Weak and vulnerable inmates may be coerced to provide sexual services, to pay money or goods for protection, to repay loans or favours at high interest, or to persuade family members to bring drugs into the institution.

For inmates in many correctional institutions, the potential for violence and exploitation is a fact of daily life. In contrast to the physical aggression that characterizes life inside institutions for male offenders, in women's facilities such aggression appears to be more indirect and to take the form of verbal bullying, threats, ostracism, intimidation, and gossip (Ireland and Archer, 1996). One Canadian study found that offenders who grew up in highly dysfunctional families tended to be more disruptive in prison and to receive a higher number of charges for assaultive behaviour (Chubaty, 2002).

Violence between inmates in institutions can be categorized as **expressive violence** or **instrumental violence.** Expressive violence is neither planned by the perpetrator nor deliberate. Rather, it is a result of specific problems that the inmate initiator is experiencing (including stress), problems in adjusting to life in the institution, and difficulties in anger management. Instrumental violence, on the other hand, is used by the perpetrator as a means to an end. The motive of the aggressor is to gain or maintain status or to intimidate other inmates in order to secure illicit goods and services (Leschied, Cunningham, and Mazaheri, 1997).

The level of violence in individual correctional institutions is a function of many factors, including conditions in the institution, the actions of correctional officers and administrators, overcrowding, and competition between inmate gangs for turf. Violence can erupt over what, in the outside community, would be a nonissue. An inmate in the Don Jail recalled watching one inmate beat another inmate to within an inch of his life over who owned a slice of toast. Prescriptions for avoiding violence include never looking at—let alone touching—other people's possessions, never whistling, never reaching over anybody's food, and never talking too much. Even making eye contact with another inmate can be dangerous, as it may signal either a sexual advance or a challenge to the power and status of an inmate (Shephard, 1997:F1).

Many inmates live in constant fear for their safety. Among the more fearful are young inmates and those who do not have strong friendship networks. Given the patterns of violence in prison, this fear is most likely justified. An examination of homicides in federal institutions revealed that victims tended to be relatively young, to have a history of violence, and to be killed by multiple assailants either out of revenge or because of drug-related matters (Porporino, Doherty, and Sawatsky, 1987).

Patterns of Victimization

It is difficult to determine the actual incidence and patterns of prison victimization. In its 2001–02 annual report, the federal Correctional Investigator (2002) noted that the CSC gathers only limited information on institutional violence and inmate injuries. A survey of Canadian inmates found that one-third of those surveyed had been threatened with assault, one-fifth had been assaulted, and a small group had been repeatedly threatened or physically assaulted (Chubaty, 2002). In actuality, it is a relatively small percentage of any inmate population that is a threat to others: "Inmates who tyrannize other inmates may benefit from violent and chaotic conditions within prisons, but the vast majority of inmates suffer terribly from such conditions. Their goal is not to instigate trouble, but rather to survive it" (Kauffman, 1988:264).

Perhaps the greatest threat to the ability of correctional institutions to effectively punish criminal offenders is the inability of correctional staff to guarantee the safety of inmates. It also undermines the legitimacy of the state to punish offenders. One inmate stated to C.T. Griffiths, "If the state has the right to punish me if I get caught violating the law, then they also have a responsibility to ensure that I serve my punishment safely. I did the crime, I'll do the time. But the state does not have the right to inflict additional punishment on me by failing to protect me while I am incarcerated."

Not all inmates, however, are at equal risk of being victimized. The degree to which an inmate is vulnerable to attack and exploitation by other inmates depends in large measure on his or her status, power, and friendship network. A study of several U.S. prisons found that "those inmates who suffered most within the prison at the hands of fellow inmates were often the meekest and least violent among them, and those who had committed the least serious offences outside the prison" (Kauffman, 1988).

Sexual Coercion and Rape

Sexual coercion and rape are two brutal realities of prison life, yet there is very little information on the perpetrators and victims of this type of violence or its prevalence in Canadian institutions. The reluctance of inmate victims to report victimization, combined with the assumption by many correctional observers that most inmate sexual activity is consensual, has hindered an understanding of this very important area of institutional corrections. More attention has been given to this topic in the United States (visit, for example, the website of Stop Prisoner Rape at www.spr.org). A study of sexual coercion in several U.S. prisons found that (1) of the inmates surveyed, 20 percent reported being the targets of sexual coercion, and (2) there was a high incidence of depression and suicidal thoughts among the inmate victims (Struckman-Johnson et al., 1996).

Perpetrators use a variety of tactics in cases of sexual coercion, including inflicting physical harm or threatening violence, intimidating the target with physical size and strength, and using persuasion. An inmate may also be successful in taking another inmate as his "punk," an exploitative relationship that, nevertheless, provides a measure of security and protection for the weaker inmate. Depending on the circumstances of the incident, such as whether there are multiple perpetrators, the target can often prevent the attack by avoiding the perpetrators, consistently refusing, using defensive threats, or fighting:

> *He was always winking, blowing kisses and always trying to talk me into letting him give me a blow job. Until one day when he grabbed ahold of my penis and said I want you. Up until then I let it ride but after dinner that night I caught him by the tennis court where no guards could be and I smiled and said so you want me and when he said yes I plant my foot upside his jaw and left him laying on the ground and that put an end to it. (cited in Struckman-Johnson et al., 1996:73)*

Such tactics of resistance, however, may not work if the target inmate is vulnerable to attack, for example, because of physical weakness or lack of a protective friendship group. There are, however, a number of factors that mitigate against inmates sexually assaulting even weaker inmates in the prison, including being investigated by prison authorities, the threat of disciplinary sanctions, and potential criminal and civil charges.

Inmate Strategies for Avoiding Violence and Victimization

Because institutional staff cannot guarantee an inmate's safety, inmates use a variety of strategies or avoidance behaviours to reduce the risk of violence and victimization. These strategies can be grouped into **passive precautions** and **aggressive precautions**. Passive precautions, which tend to be used by older, socially isolated inmates who are serving longer periods of confinement and who have been victimized in the past, include keeping to oneself; avoiding certain areas of the institution where there is a high risk of attack, such as the dining hall, recreation areas, and the yard; and spending more time in one's cell. Aggressive precautions tend to be adopted by younger inmates and include developing a tough attitude, lifting weights, and keeping a weapon (McCorkle, 1992a; 1992b). See Figure 7.1.

INMATES AS PARTNERS AND PARENTS

Discussions of corrections often overlook the fact that many inmates are fathers, mothers, and spouses (Foran, 1995). Little attention has been given to the dynamics and needs of the inmate family, both during the inmate's confinement and following release. This is somewhat surprising, since nearly half of the offenders in confinement are married at the time of admission and the majority have children or stepchildren. Further, inmate mothers are likely to be the sole caregiver for their children.

Figure 7.1

Precautionary Behaviours among Inmates

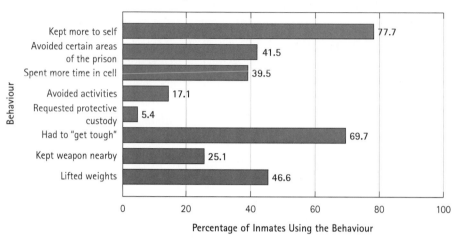

Source: McCorkle, 1992a:10.

Among the primary concerns for families of incarcerated men are:

- money
- raising children alone
- general loneliness
- fears related to release from prison
- housing
- hostility from friends
- isolation from the community
- fears related to treatment while incarcerated (Carr, 1995:31)

Systems of correction have generally not been designed to consider the needs of inmate families, who often feel isolated and neglected by correctional authorities. One family member describes the system as "unresponsive to requests for information, unconcerned about dirty washrooms and gum stuck to the floor, indifferent to worn-out furniture in private family visitation areas, intolerant of criticism and likely to take out anger against a complaining family member on the offender" (Carr, 1995:31).

For the inmate, the loss of regular family contact is one of the pains of imprisonment. An offender incarcerated for a white-collar crime describes this difficulty:

I was fortunate to have a strong family and loving wife that stayed with
me. I also have a good education and the belief in myself that I have a

future. My situation was unique. I constantly received mail from friends, talked to friends on the phone, and enjoyed their frequent visits. I was so lucky to have friends who still cared about me and my family and who allowed me to vent through the many days of intense loneliness and frustration. Most who enter prison lose their family, have no education, and ... cannot see a future. They receive no mail, no visits, and have no one to call. Time crawls in an atmosphere of little hope. (Hubbell, 1997:6)

A number of factors hinder efforts to maintain and strengthen the family ties of incarcerated offenders, including:

- the obstacles imposed by distance: even with the regional facilities, many federally sentenced women are far from their families and children, while women housed in provincial facilities may be better able to maintain close contact with their children
- the constraints imposed by long-term sentences: maintaining family ties is virtually impossible for offenders serving 10- or 25-year terms

A key resource and source of support for the families of offenders is the Canadian Families and Corrections Network, profiled in Box 7.5. The CSC offers the Parenting Skills Training Program as one of the six programs that

BOX 7.5

Canadian Families and Corrections Network

The Canadian Families and Corrections Network is an organization of citizens, volunteer groups, private agencies, inmate committees, and correctional officials. Its primary objective is to empower and strengthen inmate families through information sharing and the development of appropriate policies and programs that strengthen inmate families. Illustrative of the efforts of network members is Bridge House, located in Kingston, Ontario, which is a residence for out-of-town families visiting an incarcerated family member; the Women in the Shadows program in Fredericton, New Brunswick, which involves weekly meetings of inmate spouses; and the Relink program operated by the Salvation Army in Ottawa, which provides information and assistance to inmate families.

Source: Carr, 1995.

compose the living skills program series. Federal and provincial/territorial systems of correction also offer a number of programs to assist inmate mothers.

The Dynamics of Inmate Families

Many inmates lack parenting skills that would assist them in developing and sustaining positive relationships with their spouses and children while incarcerated. This lack of skills is a consequence of being raised in dysfunctional family environments characterized by poverty and violence, living in foster homes, or spending lengthy periods of time in youth correctional facilities.

There are also high levels of sexual, physical, and psychological abuse in many inmate families. The rates are particularly high in the families of Aboriginal inmates. Women partners are most frequently the victims of this violence and abuse, with children being victimized much less frequently (Robinson, 1995). The majority of inmates who are violent toward family members were abused themselves as children; this relationship is illustrated in Figure 7.2.

Children whose parents are incarcerated can suffer from emotional, behavioural, and academic problems, the type and severity of which vary according to the child's age, length of separation from parents, and, in some instances, gender (Caddle and Crisp, 1997; Gabel, 1995). The symptoms can

Figure 7.2

The Relationship between Childhood Victimization and Perpetration of Family Violence among Federal Inmates

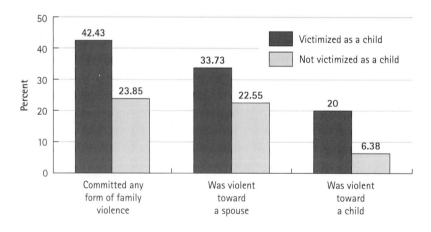

Source: Robinson, 1995:17.

mirror those evidenced by children who have experienced the death of a parent. The children of inmates may also feel responsible for their parents' incarceration, be embarrassed among their peers, and worry that they may be sent to prison one day.

Female Inmates and Their Children

> *The only thing that kept me going was the thought that I was going to see my kids again. I missed them so much I couldn't even talk about them. I almost didn't get parole because they thought I might have been mentally unstable. I felt so desperate, I might have suicided if someone had told me they were gone forever.*

> —female inmate, cited in Wine, 1992:69

Approximately 75 percent of the women in federal and provincial/territorial institutions have children. Although many male inmates are parents, their children will almost always be cared for by the other parent. Women are somewhat more likely than men to have children and are far more likely to be the sole custodial parent of their children. Accordingly, when women are incarcerated, their children are usually cared for by relatives, most commonly grandparents. When no surrogate caretaker is available, the children may be apprehended by provincial/territorial child welfare authorities and placed in foster care. If the period of incarceration is lengthy and the children are young, they may be candidates for adoption. Because of these factors, the incarceration of a female parent typically results in greater disruption in the lives of children than is the case if a father is incarcerated.

There are varying levels of in-person contact, ranging from contact visits and overnight family visits, to on-site part-time residency, to the on-site full-time residency that is a defining feature of mother–child programs (discussed below). **Private family visits** are generally available only in federal facilities. These visits, which allow the spouse and family members to spend up to 72 hours in a trailer unit or small house on prison grounds, provide the opportunity for more normal parent–child interaction than is possible on a four-hour day visit.

Mother–child programs generally allow infants to reside with their mothers in open living units for a period of up to two years. The first Canadian mother–child programs were developed in provincial institutions in British Columbia and Manitoba. The regional correctional institutions that were constructed for federally sentenced women include bedrooms for children. There are, for example, ten bedrooms at Grand Valley Institution in

Kitchener, Ontario, and the Okimaw Ohci Healing Lodge for Aboriginal women in Saskatchewan can accommodate eight to ten children, up to the age of four. A daycare was also built at the healing lodge.

Mother–child programs can involve regular part-time visits, such as on weekends, or full-time residency in the institution, which is generally available only for preschool-aged children. To be eligible to participate in the program, an inmate mother must have a positive relationship with her child or be able to demonstrate that such a relationship is possible. The determining factor in deciding whether an inmate mother can participate in the program is the best interests of the child. Despite support for mother–child programs by the CSC and various provincial/territorial correctional systems, implementation has been slow and uneven across the country. In some instances, overcrowding has resulted in female offenders being housed in space originally designated for the mother–child program.

Although mother–child programs are a core component of female offender policy at the federal level and in many provincial/territorial correctional systems, there is controversy surrounding them. Check out the following At Issue.

AT ISSUE

INMATE MOTHER–CHILD PROGRAMS: IN WHOSE BEST INTERESTS?

The development of mother–child programs in federal and provincial/territorial correctional institutions attempts to address one of the most critical issues facing women in prison. These programs, however, have also been criticized.

Proponents of mother–child programs in correctional institutions contend:
- The programs create or strengthen the bonds between mothers and their children.
- Mothers have the opportunity to provide early childhood nurturing.
- The programs allow closer monitoring of the health and safety of children than would be possible in the community.
- Inmate mothers have the chance to learn parenting skills.
- Inmate mothers are more likely to maintain family ties upon release.
- The programs assist inmates in developing prosocial attitudes and behaviours.

Opponents of mother–child programs counter that:
- The prison environment, with its attendant illicit activities such as drug use, is no place for young children.

- Inmate mothers should address their own problem behaviour before becoming involved in childcare.
- Young children who reside in correctional institutions are stigmatized.
- The prison is an artificial environment that bears little resemblance to the outside community to which the inmate mother and her child will ultimately have to adjust.
- It is unfair and disruptive to children to place them in a correctional facility, only to remove them at a later date if the inmate mother is serving a lengthy sentence.
- Mother–child programs are discriminatory toward inmate fathers, who are not allowed similar access to their children.

THE RESEARCH EVIDENCE

To date, there have been no published studies on mother–child programs in Canadian correctional institutions; thus, it is impossible to determine whether the arguments made by proponents of these programs are valid or whether the concerns of critics are justified. It is unknown, for example, what impact living in a correctional institution has on children; whether programs strengthen mother–child bonds; and whether women who participate in these programs have higher rates of success upon release. Further, and importantly, there have been no studies that have examined these programs from the perspective of the children.

QUESTIONS

1. In your opinion, should criminal court judges consider whether a female offender has children in determining whether a period of incarceration is imposed? Why or why not?
2. Are you generally supportive of mother–child programs in correctional institutions? Why or why not?
3. What would be your position if it were proposed that father–child programs be developed in correctional institutions?

Sources: Teather, Evans, and Sims, 1997; Watson, 1995.

THE CARCERAL EXPERIENCE: IN THE WORDS OF INMATES

It is a cold, dark, gloomy place. It has the stink of tobacco, the foul smell of body odour at night, and the smell that you find in a basement filled with dust and cobwebs. In prison, existence is slow, tense, and gloomy, and everybody feels everything intensely, and yet these things are small, meaningless and often trivial. You wouldn't believe how many fights I've seen in a meal line and often just because one person accidentally bumped into another. Why is that? Well, our past is dead and gone, our future is non-existent and the present is all we have, causing great pain.

—inmate's description of Kingston Penitentiary, cited in
Thompson, 2002:124

It is difficult, if not impossible, for those of us who have never been confined in a correctional institution to understand the carceral experience. The closest that we can get is the writings of inmates about their experiences doing time (see, for example, Thompson, 2002). Inmate-authored poems are reproduced in Boxes 7.6 and 7.7.

BOX 7.6

Prison Life

Aaron Collins

The cage is my brother.
It contains my heart.
It holds my soul in its hard, cold mind.
It clutches me to its iron bosom.

The walls are lovers.
They hold me in the night.
I see them when I am awake.

The cell is my teacher.
It has taught me the strength of solitude.
It has taught me the adequacy of shedding regretful tears.
It has taught me the value of freedom.

The prison is my mother.
She feeds me when I am hungry.
She disciplines me when I do wrong.
But she will have to let me go ... someday.

Source: Inmate Classified (www.inmate.com).

BOX 7.7

December Rain

A Week before Christmas

Elmo Chattman

A steady rain fell on the Max-A yard today
Cold and wet, some of the men huddled together
in one corner along the fence
to escape the frigid assault
from the angry fists of winter.

These are men who usually live
with great distances between them
like the giant saguaros of the southwest
scattered across the desert floor
to ensure they won't have to fight
for the same few drops of water.

But today, much of that distance was forgotten
Their wet captive bodies touched
became a living, breathing mass of close proximity
united in common battle
against the wet swords of the wind
trying to keep warm
trying to humor each other
trying to reclaim what has been taken from them:
a memory of what it means to live free.

Source: Inmate Classified (www.inmate.com).

INMATE COMPLAINTS, GRIEVANCE SYSTEMS, AND INVESTIGATIONS

For inmates confined in federal institutions, sections 90 and 91 of the Corrections and Conditional Release Act set out the procedures for ensuring that any complaints are dealt with in a fair and equitable manner. Grievances are to be handled fairly, in a timely fashion, and effectively. Inmates must make every attempt to resolve their grievance through the internal grievance procedure in the institution prior to filing a written complaint with the Correctional Investigator.

The Offender Complaint and Grievance System, which operates in all federal institutions, has a number of steps that inmates can follow to attempt to resolve a complaint:

Complaint lodged with institution staff
Level 1—grievance filed with Warden
Level 2—Regional Deputy Commissioner, Regional Headquarters
Level 3—Deputy Commissioner of Corporate Development (for men)/
Deputy Commissioner of Women (for women)

Thousands of complaints or grievances are filed every year by inmates in federal correctional facilities. Of the inmate population, 5 percent account for nearly 70 percent of all complaints and grievances. Box 7.8 lists the areas of concern most frequently identified by federal offenders in 2001–02.

BOX 7.8

Most Common Types of Complaints Made by Federal Offenders, 2001–02

Area of Concern	Number of Complaints
Health care	987
Transfer	761
Case preparation	731
Visits and private family visits	506
Staff responsiveness	427
Administrative segregation	418
File information (access, correction, and disclosure)	397
Cell effects	371
Grievance procedure	344
Parole decisions	254

Source: Correctional Investigator Canada, 2002:50

Similar grievance procedures and requirements are in place for inmates confined in provincial/territorial institutions. Complaints that are not resolved at the institution may be referred to the office of the provincial ombudsman. In Ontario, inmate complaints (7,697 in 2001–02) make up the bulk of the ombudsman's caseload. Box 7.9 lists the most frequent types of complaints and inquiries against the Ontario correctional system in 2001–02.

BOX 7.9

Most Common Types of Complaints and Inquiries against Correctional Services, Province of Ontario, 2001–02

Area of Concern	Number of Complaints
Staff conduct	738
Health (adequacy of care)	567
Living conditions (food/diet)	497
Classification or transfer within the provincial system	439
Health (medication)	401
Living conditions	364
Personal/inmate property	355
Yard	345
Living conditions (clothing size, condition, etc.)	301
Responses to inmate requests	272
Health (delay of treatment)	255
Living conditions (cleanliness, hygiene, sanitation)	252
Correspondence	212
Canteen	181
Administrative segregation	166
Living conditions (lockup)	165
Living conditions (overcrowding)	160
Living conditions (heating, ventilation, air)	152

BOX 7.9, continued

Area of Concern	Number of Complaints
Inmate misconduct issuance adjudication	150
Living conditions (segregation)	146
Health (prescription request)	141
Visiting privileges	133
Security (lockdown)	131

Source: Ombudsman Ontario, 2002:35.

Following is an illustration of the types of cases investigated and resolved by the provincial ombudsmen:

- Two inmates complained about an incident in which correctional officers interrupted an Aboriginal pipe ceremony and accused the participants of smoking marijuana. An Elder who was present at the ceremony denied the allegation and offered to let the officers inspect his medicine bundle. Despite this gesture, the officers terminated the ceremony. The inmates felt that the actions of the correctional officers demonstrated a lack of respect toward the Elder and the pipe ceremony. The ombudsman recommended that an Elder provide Aboriginal spiritual awareness sessions to correctional staff and that the officers involved in the incident apologize for their actions (Saskatchewan Ombudsman, 2001:18–19).
- An inmate suffering from mental illness and severe hearing loss was placed in a segregation cell for most of her two-month confinement. A third party contacted the ombudsman's office and expressed concerns that the woman could be heard screaming throughout the night. An investigation by the ombudsman found that, in a violation of correctional policy, the woman had been denied regular access to showers and daily fresh air. Correctional officials acknowledged that the conditions of the inmate's confinement were unacceptable and agreed to take steps to prevent similar situations from occurring in the future. (Ombudsman Ontario, 2002:13–14)

FAILING TO COPE WITH CONFINEMENT: SELF-INJURIOUS BEHAVIOUR AND SUICIDE

The prison suicide rate is more than twice that of the general Canadian population. Suicide is the most common cause of inmate death inside correctional institutions, accounting for approximately 61 percent of the deaths in provincial/territorial facilities and 21 percent of deaths of federal inmates (Reed and Roberts, 1999:8). Among federal inmates, there is a greater likelihood that they will die by suicide than be killed by another inmate (Larivière, 1997). Many of the inmates who attempt suicide have made previous attempts while in the community (Liebling, 1998).

Whereas many male inmates are at risk of suicide, female offenders tend to engage in self-injurious behaviour, including slashing and self-mutilation—although there is some evidence to suggest that female inmates in provincial institutions who are awaiting trial or who are serving short sentences are at greater risk to commit suicide than male offenders and the general population (Daigle, Alarie, and Lefebvre, 1999). Self-injurious behaviour among female offenders has been linked to childhood abuse and other pre-prison psychological difficulties (Snow, 1997). The risk factors associated with self-injurious behaviour include:

- social cognitive problems
- substance abuse
- psychiatric difficulties
- dysfunctional family relationships
- involvement in institutional incidents, including violence, substance abuse, and discipline problems (Wichmann, Serin, and Abracen, 2002)

Assessing the Risk of Suicide

It is often difficult to predict inmate suicides and to identify causal factors that may place an inmate at increased risk. Although prison psychologists are often able to determine that an inmate is at risk of suicide, techniques are not sufficiently developed to predict the likelihood of a suicide occurring. The task is made even more difficult by the wide variety of behaviours that may or may not be related to future suicide. These include certain gestures, self-injury, and attempted suicides.

Among the risk factors that have been found to be associated with completed suicides among inmates in institutions and offenders being supervised in the community are:

- age: young, male inmates and elderly inmates were at greater risk
- alcohol abuse: alcoholics were at five times the risk of non-alcoholics
- prior suicidal behaviour
- depression
- hopelessness
- mental illness
- education level: there was a positive relationship between higher academic achievement and suicide risk
- employment (Polvi, 1997; Rosine, 1995)

Many provincial institutions have a suicide screening protocol to identify those inmates who may be at risk of suicide. To date, the CSC has not developed a coordinated plan for the early identification and treatment of potentially suicidal inmates.

Profile of Inmates Who Commit Suicide

Inmates who commit suicide while incarcerated in Canadian institutions tend to be single, white males, aged 20–43, who are housed in medium-security institutions and who have a history of violence. Many of the deceased had alcohol and/or substance abuse problems and had been sexually or physically abused as children (Larivière, 1997).

Suicide occurs primarily among male inmates, whereas female offenders exhibit more self-mutilation, as noted above. This tendency reflects the patterns of suicide in the general population, where males have a rate of suicide that is four times that of females. Interestingly, there are regional variations in inmate suicides, with the Quebec region recording more than all other regions combined.

The most common method of death is by hanging, generally in the inmate's cell. The precipitating factor in many cases was found to be pressure from other inmates because of the inmate's offence or money owed for drugs or other debts. Inmates are particularly at risk during the initial phase of their confinement. The risk of suicide may be elevated for women who are placed in segregation (Martel, 1999).

Case Studies of Inmate Suicide

Case studies of two suicides committed in federal institutions during 1996–97 are presented in Boxes 7.10 and 7.11. Each case study includes a background profile of the inmate; the actuarial, historical, and clinical risk factors; and a narrative based on the post-death investigation that was conducted in each case. The case presented in Box 7.10 illustrates how the pressures of living inside the prison and the difficulties that inmates become involved in as a result of gambling and drug-related debts can precipitate or contribute to self-inflicted death. The case in Box 7.11 involved an Aboriginal offender who was most likely suffering from depression, owing to severe cultural shock as well as to the consequences of being confined many kilometres from home.

Inmate suicide is also a problem in many provincial/territorial systems of corrections. Among the cases included in the report of a Quebec coroner that

BOX 7.10

Death Inside: Case Study 1

Background

Method	Hanging
Institution	Archambault
Arrival at Institution (most recent)	January 31, 1996
Current offences	Break and Enter, Conspiracy to Break and Enter with Intent, Theft over $1000, Possession of Break-In Instruments, Possession of Narcotics

Predictors

Actuarial Risk Factors

Age	29
Marital status	Single
Sentence length	2 years
Time served in sentence	8 months, 8 days

BOX 7.10, continued

Historical Risk factors	Y	N	Unk.
Psychiatric history		✓	
History of alcohol or drug abuse	✓		
Prior suicide attempt(s)	✓		
History of impulsive behaviour	✓		
Family history of suicide		✓	

Clinical Risk Factors	Y	N	Unk.
Suicidal ideation and suicidal intent	✓		
Suicide plan	✓		
Hopelessness	✓		
Sudden change in psychological functioning		✓	
Stress, vulnerability, and poor coping	✓		
Depressive symptoms	✓		
Current problem with alcohol or drugs		✓	
Psychotic symptoms		✓	
Physical isolation	✓		
Psychosocial isolation	✓		

Narrative

This inmate experienced a number of difficulties living in the regular population of the institution. He had enemies among his fellow inmates, particularly among inmates associated with motorcycle gangs, and appeared to live in constant fear for his life. There were numerous self-inflicted injuries and suicide attempts prior to his death. Many of these behaviours were perceived as manipulative and thought to be strategies to avoid the pressure from other inmates.

His most recent suicide attempt occurred four days prior to his death. He was treated in hospital and eventually returned to a detention cell (non-camera equipped). A memorandum was written to detention officers asking that they pay special attention to the inmate given his higher risk to commit suicide.

The Board of Investigation found that interventions undertaken after his previous suicide attempts were poorly conducted. The surveillance of this inmate during his placement in detention was considered inappropriate. The Board also felt that there had been a lack of continuity and of uniformity in the way in which information was transmitted between staff.

From the time that the inmate was found, the emergency interventions undertaken by the institution's personnel showed a high level of diligence and professionalism.

Critical incident stress management was offered to all employees involved in the incident but was apparently refused. No such intervention was offered to inmates.

Recommendations

- that management ensure adherence to Standing Orders;
- that a complete psychological assessment be conducted on offenders with recent suicide attempts;
- that management review the means of communication between staff and ensure that these means are efficient, understood, and implemented; and,
- that management ensure the appropriate use of cells with surveillance cameras.

Source: Larivière, 1997:15–16.

BOX 7.11

Death Inside: Case Study 2

Background

Method	Hanging
Institution	Archambault
Arrival at Institution (most recent)	September 16, 1996
Current offences	Assault, Use of Force, Threats of Violence and Fail to Comply

Predictors

Actuarial Risk Factors

Age	29
Marital status	Married
Sentence length	2 years
Time served	1 month, 27 days

Historical Risk factors	Y	N	Unk.
Psychiatric history	✓		
History of alcohol or drug abuse	✓		
Prior suicide attempt(s)	✓		
History of impulsive behaviour			✓
Family history of suicide			✓

Clinical Risk Factors	Y	N	Unk.
Suicidal ideation and suicidal intent		✓	
Suicide plan			✓
Hopelessness	✓		
Sudden change in psychological functioning		✓	
Stress, vulnerability, and poor coping	✓		
Depressive symptoms	✓		
Current problem with alcohol or drugs			✓
Psychotic symptoms	✓		
Physical isolation		✓	
Psychosocial isolation	✓		

Narrative

This offender was serving a two-year sentence for assaults committed against his wife. He was only two months into his sentence when staff found him hanging from the handle of his cell's window.

The most notable feature in this case was the severe language barrier between the inmate and staff. As an Aboriginal from a remote community in northern Quebec, he spoke no French and practically no English. Consequently, very little was known about the offender's state of mental health other than his recent suicide attempt a few days prior to his death.

The Board of Investigation felt that policies relating to Aboriginal needs were perhaps not well understood by staff. Otherwise, the Board noted a professional and effective response to the incident. Critical incident stress management was offered to staff but was declined. It does not appear that it was offered to inmates.

BOX 7.11, continued

Recommendations

- that procedures relating to interpreters be established in institutions where there is a need to do so;
- that requests for interpreters be made in the very first week of arrival at the Regional Reception Centre;
- that management clearly define the role of Aboriginal Liaison Officers and their relationships with case management staff; and,
- that management highlight the very effective response by security and health services staff during this incident.

Source: Larivière, 1997:24–25.

highlighted the problem of suicide in provincial correctional facilities were the following:

- An 18-year-old inmate hanged himself with a curtain in the shower of the Roberval Detention Centre. A known glue-sniffer, the inmate had made several suicide attempts in the days leading up to his death, but he was unsupervised in the shower because the correctional worker responsible for surveillance of the shower area did not work on weekends.
- A 61-year-old inmate hanged himself in the Trois-Rivières Detention Centre by tying a sheet to the top shelf of the locker in his cell. The man had been arrested for indecent exposure and was incoherent in the days before his suicide. Although correctional officers in the facility had reported observing him in "strange positions," such as standing on his locker with a sheet, no special surveillance was made. (Picard, 1997)

Investigating Inmate Suicides and Recommendations for Prevention

Internal investigations are conducted by the CSC in all cases of self-inflicted death in federal institutions. These reports are compiled annually and the information is used to provide a general overview of the incidence and types of inmate suicides, to develop recommendations to improve institutional procedures and increase awareness among correctional staff, and to further understand the phenomenon of inmate suicide. The annual report on inmate suicides prepared by the CSC also includes general recommendations for primary and secondary suicide prevention, as well as ways in which to improve the response to these incidents.

In an attempt to reduce the incidence of suicide and self-harm, the CSC has implemented inmate peer support programs in all maximum- and medium-security institutions. The Samaritans program, which operates in Drumheller Institution (Alta.), Stony Mountain Institution (Man.), and Saskatchewan Penitentiary (Sask.), is a peer support program through which a community-based organization provides suicide prevention training for inmate peer counsellors. A similar program, VIVA, operates in Leclerc Institution (Que.).

QUESTIONS FOR REVIEW

1. Define the following terms: (a) mortification, (b) status degradation ceremonies, (c) pains of imprisonment, and (d) prisonization. Then indicate how each term assists us in understanding institutional corrections.

2. Discuss the origins and basic tenets of the inmate code. What do research studies indicate about the state of the inmate code in the contemporary prison?

3. What is an argot role, and how is this term related to the inmate social system?

4. Describe the concept of mature coping as developed by Johnson (1996). What issues have been raised about this concept?

5. Note some of the differences among long-term federal offenders discovered in the survey by Porporino (1991).

6. What is a state-raised offender, and what challenges do these offenders present to corrections?

7. Compare and contrast expressive violence and instrumental violence.

8. Summarize the findings of Struckman-Johnson et al. (1996) regarding sexual coercion in U.S. prisons.

9. Compare and contrast the inmate strategies of passive precautions and aggressive precautions for avoiding violence and victimization.

10. Identify five risk factors that have been found to be associated with completed suicides among inmates in institutions and offenders under supervision in the community.

REFERENCES

Ault, F.A.W. 1997. "Imprisoned by an Uncaring Public." *The Globe and Mail* (April 21):A14.

Caddle, D., and D. Crisp. 1997. "Mothers in Prison." *Research Findings.* No. 38. London, U.K.: Research and Statistics Directorate, Home Office.

Carr, C. 1995. "A Network of Support for Offender Families." *Forum on Corrections Research* 7(2):31–33.

Chubaty, D.E. 2002. "Victimization, Fear, and Coping in Prison." *Forum on Corrections Research* 14(1):13–15.

Clemmer, D. 1940. *The Prison Community.* Boston: Christopher.

Cloward, R.A. 1969. "Social Control in the Prison." In L. Hazelrigg (ed.), *Prison within Society: A Reader in Penology* (78–112). Garden City, N.Y.: Doubleday.

Cooley, D. 1992. "Prison Victimization and the Informal Rules of Social Control." *Forum on Corrections Research* 4(3):31–36.

Correctional Investigator Canada. 2002. *Annual Report of the Correctional Investigator, 2001–2002.* Ottawa: Public Works and Government Services Canada.

———. 2002. CSC Speakers Binder. Section 6. *Issues and Challenges Facing CSC.* Ottawa. Retrieved from www.csc-scc.gc.ca/text/pblct/guideorateur/pdf.

Crouch, B.M. 1993. "Is Incarceration Really Worse? Analysis of Offenders' Preferences for Prison over Probation." *Justice Quarterly* 10(1):67–88.

Daigle, M., M. Alarie, and P. Lefebvre. 1999. "The Problem of Suicide among Female Prisoners." *Forum on Corrections Research* 11(3):41–45.

Dube, R. 2002. *The Haven: A True Story of Life in the Hole.* Toronto: HarperCollins.

Faulkner, P.L., and W.R. Faulkner. 1997. "Effects of Organizational Change on Inmate Status and the Inmate Code of Conduct." *Journal of Crime and Justice* 20(1):55–72.

Foran, T. 1995. "A Descriptive Comparison of Demographic and Family Characteristics of the Canadian and Offender Populations." *Forum on Corrections Research* 7(2):3–5.

Gabel, S. 1995. "Behavioural Problems in the Children of Incarcerated Parents." *Forum on Corrections Research* 7(2):37–39.

Goffman, E. 1961. *Asylums: Essays on the Social Situation of Mental Patients and Other Inmates.* Garden City, N.Y.: Doubleday.

Hamilton, Associate Chief Justice A.C., and Associate Chief Judge C.M. Sinclair. 1991. *Report of the Aboriginal Justice Inquiry of Manitoba: The Justice System and Aboriginal People.* Vol. 1. Winnipeg: Queen's Printer.

Harris, M. 2002. *Con Game: The Truth about Canada's Prisons.* Toronto: McClelland and Stewart.

Hubbell, W. 1997. "Light from Darkness." *George.* August. Retrieved from www.ncianet.org/george.html.

Hughes, The Hon. E.N. (Ted). (Chair). 1996. *Report of the Independent Review of the Circumstances Surrounding the April 25–26, 1996 Riot at the Headingley Correctional Institution.* Winnipeg: Ministry of Justice, Province of Manitoba.

Ireland, J., and J. Archer. 1996. "Descriptive Analysis of Bullying in Male and Female Adult Prisoners." *Journal of Community and Applied Social Psychology* 6:35–47.

Irwin, J., and D.R. Cressey. 1962. "Thieves, Convicts, and the Inmate Culture." *Social Problems* 10(1):142–55.

John Howard Society of Alberta. 1992. *A Briefing Paper on the Effects of Long Term Incarceration.* Edmonton: John Howard Society of Alberta.

Johnson, R. 1996. *Hard Time: Understanding and Reforming the Prison.* Belmont, Calif.: Wadsworth.

Kauffman, K. 1988. *Prison Officers and Their World.* Cambridge, Mass.: Harvard University Press.

Larivière, M.A.S. 1997. *The Correctional Service of Canada 1996–97 Retrospective Report on Inmate Suicides.* Ottawa: Correctional Service of Canada.

Lawson, D.P., C. Segrin, and T.D. Ward. 1996. "The Relationship between Prisonization and Social Skills among Prison Inmates." *The Prison Journal* 76(3):293–309.

Leschied, A.W., A. Cunningham, and N. Mazaheri. 1997. *Safe and Secure: Eliminating Peer-to-Peer Violence in Ontario's Phase II Secure Detention Centres.* London, Ont.: London Family Court Clinic.

Liebling, A. 1998. "Prison Suicide and the Nature of the Environment." In A. Liebling (ed.), *Deaths of Offenders: The Hidden Side of Justice* (64–74). London, U.K.: Waterside Press.

Martel, J. 1999. *Solitude and Cold Storage: Women's Journeys of Endurance in Segregation.* Edmonton: Elizabeth Fry Society of Edmonton.

McCorkle, R.C. 1992a. "Institutional Violence: How Do Inmates Respond?" *Forum on Corrections Research* 4(3):9–11.

———. 1992b. "Personal Precautions to Violence in Prison." *Criminal Justice and Behavior* 19(2):160–73.

Murphy, P.J., and L. Johnsen. 1997. *Life 25: Interviews with Prisoners Serving Life Sentences.* Vancouver: New Star Books.

National Parole Board. n.d. "Inmate Jargon." Abbotsford, B.C.: Pacific Region.

Ombudsman Ontario. 2002. *Annual Report, 2001–2002.* Toronto: Queen's Printer.

Owens, A.M. 2002. "Prison Guards Outraged by Judge's Ruling." *National Post* (November 4):A5.

Paulus, P.B. and M.T. Dzindolet. 1992. "The Effects of Prison Confinement." In P. Seudfeld and P.E. Tetlock (eds.), *Psychology and Social Policy* (327–41). New York: Hemisphere.

Picard, A. 1997. "Quebec Anti-Suicide Plan Failing, Coroner Says." *The Globe and Mail* (September 23):A3.

Plourde, C. 2002. "Consumption of Psychoactive Substances in Quebec Prisons." *Forum on Corrections Research* 14(1):16–18.

Polvi, N.H. 1997. *Prisoner Suicide: A Review of the Literature.* Ottawa: Correctional Service of Canada.

Porporino, F.J. 1991. *Differences in Response to Long-Term Imprisonment: Implications for the Management of Long-Term Offenders.* Ottawa: Correctional Service of Canada.

Porporino, F.J., P.D. Doherty, and T. Sawatsky. 1987. "Characteristics of Homicide Victims and Victimizations in Prisons: A Canadian Historical Perspective." *International Journal of Offender Therapy and Comparative Criminology* 31(2):125–35.

Reed, M., and J.V. Roberts. 1999. "Adult Correctional Services in Canada, 1997–98." *Juristat* 19(40). Ottawa: Canadian Centre for Justice Statistics, Statistics Canada.

Robinson, D. 1995. "Federal Offender Family Violence: Estimates from a National File Review Study." *Forum on Corrections Research* 7(2):15–18.

Rosine, L. 1995. "Assessment of Suicides in Incarcerated Populations." In T.A. Leis, L.L. Motiuk, and J.R.P. Ogloff (eds.), *Forensic Psychology: Policy and Practice in Corrections* (150–63). Ottawa: Correctional Service Canada.

Saskatchewan Ombudsman. 2001. *Annual Report, 2001.* Saskatoon.

———. 2002. *Locked Out: Inmate Services and Conditions of Custody in Saskatchewan Correctional Centres.* Saskatoon. Retrieved from www.legassembly.sk.ca/officers/ombuds.htm.

Shephard, M. 1997. "'Imagine the Worst': Inmates Soon Learn That to Be Sent to a Canadian Prison Is to Be Condemned to a Term of Fear, Pain, Even Torture." *The Toronto Star* (August 31):F1.

Snow, L. 1997. "A Pilot Study of Self-Injury amongst Women Prisoners." *Issues in Criminological and Legal Psychology* 28:50–59.

Struckman-Johnson, C., D. Struckman-Johnson, L. Rucker, K. Bumby, and S. Donaldson. 1996. "Sexual Coercion Reported by Men and Women in Prison." *The Journal of Sex Research* 33(1):67–76.

Sykes, G.M. 1958. *Society of Captives: A Study of a Maximum Security Institution.* Princeton, N.J.: Princeton University Press.

Sykes, G.M., and S.L. Messinger. 1960. "The Inmate Social System." In R.A. Cloward, D.R. Cressey, G.H. Grosser, R. McCleery, L.E. Ohlin, G.M. Sykes, and S.L. Messinger (eds.), *Theoretical Studies in the Social Organization of the Prison* (5–19). New York: Social Science Research Council.

Teather, S., L. Evans, and M. Sims. 1997. "Maintenance of the Mother–Child Relationship by Incarcerated Women." *Early Child Development and Care* 131:65–75.

Terry, C.M. 1997. "The Function of Humor for Prison Inmates." *Journal of Contemporary Criminal Justice* 13(1):23–40.

Thompson, S. 2002. *Letters from Prison: Felons Write about the Struggle for Life and Sanity behind Bars.* Toronto: HarperCollins.

Watson, L. 1995. "In the Best Interest of the Child: The Mother–Child Program." *Forum on Corrections Research* 7(2):25–27.

Welch, M. 1996. *Corrections: A Critical Approach.* New York: McGraw-Hill.

Wichmann, C., R. Serin, and J. Abracen. 2002. *Women Offenders Who Engage in Self-Harm: A Comparative Investigation.* Ottawa: Research Branch, Correctional Service of Canada.

Wine, S. 1992. *A Motherhood Issue: The Impact of the Criminal Justice System Involvement on Women and Their Children.* Ottawa: Corrections Branch, Ministry of the Solicitor General of Canada.

Zamble, E., and F.J. Porporino. 1988. *Coping, Behavior, and Adaptation in Prison Inmates.* New York: Springer-Verlag.

CHAPTER 8

CLASSIFICATION, CASE MANAGEMENT, AND TREATMENT

CHAPTER OBJECTIVES

- *Discuss the tools and techniques used in classifying inmates.*
- *Discuss the case management process.*
- *Examine institutional treatment programs.*
- *Consider the principles of effective correctional treatment.*
- *Examine the effectiveness of institutional treatment programs.*
- *Identify the conditions required for effective correctional treatment.*

KEY TERMS

Classification
Correctional plan
Static risk factors
Dynamic risk factors
Criminogenic factors
Case management
Risk principle
Need principle

Responsivity principle
Differential treatment effectiveness
Differential amenability to treatment
Recidivism rates
Differential treatment availability
Program fidelity
Program drift

This chapter distills the massive amount of information that has been published on classification, case management, and treatment programs for incarcerated offenders. There are three major trends in offender classification and treatment: (1) the increasing use of sophisticated risk/needs assessment instruments; (2) the increasing domination of treatment research, policy, and programs from a psychological perspective, which includes a heavy emphasis on cognitive behaviour interventions; and (3) a differentiated treatment approach for women, Aboriginals, and specific categories of offenders.

CLASSIFICATION AND RISK ASSESSMENT

Classification is the process by which inmates are subdivided into groups based on a variety of considerations. Classification is used for:

- determination of and assignment to the most appropriate custody and security levels
- program placement
- designation to proper housing placement within the institution

The comprehensive assessment that takes place is designed to determine the risks and needs of each offender. An attempt is then made to place the offender in the institutional setting that is most compatible to these risks and needs, both in terms of security level and treatment and work programs. Ideally, the assessment process should be continued throughout the inmate's sentence and following release.

In each region of the Correctional Service of Canada (CSC), there are reception centres where offenders spend a period of time after sentencing. The primary purpose of the assessment centres is to conduct a comprehensive, standardized assessment of offender risk and needs that will provide the foundation for the offender's participation in programs and treatment. A key part of this process is gathering existing documentation on the offender from a variety of sources, including the family, corrections, the court, the police, and the victim. A variety of instruments are used to conduct psychological, substance abuse, vocational, educational, and family violence assessments; many of these instruments are deemed not appropriate for assessing female offenders and Aboriginal offenders, and are used only for male, non-Aboriginal offenders. The assessment process continues throughout the offender's sentence, from intake and incarceration, to release from custody, and up to sentence expiry. Inmates are reclassified periodically during the course of their confinement, based on their progress and performance in treatment programs and work assignments and on their behaviour in the institution. Both at the initial classification stage and in subsequent classification decisions, correctional personnel consider security and risk concerns, as well as the programmatic needs and abilities of the inmate. See Figure 8.1.

At the provincial/territorial level, classification may occur during the inmate's stay in a remand centre or upon arrival at the facility. The short period of time that inmates under provincial/territorial jurisdiction remain in confinement, however, means that determining risk and security levels is the primary objective of classification. At the Whitehorse (Yukon) Correctional

Figure 8.1

Offender Risk Assessment and Management Process

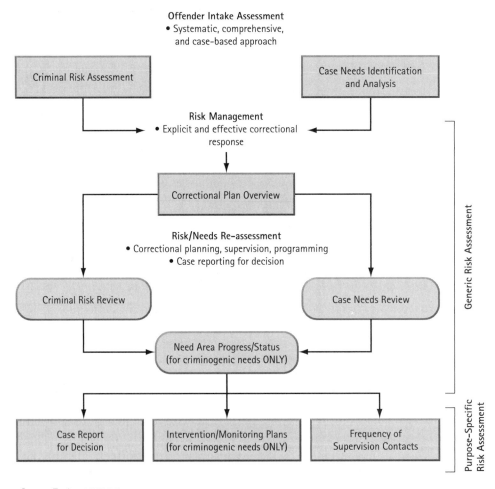

Source: Taylor, 1998:34.

Centre, for example, case managers and the integrated case management team identify offender needs and develop a program plan. In Ontario, all provincial inmates are classified as either Level 1 or Level 2. Level 1 is assigned to offenders who have committed offences that are listed in the Regulations of the Ministry of Correctional Services Act and generally include interpersonal offences involving violence. Inmates who are designated Level 1 require additional information, such as a mental-health assessment, as part of any application for release. The Level 2 designation is assigned to all other inmates.

Classification Tools and Techniques

The classification systems used by federal and provincial/territorial corrections generally include psychological, personality, and behavioural inventories that attempt to categorize offenders into certain types. At the federal level, this procedure is referred to as the Offender Intake Assessment (OIA), during which extensive information on the offender's criminal history and pattern of victimizations is gathered. Among the documents that form the OIA are the preliminary assessment, the post-sentence community assessment (the result of interviews with key community contacts), and a summary of the various inmate risk factors. The goal of the OIA is the development of the **correctional plan,** a document that summarizes the entire case record and that is generally updated every six months.

Among the factors that are considered in determining the inmate's security level during the initial classification process are:

- the seriousness of the offence
- outstanding charges
- the inmate's performance and behaviour while under sentence
- the inmate's social, criminal, and, where available, young offender history
- any physical or mental illness or other disorder
- the inmate's potential for violence
- the inmate's continued involvement in criminal behaviour

The primary tool used by the federal CSC to assess offender risk and to determine security classification is the Custody Rating Scale (CRS). This instrument is based on research that indicates not only that there are measurable differences between offenders, but also that offenders can be categorized in terms of adjustment to confinement, risk of escape, and risk to the community should they escape. The scale consists of a number of items that attempt to measure these differences. Evaluation research has revealed that the CRS is an effective classification instrument (Luciani, 1997).

In Ontario, the Level of Service Inventory–Ontario Revision (LSI-OR) is the primary classification/assessment instrument. This is a standardized interview, which contains a range of questions relating to the offender, including offence history, substance abuse, and employment history. For each of the 43 items in the inventory, the offender is scored either 0 or 1. The higher the total score of the inmate, the greater the likelihood that the inmate will have difficulties in the institution and upon release. Evaluations of the LSI-OR indicate that it is an acceptable tool for predicting the performance of inmates in both institutional and community-based programs (Gendreau, Little, and Goggin, 1996).

Another widely used assessment tool is the Static-99, developed by Phenix, Hanson, and Thornton (2000). This actuarial instrument is designed to estimate the probability of sexual and violent recidivism among males who have been convicted of at least one sexual offence against a child or non-consenting adult. The coding form for the Static-99 is reproduced in Box 8.1.

Risk and Need Profiles of Offenders

The assessment of risk is a key component of classification and case management. Risk assessments are designed to identify those offenders who are most likely to reoffend upon release from the institution if no treatment intervention occurs (Taylor, 1997:32). Risk analysis is used in a variety of ways:

- to determine which facility the offender should be confined in or moved to
- to determine the offender's treatment needs
- to identify those offenders who require higher levels of support, intervention, and supervision upon release
- to assist in release decisions

Research studies indicate that (1) the inmate's criminal history is strongly related to failure upon conditional release, (2) the number and types of offender needs are related to recidivism, and (3) the combined assessment of both risks and needs improves the ability to predict which offenders will recidivate.

In assessing the degree of risk posed by an offender, correctional personnel generally consider:

- **static risk factors:** the offender's criminal history, including prior convictions, seriousness of prior offences, and whether the offender successfully completed previous periods of supervision in the community

BOX 8.1

The Static-99: A Risk Assessment Instrument for Sex Offenders

Risk Factor	Codes		Score
Prior sex offences (same rules as in RRASOR)	Charges	Convictions	
	None	None	0
	1–2	1	1
	3–5	2–3	2
	6 +	4 +	3
Prior sentencing dates (excluding index)	3 or less		0
	4 or more		1
Any convictions for non-contact sex offences	No		0
	Yes		1
Index nonsexual violence	No		0
	Yes		1
Prior nonsexual violence	No		0
	Yes		1
Any unrelated victims	No		0
	Yes		1
Any stranger victims	No		0
	Yes		1
Any male victims	No		0
	Yes		1
Young	Aged 25 or older		0
	Aged 18–24		1
Single	Ever lived with lover for at least two years?		
	Yes		0
	No		1
Total score	Add up scores from individual risk factors		

BOX 8.1, continued

TRANSLATING STATIC-99 SCORE INTO RISK CATEGORIES

Score Label for Risk Category

0, 1	Low
2, 3	Medium-Low
4, 5	Medium-High
6 or plus	High

Source: Phenix, Hanson, and Thornton, 2000.

- **dynamic risk factors:** those attributes of the offender that can be altered through intervention (e.g., level of education and cognitive thinking abilities). As opposed to the static criminal history factors, the needs of the offender can change (for the better or, if not addressed, for the worse). Many risk/need factors are **criminogenic,** meaning if they are not addressed, future criminal behaviour may occur.

The determination of risk, then, is the result of combining static criminal history information with dynamic (or criminogenic need) factors. The role of the risk/needs assessment in the deliberations surrounding the release of offenders from confinement will be discussed in Chapter 9.

A crucial component of the classification process is the collection of information from other criminal justice agencies, including the police and the sentencing court. In addition, the community assessment conducted by the community parole officer is also used for pre-release planning. Correctional systems have historically experienced difficulties in securing and collating information about inmates, although in recent years a concerted effort has been made to implement information systems that are designed to ensure that materials are secured in a timely manner.

Questions have been raised about the effectiveness of classification in identifying the programmatic needs of inmates. One study found, for example, that only half of the program assignments were effective in targeting the criminogenic needs of offenders, and for those inmates who completed the assigned programs, the interventions were unrelated to recidivism upon release from the institution (Dhaliwal, Porporino, and Ross, 1994).

Research studies indicate that actuarial risk assessment instruments are more accurate than professional clinical judgment in predicting whether inmates will reoffend (Bonta, 2002). Effective risk/needs assessments require not only that instruments are used to identify the needs of offenders, but also that inmates have access to the programs in their identified need areas. For a variety of reasons (discussed later in this chapter), inmates are often unable to gain access to specific treatment programs.

CASE MANAGEMENT

Correctional **case management** is the process by which the needs and abilities of offenders are matched with correctional programs and services. The primary goals of case management are to:

- provide for systematic monitoring of the offender during all phases of confinement
- facilitate the graduated release of offenders into the community
- prevent reoffending by the inmate upon release into the outside community

A properly operated case management process: (1) ensures that the inmate is provided with the level of structure and supervision required while addressing identified offender needs, (2) balances the need for rehabilitative intervention with community protection, (3) prepares the inmate for successful reintegration into the community, and (4) contributes to effective supervision of the offender in the community.

An overview of the case management process is presented in Box 8.2. Note that case management is carried out both during the inmate's confinement and following release from the institution. Also, note that the process outlined in Box 8.2 is intended only as a general description of the various phases of case management. The number of phases and their specific titles may vary between systems of corrections.

The Correctional Plan

At the core of the case management process is the correctional plan, which is developed for most inmates, the exception being those serving short sentences. This plan determines the offender's initial institution placement, specific training or work opportunities, and release planning. The correctional plan is based on the risk/needs profile of the inmate and is used to guide all

BOX 8.2

The Five Phases of the Case Management Process

I. Initial Assessment and Institutional Placement

- identification of inmate risks/needs
- development of correctional plan

II. Correctional Planning and Institutional Supervision

- correctional plan initiated
- institutional programs (work, treatment, skills upgrading)
- institutional transfers
- institutional releases (temporary absences, work releases)
- ongoing monitoring of inmate progress

III. Preparing Cases for Release Decisions

- institutional progress reports
- community assessments

IV. Parole Board Decision and Release

- temporary absences, day/full parole, statutory release

V. Community Supervision

decisions made about the inmate. The plan identifies program needs, based in part on the dynamic factors discussed above. For example, if substance abuse is a contributing factor to the inmate's pattern of criminality, then the offender should be referred to a substance abuse program. The correctional plan also sets out benchmarks, including parole eligibility dates and likely program entrance dates.

The informational heart of the case management process in federal institutions is the Offender Management System (OMS), a centralized database on offenders that is used to improve efficiency in the gathering and sharing of information about offenders across the country. Such information would be helpful, for example, if a parolee from the Vancouver area absconded and was arrested in Halifax. The Halifax district parole office would have immediate access to the accumulated file information.

Provincial/territorial systems of corrections also have systems for gathering information on inmates on an ongoing basis, although, again, the relatively short period of time offenders are confined reduces the time spent on information gathering. The province of Ontario also uses the OMS system; however, it is not connected to the federal system.

Since only a small percentage of inmates in provincial/territorial systems of corrections spend more than a year in confinement, the primary focus of case management is release planning. In federal institutions, on the other hand, the case management process generally takes place over a much longer period, involves regular reviews, and is used in identifying program requirements, in making decisions to transfer inmates from one institution to another, and in release planning. To streamline the case management process, the CSC has implemented Operation Bypass (see Box 8.3).

The Role of Federal Institutional Parole Officers

In federal corrections, institutional parole officers (IPOs) have primary responsibility for case management and work as part of the unit management team, which also includes correctional officers. Their duties include assessing offender needs, as well as behaviours or attitudes that have contributed to their criminal behaviour; developing intervention plans to address these attitudes and behaviours; and helping offenders undertake and complete these intervention plans. The IPOs also make recommendations concerning offender transfers, temporary absences, and other forms of conditional release, including parole. In many institutions, IPOs spend the majority of their time doing paperwork rather than supervising and counselling inmates.

INSTITUTIONAL TREATMENT PROGRAMS

[T]he question before us is not only how stringently we want to punish people in prison but also what kind of people we want to see emerge from it.

—Talbot, 2003:100

BOX 8.3

CSC's Operation Bypass

Operation Bypass is an initiative implemented by the federal CSC on February 1, 1999. This strategy was developed to address a number of problem areas in the case management process, including the following:

- The time required to complete and read the battery of assessment instruments on inmates was too long, occupying as much as 75 percent of staff time and taking away from face-to-face interaction with offenders.
- There was an unacceptable level of duplication in assessment reports, which wasted the time of front-line staff.
- Not all of the information gathered on inmates was needed or utilized.
- All of the above factors, in combination, delayed the completion of reports, which, in turn, delayed the development of a correctional plan; this, in turn, often resulted in inmates not having timely access to treatment programs.

The changes implemented in Operation Bypass are designed to reduce the amount of time that correctional staff spend inputting information on offenders; to reduce duplication of information; to adopt a "back to basics" approach that eliminates the need to gather information that is not "value-added"; and to discard or merge several reports previously completed on offenders. A key feature is the creation of timelines, which are designed to speed up the development of the correctional plan. The preliminary assessment on new inmates must now be completed within five working days, and the Offender Intake Assessment and the correctional plan are to be completed within 70 days of the inmate's admission.

The most common types of treatment programs in federal and provincial/territorial institutions focus on living skills, anger management, substance abuse, family violence, basic education, and vocational training/industries. There is considerable variation among institutions in the specific types of programs offered. The federal CSC offers a number of core programs that are designed to address specific need areas and to prepare inmates for re-entry into the community. Many of these programs are also available in provincial/territorial institutions. The programs and research findings related to their effectiveness are discussed below.

Living Skills Programming

This treatment consists of a series of programs that are designed to provide inmates with the skills and strategies to successfully re-enter and adjust to life in the community. Programs include parenting skills training, anger and emotion management, critical thinking, interpersonal problem solving, living without violence, and leisure education. For some inmates, these programs produce positive changes that may increase their likelihood of success upon release (Marshall, 1989). The Parenting Skills Training Program, one of the programs in the Living Skills Programming series, is profiled in Box 8.4.

BOX 8.4

CSC's Parenting Skills Training Program

The Parenting Skills Program is designed to address the high levels of conflict that afflict inmate families (see Chapter 7). The program attempts to address the cognitive problems of offenders which contribute to family dysfunction, including poor communication, a lack of problem-solving skills, and ineffective parenting. Through the use of case scenarios, role playing, and group activities, inmates acquire the capacity for critical thinking, empathy, and creativity in parenting (Carpentier, 1995).

Cognitive Skills Training

This program, which is delivered by trained staff, focuses on the development of skills for effective thinking, decision making, problem solving, and goal setting, as well as interpersonal skills. There is a substantial body of evidence to suggest that many criminal offenders:

- have not acquired a number of cognitive skills that are essential to positive social adaptation
- lack self-control and are unable to self-regulate their behaviour
- tend to be action-oriented, unreflective, and impulsive
- have difficulty with social perspective taking (i.e., they are often unable to view the world from another person's perspective)
- tend to think in concrete rather than abstract terms and act without considering or calculating the consequences of their behaviour

- lack interpersonal skills, problem-solving skills, and critical reasoning and planning skills
- tend to blame others for their behaviour (Fabiano, Porporino, and Robinson 1990:1)

The underlying principle of the cognitive model of offender rehabilitation is to "target thinking, not behaviour." The cognitive model is based on the assumption that since "faulty thinking patterns" seem to be instrumental in propelling offenders toward re-involvement in criminal activities, programs should attempt to change the way offenders think in order to change the way they act. Cognitive skills programming is designed to teach inmates the connections between thoughts and actions, show them how to think logically and objectively, and give them the skills to think through their responses to situations.

Cognitive skills programming is perhaps the most promising correctional intervention. Research using control and experimental groups indicates that, if correctly matched with inmate needs, cognitive skills programs can increase critical reasoning skills, the capacity for optional thinking, and interpersonal problem solving. Acquisition of these skills is, in turn, related to reduced rates of recidivism upon release. The positive impact of cognitive skills programs extends to violent offenders and drug offenders, although inmates convicted of nonviolent offences, such as property crimes, appear to benefit little from the program. Positive outcomes have also been reported for offenders who complete the program while under supervision in the community (Robinson, 1995; Vennard, Sugg, and Hedderman, 1997).

Substance Abuse Intervention

A high percentage of inmates have a history of substance abuse, and, for many, alcohol and drugs are directly related to their criminal history. One survey of federal inmates found, for example, that just over 80 percent of Aboriginal and nearly 75 percent of non-Aboriginal inmates reported substance abuse problems of sufficient severity to warrant treatment intervention (Vanderburg, Weekes, and Millson, 1994). Therefore, substance abuse programs are offered in most federal and provincial/territorial institutions. The Computerized Lifestyle Assessment Instrument is used by the CSC to identify inmates with substance abuse problems and to determine their specific treatment needs. This instrument is a valid assessment tool for both non-Aboriginal and Aboriginal inmates.

The core program offered by the CSC is the Offender Substance Abuse Pre-release (OSAP) program. OSAP uses behavioural and cognitive-behavioural approaches in an attempt to alter patterns of substance abuse and to reduce the likelihood that the inmate will abuse drugs or alcohol upon release from the institution. Among the program components are training in cognitive and behavioural skills, problem-solving skills, alcohol and drug education, and techniques of relapse prevention. Similar programs are offered in many provincial/territorial institutions.

The potential effectiveness of these programs has been hindered by the failure to consider the variation in the severity of substance abuse problems among inmates and to ensure follow-up of offenders released from institutions. It appears that substance abuse programs are effective in educating inmates about substance abuse (Millson and Robinson, 1992; Weekes and Millson, 1994). The impact of these programs on post-release behaviour is less clear, owing in large measure to the lack of follow-up studies. One study of a sample of federal offenders found that participation in the OSAP program was unrelated to re-admission for violations of release conditions but was significantly related to re-admissions for new offences (Weekes, Millson, and Lightfoot, 1995). Those offenders who performed well in the OSAP program were less likely to be re-admitted for a new offence. No control (non-treatment) group was used in this study, however.

Violence Prevention Programs

The CSC's Violence Prevention Program consists of 120 two-hour sessions delivered over a four-month period to a group of no more than 12 offenders who are at a high risk to commit violent offences. The program, which uses a cognitive-behavioural and skills-based approach, is presented in modules on topics such as violence awareness, anger control, problem solving, positive relationships, resolving conflicts, self-control, and violence prevention. Each participant is required to develop, articulate, and manage a comprehensive violence (relapse) prevention plan (Correctional Service of Canada, 2002).

As noted in Chapter 7, inmate family life is characterized by a considerable amount of conflict and violence. The CSC's Family Violence Program, which has information and skill-building components, is directed toward inmates who either have a history of violence or are at risk of becoming abusive. The program is a feminist-informed, cognitive-behavioural approach that teaches participants about the power and control dynamics that underlie their abusive behaviour toward partners and children.

Literacy and Education Programs

As many as two-thirds of the inmates admitted to correctional institutions test at or below grade 8 levels in math and language. The education programs in correctional facilities focus on general literacy and Adult Basic Education (ABE), although most provincial/territorial facilities and all federal institutions offer secondary education (grades 11 and 12) as well as vocational training. Inmates in federal institutions may also access university-level courses via correspondence, although the inmate generally assumes the cost of these courses.

A two-year follow-up study of inmates who had completed the ABE program found high program-approval ratings from inmate participants, as well as significant literacy gains—on average, three grade levels. There was also a significant relationship between program completion and a reduced likelihood of re-admission upon release, even though offenders in the study were of higher than average risk (i.e., younger and convicted of a violent offence). Higher-risk offenders appeared to benefit more from the program than lower-risk offenders (Correctional Service of Canada, 1991). A problem area is the lack of continuity between prison education and post-release follow-up and support.

Evaluations of on-site university-level courses in Canadian federal institutions (prior to their cancellation in the early 1990s) found that, for some offenders, participation in university degree programs reduced the risk of reoffending (Duguid, 1981). No evaluations have been conducted of success after release of inmates who enroll in university-level correspondence courses while confined. U.S. studies have found that participation in postsecondary education courses reduces recidivism for some offenders (Batiuk, Moke, and Rountree, 1997).

Sex Offender Treatment Programs

The treatment of sex offenders has become a focal point of systems of corrections, owing in large measure to increasing public and political concern about this group of offenders and their increasing numbers in institutional populations. Approximately 25 percent of all federal inmates are sex offenders, and nearly 40 percent of the Aboriginal offenders confined in federal institutions have been convicted of a sex offence.

As a group, sex offenders are difficult to treat, particularly those classified as high risk. The patterns of deviance are often very entrenched and, to a greater extent than other offender groups, sex offenders tend to deny having committed an offence, to minimize the impact of the crime on the victim(s), and to attribute their behaviour to the actions and wishes of the victim(s). Therefore, sex offenders are often unmotivated to participate in treatment programs and to engage in the process of self-change.

Most treatment interventions for sex offenders take a multidisciplinary team approach, which involves psychiatrists, psychometrists, social workers, physicians, nurses, chaplains, recreational staff, and volunteers. These programs are designed to reduce the likelihood that sex offenders will recidivate upon release from the institution. Programs focus on identifying the nature and pattern of the offender's behaviour, as well as on providing skills in self-management and self-control. Many treatment programs for sex offenders use a cognitive-behavioural approach and emphasize relapse prevention. In Ontario, for example, there are a number of specialized treatment facilities for sex offenders under provincial jurisdiction, including:

- Ontario Correctional Institute: This facility accommodates 50 to 75 sex offenders in a program that emphasizes victim awareness/empathy.
- Millbrook Correctional Centre: This centre operates a variety of treatment interventions for sex offenders, including a relapse prevention program, which teaches inmates techniques for avoiding cues that are likely to result in reoffending, and various alternative coping strategies.

Programs for federal sex offenders and federal Aboriginal sex offenders are profiled in Boxes 8.5 and 8.6 respectively.

BOX 8.5

Institut Philippe Pinel de Montréal Treatment Program for Sex Offenders

This is an intensive 12-month treatment program for sex offenders, including sex murderers who have been diagnosed with several deviance disorders. The program is centred on a cognitive-behavioural approach. Program components include sex education, social skills training, stress and anger management, aversion therapy, and orgasmic reconditioning. There is an attempt to match specific program modules to individual offenders. Service delivery is 80 percent group and 20 percent individual, with groups ranging in size from six to eight. Program therapists include a criminologist-sexologist, psychiatrist, and psychologist. A number of pre- and post-treatment assessments and evaluations are used to determine whether the objectives of the treatment program, including improving social skills, understanding the aggression cycle, increasing empathy, modifying sexual preferences, and formulating strategies for relapse prevention, have been achieved.

The program, which is operated under contract with the CSC, can accommodate 15 offenders at a time and has an annual budget of $3 million.

Source: Carter and Lefaive, 1995:44–45.

The treatment of sex offenders has often been subjected to the "nothing works" criticism. There is evidence, however, that some treatment approaches, particularly those that use a group format, focus on anger management and the development of cognitive-behavioural skills, and have a relapse prevention component, are successful in reducing rates of reoffending among some categories of sex offenders (Marshall and Pithers, 1994). An evaluation of the sex offender treatment program at Warkworth Sexual Behaviour Clinic (Ont.), for example, found that the risk assessment techniques used were predictive of failure upon release and that the intervention program reduced rates of reoffending (Barbaree, Seto, and Maric, 1996).

A similar evaluation of sex offender treatment programs in the Prairie region of the CSC found that, in comparison with a national sample of released sex offenders, those sex offenders classified as high-risk who had completed the treatment program:

- had significantly lower rates of re-conviction for sexual offences
- had somewhat lower rates of re-conviction for non-sexual offences
- were less likely to return to prison for any reason compared with offenders who did not complete the program (Gordon and Nicholaichuk, 1996)

BOX 8.6

Intensive Sex Offender Program for Aboriginal Men, Mountain Institution (British Columbia)

This is a holistic treatment program, with a focus on spiritual healing, delivered by correctional practitioners and an Aboriginal spiritual adviser. A key objective of the program is to assist offenders in recognizing high-risk situations and risk factors. Program modules include thinking error and cognitive restructuring, rational emotive therapy, sexuality and human relationships, behaviour cycle, victim empathy, and relapse prevention planning. The program also offers Elder-led sessions on module issues and a Healing/Insight/Feelings Group that encourages offenders to examine their attitudes, thoughts, and behaviours.

Sources: Correctional Service of Canada (www.csc-scc.gc.ca/text/pblct/sexoffender/aboriginal/toce_e.shtml); see also Hylton, 2002.

The same study found that offenders who did not complete the treatment program were at a high risk of reoffending. These findings reaffirm the belief that high-risk offenders are most likely to benefit from treatment interventions. The serious consequences of sex offences for victims mean that the rates of recidivism among this offender group remain a concern at any level.

Vocational and Work Programs

Prison work has a long and somewhat inglorious history in Canadian corrections, and it is only in the past few decades that vocational and work programs have been considered as part of the rehabilitation regimen. You will recall from the review of the history of corrections in Chapter 2 that opposition to prison industries by outside labour groups began during the 1830s. As a consequence of this ongoing opposition, inmate labour has traditionally been confined to activities related to the maintenance of institutions and the production of goods for government organizations. In the early 1900s, industrial programs in federal institutions were labelled "a disgrace to the Dominion," owing in large measure to the absence of "healthful, purposeful, profitable work" (Edwards, 1996:6).

The federal government agency CORCAN has as its primary mandate the production and marketing of prison-made goods. The objective of CORCAN is to provide offenders in institutional settings with training and work experiences they can transfer to the private sector in the outside community. Under provisions of the Corrections and Conditional Release Act, goods and services produced by inmates can be sold only to federal, provincial, and municipal governments or to charitable, religious, and nonprofit organizations. Successive reports of the Auditor General of Canada have documented the inability of CORCAN to become a sustainable enterprise.

There is some evidence that uninterrupted participation in prison work programs during a period immediately prior to release from the institution may have some positive impact on the rates of post-release recidivism, particularly for offenders classified as low risk (Motiuk and Belcourt, 1996). A study of post-release employment and recidivism among a sample of federal inmates found that higher-risk offenders were less likely to be employed upon release and that offenders who were employed had a reconviction rate of half that of unemployed offenders (Gillis, Motiuk, and Belcourt, 1998).

Despite the recommendations of numerous commissions of inquiry over the past 75 years that industry and vocational training programs be improved and expanded, little progress has been made. Prison industry programs continue to be afflicted by poorly defined and conflicting program objectives, dull work assignments, outdated equipment, and a lack of programs that provide a realistic opportunity for inmates to secure employment upon release. The fact that inmate pay scales provide for remuneration of less than $10 per day for most jobs further reduces incentives for inmate participation and diminishes the value of work performed. The failure of correctional systems to create meaningful and productive work and vocational programs for inmates is even more unfortunate when one considers the vast untapped source of creativity and energy in inmate populations and the positive impact that meaningful employment programs could have on life inside correctional institutions.

Private-Sector Involvement in Prison Industries

One option to improve prison industry and vocational programs in Canadian institutions is to involve the private sector in locating work opportunities within institutions. This practice is widespread in the United States, where most state systems of corrections and the U.S. federal prison system have partnerships with the private sector.

The typical arrangement involves a private-sector business locating inside a correctional facility. Inmates are interviewed and screened for employment suitability and trained by the employer. Space inside the institution is generally rented for a nominal fee, which can be as low as $1 per year, and the company sells goods manufactured in the prison on the open market. Inmates earn a wage similar to that received by workers in the outside community. For its part, the prison provides security as well as a motivated workforce that has low rates of absenteeism and, owing to urinalysis testing, is generally free from alcohol and drugs. By law in most states, inmates are required to set aside a portion of their earnings to support their families, pay any court-ordered restitution to their crime victims, contribute to room and board, and contribute to their savings account for release.

The CSC has shown little enthusiasm for the development of private-sector prison industries in Canada. Nevertheless, the issues presented in the following At Issue—particularly as they relate to provincial systems of corrections—are likely to become the focus of intense debate in the coming years.

AT ISSUE

PRIVATE-SECTOR INDUSTRY IN CANADIAN INSTITUTIONS?

There are a variety of ways in which the private sector can become involved in developing and operating prison-based industries. These industrial programs could be developed in federal and provincial/territorial facilities, in privately operated prisons, or in the community.

Proponents of involving the private sector in prison industries contend:

- The correctional system/private-sector partnership is a win–win situation: industry secures access to a motivated, reliable workforce, while prisons have access to private-sector expertise and inmates develop skills that will make them employable in the outside community.
- Inmates who work in private-sector industries and earn a wage similar to their "free world" counterparts can use this money to support their families, pay restitution to victims, pay room and board, and save money for release.
- Private-sector industries reduce inmate idleness, lessen the frequency of behavioural disruptions, and create a positive institutional environment.

Opponents of private-sector prison industries counter:

- The "in-kind" subsidies for private-sector businesses, including nominal rents and security, are too generous and should not be paid for by taxpayers.
- Business and labour groups in the outside community would oppose private-sector prison industries and would try to prevent the goods produced by these industries from being sold on the open market.
- Inmates would be susceptible to exploitation by private industry.
- Private-sector industries would take jobs from workers in the outside community.
- It is immoral to profit from inmates, who are a disadvantaged group in society.

THE RESEARCH EVIDENCE

There is no current research on the viability of private-sector prison industries in Canada. A study conducted by MacDonald (1982) over two decades ago found widespread support among business and labour groups for paying inmates and allowing prison-produced goods to compete on the open market, as long as such products were not subsidized or given any other unfair competitive advantage. Private-sector industries are a central component of most systems of corrections in the United States and are viewed positively by senior correctional officials, inmates, and institutional staff. It is interesting to note that the emphasis on punishment and longer terms of confinement in the United States has not resulted in a call for terminating private-sector industries in prisons.

QUESTIONS

1. Would you support the development of private-sector industries in Canadian correctional institutions on a trial basis? Why or why not?
2. If yes, which criteria would you use to determine whether such an initiative was successful?
3. If yes, would you require inmates who worked in prison industries to contribute to the costs of their room and board? Pay victim compensation?

Religious Programs and the Chaplaincy

From the construction of the first prisons in the early 1800s to the present, religion has been a key component of institutional life. Although there are no Canadian data on the numbers of inmates who participate in religious programs and services in Canadian institutions, figures from the United States indicate that one in three inmates is involved in religious programs. It can be assumed that the numbers are much the same in Canada.

Across Canada, a wide range of religious groups and organizations are involved in offering programs on a volunteer basis to inmates. In Ontario, for example, provincial Chaplaincy Services are the equal responsibility of the Ministry of Community and Social Services, the Ministry of Public Safety and Security, and the Ministry of Health. Across the province, there are a number of Regional Multifaith Committees that address the religious and spiritual needs of inmates in adult and youth institutions and under supervision in the community. Aboriginal Elders are also involved in providing cultural and spiritual guidance to Aboriginal inmates in many institutions.

Despite the extensive involvement of inmates in religious programs and the volunteer activities of religious groups and organizations inside correctional institutions, there are few published studies on the impact of religious programs on the attitudes, values, and behaviours of inmate participants during confinement and following release. Research in the United States suggests that inmates who are committed to their religious beliefs and participate extensively in religious programs have fewer institutional infractions and are significantly less likely than those inmates who had low levels or no involvement in prison fellowship to be rearrested within the first year following release (Clear et al., 1992; Johnson, Larson, and Pitts, 1997).

Community Involvement in Institutional Programs

Community volunteers are involved in a wide range of activities in federal and provincial/territorial institutions. Many volunteers represent community service clubs and organizations, and others work one-on-one with inmates both during confinement and following release. The most active programs of this type are M2 (Man to Man) and W2 (Woman to Woman). These programs involve a citizen from the community being matched with an offender. Across the country, college and university students are also actively involved in institutional programs.

FEMALE INMATES AND TREATMENT

Historically, women in prison were subjected to gender-stereotyped programs such as hairdressing and sewing. Over the past decade, however, federal and provincial/territorial systems of corrections have given increasing attention to the distinct treatment needs of female offenders. First, the application to women of risk/needs instruments that were developed for men has been called into question. Under CSC policy, instruments such as the highly regarded Psychopathy Check List (PCL) are not applied to female offenders, despite a lack of evidence that they are gender-biased. Separate classification and risk assessment instruments have not been developed for female offenders.

Second, the entire paradigm of corrections and corrections research has been challenged. The Task Force on Federally Sentenced Women (1990) noted the inherent contradiction in a system that purports to promote responsibility and accountability but accomplishes the opposite. Using a women-centred approach, the task force outlined five principles to guide correctional responses to women: empowerment, meaningful and responsible choices, respect and dignity, supportive environment, and shared responsibility. The recommendations of the task force were criticized for not adequately addressing the social, economic, and political barriers that keep women marginalized (Hannah-Moffat, 1995). Indeed, the Women's Issues Task Force (1995) of Ontario recognized that a correctional strategy for women had to acknowledge the wider systemic barriers facing women in general—barriers that include poverty, unemployment, lack of education, and sexism.

The needs of women in conflict with the law are many and can include life-skill deficits, low educational achievement, unemployment, substance abuse, housing problems, emotional problems, and parenting struggles. Women, especially Aboriginal women and other women of colour, may suffer systemic disadvantages that compound the situation by acting as barriers to full participation in the labour force. Legal issues can include disputes over custody of their children and child welfare proceedings in family court, as well as their own troubles with the criminal justice system.

Risk/needs assessments of a sample of female offenders in Canada revealed significantly higher levels of difficulty with behavioural and emotional stability, family relations, and academic and vocational skills compared with male offenders (Blanchette and Dowden, 1998). The needs of the female offender may well be higher than those of men, despite the fact that women's offences are generally less serious. According to a Statistics Canada survey

(Robinson et al., 1998), incarcerated women are younger than their male counterparts and are less likely than male inmates to be incarcerated for an interpersonal offence.

Another feature of the population of incarcerated women that has implications for treatment is the prevalence of abuse victimization in their histories. In one Canadian study, the number of women with victimization histories was 82 percent in the federal system and 72 percent in provincial institutions (Task Force on Federally Sentenced Women, 1990). The figures were even higher for Aboriginal women. Comack (1993), studying provincial prisoners in Manitoba, found that 78 percent of those women reported childhood or partner abuse. These findings, mirrored in many other studies, reveal levels of victimization higher than those in the general population of women or among male inmates (Haskell and Randall, 1993; Weeks and Widom, 1998).

There are two paradigms for intervention with women. The first is the empowerment and consciousness-raising approach, which focuses on the social and political sources of violence against women and emphasizes the dynamics of power and control. Program material is typically delivered in a group format, in which women learn that they are not alone and that all women are affected by inequality. The second paradigm is the therapeutic or medical model, which focuses more on the individual woman and her feelings and beliefs (Correctional Service of Canada, 1995). Each approach has its critics. The first is typically criticized for immobilizing some women by failing to give them the tools to make individual changes. The psychotherapeutic approach is seen by many as disempowering and blaming and as putting too much emphasis on the need for the woman alone to change.

Increasingly, a role for both orientations is being recognized, especially with the move toward holistic treatment approaches in which the lines between program areas are blurred. This trend is consistent with the cognitive-behavioural approach, whereby everyday activities are seen as opportunities to practise problem solving, communication, and anger management skills. This is the philosophy underlying the new facilities for federally sentenced women.

ABORIGINAL INMATES AND TREATMENT

So, prison is no place to recover. From anything, either the grief of memory, or loss, or abuse, or the diseases of addiction. But if you're Native and you can get the help to seek and find and claim your spiritual name, a lot can be changed. You can discover your destiny. You life can bridge back to the origins of your family and people, you can seek out your colours, your clan, your spirit keepers. You may find the self you never knew you were.

—Yvonne Johnson, cited in Wiebe and Johnson, 1998:387

The special treatment needs of Aboriginal inmates have received increasing attention by systems of corrections, driven in large measure by the high rates of incarceration of Aboriginal offenders. In addition to sharing many of the attributes of inmates generally, such as low levels of formal education and vocational skills, Aboriginal inmates may not have a supportive family or community to return to upon release and may lack positive role models upon which to pattern their attitudes and behaviours. They may also have little knowledge of traditional Aboriginal culture and lifeways (Nuffield, 1998:13). In an attempt to address the special needs of Aboriginal offenders, new institutions and programs have been designed and implemented (see Box 8.7).

The overrepresentation of Aboriginal offenders is particularly acute in provincial/territorial institutions. Addressing the treatment needs of these offenders—many of whom have been confined in provincial/territorial facilities on previous occasions—is hindered by the relatively short periods of confinement and by the reluctance of many Aboriginal inmates to participate in treatment programs.

A wide variety of Aboriginal-specific programs can be found in federal and provincial/territorial institutions. Many of these programs are operated by

BOX 8.7

Treatment in Pê Sâkâstêw Institution

Aboriginal Elders were directly involved in reviewing and developing the rehabilitation programs at Pê Sâkâstêw, a minimum-security institution for Aboriginal male offenders on the Samson Cree Nation in Alberta. Programs are centred on Aboriginal healing and include a sweat lodge. Inmates in the minimum-security facility are called *Owiciiyisiwak*, which in the Cree language means "here to learn." Offenders are carefully screened prior to being sent to the institution and must have demonstrated an interest in rehabilitation programs and have a history of positive interaction with correctional staff. Generally, inmates have less than two years remaining until release when they arrive at the institution and spend about eight months preparing for release by participating in a variety of programs and activities.

systems of corrections, while others are sponsored by outside Aboriginal organizations and agencies. In many institutions, Native liaison workers and Elders play key roles in program delivery (Waldram, 1997). Many of the programs for Aboriginal inmates in federal and provincial/territorial correctional facilities incorporate elements of culture and spirituality, reflecting "the belief that unique solutions are required to reflect the unique cultural backgrounds of aboriginal inmates, and that loss of cultural roots and identity are the primary causes of involvement in the criminal justice system" (LaPrairie, 1996:79). The Aboriginal Gang Initiative, a program developed by the CSC to address the reintegration needs of the estimated 300 Aboriginal gang members confined in federal institutions in the Prairie region, assists gang members in finding a new identity that is rooted in their traditional culture and spirituality (Phillips, 2002).

Programs designed to address the needs of Aboriginal inmates and offenders have taken a variety of approaches. Whereas many programs and agencies focus on Aboriginal spiritual and cultural activities, others emphasize providing offenders with the skills to survive upon release, particularly those who will be returning to urban areas. The emerging consensus is that programs for Aboriginal offenders should combine traditional Aboriginal approaches with contemporary treatment methods (Zellerer, 1994).

Among the more common Aboriginal-specific programs that may be found in correctional institutions across the country are sweat lodges, healing circles, Native and cultural awareness, substance abuse treatment, and programs designed to address family violence. Among the First Nations programs offered in the Whitehorse Correctional Centre, for example, are the Elders Program/Traditional Medicine Program, in which traditional medicine, spirituality, and healing are used to assist offenders; the Solstice/Equinox program, which involves feasts to celebrate the changing of the seasons; sweat lodge ceremonies, which assist inmates in connecting with their spirituality and in building inner strength; and the Sharing Circle, a group meeting in which inmates share their problems and ideas with a facilitator and one another. Among a sample of federal Aboriginal inmates, two-thirds held positive views toward programs such as sweat lodge ceremonies that promoted personal healing and cultural awareness, and there were high rates of participation in these programs (Johnston, 1997). One of the more innovative programs for Aboriginal inmates in presented in Box 8.8.

There have been few formal evaluations of programs and little follow-up of inmates who participated in them. Evaluation of a pilot project for Aboriginal offenders offered in federal institutions in the Ontario region found that the program improved inmates' attitudes toward Aboriginal culture, created a safer institutional environment, and raised awareness among

An Aboriginal Elder (left) and an inmate helper prepare for a sweat lodge ceremony at Mission Institution, British Columbia.

Aboriginal employees, although no follow-up of inmate participants was conducted after their release. An evaluation of the Ma Mawi Wi Chi Itata family violence program in Stony Mountain Institution (described in Box 8.8) found high levels of inmate satisfaction with the content and process of the program and a widely shared view among inmate participants that the program had significantly affected their behaviour, attitudes, and emotions. Similarly positive assessments were provided by staff involved in the program. No attempt was made to measure post-release outcomes (Proulx and Perrault, 1996). There is some evidence to suggest that community-based approaches are more effective and cost-efficient than healing circles and sweat lodges (Lane et al., 2002).

Aboriginal-Specific versus Generalist Programs for Aboriginal Inmates

The lack of evaluations of treatment programs for Aboriginal offenders makes it difficult to determine whether Aboriginal-specific programs are more effective than generalist programs that are offered to both Aboriginal and non-Aboriginal inmates. Although the belief is widespread that Aboriginal-specific treatment interventions are more effective than general programs, LaPrairie

BOX 8.8

The Ma Mawi Wi Chi Itata Family Violence Program, Stony Mountain Institution (Manitoba)

This program for Aboriginal inmates is designed to address the issues related to violent behaviour and attempts to alter inmates' patterns of violent behaviour toward spouses and family members, as well as disruptive behaviour in the institutional setting. Education, counselling, healing, and prevention is the primary focus of the program, which incorporates contemporary and traditional treatment approaches.

The program is divided into four sections, each representing a geographical direction on the Medicine Wheel:

- *The East:* represented by the eagle; the primary objective is "to see"; focus is on the cycle of violence, the role of socialization in committing violence, and the relationship between violence and substance abuse
- *The South:* represented by the mouse; the primary objective is "to do"; focus is on offender's expressing negative emotions, including childhood experiences and family origin; exploration of feelings of shame and guilt for past behaviour, including discussion of inmate's most violent incident
- *The West:* represented by the bear; primary objective is "to think"; education on and discussion of the impact of violence on children and families; consideration of the various dimensions of relationships and skills in substituting assertiveness for aggression
- *The North:* represented by the buffalo; purpose is "to know"; focus is on taking the middle way; inmates meet in sharing circles to establish goals, share stories, and relate feelings

At the completion of the program, there are a number of ceremonies, including a sweat lodge ceremony and a feast. These ceremonies and the program itself are designed to provide the Aboriginal inmate with a new identity.

Source: Proulx and Perrault, 1996.

notes that "the evidence for this is often anecdotal and often put forward by the people who write policy or deliver programs" (1996:82).

Despite the proliferation of programs and services for Aboriginal offenders, there are a number of unanswered questions about the needs of

Aboriginal offenders and how to develop and deliver effective treatment programs for Aboriginal inmates:

- Does a policy of cultural-specific programming inhibit Aboriginal participation in mainstream programs that might be beneficial?
- How much does Aboriginal-specific programming reflect the desires and needs of Aboriginal offenders as identified *by them*, and how much does it reflect a larger Aboriginal political/service delivery agenda?
- What criteria are to be used in determining whether a program is culturally appropriate, given the diversity of Aboriginal cultures in Canada?
- How and by whom is the legitimacy of spiritual healers and Elders and other deliverers of spiritual programs to be established?
- To what extent should one cultural group's practices, such as the sweat lodge, be used by Aboriginal offenders from other groups? (LaPrairie, 1996:83–84)

COMMUNITY SERVICE PROJECTS AND ACTIVITIES

The media's focus on the more sensational events in corrections, such as escapes, riots, and heinous crimes committed by offenders under supervision in the community, tends to obscure the extensive involvement of inmate populations in community service projects (see Box 8.9). These activities not only benefit various groups of community residents, but also provide an outlet for the energies and talents of inmates. Participation in community projects may also assist inmates in developing prosocial attitudes and behaviours.

PRINCIPLES OF EFFECTIVE CORRECTIONAL TREATMENT

There are five core principles that provide the basis for effective correctional treatment.

The Risk Principle

As previously noted, there are two categories of risk factors: static factors, including the inmate attributes of age, offence history, and prior confinements; and dynamic factors (or criminogenic needs), including antisocial values, attitudes, and behaviours. Although static factors are predictive of recidivism for many offenders, these attributes cannot be changed. Dynamic factors, which may also be related to reoffending, are amenable to change and are the target of treatment interventions.

Inmate and developmentally challenged youth, Community Sports
Day, Mission Institution, British Columbia

The **risk principle** holds that treatment interventions have a greater
chance of success when they are matched with the risk level of the offender.
Higher levels of service are reserved for higher-risk inmates; lower-risk
inmates do not require the same level of service to benefit from treatment
interventions and may, in fact, be negatively affected by intensive service
delivery. Among the risk factors that have been identified are:

- antisocial attitudes, values, beliefs, rationalizations, and cognitive-emotional states (such as anger, resentment, defiance, or despair)
- antisocial associates
- a history of antisocial behaviour
- temperamental aggressiveness, callousness, egocentricity, impulsiveness, psychopathy, and weak socialization
- a lack of problem-solving or self-management skills
- general problems at home, school, work, or leisure
- lower-class origins
- personal distress indicators
- biological and neurophysiological factors (Andrews, 1995:43)

BOX 8.9

Selected Inmate Community Service Projects

- Inmates at Dorchester Penitentiary (N.B.) and at the Nova Institution for Women (N.S.) participated in the Toys for Tots program by making and repairing toys for distribution at Christmas to needy families in the local community.
- Offenders at Beaver Creek Institution in Gravenhurst, Ontario, cleaned up parks, bagged candies for the annual Santa Claus parade, and assisted in the maintenance and repair of cottages for citizens who attend a dialysis camp.
- Offenders at the Okimaw Ohci Healing Lodge in Maple Creek, Saskatchewan, provided homemade blankets to a shelter for persons with disabilities.
- Offenders at Mountain Institution in Agassiz, British Columbia, volunteered to repair wheelchairs for senior citizens and persons with disabilities.

Source: Correctional Service of Canada, 2000, 2001.

The Need Principle

The **need principle** holds that to be effective, treatment interventions must also address the criminogenic needs of inmates. These include such attributes as alcohol or substance abuse, relations with peers, and attitudes toward and experience with employment. The objective of targeting criminogenic needs is to alter personal attributes of the offender to reduce the likelihood of reoffending.

The Responsivity Principle

The **responsivity principle** states that treatment interventions must be matched to the learning styles and abilities of individual inmates. In practice, this may mean that certain offenders, such as those with lower IQs, will require special programs.

Professional Discretion

Effective treatment interventions require that correctional personnel consider the unique attributes of individual inmates and apply the above three principles in an appropriate manner. There is considerable heterogeneity even among inmates convicted of the same crimes, such as sex offenders, or with similar histories, such as substance abuse, and these must be considered by the treatment professional.

Program Integrity

This principle states that efforts must be made to ensure that treatment programs are designed and delivered by qualified professionals whose adherence to the treatment model is monitored.

CREATING THE CONDITIONS FOR EFFECTIVE CORRECTIONAL TREATMENT

In addition to incorporating the above principles into the design and delivery of correctional treatment programs, there are a number of additional related factors that may enhance treatment effectiveness (see Palmer, 1994).

Correctional Officers and Correctional Staff

Effective program interventions require correctional officers and staff who understand and support the objectives of correctional treatment. This ensures that institutional staff reinforce, rather than undermine, treatment efforts. You will recall from the discussion in Chapter 6, however, that, in comparison with other institutional staff, correctional officers are more punitive in their attitudes toward inmates and are less supportive of rehabilitation programs. Correctional officers also may provide various types of assistance to inmates and, in so doing, act as change agents. The level of motivation, attitudes, training, experience, and other attributes of correctional staff and treatment personnel all contribute to successful treatment interventions (Lösel, 1995:96).

There are other correctional personnel within institutions, including civilians who supervise industry and agricultural programs, who may also have an impact on the attitudes and behaviours of inmates. A study of the CSC industry program, CORCAN, for example, found that shop instructors who had dynamic leadership styles and encouraged inmates had a significant impact on inmate behaviour in the institution (Gillis et al., 1995).

Matching Inmate Needs with Programs

One of the challenges confronting systems of corrections is how to address the needs of a client population that is marginal in terms of lifestyle, skills, and abilities. Historically, treatment programs were delivered to inmate populations within a "one size fits all" framework, the assumption being that all inmates would benefit equally from exposure to a specific intervention.

Although inmate populations share some general attributes—for example, low levels of education and skill development and histories of alcohol and substance abuse—each inmate is first and foremost an individual with unique needs and requirements. Heterogeneity, rather than uniformity, characterizes inmates, even those who have committed the same type of offence. To be effective, treatment interventions must be multifaceted and matched to the specific needs of individual offenders. This is the notion of **differential treatment effectiveness.** Classification and case management are designed to assist in determining the needs of individual offenders.

Inmate Amenability to Treatment

The inmate is a key component of the treatment process. For any program to have a significant impact on the attitudes and behaviours of the inmate, the offender must be amenable to treatment. Among the inmates in any institutional population there is a **differential amenability to treatment.** That is, for a variety of reasons, including mental deficiency or learning disability, a deeply rooted attitudinal and behavioural pattern centred on a criminal lifestyle, an extensive history of confinement in institutions, and/or a general lack of interest in making the effort to change, not all inmates are receptive to treatment. Many offenders are in a state of denial about the offence for which they have been convicted, and this frame of mind may make effective treatment intervention more difficult. Among the more common attributes of sex offenders, for example, are denial of the offence and a tendency to blame the victim for the incident.

Until recently, offenders were generally excluded from having input into determining the specific treatment programs they would take part in while in the care and control of correctional systems. It is now an accepted principle of correctional practice that inmates must be active participants in their treatment and, importantly, that such participation reflects a desire to change, rather than a manipulation of the treatment process to secure conditional release.

A challenge for systems of corrections and treatment personnel is to develop strategies that will interest and motivate inmates to become involved in treatment programs as part of a concerted effort to alter their attitudes and values. The Northern Treatment Centre in Ontario, profiled in Box 8.10, is an innovative approach to correctional treatment.

BOX 8.10

Northern Treatment Centre (Sault Ste. Marie, Ont.): A Unique Correctional Institution

The Northern Treatment Centre (NTC) is a 96-bed, medium-security facility for federal and provincial inmates operated by the Ontario Ministry of Public Safety and Security, Correctional Services. The entire structure and organization of the centre is directed toward the treatment of offenders, and programs are based on a psychoeducational and cognitive-behavioural approach. Inmates must apply for admission to the centre from their home institution, and priority is given to offenders from Northern Ontario, particularly Aboriginal inmates.

Once accepted, offenders are assessed for potential referral to the five core program areas: substance abuse, criminal beliefs and attitudes, anger management, personal relationships, and domestic violence. There is also a series of programs for Aboriginal inmates, focusing on substance abuse, community, family and child care, and cultural awareness. NTC programs are delivered by staff trained in social work and psychology and are designed to be completed within a 90- to 120-day period. Correctional officers are involved in security and control as well as case management. The NTC is an example of a correctional institution based on an integrated treatment model. This model is illustrated in Figure 8.2.

Source: Leschied and Cunningham, 1998.

Figure 8.2

Integrated Treatment Model of the Northern Treatment Centre

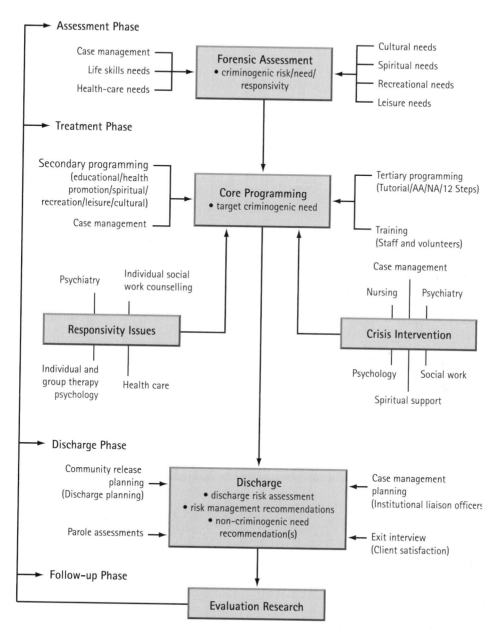

Source: L. Rosine, Chief Psychologist, Northern Treatment Centre, 1998.

Continuity of Treatment Interventions from Institution to Community

A longstanding challenge to systems of corrections has been to ensure continuity between treatment interventions in institutional settings and in the community following release. The absence of resources, the lack of communication between institutional treatment personnel and their community-based counterparts, and the loss of eligibility to participate in community-based programs upon warrant expiry have all contributed to the lack of treatment continuity. There is evidence to suggest, for example, that when institutional treatment interventions for substance abusers is part of a continuum with community-based treatment following release, there are higher rates of long-term abstinence (Inciardi, 1996). Continuity of treatment is a major issue when Aboriginal inmates return to northern or remote communities.

THE EFFECTIVENESS OF CORRECTIONAL TREATMENT

Since the introduction of treatment programs into correctional institutions in the 1950s, there has been an ongoing (and still unresolved) controversy over their effectiveness. The debate has involved politicians, community interest groups, correctional scholars, and senior and line-level correctional personnel.

"Nothing Works": The Legacy of Robert Martinson

For the past 25 years, no discussion of the effectiveness of correctional treatment programs has been complete without mention of Robert Martinson, a scholar who conducted a survey of over 200 treatment programs and concluded that "with few and isolated exceptions, the rehabilitative efforts that have been reported so far have had no appreciable effect on recidivism" (1974:25). The "nothing works" finding, as it became known, had a significant impact on correctional policy for many years, even though, in a less publicized effort, Martinson (1979) himself re-evaluated the treatment programs five years later using more valid criteria and concluded that some treatment did have an effect on recidivism.

Martinson's name and study continue to be invoked by correctional observers who contend that rehabilitation programs are ineffective in altering the attitudes and behaviours of inmates and in reducing rates of reoffending.

"Some Things Work": Evaluations of Correctional Treatment Programs

The "nothing works" doctrine is a fiction that is not based on science.

—Cullen and Gendreau, 2001:332

Over the past decade, numerous research studies have shown that *some treatment programs are effective with some offenders.* In fact, effective treatment interventions have been found to reduce rates of reoffending by as much as 50 percent (Lurgio, 2000), although other observers have placed the reductions in the range of 10 percent (Bonta, 1997; Lösel, 1996; Sherman et al., 1997). That said, determining which interventions are the most effective with which inmates remains a challenge. As one observer has noted, even with some "rather promising results, we are still far from a conclusive answer with respect to what works best, with whom and under what conditions ... offender treatment research is still in its infancy" (Lösel, cited in Roberts, 1995:233).

Bonta (1997:8) has summarized what the research tells us about rehabilitation programs:

- Direct treatment services are more likely than criminal sanctions to reduce recidivism.
- Effective treatment programs follow the principles of risk and need.
- Effective treatment programs are cognitive-behavioural in nature.

A review of the effectiveness of selected treatment interventions is presented in Box 8.11.

BOX 8.11

Research Summary: The Effectiveness of Selected Treatment Interventions

Adult Basic Education: A significant relationship exists between program completion and reduced likelihood of recidivism upon release, even among high-risk inmates. Effectiveness may be improved with more continuity between prison education and post-release follow-up and support.

BOX 8.11, continued

University-Level Education: For some offenders, participation in university degree programs reduces the risk of reoffending.

Vocational and Work Programs: There is some evidence that participation in vocational and work programs reduces levels of misconduct in the institution, increases the likelihood that the offender will find employment when released, and increases the chances of success in the community.

Cognitive Skills Programs: This is a very successful intervention when appropriately matched with inmate needs. Acquisition of skills results in reduced rates of recidivism upon release, even for violent offenders. This is also an effective intervention for offenders under supervision in the community.

Life Skills Programs: For some inmates, these programs are effective in increasing post-release success.

Anger Management Programs: There is some evidence that high-risk offenders who participate in these programs have significantly reduced rates of nonviolent and violent recidivism upon release.

Substance Abuse Programs: There is evidence that federal offenders who complete these programs have lower rates of re-admission and fewer new convictions.

Sex Offender Treatment Programs: Research evidence shows that some treatment interventions, particularly those using a cognitive-behavioural approach and containing a relapse prevention component, are successful in reducing rates of reoffending among some categories of sex offenders.

Violent Offender Programs: Group-centred interventions that focus on anger management and cognitive-behavioural skills development are successful in reducing institutional misconduct and post-release recidivism among violent offenders.

Religious Programs: Although there are no published evaluations in Canada, findings from the United States suggest that participation in religious programs has a positive impact on the attitudes, values, and behaviour of inmates, resulting in fewer incidents of institutional misconduct and reduced likelihood of recidivism upon release.

Aboriginal Treatment Programs: There have been few formal evaluations of treatment interventions for Aboriginal offenders and the impact of these programs on institutional and post-release behaviour, attitudes, and values. There is no empirical evidence that healing programs are effective in reducing the risk of reoffending upon release. Anecdotal evidence regarding some programs is positive.

Source: Motiuk, Boe, and Nafekh, 2002.

MEASURING THE EFFECTIVENESS OF CORRECTIONAL TREATMENT

Efforts to assess the effectiveness of treatment programs have been afflicted by a number of difficulties.

The Absence and Poor Quality of Program Evaluations

A major obstacle in determining "what works" is the absence of a standardized evaluative framework. The failure of studies to use such a framework makes it difficult to determine whether those offenders who participated in a particular treatment program benefited from the experience in comparison with a matched group of inmates who did not participate in the program. In addition, program evaluations often focus on program design while paying insufficient attention to treatment outcomes (Lane et al., 2002).

Studies of the effectiveness of treatment interventions in provincial/territorial institutions are virtually nonexistent. These systems of corrections have the added difficulty of high inmate turnover, which is an obstacle not only to the delivery of treatment programs, but also to any attempts to determine program success.

Measuring Treatment Success: A Difficult Task

The traditional method used to determine success is **recidivism rates**—the number of offenders who, once released from confinement, are returned to prison either for a technical violation of a condition of their parole or statutory release or for the commission of a new offence. The use of recidivism rates as a measure of program effectiveness has been criticized on a number of counts:

- Using legal criteria of subsequent contact with the criminal justice system makes no provision for the "relative" improvement of the offender. Offenders who previously committed serious crimes and are subsequently returned to confinement for a relatively minor offence might be viewed as a "relative success," rather than as a failure.
- The question of how long after release from confinement the offender's behaviour is to be monitored is undecided. Many types of sex offenders, for example, remain a high risk to reoffend for a decade or longer following release.
- Recidivism rates are a result of detection of the released offender by parole or police officers. In fact, the offender may have returned to criminal activity and not have been detected, a not unlikely scenario

given that clearance rates of the police for most nonviolent offences is less than 20 percent and often as low as 5 percent.

- The success or failure of an offender upon release may be due in large measure to the level and types of supervision that he or she receives. Among parole officers there are a variety of supervision styles, ranging from officers who have a more punitive orientation to those who focus on providing services and assistance (more on this in Chapter 10).
- It is difficult to relate the offender's behaviour upon release to specific treatment interventions that he or she received while incarcerated. There are many reasons why an individual may cease violating the law, including the efforts of a supportive family and/or spouse, success in securing stable employment, and maturation.

The use of control groups within a standardized evaluative framework eliminates many of the problems associated with using recidivism as an outcome measure.

The Notion of "Relative" Success upon Release

In an attempt to address many of these difficulties with using recidivism rates to measure the effectiveness of treatment interventions, several observers have suggested the use of more refined indicators of post-institution behaviour, including the following:

- *clear reformation:* offenders who have been on parole, have stable employment, and are not associating with persons involved in criminal activity
- *marginal reformation:* offenders who have not been returned to a correctional institution but have failed to maintain employment, are associating with persons involved in criminal activities, and/or have committed minor offences
- *marginal failures:* offenders who are returned to correctional institutions for violating the conditions of their release or for minor crimes
- *clear recidivists:* offenders who commit a major crime and are returned to prison (Glaser, 1964:31–58)

This scheme was proposed four decades ago and, in recent years, correctional researchers have distinguished between those offenders returned to institutions for violations of release conditions and those who committed new offences.

POTENTIAL OBSTACLES TO EFFECTIVE CORRECTIONAL TREATMENT

There are a number of potential obstacles to the delivery of effective treatment programs in correctional institutions. These include the following:

Punishment versus Treatment

The primary mandate of correctional institutions—to securely confine offenders—often undermines the objectives of treatment programs. You will recall from the discussion in Chapter 5 that a defining attribute of correctional institutions is that they are public and political institutions. The availability of treatment resources may be limited by politicians, legislatures, and community interest groups:

> *The kinds of treatments which the correctional authorities are able to offer are often limited by society's demands for painful prison conditions.... Programs that attempt to create an environment where a useful treatment atmosphere can be developed are commonly attacked as "country club prisons" that do not provide enough pain. (Travis, Schwartz, and Clear, 1983:178–79)*

In recent years, community interest groups and politicians have voiced concerns about the living conditions in correctional institutions and the privileges accorded to inmates. The cancellation of the on-site university-level education program offered by the CSC was a response to the argument that inmates were getting a free education while citizens in the outside community were required to assume the costs of education. Currently, inmates may enroll in university-level correspondence courses but must assume the costs of tuition and books.

Resistance to rehabilitation programs for inmates is likely to be most pronounced when crime rates are perceived to be high, when governments are experiencing fiscal restraint, and when the economy and rates of employment have slowed.

Doing Time and Doing Treatment

> *Our contemporary prisons basically replicate the social order that produced the offenders to begin with. Their signal qualities are violence, idleness, and noise.*

—Mark A.R. Kleiman, professor of public policy, cited in Talbot, 2003:97

The discussion in Chapter 7 revealed that inmates are confronted with a variety of pains of imprisonment, as well as with the need to develop coping and survival strategies for doing time. Although inmate adherence to the convict code has eroded in recent years, the inmate social system, with its attendant activities in securing illicit goods and services, and the violence and coercion that exist in many institutions are major obstacles to correctional treatment. For those inmates who must spend a considerable portion of their time and energy coping with confinement and avoiding victimization, pursuing self-change through participation in treatment programs may be difficult. Inmates may also be subject to pressure from other inmates, in the form of threats or intimidation, not to participate in treatment programs.

As noted in Chapter 5, the CSC has recently opened a number of Intensive Support Units (ISUs)—drug-free units that house inmates who want to avoid the violence, intimidation, and other problems associated with illicit drug use and distribution. Although it is hoped that the establishment of ISUs will remove some of the barriers to correctional treatment, there has been no evaluation of their effectiveness to date.

The Institutional Environment

Ironically, one of the biggest potential obstacles to the delivery of effective correctional treatment may be the institution itself and the dynamics of life inside correctional institutions. As previously noted, all correctional institutions are total institutions, a primary attribute of which is the strict control exercised over all facets of the inmate's daily life. Such control is antithetical to the goals of treatment, rehabilitation, and self-change, which require that inmates assume responsibility for their behaviour and develop effective decision-making and problem-solving skills.

However, the environment of correctional institutions may not have a uniformly negative impact on treatment efforts. There are a number of factors related to the correctional facility and the individual inmate that may moderate the potentially negative attributes of the institution. Recall from the discussion of prison architecture in Chapter 5 that many of the federal correctional institutions constructed in recent years have been designed to create more positive environments for staff and inmates. For individual inmates, the use of successful coping mechanisms may also moderate the more negative features of prison life and increase the inmate's amenability to treatment interventions. The integrity of program delivery, whether in an institutional or community setting, remains a key factor in effectiveness.

Inmate Access to Programs

How treatment programs are delivered, including the timeliness of program offerings and the extent to which programs attract and retain inmate participants, can affect treatment outcomes. For treatment interventions to be effective, the inmate must have the opportunity to participate in and complete the particular treatment program. Generally, treatment programs operate on one of two types of schedules: *closed group*, which means that the treatment program begins and ends on specified dates and inmates must participate in all of the sessions; and *open group* (or continuous intake programs), which allow inmates to join the treatment program at any time if space is available. Most treatment programs are of the closed group variety, which often makes it difficult to match offenders with programs. These designations do not apply to treatment programs that involve one-on-one interventions with inmates.

Access to and completion of programs is a problem for many inmates in federal institutions. A lack of space and program resources often results in inmates waiting months or even years to gain access to specific programs. Although the classification process is able to determine the programming needs of inmates, many offenders either never enroll or fail to complete the recommended programs. A study of high-risk offenders participating in a violent offender program found that one in three inmates failed to complete the program; non-completers tended to be high-risk inmates with low levels of education and a poor employment record (Wormith and Olver, 2002). Figure 8.3 illustrates the "timeline" problems encountered by a sample of 1,800 federal inmates.

In provincial/territorial correctional facilities, the relatively short period of confinement is a major impediment to the delivery of effective correctional treatment. The majority of inmates spend only a few months in a controlled institutional environment prior to being transferred to minimum-security facilities or released under some form of supervision in the community. This limited time precludes participation in treatment programs or limits program participation to short periods, despite the fact that offenders in these facilities have many of the same deficiencies as federal inmates, including low levels of education, a propensity for violence, and a variety of substance abuse, anger management, and mental-health problems.

The levels of program participation are also a potential obstacle to treatment success, particularly for Aboriginal inmates, who may feel that treatment programs are not relevant to them or be uncomfortable interacting with non-Aboriginal staff and inmates. This hesitancy may be most pronounced among high-risk inmates.

Figure 8.3

Average Time to Achieve Milestones in the Case Management Process

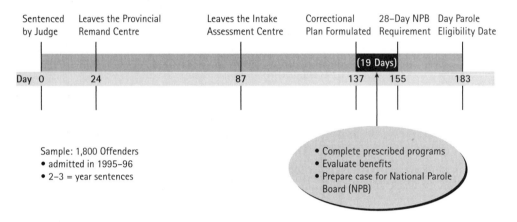

Source: Auditor General of Canada, 1996:16 (ch. 30). Reproduced with permission of the Minister of Public Works and Government Services Canada, 1999.

There is also **differential treatment availability,** both within provincial/territorial jurisdictions and between the various regions of the CSC. This results in situations, for example, where a high-risk sex offender would receive a year of treatment in a specialized program in one CSC region, while a sex offender in another region might complete only a six-month, nonresidential program. In fact, the CSC spends only 7 percent of its $1.5-billion budget on treatment programs.

Program Fidelity and Program Drift

A key factor in the development of effective correctional treatment is program implementation (Gendreau, Goggin, and Smith, 1999). Correctional authorities must ensure that there is **program fidelity**—that is, that a treatment program is delivered in the way it was originally designed. Program fidelity can be assured by having a clear program manual and appropriate training and supervision of treatment staff.

The comments of one federal inmate illustrate the problem of program fidelity:

The Substance Abuse Program I attended involved nothing more than watching a series of videotapes two days a week for 10 weeks. Our group viewed the tapes, then were dismissed. There was no discussion; there was no interaction between facilitator and group; there was no attempt to talk about anything. After the program was over I had an idea what abuse of drugs and alcohol would do to my body, but I had no idea why I ever wanted to use them. (Kowbel, 1995:A20)

It is also important to use outcome measures that can detect **program drift.** For example, if a substance abuse program has shown to be effective in reducing levels of substance abuse among released offenders, an increase in substance use among program completers can indicate that program delivery is drifting, and the necessary steps can be taken to correct this.

The notion of program fidelity is still a relatively new idea in corrections. One way to address the issue is through the process of site accreditation. There is a trend in many Western countries, including the United States and England, for correctional institutions to be assessed against pre-set standards. For example, the American Correctional Association will perform site audits and accredit facilities that meet set levels of mandatory and optional standards. Where treatment programs are concerned, the process involves ensuring that treatment providers have sufficient education and training, they are adequately supervised, outcomes are monitored, the culture of the institution is supportive of the treatment program, and non-treatment staff understand the program.

THE ETHICS OF CORRECTIONAL TREATMENT

Historically, inmates had no power to resist the sanctions imposed on them, and a wide variety of punishments have been inflicted on inmates under the guise of treatment. These punishments included electroshock therapy, which was administered to many inmates without their consent until the 1980s. Inmates were also used as subjects in a variety of experiments, including studies of the effects of LSD. Although the inmates in this series of studies did provide consent, the issue is whether a captive person is able to provide informed consent. The enactment of the Canadian Charter of Rights and Freedoms (1982) has provided inmates with some degree of legal protection. One issue is whether inmates have the right to refuse treatment while confined. Check out the following At Issue.

AT ISSUE

SHOULD INMATES HAVE THE RIGHT TO REFUSE TREATMENT?

Consider the following scenario: An inmate convicted of a sex offence is sentenced to 15 years in prison. During confinement, he refuses to participate in treatment programs. As a consequence, he does not receive any form of conditional release, is denied statutory release after having served two-thirds of the sentence, and serves his entire sentence in prison. Upon his warrant expiry date, he is released, untreated, from the correctional institution, at high risk of reoffending.

This raises the issue of whether inmates have a legal right to refuse treatment. A provision of the Corrections and Conditional Release Act states that inmates must provide informed consent, both at the onset and during treatment, and that the inmate has the right to refuse treatment or to withdraw from a treatment program at any time. The Canadian Charter of Rights and Freedoms also guarantees that all persons have the right to life, liberty, and security of the person—rights that would most likely be violated by any provision of mandatory treatment (McKinnon, 1995).

QUESTIONS

1. What is your position on the right of inmates to refuse treatment? Would you, for example, support an attempt to impose mandatory treatment on certain categories of offenders (e.g., sex offenders and violent offenders)?
2. Inmates who refuse treatment may have applications for conditional release denied and may also be prohibited from being released on their statutory release date. This means they will serve their entire sentence in confinement and be released with no conditions or supervision. Given this, would you support the release of serious offenders on either conditional release or statutory release even if they have refused to participate in treatment programs?

QUESTIONS FOR REVIEW

1. Define classification and its role in corrections.
2. What factors are considered in determining an inmate's security level during the initial classification stage?
3. What is the role of risk analysis in the classification process?
4. Compare and contrast static risk factors and dynamic risk factors, and note the role of each type of factor in the classification process.
5. Define and discuss the goals of correctional case management.
6. Describe the basic tenets of cognitive skills training for inmates.

7. Define (a) the risk principle, (b) the need principle, and (c) the responsivity principle, and then discuss the role that each plays in the creation of effective correctional treatment.

8. What is meant by (a) differential treatment effectiveness and (b) differential amenability to treatment, and how do each of these notions contribute to our understanding of correctional treatment for inmates? Why is measuring treatment success so difficult?

9. Discuss the issues surrounding treatment programs for female offenders.

10. Describe what research studies indicate about the effectiveness of the following treatment interventions: (a) adult basic education, (b) cognitive skills programs, (c) sex offender treatment programs, and (d) religious programs.

REFERENCES

Andrews, D.A. 1995. "The Psychology of Criminal Conduct and Effective Treatment." In J. McGuire (ed.), *What Works: Reoffending—Guidelines from Research and Practice* (35–62). Chichester, U.K.: John Wiley and Sons.

Auditor General of Canada. 1996. "Correctional Service of Canada—Reintegration of Offenders." *Report of the Auditor General to the House of Commons, Chapter 30.* Ottawa: Minister of Public Works and Government Services Canada.

Barbaree, H.E., M.T. Seto, and A. Maric. 1996. "Effective Sex Offender Treatment: The Warkworth Sexual Behaviour Clinic." *Forum on Corrections Research* 8(3):13–15.

Batiuk, M.E., P. Moke, and P.W. Rountree. 1997. "Crime and Rehabilitation: Correctional Education as an Agent of Change: A Research Note." *Justice Quarterly* 14(1):167–80.

Blanchette, K., and C. Dowden. 1998. "A Profile of Federally Sentenced Women in the Community: Addressing Needs for Successful Integration." *Forum on Corrections Research* 10(1):40–43.

Bonta, J. 1997. *Offender Rehabilitation: From Research to Practice.* Ottawa: Department of the Solicitor General of Canada.

———. 2002. "Offender Risk Assessment: Guidelines for Selection and Use." *Criminal Justice and Behavior* 29:355–79.

Carpentier, M. 1995. "Offenders Learning to Be Better Parents." *Forum on Corrections Research* 7(2):23–24.

Carter, W., and P. Lefaive. 1995. *Sex Offender Programs in CSC: Program Inventory and Description, Resourcing and Capacities.* Ottawa: Sex Offender Programs, Correctional Service of Canada.

Clear, T.R., D.B. Stout, H.R. Dammer, L. Kelly, P.L. Hardyman, and C. Shapiro. 1992. "Does Involvement in Religion Help Prisoners Adjust to Prison?" *NCCD Focus* (November):1–7.

Comack, E. 1993. *Women Offenders' Experiences with Physical and Sexual Abuse: A Preliminary Report.* Winnipeg: Criminology Research Centre, University of Manitoba.

Correctional Service of Canada. 1991. "Adult Basic Education: Can It Help Reduce Recidivism?" *Forum on Corrections Research* 3(1):4–7.

———. 1995. *Program Development for Survivors of Trauma and Abuse: Discussion Paper.* Ottawa: Correctional Service of Canada.

———. 2000. *Contact* 8(12). Ottawa.

———. 2001. *Contact* 9(2). Ottawa.

———. 2002. *Violence Prevention Programs.* Retrieved from www.csc-scc.gc.ca/text/prgrm/correctional/vp_e.shtml.

Cullen, F.T., and P. Gendreau. 2001. "From Nothing Works to What Works: Changing Professional Ideology in the 21st Century." *The Prison Journal* 81(3):313–38.

Dhaliwal, G.K., F. Porporino, and R.R. Ross. 1994. "Assessment of Criminogenic Factors, Program Assignment, and Recidivism." *Criminal Justice and Behavior* 21(4):454–67.

Duguid, S. 1981. "Moral Development, Justice and Democracy in the Prison." *Canadian Journal of Criminology* 23(1):147–62.

Edwards, J. 1996. "Industry in Canadian Federal Prisons: Glimpses into History." *Forum on Corrections Research* 8(1):6–7.

Fabiano, E.A., F.J. Porporino, and D. Robinson. 1990. *Rehabilitation through Clearer Thinking: A Cognitive Model of Correctional Intervention.* Ottawa: Research and Statistics Branch, Correctional Service of Canada.

Gendreau, P., C. Goggin, and P. Smith. 1999. "The Forgotten Issue in Effective Correctional Treatment: Program Implementation." *International Journal of Offender Therapy and Comparative Criminology* 43(2):180–87.

Gendreau, P., T. Little, and C. Goggin. 1996. "A Meta-analysis of the Predictors of Adult Offender Recidivism: What Works!" *Criminology* 34(4): 575–95.

Gillis, C., M. Getkate, D. Robinson, and F.J. Porporino. 1995. "Correctional Work Supervisor Leadership and Credibility: Their Influence on Offender Work Motivation." *Forum on Corrections Research* 7(3):15–17.

Gillis, C.A., L.L. Motiuk, and R. Belcourt. 1998. *Prison Work Program (CORCAN) Participation: Post-Release Employment and Recidivism.* Ottawa: Research Branch, Correctional Service Canada.

Glaser, D. 1964. *The Effectiveness of a Prison and Parole System.* Indianapolis, Ind.: Bobbs-Merrill.

Gordon, A., and T. Nicholaichuk. 1996. "Applying the Risk Principle to Sex Offender Treatment." *Forum on Corrections Research* 8(2):36–38.

Hannah-Moffat, K. 1995. "Feminine Fortresses: Women-Centered Prisons?" *The Prison Journal* 75(2):135–64.

Haskell, L., and M. Randall. 1993. *The Women's Safety Project: Summary of Key Statistical Findings.* Ottawa: Canadian Panel on Violence Against Women.

Hylton, J. 2002. *Aboriginal Sex Offending in Canada.* Ottawa: Aboriginal Healing Foundation.

Inciardi, J.A. 1996. "A Corrections-based Continuum of Effective Drug Abuse Treatment." *National Institute of Justice Research Preview.* June. Washington, D.C.: Office of Justice Programs, U.S. Department of Justice.

Johnson, B.R., D.B. Larson, and T.C. Pitts. 1997. "Religious Programs, Institutional Adjustment, and Recidivism among Former Inmates in Prison Fellowship Programs." *Justice Quarterly* 14(1):145–66.

Johnston, J.C. 1997. *Aboriginal Offender Survey: Case Files and Interview Sample.* Ottawa: Research Branch, Correctional Service Canada.

Kowbel, R.D. 1995. "Self-Help Programs Are Part of Jailhouse Games." *The Globe and Mail* (January 13):A20.

Lane, P., M. Bopp, J. Bopp, and J. Norris. 2002. *Mapping the Healing Journey: The Final Report of a First Nation Research Project on Healing in Canadian Aboriginal Communities.* Ottawa: Solicitor General Canada and the Aboriginal Healing Foundation.

LaPrairie, C. 1996. *Examining Aboriginal Corrections in Canada.* Ottawa: Aboriginal Corrections, Ministry of the Solicitor General.

Leschied, A.W., and A. Cunningham. 1998. *Northern Treatment Centre Evaluation: Interim Report.* London, Ont.: London Family Court Clinic.

Lösel, F. 1995. "The Efficacy of Correctional Treatment: A Review and Synthesis of Meta-evaluations." In J. McGuire (ed.), *What Works: Reducing Reoffending: Guidelines from Research and Practice* (79–111). Chichester, U.K.: John Wiley and Sons.

———. 1996. "Effective Correctional Programming: What Empirical Research Tells Us and What It Doesn't." *Forum on Corrections Research* 8(3):33–37.

Luciani, F. 1997. "Tried and True: Proof That the Custody Rating Scale Is Still Reliable and Valid." *Forum on Corrections Research* 9(1):13–17.

Lurgio, A. 2000. "Drug Treatment Availability and Effectiveness: Studies of the General and Criminal Justice Populations." *Criminal Justice and Behavior* 27:495–528.

MacDonald, G. 1982. *Self-Sustaining Prison Industries.* Vancouver: Institute for Studies in Criminal Justice Policy, Simon Fraser University.

Marshall, W.L. 1989. *Evaluation of Life Skills Training for Federal Penitentiary Inmates.* Ottawa: Solicitor General of Canada.

Marshall, W.L., and W.D. Pithers. 1994. "A Reconsideration of Treatment Outcome with Sex Offenders." *Criminal Justice and Behavior* 21(1):10–27.

Martinson, R.M. 1974. "What Works? Questions and Answers about Prison Reform." *The Public Interest* 35 (spring):22–54.

———. 1979. "New Findings, New Views: A Note of Caution Regarding Sentencing Reform." *Hofstra Law Review* 7:243–58.

McKinnon, C. 1995. "The Legal Right of Offenders to Refuse Treatment." *Forum on Corrections Research* 7(3):43–47.

Millson, B., and D. Robinson. 1992. *An Assessment of the Offender Substance Abuse Pre-Release Program at Drumheller Institution*. Ottawa: Research and Statistics Branch, Correctional Service of Canada.

Motiuk, L.L., and R.L. Belcourt. 1996. "CORCAN Participation and Post-Release Recidivism." *Forum on Corrections Research* 8(1):15–17.

Motiuk, L., R. Boe, and M. Nafekh. 2002. *The Safe Return of Offenders to the Community*. Ottawa: Research Branch, Correctional Service of Canada. Retrieved from www.csc-scc.gc.ca/text/faits/facts08-04_e.shtml.

Nuffield, J. 1998. *Issues in Urban Corrections for Aboriginal People: Report of a Focus Group and an Overview of the Literature and Experience*. Ottawa: Aboriginal Corrections Policy Unit, Solicitor General Canada.

Palmer, T. 1994. *A Profile of Correctional Effectiveness and New Directions for Research*. Albany: State University of New York Press.

Phenix, A., R.K. Hanson, and D. Thornton. 2000. *Coding Rules for the Static-99*. Ottawa: Corrections Research, Solicitor General of Canada. Retrieved from www.sgc.gc.ca/publications/corrections/CodingRules_e.asp.

Phillips, D. 2002. "The Aboriginal Gang Initiative." *Let's Talk* 27(2):1–4. Retrieved from www.csc-scc.gc.ca/text/pblct/letstalk/2002/no2/16_e.shtml.

Proulx, J., and S. Perrault. 1996. *An Evaluation of the Ma Mawi Wi Chi Itata Centre's Family Violence Program: Stony Mountain Project*. Ottawa: Winnipeg: Ma Mawi Wi Chi Itata Family Violence Program.

Roberts, C. 1995. "Effective Practice and Service Delivery." In J. McGuire (ed.), *What Works: Reducing Reoffending: Guidelines from Research and Practice* (221–36). Chichester, U.K.: John Wiley and Sons.

Robinson, D. 1995. *The Impact of Cognitive Skills Training on Post-Release Recidivism among Canadian Federal Offenders*. Ottawa: Correctional Service of Canada.

Robinson, D., W.A. Millson, S. Trevethan, and B. MacKillop. 1998. "A One-Day Snapshot of Inmates in Canada's Adult Correctional Facilities." *Juristat* 18(8). Cat. no. 85-002-XPE. Ottawa: Canadian Centre for Justice Statistics, Statistics Canada.

Sherman, L.W., D. Gottfredson, D. MacKenzie, J. Eck, P. Reuter, and S. Bushway. 1997. *Preventing Crime: What Works, What Doesn't, What's Promising*. Washington, D.C.: Office of Justice Programs, U.S. Department of Justice.

Talbot, M. 2003. "Catch and Release." *Atlantic Monthly* 291(1):97–100.

Task Force on Federally Sentenced Women. 1990. *Creating Choices: The Report of the Task Force on Federally Sentenced Women*. Ottawa: Correctional Service of Canada.

Taylor, G. 1997. "Implementing Risk and Needs Classification in the Correctional Service of Canada." *Forum on Corrections Research* 9(1):32–35.

———. 1998. "Preparing Reports for Parole Decisions: Making the Best of Our Information—and Time." *Forum on Corrections Research* 10(2):30–34.

Travis, L.F., M.D. Schwartz, and T.R. Clear. 1983. *Corrections: An Issues Approach*. 2nd ed. Cincinnati, Ohio: Anderson.

Vanderburg, S.A., J.R. Weekes, and W.A. Millson. 1994. *Native Offender Substance Abuse Assessment: The Computerized Lifestyle Assessment Instrument*. Ottawa: Research and Statistics Branch, Correctional Service of Canada.

Vennard, J., D. Sugg, and C. Hedderman. 1997. *Changing Offenders' Attitudes and Behaviour: What Works?* Home Office Research Study 171. London, U.K.: Home Office Research and Statistics Directorate.

Waldram, J.B. 1997. *The Way of the Pipe: Aboriginal Spirituality and Symbolic Healing in Canadian Prisons*. Peterborough, Ont.: Broadview Press.

Weekes, J.R., and W.A. Millson. 1994. *The Native Offender Substance Abuse Pre-treatment Program: Intermediate Measures of Program Effectiveness*. Ottawa: Research and Statistics Branch, Correctional Service of Canada.

Weekes, J.R., W.A. Millson, and L.O. Lightfoot. 1995. "Factors Influencing the Outcome of Offender Substance Abuse Treatment." *Forum on Corrections Research* 7(3):8–11.

Weeks, R., and C.S. Widom. 1998. *Research Preview: Early Childhood Victimization among Incarcerated Adult Male Felons*. Washington, D.C.: National Institute of Justice, U.S. Department of Justice.

Wiebe, R., and Y. Johnson. 1998. *Stolen Life: The Journey of a Cree Woman*. Toronto: Vintage Canada.

Women's Issues Task Force. 1995. *Women's Voices, Women's Choices: Report of the Women's Issues Task Force*. Toronto: Ministry of Solicitor General and Correctional Services.

Wormith, J.S., and M.E. Olver. 2002. "Offender Treatment Attrition and Its Relationship with Risk, Responsivity, and Recidivism." *Criminal Justice and Behavior* 29(4):447–71.

Zellerer, E. 1994. *A Review of Aboriginal Family Violence Treatment Programs for Men*. Ottawa: Correctional Service of Canada.

CHAPTER 9
RELEASE FROM PRISON

CHAPTER OBJECTIVES

- *Discuss the purpose and principles of conditional release.*
- *Identify the types of conditional release.*
- *Discuss the release options for provincial/territorial inmates.*
- *Discuss the release options for federal inmates.*
- *Consider the issues surrounding crime victims and conditional release.*
- *Examine the dynamics of parole board decision making.*
- *Consider the issues surrounding the prediction of recidivism.*

KEY TERMS

Parole eligibility date
Warrant expiry date
Temporary absence
Day parole
Full parole
Remission/discharge
Statutory release
Cold turkey release
Accelerated parole review

Faint-hope clause
Detention during the period of
   statutory release
One-chance statutory release
Community assessment
Clinical prediction
Actuarial prediction
Ecological fallacy

As noted in the opening pages of this text, nearly everyone who is sent to a correctional institution will eventually be released. Most inmates are released sooner, rather than later, in their sentence: it is the small percentage of offenders who receive sentences of two years or more who present the greatest challenges in terms of the timing and conditions of release and re-entry into the community. This chapter examines the decisions surrounding the timing and conditions of conditional release. Chapter 10 will consider the issues related to the re-entry of offenders into the community.

THE PURPOSE AND PRINCIPLES OF CONDITIONAL RELEASE

Section 100 of the Corrections and Conditional Release Act states:

> *The purpose of conditional release is to contribute to the maintenance of a just, peaceful and safe society by means of decisions on the timing and conditions of release that will best facilitate the rehabilitation of offenders and their reintegration into the community as law-abiding citizens.*

The Act also sets out a number of principles to be followed by the parole boards in pursuing the objectives of conditional release:

- The protection of society is the primary consideration in every case.
- Parole boards are to consider all available information that is relevant to the case, including recommendations from the sentencing judge, the results of assessments completed during the case management process, and information from victims and the offender.
- Parole boards can enhance their effectiveness by sharing information with other criminal justice agencies and by ensuring that information on policies and programs is communicated to offenders, victims, and the public.
- Parole boards should, in their decision making, make the least restrictive determination required to ensure the protection of society.
- Parole boards are to be guided by appropriate policies and ensure that members receive sufficient training to effectively implement these policies.
- Offenders are to be provided with all relevant information relating to the decisions of parole boards, the reasons for the decision, and the conditions of any conditional release.

With respect to the conditional releases decided by parole boards, section 102 of the Corrections and Conditional Release Act states:

The [National Parole] Board or a provincial parole board may grant parole to an offender if, in its opinion,

(a) the offender will not, by reoffending, present an undue risk to society before the expiration, according to law, of the sentence the offender is serving; and

(b) the release of the offender will contribute to the protection of society by facilitating the reintegration of the offender into society as a law-abiding citizen.

In practice, this means that conditional release can be granted under either of two conditions:

- if the applicant is unlikely to reoffend between the release and warrant expiry
- if there is a risk of reoffending but that risk can be managed by the specific interventions, such as a residential treatment program, that would be unavailable except as part of a conditional release.

The specific conditional release options available to inmates depend on the length of the offender's sentence and whether he or she is under the supervision and control of provincial/territorial or federal systems of corrections. Generally, conditional release is granted in cases in which it can be demonstrated that the community will not be placed at risk by the release of the inmate from confinement. For some offenders, the risk of reoffending is rated as low because of their particular sociobiographical backgrounds and absence of previous convictions. Other offenders who are at a high risk to reoffend must demonstrate that they have taken steps to address those aspects of their lives (criminogenic risk factors) that would increase their likelihood of reoffending. However, parole board members have considerable discretion in making decisions to grant or deny parole and may choose to disregard risk assessments.

The underlying premise of conditional release programs is that the likelihood of recidivism is reduced. More specifically, it is argued, the prospect of early release serves as an incentive for inmates to participate in institutional programs; the threat of being returned to confinement helps deter criminal behaviour; conditional release programs assist in minimizing the negative impact of incarceration; and supervision by a parole officer will be beneficial for the inmate. The absence of research studies, however, makes it difficult to determine the validity of these assumptions. The discussion in Chapter 7, for example, revealed that not all inmates are equally, or negatively, affected by the carceral experience, and the examination of correctional treatment in

Chapter 8 illustrated the difficulties of connecting participation in institutional treatment programs with post-release behaviour.

THE TYPES OF CONDITIONAL RELEASE

The release of an offender from custody can occur at one of three points in the sentence:

- the **parole eligibility date** (for either day parole or full parole)
- the discharge possible date, which generally occurs at the two-thirds point in a sentence
- the **warrant expiry date,** which marks the end of the sentence imposed by the court

The types of conditional release available to inmates incarcerated in federal and provincial/territorial correctional institutions are:

- **temporary absence** (TA), which may (1) be either escorted or unescorted, (2) begin very soon after admission and extend to the end of the sentence, and (3) involve the offender being placed under electronic monitoring
- **day parole,** generally at the one-sixth point in a sentence
- **full parole,** available at the one-third point in a sentence
- **remission/discharge,** available to provincial inmates at the two-thirds point
- **statutory release,** available to federal inmates at the two-thirds point

Inmates may also be released from confinement without any conditions or supervision. Often referred to as **cold turkey release,** this occurs when:

- provincial inmates are discharged from confinement at the two-thirds point of their sentence
- federal inmates are released at their warrant expiry date at the end of their court-imposed sentence

RELEASE OPTIONS FOR PROVINCIAL/TERRITORIAL INMATES

Except in Ontario, provincial inmates are released before their warrant expiry date in one of three ways: temporary absence, parole, or remission/discharge. Temporary absences and parole are forms of conditional release, whereas discharge is automatic and does not involve the imposition of conditions. Figure 9.1 illustrates the timeline for an 18-month provincial sentence.

Figure 9.1

Timeline for an 18-Month Provincial Sentence

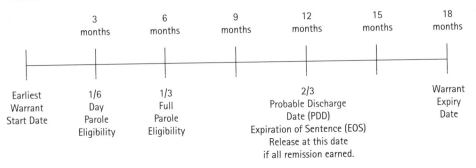

Source: British Columbia Board of Parole (www.gov.bc.ca/bcparole/manual).

In Ontario, inmates may be incarcerated until their warrant expiry date. Under the province's Corrections Accountability Act, inmates must earn the privilege of early release by:

- participating in work, skills/trade training, community service, treatment programs, and other "purposeful activities"
- abiding by institutional rules and standards of positive behaviour, including zero tolerance for acts of violence

An inmate who does not meet these criteria will fail to earn remission, also known as "good time" (www.mpss.jus.gov.on.ca/english/corr_serv/adult_off/earned_rem.html).

Temporary Absences

Temporary absences are the most common type of conditional release for provincial offenders, and although detailed statistics are unavailable, the practice appears to be on the increase. Each province/territory has its own form of TA program.

A TA can be an escorted pass of a few hours duration to attend a family funeral or a college class, but it can also span almost the full length of a provincial sentence, strung back-to-back in intervals that can run as long as 60 days. There may be a waiting period before eligibility, often one-sixth of the sentence, but inmates in some jurisdictions can apply for a TA immediately after entering the correctional system. In Ontario, for example, there are six types of temporary absence:

- humanitarian
- medical
- program/rehabilitative
- permission to live in a community residential agency
- immediate temporary absence (ITA)
- extended temporary absence for long-term inmates

All applications are reviewed and investigated by a TA coordinator, and most are reviewed by a TA committee. Cases recommended by the committee are forwarded to the superintendent of the institution for final approval. The entire process (except for ITAs) takes about two weeks after the application is made. Successful applicants must agree to the prescribed conditions and carry their TA permits at all times.

Among the assumed benefits of TAs is that it is more desirable for qualifying inmates to serve their sentences in a community setting rather than in confinement. The use of TAs may also provide a mechanism to control overcrowding. The absence of research studies makes it difficult to assess these assumptions, although the per diem costs for inmates on TAs are much lower than for inmates in confinement.

Eligibility Criteria and TA Decision Making

In Ontario, all provincial inmates, including fine defaulters, are eligible to apply for a TA as long as they are not facing outstanding charges for which they have been denied bail. Decisions on escorted and unescorted TAs of up to 72 hours are made by the superintendents of correctional facilities. The Ontario Parole and Earned Release Board has responsibility for unescorted TAs of 72 hours or longer.

Each applicant is assessed for suitability with reference to criminal history, particulars of the current offence, information from any pre-sentence report prepared by a probation officer, the victim impact statement (if one exists), and the most recent score from the Level of Service Inventory–Ontario Revision (LSI-OR). In screening inmates for suitability for a TA, consideration is generally given only to those inmates who are classified as being at a low risk to reoffend. Some types of offenders, including sex offenders and others with histories of violence, are not eligible for TAs in many provinces.

Some TAs are terminal in that they are expected to run until the end of the sentence, renewed every 60 days. Offenders released on a TA may be required to live in a community residential facility, or, if allowed to live at their own residence, they must remain at home when not at school, work, or another approved activity. Unannounced visits and calls may be made by correctional personnel, depending on the jurisdiction. These visits to offenders' residences or places of work/education are undertaken to verify that the conditions of the TA are being followed. In some provinces, offenders on TAs may be subject to electronic monitoring or be required to participate in programs offered by community agencies such as the John Howard Society. Under Alberta's Surveillance Supervision Program, for example, unemployed offenders must report daily to an attendance centre for programs or community service and be at home from 6 p.m. to 6 a.m. every day. As with any type of conditional release, violation of TA conditions can result in revocation and the offender can be returned to the institution.

Electronic Monitoring and TAs

In addition to being used as an alternative to confinement, as discussed in Chapter 4, EM can be used as a condition of temporary absences (back-end EM) or as a sentencing option ordered by the judge (front-end EM). There is considerable variation among the provinces in how EM is used. In British Columbia, the use of EM is limited to offenders on day parole or full parole. In Ontario, EM may be a requirement for offenders on TAs.

Parolees who have EM as a condition of release are required to abide by a curfew and to be at their residence during specified hours. Compliance is monitored by random, computer-generated telephone calls made to the residence. In addition, correctional staff make random visits and telephone calls, the frequency of which is determined by the results of a risk/needs assessment of the inmate.

Provincial Parole

Parole is a form of conditional release granted at the discretion of a parole board. Provincial inmates may apply for day parole consideration after serving one-sixth of their sentence and for full parole consideration after serving one-third of their sentence. Figure 9.2 illustrates the parole process in British Columbia. The process is similar for provincial inmates in other jurisdictions.

Inmates who appear before a parole board present a release plan and explain to board members why they would be good candidates to resume independent living, subject to monitoring by a parole officer. In accepting parole, provincial inmates forfeit all accumulated remission and so are subject to supervision until warrant expiry (the end of their sentence). Successful applicants agree to abide by a set of general and, depending on the case, specific conditions and to report to a parole supervisor.

Figure 9.2

Parole Flow Chart

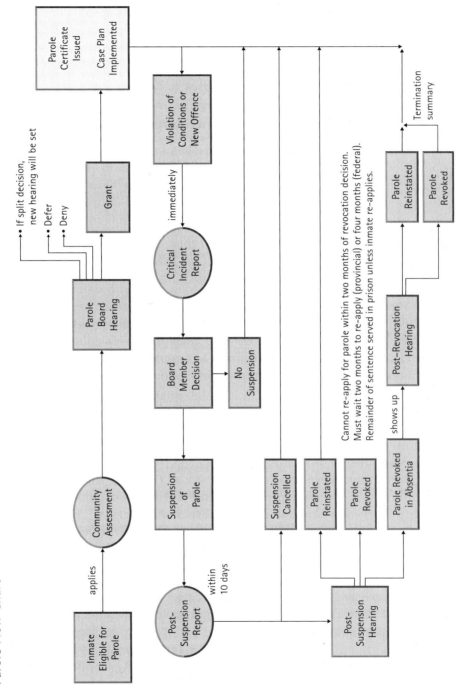

Source: Copyright © 1998 Corrections and Community Justice Division, Province of British Columbia.

The number of provincial offenders on parole has steadily declined over the past decade. The parole grant rate in Ontario has experienced the greatest decline, falling from approximately 60 percent to 28 percent. This precipitous decrease has been due in large measure to the province's get-tough approach to community corrections, which places a premium on public safety and security. Also contributing to the declining parole grant rate is the fact that the vast majority of parole-eligible inmates do not apply for parole, in large part because of their relatively short custodial sentences.

The majority of provincial parolees are in the three provinces that have their own parole boards: Quebec, Ontario, and British Columbia. These parole boards are independent of the correctional system. The British Columbia Board of Parole is a community board; parole board members are limited to a four-year term and conduct hearings on a part-time basis. The provincial parole boards in Ontario and Quebec have full-time and part-time members. In Ontario, offenders who are serving sentences of six months or longer are automatically scheduled for an in-person hearing before the parole board, while those offenders serving sentences of less than six months must apply, in writing, to appear before the board. In Quebec, the parole board automatically reviews the case of all offenders (even those who do not apply for parole) once they have served one-third of their sentence. In British Columbia, offenders must apply, in writing, to appear before the parole board.

Outside of these provinces, parole applicants have hearings before one member of the federal National Parole Board (NPB). (The grant rates and other comparative data for the provincial parole boards are presented in Table 9.1.) Provincial inmates who are in provinces without a provincial parole board and inmates in Yukon Territory, the Northwest Territories, and Nunavut may be able to apply to the NPB for release on day parole after serving one-sixth of their sentence in confinement and for full parole after serving one-third of their sentence in a provincial correctional institution. The British Columbia Board of Parole is the only provincial board that grants day parole.

Remission/Discharge

Another option for provincial inmates is to serve their entire sentence in confinement, minus remission, which is earned at a rate of one day for every two days served. This type of release can occur by default (because the sentence was so short), by choice (because the offender did not seek conditional release), or because all applications for TAs and parole were denied. With the exception of Ontario, as long as the inmate does not lose remission because of

Table 9.1   Comparison of Three Provincial Parole Boards and the National
Parole Board

	British Columbia Board of Parole	Ontario Board of Parole	Commission québécoise des libérations conditionelles	NPB Hearing Applications from Provincial Inmates*
Qualification for day parole	One-sixth	Not available (inmates may apply for a temporary absence after one-sixth)	Not available	One-sixth
Qualification for full parole	One-third	One-third	One-third	One-third
Victim observation of parole hearing	Yes	Yes	No	Yes
Victim allowed to make oral statement	Yes	Yes	No	Yes
Grant rate, full parole	67% (2000/01)**	28% (2000/01)**	48% (2001/02)	56% (2001/02)

* Except in British Columbia, Ontario, and Quebec.
** The last year for which figures were available.

Sources: British Columbia Board of Parole (www.gov.bc.ca/bcparole/manual); Commission québécoise des libérations conditionnelles (www.msp.gouv.qc.ca); National Parole Board (www.npb-cnlc.gc.ca); Ontario Parole and Earned Release Board (www.operb.gov.on.ca).

institutional misconduct, he or she is released from confinement after serving two-thirds of the sentence and is *not* subject to supervision by a parole officer. This type of release is often referred to as *cold turkey release*, although some offenders will have been sentenced to complete a period of probation following confinement that begins at discharge.

Victims and the Release of Provincial Inmates

Despite public education campaigns aimed at both victims and the general population, there are many gaps and inaccuracies in their knowledge of the correctional process. It is unlikely, for example, that most crime victims and community residents are aware that a provincial offender can be released on a TA. This lack of awareness has resulted in situations where crime victims encounter their perpetrators in public only weeks, or days, after witnessing the sentencing in court. Even worse, victims may have their feelings of safety shattered when the perpetrator shows up on their doorstep. Crime victims may also not understand the parole process and the criteria that are used by parole board members in making release decisions. Attending a parole hearing and being in the same room as the offender can be a difficult experience for crime victims.

Correctional authorities in several provinces have taken a number of steps to minimize the likelihood of re-victimization, particularly in cases where the offender and victim are acquainted:

- Offenders convicted of interpersonal crimes are often disqualified from applying for extended or unescorted TAs.
- There may be a requirement that the offender complete certain programs prior to being considered for a TA.
- The directive that the offender not contact the victim is a near-universal condition of all types of conditional release.
- Crime victims are able to contact the parole board and/or correctional officials and ask to be informed about the timing and specifics of any release.
- Crime victims can express their concerns to correctional authorities and/or the parole board.
- Except in Quebec, crime victims can ask to observe and make a written or oral submission at parole hearings (see Table 9.1).

In Manitoba, correctional officials are proactive in attempting to locate and contact victims who may be at risk of re-victimization. In Ontario, qualifying victims who register with the Victim Notification Service are given a personal identification number, which allows them to access, via telephone, case-specific information about an offender in the provincial correctional system.

RELEASE OPTIONS FOR FEDERAL INMATES

The discussion of Operation Bypass in Chapter 8 noted that the planning process for release of federal inmates begins within the first five days of the inmate's sentencing. To facilitate this process, every federal correctional institution has a reintegration manager. The Correctional Service of Canada (CSC) has defined as one of its key objectives a substantial increase in the number of offenders on conditional release, a strategy that has raised concerns among victim-rights groups. Figure 9.3 shows a recent decline in the number of offenders on conditional release after several years of increase in the mid- to late 1990s. The number of federal offenders on day parole, full parole, and statutory release are presented in Figure 9.4.

Early in the federal inmate's sentence, a reintegration-potential rating is established, based on information gleaned from the Custody Rating Scale, the Static-99, the Statistical Information on Recidivism Scale (discussed later in this chapter), and other static and dynamic risk factors (see Chapter 8). This rating places the individual inmate into one of three categories: high, medium, or low reintegration potential. The majority of the inmates with high reintegration potential will not require core programming. The existence of this category reflects the concern that some inmates are being steered into programs unnecessarily, wasting their time and system resources. For members of this

Figure 9.3

Federal Offender Population, 1991/92 to 2001/02

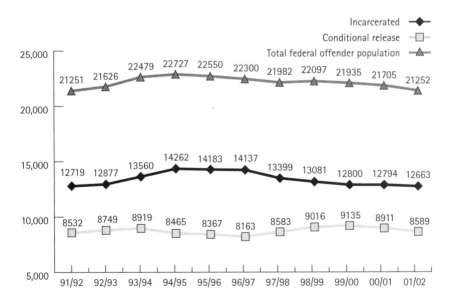

Source: National Parole Board, 2002:ix.

Figure 9.4

Federal Conditional Release Population, 1991/92 to 2001/02

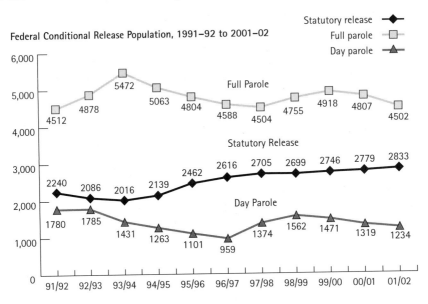

Federal Conditional Release Population, 1991–92 to 2001–02

Statutory release ◆

Full parole ▢

Day parole ▲

Source: National Parole Board, 2002:17.

group, any programs that are required can be accessed in the community. Accordingly, these inmates are viewed as candidates for conditional release as soon as they meet the eligibility criteria.

Federal inmates with a medium reintegration potential are directed to core programs in the institution (see Chapter 8 for a discussion of core programs) and to follow-up programs in the community once they are released. (High-risk inmates are required to complete an extensive program of treatment intervention and are viewed cautiously by correctional personnel and by the parole board.) Federal inmates, who serve longer periods of time behind bars in comparison with their provincial counterparts, tend to be released in gradual stages. This begins with escorted or unescorted temporary absences, decisions about which are usually made at the institutional level (for a discussion of federal TAs, see Grant and Johnson, 1998; Grant and Millson, 1998). They are also eligible for work releases and community development releases. Two types of conditional release (day parole and full parole) are discretionary, while one (statutory release) is not. These release options are described in Box 9.1.

BOX 9.1

Release Options for Federal Offenders

Temporary Absences

- TAs are usually the first type of release an offender may be granted.
- TAs may be escorted (ETA) or unescorted (UTA).
- TAs are granted so the offender may receive medical treatment, have contact with family, undergo personal development and/or counselling, and participate in community service work projects.

Eligibility

- Offenders may apply for ETAs at any time throughout their sentence.
- UTAs vary, depending on the length and type of sentence. Offenders classified as maximum security are not eligible for UTAs.
- For sentences of three years or more, offenders are eligible to be considered for UTAs after serving one-sixth of their sentence.
- For sentences of two to three years, UTA eligibility is at six months into the sentence.
- For sentences under two years, eligibility for TAs is under provincial jurisdiction.
- Offenders serving life sentences are eligible to apply for UTAs three years before their full parole eligibility date.

Day Parole

- Day parole prepares an offender for release on full parole or statutory release by allowing the offender to participate in community-based activities.
- Offenders on day parole must return nightly to an institution or a halfway house unless otherwise authorized by the NPB.

Eligibility

- Offenders serving sentences of three years or more are eligible to apply for day parole six months prior to full parole eligibility.
- Offenders serving life sentences are eligible to apply for day parole three years before their full parole eligibility date.
- Offenders serving sentences of two to three years are eligible for day parole after serving six months of their sentence.
- For sentences under two years, day parole eligibility comes when one-sixth of the sentence has been served.

BOX 9.1, continued

Full Parole

- The offender serves the remainder of the sentence under supervision in the community.
- The offender must report to a parole supervisor on a regular basis and must advise on any changes in employment or personal circumstances.

Eligibility

- Most offenders (except those serving life sentences for murder) are eligible to apply for full parole after serving either one-third of the sentence or seven years.
- Offenders serving life sentences for first-degree murder are eligible after serving 25 years.
- Eligibility dates for offenders serving life sentences for second-degree murder are set between 10 and 25 years by the court (at the time of sentencing).

Statutory Release

- By law, most federal inmates are automatically released after serving two-thirds of their sentence if they have not already been released on parole. This is called statutory release.
- Statutory release is not the same as parole because the decision for release is not made by the NPB.

Eligibility

- Offenders serving life or indeterminate sentences are not eligible for statutory release.
- The CSC may recommend an offender be denied statutory release if they believe the offender is likely to:
  (a) commit an offence causing death or serious harm to another person;
  (b) commit a sexual offence against a child; or
  (c) commit a serious drug offence before the end of the sentence.

In such cases, the NPB may detain that offender until the end of the sentence or add specific conditions to the statutory release plan.

The conditional release eligibility dates for federal offenders and federal inmates serving life sentences are presented in Figure 9.5 and Table 9.2, respectively.

Source: National Parole Board, 1997.

Figure 9.5

Overview of Conditional Release Eligibility Dates for Federal Offenders

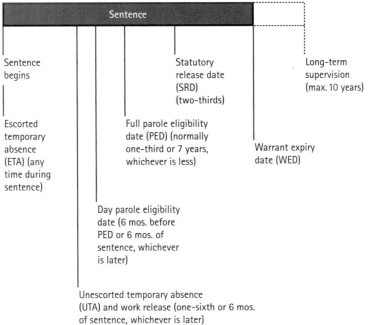

Source: Solicitor General Canada, 1998a:17.

National Parole Board

The National Parole Board was created in 1959 following the report of the Fauteux Committee (1956) which found that the ticket of leave system (discussed in Chapter 2) was prone to political interference. It is a division within the Ministry of the Solicitor General, but it is independent of the CSC and can authorize conditional release of federal offenders. Parole board members are order-in-council appointments who serve for limited terms and are paid on a per diem basis. They may or may not have prior training or experience in the criminal justice field. Members are centralized in five regional offices and travel to the institutions for in-person hearings with parole applicants.

The NPB's conditional release program comprises seven operational areas:

- temporary absence
- day parole
- full parole
- statutory release
- detention
- long-term supervision
- appeal decisions

Table 9.2   Conditional Release Eligibility Dates for Inmates Serving Life Sentences

	Unescorted TAs	Day Parole	Full Parole	Statutory Release
First-degree murder after July 26, 1976*	3 years before PED**	3 years before PED	25 years***	N/A
Second-degree murder after July 26, 1976*	3 years before PED	3 years before PED	10–25 years*** (set by judge)	N/A
Murder 1974–76, death penalty commuted*	3 years before PED	3 years before PED	10–20 years***	N/A
Capital murder, death penalty not commuted by 1976*	3 years before PED	3 years before PED	25 years*	N/A
Young offender after May 1982 (murder)*	4/5 of PED	4/5 of PED	5–10 years (set by judge)	N/A
Life sentence maximum*	3 years before PED	6 months before PED	7 years	N/A
Dangerous offenders *pre–Bill C-55*	3 years	3 years	3 years	N/A
Dangerous offenders post–Bill C-55*	3 years	3 years	7 years	N/A

* Eligibility is calculated to include time spent in custody following arrest

** PED = parole eligibility date

*** Eligible to apply for judicial review of PED after 15 years

Source: National Parole Board (www.npb-cnlc.gc.ca).

In 2001–02, the NPB heard approximately 4,400 applications for day parole and 3,800 applications for full parole. Although the number of day parole decisions has remained fairly consistent over the past decade, there has been a decline in the number of full parole decisions. In 1994–95, the NPB made 6,500 full parole decisions, compared with about half that number in 2001–02. The federal day parole grant rate has remained fairly stable (ranging from 42 percent to 44 percent) over the past decade.

Day Parole

Day parole dates back to 1969 but has undergone many legislative changes that affect the rate at which it is used (Brunet, 1998; Grant, 1998). Currently, the use of day parole is on the increase. This is most likely a result of the use of accelerated day parole review, which streamlines the release of some offenders, depending on their offences of conviction. Federal inmates who qualify for accelerated parole review (discussed below) may be released on accelerated day parole after serving six months, or one-sixth of their sentence, whichever is longer (with some differences for special categories of offenders, such as lifers, as can be seen in Table 9.2).

Inmates on day parole typically live in a community residential facility, and most apply for full parole when they reach the one-third point in their sentences. Day parole is meant to aid transition and, therefore, is seen as a short-term option for the period immediately prior to the granting of full parole. Day paroles are normally no longer than six months. Statistics on day parole for reveal that in Canada during 2001–02:

- the grant rate for day parole was 72 percent
- 71 percent of men and 87 percent of women who appeared before the NPB were granted day parole
- on average, offenders granted day parole had served about 32 percent of their sentence in confinement
- there was a slight increase in the number of Aboriginal offenders who were granted day parole (Solicitor General Portfolio, 2002)

Full Parole

Full parole is the most common means of release of federal offenders. Most full parolees will live in their own residences with their families, with friends, or independently. Again, with exceptions listed in Table 9.2, the parole eligibility date of most federal offenders is at the one-third point in the sentence (or seven years, whichever is less). Remember also from Chapter 3 that in some cases a sentencing judge has made a judicial determination that the offender must serve half of the sentence (but never more than 10 years) before being eligible to apply for parole.

Some first-time federal offenders are eligible for **accelerated parole review.** Although these inmates must still serve one-third of their sentence before being eligible, the parole approval process is streamlined by flagging these cases early in the process and expediting the development of a release plan. All of these cases are considered by one member of the NPB at an in-office review. A parole hearing is not required. The NPB will direct a parole release if it is "not convinced" that an offender will commit a violent offence prior to warrant expiry. If the decision is not to direct release, a full hearing will be held, at which the offender is present.

Provincial parole boards and the NPB may also issue a Parole to Deportation certificate. This decision is made when federal immigration authorities place a "hold" on an offender who is not a Canadian citizen and have secured the necessary approvals to remove the person from the country. In such cases, the inmate applicant will be released to the custody of immigration authorities for removal.

Statistics on full parole indicate that during 2001–02:

- the grant rate for full parole was 43 percent
- 43 percent of men and 74 percent of women were granted full parole
- there was a significant increase in the number of Aboriginal offenders who were granted full parole
- on average, offenders granted a full parole had served about 40 percent of their sentence in confinement
- Aboriginal offenders served a higher proportion of their sentences before being released on full parole
- Compared with men, women served a lower proportion of their sentences before being released on parole (Solicitor General Portfolio, 2002)

Judicial Review (Section 745)

Often called the **faint-hope clause,** this provision allows murderers serving a life sentence with no eligibility for parole for at least 15 years to apply for a reduction of this ineligibility period. The offender must first convince a superior court judge that there is a "reasonable prospect of success." If the offender passes this hurdle the case will be heard in front of a jury for a decision.

The offender can apply for judicial review only after having served 15 years of the sentence. The judicial review procedures thus apply to (1) offenders convicted of first-degree murder who are required to serve at least 25 years in prison before being eligible for parole, and (2) offenders who have been convicted of second-degree murder and sentenced to life in prison, with parole eligibility set at 15 years or longer. Offenders who have been convicted of multiple murders are not eligible to apply. This and other restrictions are not retroactive.

The judicial review must take place in the community where the crime was committed. A jury of community residents determines whether the parole eligibility date should be reduced (not whether the offender should be released). A hearing is held in which information is presented by the applicant and by the Crown counsel, although the onus is on the offender applicant to convince the jury to reduce the parole eligibility date. The main focus is on the offender's conduct during the 15 years of confinement and assessments about the risk of future offences. Both the offender applicant and the Crown counsel may call and question witnesses and experts. The offender applicant is required to testify and members of the victim's family have the option of doing so. All members of the jury must agree before the parole eligibility date can be reduced (but only a two-thirds majority is required in cases for offenders sentenced before 1997). Among the decisions that the jury can make are:

- make no change to the parole eligibility date, but set a date when another application can be made (at least two years hence)
- reduce the period of parole ineligibility to less than what it was but more than 15 years
- reduce the period of parole ineligibility to 15 years, which generally makes the offender immediately eligible to apply for parole

There is considerable variation across the country in the numbers of applications and the rates of applicant success. As of late 2002, only about one-fourth of the offenders eligible for judicial review had applied for a hearing. In 80 percent of the cases that have been heard, the lifers had their period of parole ineligibility reduced. Although the recidivism rate of these offenders has been very low to date (Solicitor General Portfolio, 2002:89), section 745 continues to be the focus of considerable controversy. See the following At Issue.

AT ISSUE

SECTION 745: THE FAINT-HOPE CLAUSE

Section 745 was added to the Criminal Code in 1976 amid the debate over the abolition of capital punishment. At that time, those serving life sentences for murder were eligible for parole after seven years. The increase to a mandatory 25 years was so dramatic that Parliament created the judicial review option. In recent years, the federal government has been under increasing pressure from community interest groups such as the Canadian Police Association and the federal Canadian Alliance Party to abolish section 745. Largely in response to this pressure, Parliament made a number of modifications in 1997 but did not repeal the provision itself.

Proponents argue that section 745:
- reflects enlightened correctional policy
- provides an incentive to offenders to participate in rehabilitation programs
- assists correctional personnel in managing long-term offenders
- does not guarantee release, even if the application is successful, but rather makes the offender *eligible* for parole consideration
- provides that offenders whose applications are successful and who are granted parole must still remain under supervision the rest of their lives

Critics of section 745, many of whom have argued that the section should be deleted in its entirety from the Criminal Code, counter that the provision:
- undermines the potential impact of life sentences as a general and specific deterrent to crime
- results in the re-victimization of crime victims and their families during the section 745 hearing, during subsequent parole hearings, and when the offender is released on parole prior to the 25-year point
- makes a mockery of the law and that "life means life"
- results in violent offenders being released into the community

QUESTIONS

1. What is your position on section 745 of the Criminal Code? Would you favour its abolition, or do you feel that the current provisions are adequate?
2. How would you respond to the criticisms of section 745?

Statutory Release

Statutory release occurs when a federal inmate has served two-thirds of the sentence and is still in confinement. This situation arises because the inmate chose not to apply for parole, applied for parole but was unsuccessful, or had an earlier release revoked and was not released again. Since 1969, first with mandatory supervision and now with statutory release, federal offenders are released at the two-thirds point but are subject to parole supervision until warrant expiry. As Figure 9.4 reveals, statutory release is a fairly common means of release (accounting for 33 percent of the federal conditional release population in 2001–02) and is growing in frequency. Statutory releases do not involve the NPB but, under the Corrections and Conditional Release Act, that body may impose a residency requirement when there is evidence that the offender is at a high risk to reoffend prior to warrant expiry. The NPB may also be asked to consider denying a statutory release.

Detention during the Period of Statutory Release

There is a small group of federal inmates (271 in 2001–02) who have been judged by the CSC to be at such risk of reoffending if released that they should be confined for the entire sentence (to warrant expiry). In these cases, concern for community safety outweighs the many undesirable aspects of a cold turkey release. As the inmate's statutory release date draws near, the CSC applies to the NPB for a detention hearing. The NPB will order the inmate detained if the board is convinced he or she will commit an offence that causes death or serious harm, a sexual offence involving a child, or a serious drug offence before warrant expiry. This detainment is called **detention during the period of statutory release.**

The NPB approves the CSC recommendation for detention in the majority of cases, about 88 percent on average. In 2001–02, 257 (95 percent) of reviewed cases were detained (Solicitor General Portfolio, 2002). The others may be released with special conditions such as **one-chance statutory release,** which means that if the release is revoked, the offender is ineligible for a subsequent statutory release prior to the warrant expiry date. Another option is to release the offender with a residency requirement that he or she live in a community facility with supervision.

Inmates referred to detention hearings tend to be serving longer sentences and are likely to have been convicted of a sexual offence and/or assault. Female offenders are rarely the subject of detention hearings. In the period 1997–2002, only 11 women were referred to a detention hearing, and all were detained. Aboriginal offenders composed 30 percent of the offenders referred to a detention hearing (Solicitor General Portfolio, 2002:87).

The purpose of detention is public protection through incapacitation. The question is whether detention is meeting that goal. See Box 9.2.

Victim Involvement in Federal Parole

There are several provisions in the Corrections and Conditional Release Act designed to increase the input and participation of crime victims in the federal parole process, as well as to provide victims with general and case-specific information. In response to the requirements of the Act, the NPB has undertaken the following initiatives:

- Each regional office is staffed with community liaison officers who provide victims with services and information.

BOX 9.2

Research Summary: The Effectiveness of Detention

Researcher Brian Grant (1997) examined all the cases referred by the CSC to the NPB for detention hearings during the four-year period 1989–90 to 1993–94. Tracking the outcome of these cases, Grant found that 23 percent of inmates were released on statutory release, 15 percent were detained but released sometime later before their warrant expiry, and 62 percent were detained until the end of the sentence.

Grant then gathered information on these offenders for two years following release and compared the outcomes with three other inmate groups: (1) those released on full parole, (2) those released on statutory release who were not referred to detention, and (3) those whose earlier release was revoked and followed by a statutory release.

It might be expected that, in terms of likelihood of reoffending upon release, the groups would rank as follows:

Offenders at Highest Risk to Reoffend

detained to end of sentence
detained then released
referred but released
statutory release only
statutory release and other
full parole

Offenders at Lowest Risk to Reoffend

The actual outcomes are illustrated in Figure 9.6. From these findings, Grant concluded that the selection process for detention has not resulted in the highest-risk offenders being detained in confinement. These findings suggest that detention, as practised by the CSC and NPB, is not meeting the goal of public protection through incapacitation.

Source: Grant, 1997.

- At their request, victims can be advised of eligibility dates, parole board decisions, and release status.
- Victim impact statements and expressions of concern for post-release safety will be considered by the NPB.
- Victims may attend parole hearings and make an oral presentation to the NFB.
- Interested parties can request written copies of NPB decisions from the Decision Registry.

A number of concerns have been raised about these policies, including the fear that correspondence from victims could be accessed by the offender, which may place victims at risk of retaliation. The lack of proactive contact by correctional authorities forces victims to learn about their rights and take steps to contact authorities. This latter point has been addressed in part with a public education campaign and toll-free numbers for questions and requests.

Figure 9.6

Offenders with a New Offence within Two Years of Release

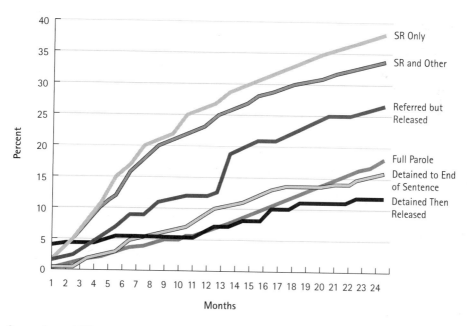

Source: Grant, 1997:23.

Parole and the Long-Term Offender

As noted in Chapter 3, sentencing judges have the option to designate certain offenders as long-term offenders, which involves appending a long-term supervision order to the end of a federal sentence. Such an order can run as long as 10 years, beginning at warrant expiry, with the specific period determined by the sentencing judge. As such, it does not affect the inmate's parole eligibility.

The CSC is responsible for supervising long-term offenders, and the NPB can set standard and special conditions for the offender, which must be adhered to during this period. If offenders violate a condition of the order, they may be re-admitted to custody for a period not longer than 90 days or admitted to a halfway house or to a mental-health facility. The CSC can also refer the matter to the NPB, which can cancel the suspension (and release the person), cancel the suspension and add new conditions, or recommend (with the approval of the provincial attorney general) that the offender be charged with "breaching long-term supervision" without reasonable excuse. This offence carries a maximum penalty of 10 years.

This measure had as its origins the observation that the ability to detain offenders during the period of statutory release leaves the most dangerous offenders with the least supervision at release. However, this designation cannot be applied retroactively and is available only at the time of sentencing. As of 2001–02, 20 offenders were under long-term supervision and 112 offenders were scheduled to be subject to long-term supervision orders once they reach warrant expiry (National Parole Board, 2002:72).

The Release of Dangerous Offenders

Inmates who have been designated as dangerous offenders (see Chapter 3) by a criminal court serve indeterminate sentences of imprisonment and can be released only by the NPB. Only about 200 people have ever been so designated, all but two of them men. The majority are sex offenders, and many have been diagnosed with antisocial personality disorder (Bonta et al., 1996; Bonta et al., 1998). Their eligibility dates are listed in Table 9.2.

Statutory release is not available to dangerous offenders, and these inmates can, literally, spend the rest of their lives in prison, repeatedly being denied release at successive parole board hearings. The NPB is not to release a dangerous offender unless it is assured that the community would not be at risk. In practice, release is rarely granted.

THE PAROLE FILE

In its deliberations, the parole board considers a number of documents contained in the inmate applicant's parole file. These include:

- *institutional reports* that provide information on work performance, rule infractions, attitudes toward and interaction with staff and other inmates, participation in core programs, and assessments prepared by treatment staff and case managers
- *victim impact statements* prepared for the sentencing judge and for the parole hearing
- *court transcripts* such as, most often, the comments of the judge at sentencing
- *police reports*
- *pre-sentence reports* prepared by probation or parole officers for the sentencing judge
- *an official offence record* from the Canadian Police Information Centre
- *materials prepared by the inmate applicant*, including, for sex offenders, a relapse prevention plan and the proposed release plan
- *letters of support* from family and friends, community support persons, and employers, among others
- *a community assessment* (discussed below)

Historically, there been a problem assembling the relevant documentation and ensuring that an offender's parole file is complete. Provincial parole boards in particular often have difficulty securing records from the CSC and the NPB in cases where the offender has previously served time in the federal system.

A key document in the parole file is the **community assessment,** which is prepared by parole officers (probation officers in British Columbia, Quebec, and Ontario). The community assessment is best described as an investigation that is designed to evaluate the feasibility of the inmate applicant's proposed community plan in terms of the level of supervision required and the availability of community resources. The standard areas addressed by the community assessment are outlined below:

Assessment of the Proposed Plan
- proposed residence (location, suitability, availability of placement in a community-based facility, etc.)
- education and/or employment activities (verification of availability, suitability to inmate, confirmation of acceptance, etc.)
- proposed treatment or counselling programs

Community Information
- significant relationships (family, friends, others)
- financial situation (expected income, assets and debt obligations)
- support services available to the inmate
- community reaction (including police opinion) to the release of the inmate

Response to Previous Corrections
- performance and compliance on supervision in the community, including probation, conditional sentences, and provincial/federal day parole

Victim Information
- victim impact and concerns
- Results of Protection Order Registry check

Areas of Risk and Supervision Issues
- factors that support, and weigh against, the offender's release

Recommended Special Conditions
- special conditions on the parole certificate (discussed later in the chapter) that address risk/needs factors and provide for the level of supervision required to access appropriate community resources

Although the community assessment is designed to be an review of the inmate's plan, the probation officer or parole officer preparing the report may on occasion express an opinion as to whether release should be granted. A community assessment, with key identifiers removed, is reproduced in Box 9.3.

DYNAMICS OF PAROLE BOARD DECISION MAKING

The decision of a parole board to release an inmate back into the community is, along with the trial verdict of the criminal court, perhaps the most important decision that is made in the correctional process. Despite this, little attention has been given to the composition of parole boards, the relationship between member characteristics and the accuracy of their predictions, how parole board members apply the statutory criteria when assessing applications for conditional release, or what weight they give to risk assessment instruments.

NPB hearings, where two members usually preside, are held in all federal penitentiaries across the country. The inmates appear with their case managers as assistants. Lawyers also may attend. The victim of the offence committed by the inmate applicant may observe the hearing but cannot make a statement. The victim's presence is rare, in part because most people would have to travel

BOX 9.3

Community Assessment (B.C.)

BRITISH COLUMBIA

Day Parole ☐   Full Parole [X]   Statutory Release ☐

Name: ██████████████   **Alias:** ████████████

Date of Birth: ████████   **FPS No.:** ████████

Court File #: ████████

CS No.: ████████

Court Location:

Offence: Possess/Use Stolen Card sec 342.1(c)
Theft Over $5000 sec 334(a)
Mischief Over $5000 430.3(a)
Driving While Prohibited/Licence Susp sec MVA 95.1
Occupying Vehicle in Which There is a Firearm sec 94.1(a)(i)

ASSESSMENT PROPOSED PLAN: *(Employment, Education, Treatment, Residence, Other)*

Mr. ██████ proposes that he will reside with his mother and step-father at the following address:

████████████

The address was confirmed and the offender's mother, Ms. ██████, states that her husband and ██ year old son ██████ welcome Mr. ██████ into their home. There are no other individuals residing in the home.

It should be noted that this arrangement of having Mr. ██████ return to the family home has occurred on many occasions with negative results. Either Mr. ██████ has been asked to leave by his mother for breaking the house rules or he has simply left. According to his mother, he usually makes up a story about finding employment elsewhere, and then leaves the family home.

Protecting Communities, Assisting Families

Ministry of Public Safety and   Corrections Branch
Solicitor General

Phone:
Fax:

BOX 9.3, continued

BRITISH COLUMBIA

Mr. ▮▮▮▮ proposes that he will be employed with ▮▮▮▮▮▮▮ , which is a family run business the ▮▮▮ and their extended family own. Ms. ▮▮▮ states that there will always be employment available if ▮▮▮ is in need of it. She also confirmed that he will be paid $10 per hour and will have approximately 70 hours per week.

As far as the education and treatment proposed plans, Mr. ▮▮▮ has not confirmed them and has not provided telephone numbers for the trauma counselling contact.

RESPONSE TO PREVIOUS COMMUNITY SUPERVISION BY CORRECTIONS:

Mr. ▮▮▮ past performance on community supervision has been poor. He has breached community orders on at least 10 occasions as well as failing to appear and breaching his parole thus having it revoked.

Mr. ▮▮▮ has 4 assault convictions, including assault with a weapon as well as escaping lawful confinement and being at large.

COMMUNITY INFORMATION *(Support Services, Personal Relationships, Community Reaction)*

Mr. ▮▮▮ lists a number of individuals as his community supports. One of them, Ms. ▮▮▮, was listed as a friend and *counselling help*, stated that she "likes to figure people out" and has been counselling Mr. ▮▮▮ since he was a teenager. Although she has no formal counselling training, and in respect to Mr. ▮▮▮ numerous convictions over the years, she still believes strongly that she is able to counsel him through his problems.

His sister, ▮▮▮, states that she is supportive of him and recognizes that he needs to communicate more effectively with the family. ▮▮▮ also stated that Mr. ▮▮▮ has informed her that when he is making positive changes in his life, he tends to receive negative feedback from the police which makes him give up and turn the wrong way. However, she has noticed that he now states that regardless of what the police do or say he realizes that he has to prove himself to those around him.

Protecting Communities, Assisting Families

Ministry of Public Safety and   **Corrections Branch**   Phone:
Solicitor General   Fax:

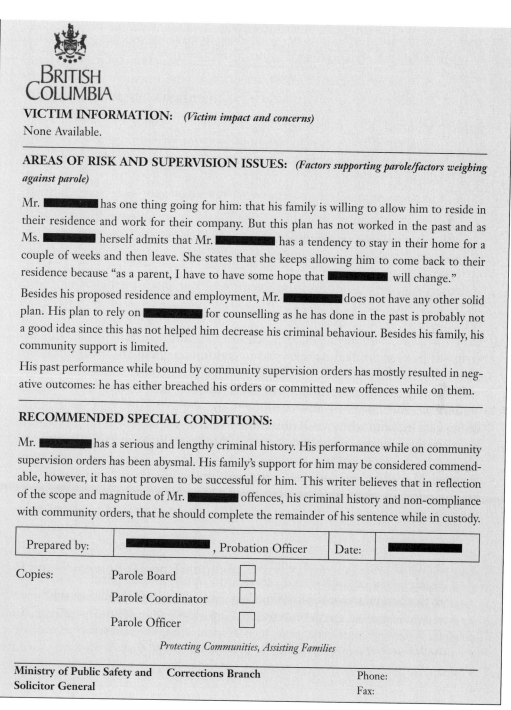

BRITISH COLUMBIA

VICTIM INFORMATION: *(Victim impact and concerns)*
None Available.

AREAS OF RISK AND SUPERVISION ISSUES: *(Factors supporting parole/factors weighing against parole)*

Mr. ███████ has one thing going for him: that his family is willing to allow him to reside in their residence and work for their company. But this plan has not worked in the past and as Ms. ███████ herself admits that Mr. ███████ has a tendency to stay in their home for a couple of weeks and then leave. She states that she keeps allowing him to come back to their residence because "as a parent, I have to have some hope that ███████ will change."

Besides his proposed residence and employment, Mr. ███████ does not have any other solid plan. His plan to rely on ███████ for counselling as he has done in the past is probably not a good idea since this has not helped him decrease his criminal behaviour. Besides his family, his community support is limited.

His past performance while bound by community supervision orders has mostly resulted in negative outcomes: he has either breached his orders or committed new offences while on them.

RECOMMENDED SPECIAL CONDITIONS:

Mr. ███████ has a serious and lengthy criminal history. His performance while on community supervision orders has been abysmal. His family's support for him may be considered commendable, however, it has not proven to be successful for him. This writer believes that in reflection of the scope and magnitude of Mr. ███████ offences, his criminal history and non-compliance with community orders, that he should complete the remainder of his sentence while in custody.

Prepared by:	███████, Probation Officer	Date:	███████

Copies: Parole Board   ☐

            Parole Coordinator   ☐

            Parole Officer   ☐

Protecting Communities, Assisting Families

Ministry of Public Safety and   Corrections Branch   Phone:
Solicitor General   Fax:

great distances and bear related costs. When victims do attend, a staff member of NPB accompanies them into the hearing and debriefs them afterward.

Before the hearing, the board members review the parole file and make notes on key points. During the hearing, the board members ask the inmate about the release plan and other questions to ascertain suitability of release. The board may pay a great deal of attention to the inmate's version of the offence, looking for some insight into why it was committed and why it would not happen again. (The inmate's participation in treatment programs and skills/trade training, as well as any other positive steps taken while in custody, are key factors here.) Indications of remorse and victim empathy are also considered important by board members. The file review and interview are designed to determine whether the offender can be managed at an acceptable level of risk in the community.

Following the interview, the inmate is asked to wait outside the hearing room while members deliberate and come to a decision. The inmate returns to the room to be told the outcome—whether the release is granted or denied or if the decision is deferred pending the gathering of additional information. If denied, specific reasons must be given so the inmate can understand how to increase the likelihood of success if another application is made, such as by participating in a treatment program, completing a program already in progress, or developing a different release plan. For example, if the plan was to live with friends who might not be a good influence, the board may recommend that the inmate look for a more suitable place to live.

Provincial parole boards in British Columbia, Ontario, and Quebec follow a decision-making process similar to that of the NPB. The observations of a journalist who spent a day observing a hearing of the NPB in the Ontario region are presented in Box 9.4.

If the parole board determines that the level of risk that the inmate applicant presents is not manageable in the community, the application for release on day parole or full parole will be denied. In such cases, provincial inmates must wait for 60 days before re-applying for release. However, given the relatively short sentences that provincial inmates serve in custody, the board may waive the 60-day waiting period. A "mock" parole grant decision sheet, with key identifiers removed, is presented in Box 9.5.

Many provincial/territorial inmates do not apply for parole, but rather serve their sentences in custody. These inmates are eligible to be released after serving two-thirds of their sentences in custody under statutory release. In contrast to federal offenders, provincial/territorial inmates on statutory release are not supervised by parole officers. Provincial parole boards are often faced with the difficult choice of releasing an offender on parole with a plan that is

BOX 9.4

Inside Hearings of the National Parole Board

Like Santa, a parole board is supposed to know who's been good or bad, and so by the time the hearing arrives parole panelists (called directors) already know more about the prisoner than they perhaps care to—and a lot of it is not very nice.

On this particular day, three board directors—former prison warden Kenneth Payne, career correctional-service employee Sheila Henriksen and social worker John Brothers—have the final say.

Armed with documents describing the parole-seeker's criminal history, psychological assessments, education, family situation, other relationships, behaviour while in prison and the recommendation from Correctional Services Canada, the members try to evaluate what risk these individuals pose to society and determine if that risk is manageable in the community.

The first up to bat on this day is a 36-year-old Kingston man who was sentenced to life on a charge of second-degree murder for killing a friend in a dispute over a woman.

At 8:30 a.m., the slight, frail-looking man is waiting outside the hearing with his case management officer and a university law student as the morning announcements play over the intercom. The atmosphere is weirdly like high school.

When the door to the hearing room opens, the brief window of opportunity has arrived that the convict has been waiting for—make-or-break time. The parole panel will soon begin its grueling interview. No holds are barred, and no part of a convict's life is off limits.

Sitting a couple of metres from the convicts, looking them in the face, panel members have to sift through what they're hearing and judge what is sincere and what is contrived, remembering that people seldom get to this point in their lives by being totally honest.

The members take in the convict's appearance and mannerisms, dissect his answers, ask questions in different ways to get a better read and compare the answers to facts provided by the professions.

They often caution the convicts against lying, because their replies must be consistent with what's in their files.

BOX 9.4, continued

This morning, the murderer from Kingston slouches, his hair slicked back tightly like people wore in the 1950s. He is wearing dark clothes, a tweed sports jacket and unmatching light-coloured socks.

The case management officer sits at a table to his left. Right as the hearing starts, the convict withdraws his application for full parole. He says day parole will suffice.

The man has spent time in a number of jails and prisons since the murder. He stares straight ahead as the case management officer outlines his criminal record, all of it minor and non-violent up to the killing. He also relates how the convict was granted full parole twice, in 1992 and again in 1995, and violated it both times.

A doctor's report rates the probability he will reoffend within a year of release at 40 per cent, saying he suffers from an anti-social personality disorder.

A panel member asks why he withdrew his application for full parole. In a low, frail voice, the convict states the obvious: "In a realistic view, I don't think you guys would send me to full parole."

A member jokes, "You have already done some of our work for us." Mr. Payne asks the convict about the bad choices he has made through his life, and there are many. The convict says his worst was getting involved in a relationship with the woman he killed for and, as he puts it, his "negative thinking."

The focus shifts to what he might have learned from his failures. "I needed to change the way I view things," the convict says. "I used to go through distorted thinking patterns. I have a problem over-complicating things.

"I used to take on other people's problems and make them my own." In discussing an anger-management course he has just repeated, he is asked: "When was the last time you felt really angry?" "When I got the letter from the parole board that media would be at my hearing," he answers. He adds, "Nothing personal," as he turns toward the observers behind him.

Asked about the killing, the convict says he doesn't recognize the man who did it, that there are "some pretty blank spots surrounding that time."

Ms. Henriksen questions his integrity. "I have got a sense you have an ability to fool people," she said. He replies: "Sitting in the position I am in, it doesn't seem right for me to say, 'Trust me.'"

But the board chooses to trust him anyway. Following brief deliberations it grants the man once-a-month [unescorted temporary absences]. If he does well on those, the next step will be day parole and then full parole without any further hearing.

"The board is satisfied you have benefited from our programs," says Mr. Payne.

The convict thanks the directors and, as he leaves, passes the bank robber waiting outside. And the process repeats itself.

The day ends with the case of the Stratford father, a 29-year-old first-time offender who smashed up his truck after a night of partying and nearly killed his passenger. His sentence was two years for criminal negligence causing bodily harm. He has served about a year.

If there is a common thread among these convicts it is the way they handle stress: Drugs and alcohol are their mainstays.

Oddly enough, the convict doesn't do a very good job of selling his case. Lucky for him it sells itself.

The case management officer gives an exemplary report on his prison behaviour, noting he attends night school and wants to pursue a trade in college.

The convict shakes as he appears before the panel members, who at times try to relax him.

One thing that works against him is a compelling victim impact statement. The victim is suing the convict. "I know he's mad but I have gone and tried to talk with him and all he does is yell at me or make rude gestures when he drives by," the convict explains. "I just wish it was me who got injured that night."

"All I know is I have two young kids I haven't seen in a month and I want to get back to them," says the man. "I can't wait."

Another quick verdict: immediate full parole. The directors deliver their judgment. And then they just hope.

Source: Campbell, 1997:A3. Reprinted by permission of the *Ottawa Citizen*.

BOX 9.5

Decision of the British Columbia Board of Parole to Grant Parole

**BC BOARD OF PAROLE
DECISION**

HEARING: ☒   FILE REVIEW: ☐

VICTIM(S): ATTENDED (NO)   PARTICIPATED (NO)   WRITTEN SUBMISSION (NO)

Name: MR. C.   CS: 00.695.720   FPS: 123456T

Place of Review: FRASER REGIONAL CORRECTIONAL CENTRE   Type of Review: APH

All relevant information was shared with the offender: YES   Date: MARCH 25, 2003

Criteria for parole ☐ (a) the offender will not, by reoffending, present an undue risk to society before the expiration according to law of the sentence is serving; and (b) the release of the offender will contribute to the protection of society by facilitating the reintegration of the offender into society as a law-abiding citizen. The following decision is based on the two criteria for parole and an assessment of risk using all relevant information available to the reviewing Board members.

Part 1 – Community Release Plan (Summary of the offender's release plan.)

Residence: Private home in Port Coquitlam with mother, step father and younger brother.
Education: No educational plans noted.
Employment: To work as a labourer for D- Bay Construction.
Treatment/Counseling: Comox Valley Recovery Centre - 28 day program followed by AA and counselling in the community.
Additional information:

Part 2 – Criminal History (Current offence, sentence length, probation, restitution, no contact orders, analysis of criminal history, contributing factors)

Current offence: CCC 403(b) Personation with intent to obtain property and CCC 344(b) Robbery (546 days).

Criminal history: Criminal record starts in 1997 as a youth and contains 6 youth charges and 3 adult charges for offences of Fraud, Theft, Drugs and Possession of stolen property.

Contributing factors: A drug addiction, alcohol and negative peers.

Part 3 - Summary of Assessments & Submissions (Note reference and significant information considered in forming the decision.)

Mr. C. applied for parole on an earlier date and was denied as his plan was deficient in treatment and counselling. Following the hearing, Mr. C. met with the D&A counsellor and arranged for treatment at Maple Ridge for 35 days followed by Comox Recovery for a further 28 days. This is confirmed. There is ongoing 1 on 1 counselling planned to follow at Port Coquitlam with AA and NA on a weekly basis.

Community Assessment: Mr. C. has the support of his family, relatives and friends. His step-dad is willing to provide employment and will assist in an apprenticeship to become a crane operator. This employment requires an early morning start (4am), work all day at a remote location, and return to the residence about suppertime.
Mr. C. requires two more courses to complete his grade 12, English 12 and Math 11. He has the ability to work on these courses in treatment, recovery and in the community of Port Coquitlam. Ms. L. (mother) and Ms. D. (sister) attended the hearing and both expressed a willingness to hold Mr. C. immediately accountable for his actions. Both have noticed a change in him and describe him as more mellow and mature. Crimes were committed while under the influence of a substance. This assessment does not support parole and was written prior to confirmation of treatment and recovery. It is the Board's understanding that the community is in favour of treatment at this point in time.

Institutional Assessment: The institution supports Parole based on institutional behaviour, completion of all available institutional programming and confirmed treatment.

CRNA: medium.

Part 4 - Board Analysis, Reasons and Decision (Relate analysis to the two criteria, instructions to the Parole Supervisor and explain the reasons for special conditions imposed.)

Before the Board is a sincere, 20 year-old male, remorseful and wanting to apologise for his crimes. He has a plan that addressess his addiction with recovery to follow. Following Comox Valley, Ms. L. (mother) has advised that her son is welcome home and there is no drugs or alcohol permitted. There is employment waiting with the opportunity of an apprenticeship as a crane operator.

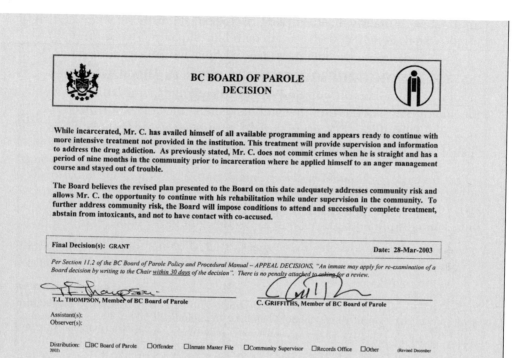

BC BOARD OF PAROLE
DECISION

While incarcerated, Mr. C. has availed himself of all available programming and appears ready to continue with more intensive treatment not provided in the institution. This treatment will provide supervision and information to address the drug addiction. As previously stated, Mr. C. does not commit crimes when he is straight and has a period of nine months in the community prior to incarceration where he applied himself to an anger management course and stayed out of trouble.

The Board believes the revised plan presented to the Board on this date adequately addresses community risk and allows Mr. C. the opportunity to continue with his rehabilitation while under supervision in the community. To further address community risk, the Board will impose conditions to attend and successfully complete treatment, abstain from intoxicants, and not to have contact with co-accused.

Final Decision(s): GRANT   Date: 28-Mar-2003

Per Section 11.2 of the BC Board of Parole Policy and Procedural Manual – APPEAL DECISIONS, "An inmate may apply for re-examination of a Board decision by writing to the Chair within 30 days of the decision". There is no penalty attached to asking for a review.

T.L. THOMPSON, Member of BC Board of Parole   C. GRIFFITHS, Member of BC Board of Parole

Assistant(s):
Observer(s):

Distribution: ☐BC Board of Parole   ☐Offender   ☐Inmate Master File   ☐Community Supervisor   ☐Records Office   ☐Other   (Revised December 2002)

not optimal or having the inmate serve until the statutory release date and then leave custody with no supervision or program.

THE PAROLE CERTIFICATE

If parole is granted, a certificate of parole is prepared. The parole certificate contains both mandatory conditions and additional conditions. Mandatory conditions include reporting regularly to a parole officer, obeying the law, and securing permission from the supervising parole officer prior to leaving a specified geographic area. There are mandatory conditions for all federal offenders on conditional release:

- On release, travel directly to the offender's place of residence, as set out in the release certificate, and report to the parole supervisor immediately and thereafter as instructed.
- Remain at all times in Canada, within territorial boundaries prescribed by the parole supervisor.
- Obey the law and keep the peace.

- Inform the parole supervisor immediately if arrested or questioned by the police.
- Always carry the release certificate and the identity card provided by the releasing authority and produce them on request for identification to any peace or parole officer.
- Report to the police if and as instructed by the parole supervisor.
- Advise the parole supervisor of address of residence on release and thereafter report immediately:
  - any change in address of residence
  - any change in occupation, including employment, vocational or educational training, and volunteer work
  - any change in the family, domestic, or financial situation
  - any change that may reasonably be expected to affect the ability to comply with the conditions of parole or statutory release.
- Do not own, possess, or have the control of any weapon. (National Parole Board, 1994:14–15)

Additional conditions are applied to the specific needs of individual offenders and designed to reduce or manage his or her specific risk factors. (The assessed need areas for federal and provincial male and female inmates are presented in Figure 9.7.) The most frequently applied additional conditions for federal parolees are:

- avoid certain persons (either a specific person such as a co-accused or people with criminal records in general)
- complete the treatment plan
- abstain from intoxicants
- undergo psychological counselling
- avoid certain places (Solicitor General Canada, 1998a)

Other common additional conditions include the requirement that the parolee seek and maintain employment or schooling, remain in a defined area, and not contact the victim(s) of their crime. Offenders convicted of sexual offences against children are often prohibited from being in the company of anyone under 14 (except when accompanied by an approved adult) and living near or being in the vicinity of schools, playgrounds, parks, or any other area where there is a reasonable expectation that children are present. The parole board can also require that the offender live in a community residential facility or other approved residence. In addition, a parolee may be required to submit to a urinalysis test when there are reasonable grounds to believe that he or she has breached the condition to abstain from all intoxicants.

Figure 9.7

Assessed High Needs of Male and Female Provincial/Territorial and Federal Inmates

Assessed High Needs — Provinces/Territories

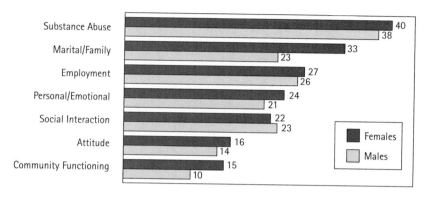

Assessed High Needs — Federal

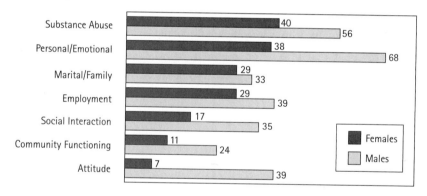

Source: Trevethan, 1999:11.

A parole certificate issued by the British Columbia Board of Parole is presented in Box 9.6.

INMATE APPEALS

Section 147 of the Corrections and Conditional Release Act provides that an inmate applicant who is denied parole may appeal on the grounds that, in making its decision, the parole board:

BOX 9.6

Certificate of Parole, British Columbia Board of Parole

Office of the Chair
#303 - 960 Quayside Drive
New Westminster BC V3M 6G2
Telephone: (604) 660-8846
Fax: (604) 660-2356
www.gov.bc.ca/bcparole/

CERTIFICATE OF PAROLE - BRITISH COLUMBIA BOARD OF PAROLE

Prisoners and Reformatories Act, Canada
Corrections and Conditional Release Act, Canada

F.P.S. No. 123456T
D.O.B. 16-APR-1983
C.S. No. 00.695.720

This is to certify that __MR. C.__ who is serving a term of imprisonment in __FRASER REGIONAL CORRECTIONAL CENTRE__, for the following offences: __S.403(B) CCC PERSONATION WITH INTENT TO OBTAIN; S.344(B) CCC ROBBERY__, was granted parole effective on __MARCH 28, 2003__ which will expire on __DECEMBER 28, 2003__ provided the parole is not sooner suspended and revoked.

CONDITIONS OF PAROLE

1. Report immediately upon release to the Parole Supervisor on __29 MARCH 2003__ at:
   MAPLE RIDGE COMMUNITY CORRECTIONS, #150-11960 HANEY PLACE, COURTHOUSE, MAPLE RIDGE, BC V2X 6G1
   PHONE NO: 604-466-7438

2. Report to the parole supervisor a minimum of __TWICE__ per __MONTH__ in person, or as directed by the parole supervisor.

3. Remain within the area of **British Columbia** namely: __LOWER MAINLAND__, or as directed by the Parole Supervisor.

4. Obey the law and keep the peace.

5. Immediately inform the parole supervisor on being questioned or arrested by the police.

6. Carry the release certificate at all times and produce it on request by the peace officer or parole supervisor for identification.

7. Report to the police at the time and place as directed by the parole supervisor, if so directed.

8. Advise the parole supervisor on release of the address of residence, namely: __MAPLE RIDGE TREATMENT CENTRE,__
   __FOLLOWED BY COMOX VALLEY RECOVERY__, and thereafter obtain permission, in advance, from the parole supervisor for:

   (i)   a change in address of residence
   (ii)   a change in occupation including a change in employment, vocational or educational training or in volunteer work.
   (iii) a change in living arrangements or financial situation and a change in family situation, or
   (iv)   a change that may reasonably be expected to affect compliance with conditions of the release.

9. Not own, possess or have control of a weapon as defined in section 2 of the Criminal Code except as authorized by the parole supervisor.

10. Special Conditions:
    a. Abstain from all intoxicants.
    b. Submit to a breathalyzer and/or urinalysis test on demand of the parole supervisor or peace officer where reasonable and probable grounds exist to believe the offender is violating the condition to abstain from intoxicants.
    c. Do not enter any premises where the primary commodity for sale is alcoholic beverages.
    d. Seek and maintain employment and/or educational opportunities.
    e. Actively participate in, and complete such substance abuse treatment, counselling and programs as you may be directed to attend by the parole supervisor.
    f. Do not have contact directly or indirectly with the victims unless assisted by your Parole Supervisor.
    g. Do not associate with; Ted Sutar, Brad Reshire and Ryan Blair.
    h. Do not associate with known criminals, except as approved by the parole supervisor.
    i. Attend and successfully complete Maple Ridge Treatment Centre and Comox Valley Recovery.
    j. Following treatment, abide by a curfew of 9:00 p.m. to 4:00 a.m. unless you have written permission from your parole supervisor to vary these hours for a specific purpose.
    k. Provide monthly updates to your Parole Supervisor on your apprenticeship and employment.

This Certificate of Parole is granted under the authority of the British Columbia Board of Parole subject to the Conditions set out on the Certificate. Failure to comply with any of these Conditions may result in the parole being suspended and/or revoked.

Issued at MAPLE RIDGE, BC   this 28 day of MARCH, 2003.

T.L. THOMPSON, *Member of BC Board of Parole*   C. GRIFFITHS, *Member of BC Board of Parole*

I have read and understand the contents of this document and accept all the above conditions and will abide by them. I acknowledge that I am the person to whom the statements contained herein refer and agree that the said statements are correct. I further acknowledge that I have been made aware of the forfeiture of earned remission upon my accepting this parole release.

Signed _____
Witnessed _____

Released from __FRASER REGIONAL CORRECTIONAL CENTRE__   on __MARCH 29, 2003__ _____
Officer in Charge _____

pc: BC Board of Parole (*original*)
       Parolee
       Inmate Master File
       Operational Communications Centre, RCMP
       Community Supervisor

(Revised December 2002)

- failed to observe a principle of fundamental justice;
- made an error of law;
- breached or failed to apply a board policy;
- based its decision on erroneous or incomplete information; or
- acted without jurisdiction or beyond its jurisdiction, or failed to exercise its jurisdiction.

In considering those cases that meet one or more of the above criteria, the appeal division of the parole board may:

- affirm the decision;
- affirm the decision but order a further review of the case by the board on a date earlier than the date otherwise provided for next review;
- order a new review of the case by the board and order the continuation of the decision pending the review; or
- reverse, cancel, or vary the decision.

In 2001–02, there were just under 500 federal inmate appeals to the NPB. In 94 percent (440/468) of the cases reviewed on appeal, the initial decision of the NPB was affirmed, while a new review was ordered in 6 percent of the cases (26/468). The initial decision was altered in two federal cases. Four appeals from provincial inmates whose cases were decided by the NPB were reviewed, and the initial decision was affirmed in three of the cases (National Parole Board, 2002:77). Comparable figures are not available from the provincial parole boards.

ISSUES IN PAROLE BOARD DECISION MAKING

Given that correctional institutions are public and political institutions, the internal operations of prisons can be significantly affected by elements in the external environment. Among the potential influences are the media, politicians and legislatures, and community interest groups (see Figure 5.3 on page 176).

Parole boards can also be described as public and political institutions, subject to influences from a variety of sources. In fact, considerable controversy often surrounds the decision making of parole boards, particularly when an inmate on conditional release commits a heinous crime. The general criticisms of parole and parole board decision making include the following:

- Parole extends rather than reduces correctional surveillance over an offender.
- Too much discretion is vested in non-judicial, unscrutinized decision makers.

- Parole boards are too sensitive to public opinion.
- Capricious and arbitrary decisions are demoralizing and can harden the distrust of inmates toward authority figures.
- Manageability and good institutional conduct may not be good indicators of suitability for release.
- The process is too one-sided (i.e., not adversarial).
- Some inmates manipulatively play the "parole game" to create the impression of rehabilitation, while those who choose not to play that game can be judged harshly.
- Sentencing someone to nine years when everyone knows they will serve only three creates disrespect for the administration of justice.
- The public lacks confidence in correctional and parole authorities in part because of the authorities' failure to acknowledge and learn from past errors. (Benzvy-Miller and Cole, 1990; Greenspan, Matheson, and Davis, 1998; Newark, 1996)

Some of the specific criticisms that that have been levelled at parole boards and their decisions are discussed below.

The Appointment of Parole Board Members

Historically, positions on parole boards were most often patronage appointments—that is, a reward for supporters of the federal government of the day. In recent years, however, there has been a shift to the appointment of people with some special training in corrections, criminal justice, and related fields (law, criminology, psychology, etc.). Today, one is as likely to find a board member with extensive experience in corrections as a person from the private sector or political realm. Recent appointments to the British Columbia Board of Parole, for example, have included a therapist with 25 years' experience working with female offenders and sex offenders, a retired senior manager from community corrections, and an Aboriginal person with extensive experience in social services and community development.

The Absence of Clearly Defined Release Criteria

As noted near the beginning of this chapter, the Corrections and Conditional Release Act sets out two general criteria that are to guide the decision as to whether an offender should be released from confinement on conditional release. This generality has traditionally been a source of difficulty for correctional staff, inmates, and parole board members themselves. Although board members have access to an extensive amount of information on each inmate applicant (including police reports, pre-sentence reports, the reasons for the sentence as set out by the presiding judge, the risk/needs assessment and other materials produced during the case management process, and the community assessments completed by the parole officer), it is often difficult for members to assess how to prioritize or weigh the importance of this information. Combined with the discretion exercised by board members, this lack of guidance can result in individual styles of parole decision making, which may, in turn, create disparity in decisions on applications for conditional release between board members or between boards, even within the same jurisdiction.

The absence of more specific release criteria also contributes to a lack of predictability in parole board decision making that may undermine the credibility and effectiveness of case managers and treatment staff, who may have encouraged the inmate and written positive recommendations, only to have the parole board deny the application for conditional release.

The Absence of Information Feedback to Parole Board Members

There are few, if any, mechanisms in place for parole board members to receive feedback on the ultimate outcome of their decisions—that is, what happens to the offender while under supervision in the community and after warrant expiry and the end of supervision. Generally, the only instance in which individual parole board members may learn of an inmate's behaviour on conditional release is in those cases where the parolee commits a high-profile crime. Discussion in the media about these tragic cases can provide board members with a skewed perspective and, in certain instances, may result in an increase in denying inmate applications for conditional release.

The Inmate and Parole Hearings

For inmates applying for conditional release, the appearance before the parole board can be an intimidating experience, accompanied by a high level of stress and anxiety. In essence, inmates have only a few minutes to state their case to the board, a particular challenge for inmates with limited language skills and vocabulary. Although inmate applicants are allowed to have legal representation or other persons in attendance for support, parole board hearings are not a court of law, and the role of lawyers is limited. Current restrictions on legal aid have limited access to legal counsel in many provinces for all but those who can afford to pay their lawyers to attend. Most provincial parole applicants appear on their own.

There are no restrictions on the nature and range of questions that board members may ask an inmate applicant, and these may include questions relating to past criminal activities and convictions, the present offence, and participation in treatment programs, as well as more personal questions about family of origin and current family members and friendships. The severe time constraints under which many parole boards operate places an added burden on both board members and the inmate applicant, which may lead to superficial coverage of some topics. In addition, there may be educational and cultural differences (including language barriers) that make it difficult, or impossible, for board members and the inmate to communicate clearly and openly with one another.

There is more knowledge of the role of the parole board and of the dynamics of parole hearings among federal offenders who have served multiple terms in custody. A lifer on parole who had appeared before the parole board on numerous occasions offered the following opinion:

> *Parole hearings for me now are old hat. I know how to present myself, what to do, what they want to hear, why they want to hear things. I have a good understanding of what their role is, and what they think their role is and how to approach that…. I think they have a really difficult job in trying to gauge the threat to society of the people who are there. They're responsible for the decisions they make. Just looking at a file doesn't give you a very good indicator of who people are. But if you put a person in a stressful situation and crank them up a little bit and see how they react and see how they handle a situation, then you get a pretty good view of who that person is. I think the board does that quite often…. If you're able to handle yourself in those situations and still be able to supply the things that are necessary, and make them feel comfortable with the idea of actually letting the person out, then you've done your job as a presenter to the board of your case. (cited in Murphy, Johnsen, and Murphy, 2002:93)*

The difficulties inmates encounter at parole hearings are often reflected in the complaints or appeals filed by inmate applicants who have been denied parole. The findings from a U.S. study of inmate complaints following denial of parole are presented in Table 9.3. One inmate who made a complaint stated: "I was denied for the third time by the parole board even though I have completed all recommended classes…. I have a place to parole to [mother's house], a good job and a very strong support group consisting of family and friends" (cited in West-Smith, Pogrebin, and Poole, 2000:7).

Aboriginal Inmates and the Parole Board

Although overrepresented in provincial/territorial and federal institutions, Aboriginal offenders tend to receive shorter sentences than non-Aboriginals

Table 9.3   Inmate Complaints about Parole Hearings: Frequency of Complaints and Percentage of Inmates Having Complaint

Nature of Complaint	Frequency of Complaints	Percentage of Inmates with Complaint
1. Inadequate time served, yet beyond P.E.D.	61	48%
2. Completed required programs	45	35%
3. Denied despite parole plan	35	27%
4. Board composition and behaviour	27	21%
5. Longer setbacks after parole violation	26	20%
6. Family need for inmate support ignored	22	17%
7. Case manager not helpful	17	13%
8. New sex offender laws applied retroactively	16	12%
9. Required classes not available	11	9%
10. Few inmates paroled on same day	7	5%
11. Appeals considered on individual basis	6	4%
12. Miscellaneous	12	9%
	N = 285	*N* = 128

*PED = parole eligibility date

Source: West-Smith, Pogrebin, and Poole, 2000:6.

and to serve less time in confinement. However, Aboriginal inmates are less likely to be successful in their applications for conditional release and may choose not to apply at all. Although Aboriginal peoples represent approximately 17 percent of the federal institutional population, only about 10 percent of federal offenders on parole are Aboriginal (LaPrairie, 1996). In addition, Aboriginal parolees are less likely than non-Aboriginals to successfully complete parole (Hamilton and Sinclair, 1991).

A number of factors have been identified as contributing to the difficulties that Aboriginal offenders experience on parole, including a lack of understanding of the parole process, feelings of alienation, a lack of self-confidence in the ability to successfully complete conditional release, and a lack of assistance for Aboriginal inmates wishing to apply for parole. They are more likely to be on statutory release than on other types of release, in part because of a high rate of waiving the right to a parole hearing.

There may be particular difficulties between Aboriginal inmate applicants and parole boards. Across the country, there are very few Aboriginal parole board members, raising the possibility of a lack of cultural sensitivity among non-Aboriginal board members and inequity in the hearing process.

These problems are reflected in the observations of Lisa Hobbs Birnie, a non-Aboriginal former member of the NPB in the Prairie region:

> *When I found myself sitting opposite Samuel Grey Hawk, or Amos Morning Cloud, or Joseph Brave Bear, or when I caught the shy, uncertain eyes of a Cree-speaking teenager from the far North attempting to follow, through an interpreter, our ritualistic procedures and answer our thoroughly white middle-class questions, I felt a little like a fraud. It seemed incalculably unfair that these men had the misfortune to have to depend upon the decisions of people who might as well have come from another planet, as far as the similarities in culture and lifestyle were concerned. (Birnie, 1990:195)*

A number of initiatives have been undertaken in an attempt to address these difficulties, including conducting Elder-assisted parole hearings in some areas, increasing the number of Aboriginal parole board members, and providing cultural-awareness training for board members (Solicitor General Canada, 1998b).

Particular difficulties may be encountered by Aboriginal inmate applicants from northern and remote regions:

> *Sometimes the inmate was ready to go out, and if he was from a city, we would release him. Another inmate, just as ready, would be denied release simply because he was from a community in the Far North with no supports available to him—not only no work, but also no self-help group of former alcoholics, no local hospital with a mental health program, no drug counselors, no sex offender programs. (Birnie, 1990:196)*

Other explanations for the lower grant rate for Aboriginal inmates focus on the higher level of seriousness of their offences of conviction and the fact that they are more likely to be classified as high risk. However, LaPrairie (1996) posits that Aboriginal-specific risk assessment instruments may be required, even different instruments for urban and on-reserve Aboriginal offenders. The Statistical Information on Recidivism Scale is no longer used with Aboriginal inmates.

Half of the Aboriginal inmates surveyed by LaPrairie (1996) indicated that correctional staff had not accurately identified their problems and need areas. While 58 percent self-identified as having an alcohol problem, this area was not typically what they believed was their greatest need. Two-thirds of the sample identified employment/education as their greatest need, followed in frequency by spirituality, culture, life skills, and assistance with literacy. As discussed in Chapter 8, one issue yet to be resolved is the extent to which Aboriginal offenders require culturally specific intervention techniques. The current trend is to consider cultural factors in program design, even for specific groups such as Aboriginal sex offenders (Ellerby and Stonechild, 1998). Aboriginal inmates themselves express differing views on the issue and, interestingly, do not evidence a high rate of program participation in Aboriginal programs (LaPrairie, 1996; Solicitor General Canada, 1998b).

PREDICTING RECIDIVISM: A CHALLENGING TASK

In contemporary corrections, the process of determining which inmates should qualify for conditional release is forward-looking, asking two basic questions: (1) if released, will the inmate commit an offence that he or she would not have committed if kept in confinement?; and (2) will conditional release with supervision reduce the risk for reoffending compared with a cold turkey release? To answer these questions, decision makers must know the factors that contribute to and reduce the probability of reoffending.

Clinical and Actuarial Prediction of Recidivism

Predicting future behaviour has always been fraught with difficulties. Early studies on prediction of violent behaviour among men with histories of violence produced repeatedly dismal results (see Webster et al., 1994, for an excellent review). Two key problems were the low base rate of violence, even among men with histories of violence, and the false positives. In other words, most of the subjects did not reoffend, and many of those predicted to be violent were not. These studies utilized **clinical prediction,** which involved mental-health professionals conducting assessments and making recommendations. One finding from these studies was that some professionals were more adept at making predictions than others. Some assessors, for example, were fairly accurate in their clinical judgments, whereas the accuracy of other assessors would have been improved by flipping a coin. This led some treatment specialists to argue that clinical prediction should be abandoned (Quinsey et al., 1998).

Another approach is **actuarial prediction,** which is created by examining a large group of inmates and identifying the factors that distinguish offenders who reoffend following release from those who do not. Among the factors that have been found to be most predictive of recidivism are:

- number of prior convictions
- number of prior admissions to prison
- age at offence leading to first imprisonment
- absence of a recent three-year prison-free period
- history of new offence or revocation while on parole
- a history of heroin or opiate dependence

These findings suggest that the past behaviour of the inmate may be the best predictor of future behaviour. This fact poses a problem for correctional officials because static risk factors, such as an inmate's criminal history, are not amenable to change. If static risk factors were the basis of granting conditional release, the outcome of any parole hearing would be a foregone conclusion. No effort on the inmate's part would improve the probability of achieving conditional release. Therefore, inmates would be discouraged from participating in institutional treatment programs or even from conducting themselves in an appropriate manner during confinement.

Risk Assessment and Dynamic Risk Factors

There are several risk assessment instruments in widespread use by correctional authorities that are based partially on dynamic risk factors—variables that are associated with a probability for offending but that are amenable to change (see Chapter 8). From a statistical survey of 131 studies of offending conducted between 1970 and 1994, Gendreau, Little, and Goggin (1996) identified several dynamic risk factors that were the most predictive of adult recidivism:

- antisocial values and attitudes
- antisocial personality
- antisocial companions
- interpersonal conflict
- social achievement (e.g., education and employment)
- substance abuse

It appears, then, that dynamic factors are as predictive as static factors and that both should be used by release authorities.

The Level of Service Inventory–Ontario Revision (LSI-OR) uses both static and dynamic factors. This 43-item instrument results in a summary score corresponding to one of five risk categories ranging from "very low" to "very high." Correctional personnel scoring the LSI-OR can exercise professional discretion and override the summary score if, in their opinion, the final risk category is incompatible with their sense of the inmate's prognosis. Overrides occur in approximately one in every ten cases and are split nearly equally between moving the inmate to a higher-risk category or to a lower-risk category than indicated by the LSI-OR summary score (Wormith, 1997).

The Prediction of Future Behaviour: *Caveat Emptor*

Even the strongest supporters of recidivism prediction admit that it is not an infallible science. Webster et al. (1994) frame the issue in terms of two dilemmas. First, research has not identified a scheme that can reliably predict future offending, yet the criminal justice system wants these predictions made for use in important decisions such as release from confinement. Second, assessors must be aware of the enormous problem of false positive prediction (predicting someone will be violent when in reality he or she will not); on the other hand, the fallout from making a false *negative* prediction—predicting no violence when violence does subsequently occur—can be significant and can include legal liability, media attention, and commissions of inquiry (see del Carmen and Louis, 1988; Gurberg, Vantour, and Christy, 1997; Smith and Smith, 1998).

As previously noted, parole board members are granted complete discretion in conditional release decisions, and it is difficult to determine the extent to which recidivism prediction tools are used in making release decisions. When risk instruments *are* used to predict recidivism, there are several issues that must be considered.

Reliability

One of the most common criticisms of risk prediction schemes is that different raters can achieve different scores for the same case and the same rater can achieve different scores over time. In practice, it is possible that an inmate's risk score can increase over time as criminal justice personnel gather more social history information and/or the inmate discloses additional background and offence information.

It is important that sufficient offence and social history data be available; otherwise, the score could be too low (i.e., incorrect). The need to have all relevant information before assessing risk is one of the lessons learned from retroactive investigations of tragic incidents such as murders by parolees. It is also crucial that assessors are adequately trained in the scoring and interpretation of the instruments. In addition, many items on risk scales are actually quite subjective, and different assessors can create different scores for the same offender, meaning that decision makers are often presented with information on the offender that is inconsistent.

The Ecological Fallacy

Actuarial prediction schemes are, by definition and design, used to predict the behaviour of groups of inmates and therefore are inappropriate for predicting the future behaviour of individuals. As Shannon (1985:161) states, "We must not claim the ability to predict who will engage in delinquent and criminal behaviour in the future when we have only the ability to state that the members of some risk groups have a greater probability of doing so than do others." Using data from one unit of analysis (i.e., groups) to draw conclusions about another unit of analysis (i.e., individuals) is called the **ecological fallacy** and is a major problem in predicting risk and future behaviour.

"Significant" May Not Be Significant

The predictive validity of instruments such as the LSI-OR has been tested by comparing the scores of groups of inmates with the rates of reoffending of the sample following release. Gendreau, Little, and Goggin (1996) found that the predictive power of the LSI-OR was .33, a figure higher than the other instruments reviewed and "statistically significant." It is clear that one of the best instruments available leaves a great deal of recidivist behaviour unpredicted, whether as a consequence of random factors or variables not considered in the prediction scheme. Greater than nothing can be far from something.

Killing Two (or Three or Four) Birds with One Stone

Wormith (1997) notes that risk instruments such as the LSI-OR can be used for four purposes: (1) classification, (2) program planning, (3) conditional release decisions (i.e., prediction), and (4) decisions about supervision in the community. The question is, however, whether one assessment instrument can effectively serve all of these purposes. More specifically, can one instrument be used for all types of offenders?

In British Columbia, for example, a series of instruments is used in provincial corrections to perform different functions. These instruments include the Inmate Classification Assessment (for classification), the Inmate Needs Assessment (for case planning), the Inmate Risk Assessment (for behaviour management in the institution), and the Community Risk/Needs Assessment Scale for conditional release and parole supervision. Each instrument uses static or dynamic factors or a combination of these two types of factors, as required. There are also separate assessment instruments for specific groups of offenders, including sex offenders, spouse abusers, and young offenders.

One Size Doesn't Necessarily Fit All

Another concern is that risk assessment instruments were developed using the offender group that composes the largest portion of the inmate population: white males. There is increasing concern that these instruments are less effective with other offender groups, including female offenders and Aboriginal offenders. For example, a history of attempted suicide was the strongest predictor of violent recidivism in one group of female inmates, while a history of self-injury was correlated with recidivism in another (Blanchette, 1997). Neither of these factors is likely to be predictive for recidivism of male offenders. The validity of male-derived classification instruments for women is also being questioned (Brennan and Austin, 1997). An Ontario study of the LSI-OR suggested that the cutoff scores used with male inmates are inappropriate for female offenders (Coulson et al., 1996).

In recognition of these potential difficulties, the Statistical Information on Recidivism Scale is no longer used for Aboriginal offenders or for female offenders, and doubts have also been raised about its utility with violent offenders and sex offenders (Cormier, 1997).

Overpredicting the Level of Risk

The identification of factors related to the risk of reoffending via various assessment instruments was viewed as a positive development for inmates who would benefit from the efforts to reduce the likelihood of recidivism and re-incarceration. Indeed, low-risk offenders enjoy the advantages associated with conditional release. The flip side of the coin, however, is that those inmates who are classified as high-risk may be penalized, a significant concern if assessment instruments over-predict the level of risk. Support for this concern is provided by the fact that, even in provincial systems of corrections, almost half of assessed inmates were identified as being at a high risk to reoffend (Robinson, Porporino, and Millson, 1998). Risk prediction has the potential to be misused to justify selective incapacitation, identifying who should stay in prison longer—or forever. If this is the case, errors in prediction have tremendous human as well as economic costs. In the next (and final) chapter, the re-entry of offenders into the community is examined.

QUESTIONS FOR REVIEW

1. Name the two circumstances, set out in the Corrections and Conditional Release Act, under which the National Parole Board or a provincial parole board may grant a conditional release.

2. What are the types of conditional release available to inmates incarcerated in federal correctional institutions? In provincial/territorial correctional institutions?

3. What is cold turkey release and what challenges does it present to provincial parole boards?

4. Why has the parole grant rate in Ontario declined in the past decade?

5. What steps have correctional authorities in some provinces taken to reduce the likelihood of re-victimization in cases where the offender and victim are acquainted?

6. Discuss the issues surrounding section 745 of the Criminal Code (faint-hope clause).

7. What did researcher Brian Grant's study indicate about the effectiveness of detention as a strategy for protecting the public?

8. Discuss the role of the inmate applicant's parole file and the community assessment in parole board decision making.

9. Identify and discuss three criticisms of parole board decision making.

10. What are the differences between clinical prediction and actuarial prediction?

REFERENCES

Benzvy-Miller, S.H., and D.P. Cole. 1990. "Integrating Sentencing and Parole." *Canadian Journal of Criminology* 32(3):493–502.

Birnie, L.H. 1990. *A Rock and a Hard Place: Inside Canada's Parole Board.* Toronto: Macmillan.

Blanchette, K. 1997. Classifying Female Offenders for Correctional Interventions. *Forum on Corrections Research* 9(1):36–41.

Bonta, J., A. Harris, I. Zinger, and D. Carriere. 1996. *The Crown Files Research Project: A Study of Dangerous Offenders.* Ottawa: Solicitor General Canada.

Bonta, J., I. Zinger, A. Harris, and D. Carriere. 1998. "The Dangerous Offender Provisions: Are They Targeting the Right Offenders?" *Canadian Journal of Criminology* 40(4):377–400.

Brennan, T., and J. Austin. 1997. *Women in Jail: Classification Issues.* Washington, D.C.: National Institute of Corrections, U.S. Department of Justice.

Brunet, L. 1998. "Highlights in the History of Day Parole." *Forum on Corrections Research* 10(2):7–10.

Campbell, D. 1997. "A Journalist Goes to Prison to See for Himself How Parole Boards Decide Which Convicts Are Good Risks and Which Ones Are Not." *Ottawa Citizen* (November 3):A3.

Cormier, R. 1997. "Yes SIR! A Stable Risk Prediction Tool." *Forum on Corrections Research* 9(1):3–7.

Coulson, G., G. Flacqua, V. Nutbrown, D. Giulekas, and F. Cudjoe. 1996. "Predictive Utility of the LSI for Incarcerated Female Offenders." *Criminal Justice and Behavior* 23(3):427–39.

del Carmen, R.V., and P.T. Louis. 1988. *Civil Liabilities of Parole Personnel for Release, Non-Release, Supervision and Revocation.* Longmont, Colo.: National Institute of Corrections.

Ellerby, L., and J. Stonechild. 1998. "Blending the Traditional with the Contemporary in the Treatment of Aboriginal Sexual Offenders: A Canadian Experience." In W.L. Marshall, Y.M. Fernandez, S.M. Hudson, and T. Ward (eds.), *Sourcebook of Treatment Programs for Sexual Offenders* (399–415). New York: Plenum Press.

Fauteux, G. 1956. *Report of a Committee Appointed to Inquire into the Principles and Procedures Followed in the Remission Service of the Department of Justice of Canada.* Ottawa: Queen's Printer.

Gendreau, P., T. Little, and C. Goggin. 1996. "Meta-Analysis of the Prediction of Adult Offender Recidivism: What Works!" *Criminology* 34(4): 575–607.

Grant, B.A. 1997. "Detention: Is It Meeting Its Goal?" *Forum on Corrections Research* 9(2):19–24.

———. 1998. "Day Parole: Effects of the Corrections and Conditional Release Act." *Forum on Corrections Research* 10(2):23–26.

Grant, B.A., and S.L. Johnson. 1998. *Personal Development Temporary Absences.* Ottawa: Correctional Service of Canada.

Grant, B.A., and W.A. Millson. 1998. *The Temporary Absence Program: A Descriptive Analysis.* Ottawa: Correctional Service of Canada.

Greenspan, E., A. Matheson, and R. Davis. 1998. "Discipline and Parole." *Queen's Quarterly* 105(1):9–27.

Gurberg, T.N., J. Vantour, and R. Christy. 1997. "When the Risks Become Reality: Messages for Practitioners and Researchers from National Investigations." *Forum on Corrections Research* 9(2):57–60.

Hamilton, Associate Chief Justice A.C., and Associate Chief Judge C.M. Sinclair. 1991. *Report of the Aboriginal Justice Inquiry of Manitoba: The Justice System and Aboriginal People.* Vol. 1. Winnipeg: Queen's Printer.

LaPrairie, C. 1996. *Examining Aboriginal Corrections in Canada.* Ottawa: Aboriginal Corrections, Solicitor General Canada.

Murphy, P.J., L. Johnsen, and J. Murphy. 2002. *Paroled for Life: Interviews with Parolees Serving Life Sentences.* Vancouver: New Star Books.

National Parole Board. 1994. *Parole: Balancing Public Safety and Personal Responsibility.* Ottawa: National Parole Board.

———. 1997. *Facts: Types of Release.* Ottawa: National Parole Board.

———. 2002. *Performance Monitoring Report, 2001–02.* Ottawa: National Parole Board.

Newark, S. 1996. "The Future of Corrections and Parole." *CPA [Canadian Police Association] Express* 38(winter):18–19.

Quinsey, V.L., G.T. Harris, M.E. Rice, and C.A. Cormier. 1998. *Violent Offenders: Appraising and Managing Risk.* Washington, D.C.: American Psychological Association.

Robinson, D., F.J. Porporino, and W.A. Millson. 1998. "A One-Day Snapshot of Inmates in Canada's Adult Correctional Facilities." *Juristat* 18(8). Cat. no. 85-002-XPE. Ottawa: Canadian Centre for Justice Statistics, Statistics Canada.

Shannon, L.W. 1985. "Risk Assessment vs. Real Prediction: The Prediction Problem and the Public Trust." *Journal of Quantitative Criminology* 1(2):159–89.

Smith, W.R., and D.R. Smith. 1998. "The Consequences of Error: Recidivism Prediction and Civil Libertarian Ratios." *Journal of Criminal Justice* 26(6):481–502.

Solicitor General Canada. 1998a. *Sentence Calculation: How Does It Work?* Ottawa.

———. 1998b. *CCRA Five-Year Review: Aboriginal Offenders.* Ottawa.

Solicitor General Portfolio Corrections Statistics Committee. 2002. *Corrections and Conditional Release Statistical Overview.* Ottawa: Solicitor General Canada.

Trevethan, S. 1999. "Women in Federal and Provincial/Territorial Correctional Facilities." *Forum on Corrections Research* 11(3):9–11.

Webster, C.D., G.T. Harris, M.E. Rice, and C. Cormier. 1994. *The Violence Prediction Scheme: Assessing Dangerousness in High Risk Men.* Toronto: Centre of Criminology, University of Toronto.

West-Smith, M., M.R. Pogrebin, and E.D. Poole. 2000. "Denial of Parole: An Inmate Perspective." *Federal Probation* 64(2):3–10.

Wormith, J.S. 1997. "Research to Practice: Applying Risk Needs Assessment to Offender Classification." *Forum on Corrections Research* 9(1):26–31.

CHAPTER 10

RE-ENTRY AND LIFE AFTER PRISON

CHAPTER OBJECTIVES

- *Understand reintegration as a process that begins before release.*
- *Consider the "pains of re-entry" faced by newly released offenders.*
- *Examine parole supervision.*
- *Consider the circumstances of selected offender groups on release.*
- *Review the process of revocation of conditional release.*

KEY TERMS

Reintegration

Pains of re-entry

Community correctional centres

Community residential centres

Community-based residential facilities

Community notification

Judicial recognizance

Suspension of conditional release

Revocation of conditional release

The overarching goal of reentry … is to have returned to our midst an individual who has discharged his legal obligation to society by serving his sentence and has demonstrated an ability to live by society's rules.… The primary objective, for offender and criminal justice agency alike, is to prevent the recurrence of anti-social behavior.

—criminologist Jeremy Travis, cited in Travis, 2000:2

A tremendous feeling of exhilaration filled my whole being the moment that I stepped through that big front gate [of Kingston Penitentiary] into a perfect summer day. I stood at the edge of the old road that led into the city as shivers of anxiety made my legs tremble and perspiration break out on my brow. For the first time in five years I was about to venture into the world and I wasn't sure if I could make the grade or stand the pressures.

—Roger Caron, author and offender, cited in Caron, 1978:159

It was June of 1959, the same year the National Parole Board came into being, but Roger Caron had served every day of his sentence. Picked up by his sister at the gate and driven to their parents' house, he moved back into his old room, to try to fit in and get on with life where he left off at age 17. He tried to break the conditioning of a rigid routine and learn to relax in the company of women. He had trouble sleeping. He quickly found and lost a job, owing in great measure to an inability to control his temper. In the end, he couldn't make the grade or stand the pressures. Less than two weeks after walking through the prison gates into the sunshine, he committed a well-planned but ill-fated robbery that led to a fourth prison term. Years later he wrote the award-winning *Go Boy!* (1978) and two other prison-related books. Despite his literary success, he resumed bank robberies in 1991. This was followed by another prison term, and in 2001, three years after his release, another arrest for plans to commit armed robbery.

THE PROCESS OF REINTEGRATION

What could have been done differently for Roger Caron to increase his chances of staying out of prison in 1959 and on subsequent occasions? Today, systems of corrections recognize two equally important responsibilities. The first is to maintain sentenced offenders securely and safely while they are incarcerated. The second is to release them in a way that maximizes their chances for success after prison. Risk assessment while an offender is confined is much easier than risk management in the community. Ideally, there should be continuity between the inmate's participation in institutional programming and the services an offender receives on conditional release in the community.

Reintegration is a process, not an event. It has been defined as "all activity and programming conducted to prepare an offender to return safely to the community as a law-abiding citizen" (Thurber, 1998:14). It begins with the treatment programs described in Chapter 8 and also includes the development of a release plan that sets out where the inmate will live, employment and/or education opportunities, and, if required, participation in post-release treatment programs (see Figure 10.1). The goal of reintegration is to avoid recidivism in the short term (until warrant expiry) and, ideally, in the long term as well. Most inmates who reoffend do so within the first two years following release from a correctional institution.

There are a number of challenges in developing effective reintegration policies and programs, including:

Figure 10.1

The Reintegration Process for Federal Offenders

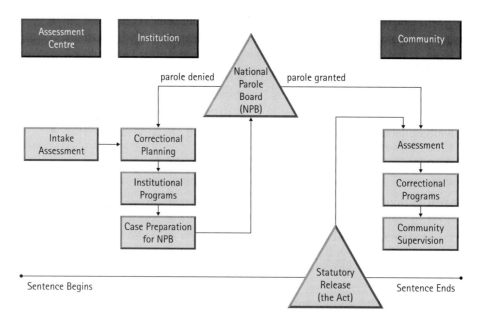

Source: Auditor General of Canada, 1996:31 (ch. 30). Reproduced with permission of the Minister of Public Works and Government Services Canada, 1999.

- maintaining continuity between institutional and community-based treatment programs
- balancing the resources available to inmates in institutions and in the community
- ensuring that offenders have access to community-based programs in all regions of the country, including remote and northern areas
- maintaining high levels of training for parole officers and ensuring that caseloads and workloads remain within reasonable levels
- allowing the participation of nonprofit agencies and the community in providing services to offenders on conditional release
- increasing public confidence in the ability of correctional agencies to reintegrate offenders safely
- encouraging Aboriginal communities to play a role in the reintegration process
- remembering to use inmates' strengths as levers for change instead of focusing solely on problems

A critical issue is how assessed risk and need factors are translated into effective strategies to proactively manage the risk presented by offenders with the greatest likelihood of failure after release.

THE PAINS OF RE-ENTRY

There's a saying, "You may be out of prison, but the prison is never out of you."

—female parolee serving a life sentence, cited in Murphy, Johnsen, and Murphy, 2002:167

In Chapter 7, the pains of imprisonment were identified and discussed. Offenders who are released from confinement also experience **pains of re-entry,** which highlights the irony of reintegration. That is, a sentence of imprisonment triggers a process whereby individuals are extracted from society and forced to adjust to a closed, structured, and artificial environment, where an antisocial value system predominates and inmates have little responsibility. Then, upon release, these same inmates are expected to resume life in the community and to hold prosocial values, exercise independence of thought and decision making, and display life skills that enable them to cope with the complexities of daily life in a fast-paced society. Such a dramatic transition, which would challenge even the most gifted individual, is particularly difficult for marginalized, socially isolated offenders who have been incarcerated for long periods. As one long-term offender commented to C.T. Griffiths, "The values, attitudes and behaviours that I learned inside were just the opposite of what I needed to make it in the free world."

Imagine the difficulties you would encounter in adjusting to a law-abiding lifestyle in the community if you were a parolee with a grade 9 education, a poor record of employment, tenuous or nonexistent family support, a substance abuse problem, and few or no non-criminal friends. Unfortunately, a record of positive conduct inside a correctional institution, including completion of various treatment programs, may not adequately prepare an inmate for the challenges that await upon re-entry into the community. A survey of federal and provincial correctional personnel found that the most frequently mentioned problems facing offenders upon re-entry were a lack of education and job skills, the absence of family support, poverty, drug and alcohol problems, and low self-esteem (LaPrairie, 1996).

Inmates spend a considerable amount of time planning for, thinking about, and speaking with fellow inmates about freedom and life on the streets. Often, thoughts of release focus on the quick acquisition of long-denied commodities, such as heterosexual sex, fast food, and a cold beer. Life on the outside is everything prison isn't—unpredictable, fast paced, filled with choices. As the release date approaches, however, this positive outlook may be replaced by feelings of anxiety and even fear. These emotions may be particularly intense among inmates who have spent a lengthy time in confinement and/or who have failed on previous releases. Statements of bravado and an external display of optimism may conceal self-doubt and apprehension. As a community sponsor, C.T. Griffiths has witnessed numerous instances of released offenders becoming physically ill as they walked through the outside gate of the correctional institution.

Back on the Street

In his classic work, *The Felon*, John Irwin offers an account of the re-entry process from the inmate's perspective:

> *The ex-convict moves from a state of incarceration where the pace is slow and routinized, the events are monotonous but familiar, into a chaotic and foreign outside world. The cars, buses, people, buildings, roads, stores, lights, noises, and animals are things he hasn't experienced at firsthand for quite some time. The most ordinary transactions of the civilian have dropped from his repertoire of automatic maneuvers. Getting on a streetcar, ordering something at a hot dog stand, entering a theater are strange. Talking to people whose accent, style of speech, gestures, and vocabulary are*

slightly different is difficult. The entire stimulus world—the sights, sounds, and smells—is strange. Because of this strangeness, the initial confrontation with the "streets" is apt to be painful and certainly is accompanied by some disappointment, anxiety, and depression. (1970:113–14)

Planning a day without the rigid timetable of prison routine can be a daunting task. A newly released offender can feel like the proverbial stranger in a strange land—embarrassed, inadequate, and convinced that every person on the street can tell he or she has been in prison by appearance alone. A female parolee serving a life sentence recalled: "I didn't feel like I was back. I didn't feel like I belonged.... I didn't feel part of this world anymore, I was still inside. In some respects, part of me will always be inside" (cited in Murphy, Johnsen, and Murphy, 2002:166–67). Ironically, given the violence that so often characterizes prison life, offenders may experience feelings of paranoia and fear for their safety upon re-entering the community.

The stress of re-entry may be particularly acute for the state-raised offender (see Chapter 7). These individuals have very little experience living in the outside community, have few or no family ties, and, importantly, have no "stake" in the community. Rather, their friends, identity, status, and power are all inside the correctional institution. Outside, in the free community, there are no guarantees of status, security, or a routine that provides for one's basic needs. In such cases, the pull of the institution may be greater than that of freedom on the streets. Close friendships are in danger of being lost and there is often a sense that comrades are being abandoned. As one ex-offender stated to C.T. Griffiths, "I have never had the intensity of friendships, the trust, the companionship, in the outside community that I had when I was incarcerated." These feelings may be particularly acute when the soon-to-be-released inmate realizes that he or she has no friends on the outside who can be relied upon for assistance, protection, and security. And it may be difficult for the inmate not to feel that he or she is abandoning close friends, confidants, or lovers inside.

One parolee, who had been incarcerated almost continuously from age 7 to 32, related an incident to C.T. Griffiths that illustrates the anxiety and panic that ex-offenders may experience in completing tasks that people in the outside, free community take for granted. The situation occurred during his first trip to the grocery store soon after being released on day parole to live in a halfway house:

I wanted to buy some groceries, so I went to Safeway. I must have been in the store for hours. There were so many choices, I had no idea of what to put in my cart. Finally, my cart was full and I pushed it up to the checkout counter. The store was really crowded, and I was so focused on deciding *what to buy that I hadn't given any thought to the price of the things I was putting in the cart. I think I had about $50 in my pocket. When the cashier rang up the total, it came to over $150. When she told me the total, I just froze. Everyone was looking at me. I stood there for what seemed like an eternity and then, without saying a word, ran out of the store. At the bus stop, my heart was racing and I was sweating. I never went back to that store. And, it was a long time before I went grocery shopping for more than one or two items.*

Even offenders who, prior to confinement, had relatively conventional lifestyles (with the exception of their lawbreaking) can find it hard to unlearn the automatic responses acquired in an environment where physical aggression is a survival skill. Compounding this, the ex-offender may miss the thrill and the rush of committing crimes.

There are more practical considerations as well. Criminal records disqualify people from some professions, including those that require being bonded (insured). Released offenders may not have suitable clothes for job interviews or job-specific gear such as steel-toed boots and special tools. Parolees may also experience job discrimination if employers are reluctant to hire them because of their prison record. As result, they may be forced to lie about their criminal history when applying for jobs.

The longer their term of confinement, the less prepared offenders are for re-entry. Parents are frequently the primary source of support, but they are also a source of stress. Out of financial necessity, parolees may have to live with parents longer than desired. Resuming family relations with a partner and children may also be difficult, with parolees being required to find a new role in a family unit that has functioned without them.

In an attempt to cope with the pains of re-entry, the parolee may revert to high-risk behaviour, including heavy drinking, drug use, resuming friendships with former criminal associates, and spending time with old friends from prison. All the plans to go straight can crumble like a New Year's resolution in February. Though most will complete their period of conditional release without committing a new offence, many will be re-convicted of a criminal offence within three years of release.

Reintegration may be more difficult for certain categories of offenders. The special circumstances of Aboriginal offenders, female offenders, the mentally disordered, sex offenders, and those inmates serving life sentences or sentences longer than 10 years will be discussed later in the chapter.

An ex–bank robber in the United States describes his experiences in Box 10.1.

BOX 10.1

Life after Hard Time: An Ex–Bank Robber Reflects on Freedom's Down Side

An accurate accounting is always a confusing business, so let's just say I robbed a lot of banks. The FBI estimated between 30 and 40. Even I lost count. But I do remember this: Robbing banks was a cool thrill. And easy enough for any literate thug to commit.

A little-known fact: Stalin began his political life robbing the czar's banks. But unlike Uncle Joe, I didn't rob banks to help finance some great social cause. I robbed banks to support a lifestyle. I was the guy who always picked up the check and rented the limo for dinner at Circus and paid for all the trips to Vegas. I kept a Chinese tailor and several cars. I entered malls and left four hours later, $6,000 lighter. I was a hedonist. And popular, too.

On the morning of a robbery, I'd be naked in front of the bathroom's steamy mirror. I'd wipe off a circle big enough for me to stare at my wet image, at my dark sexy face, my collegiate haircut, the small scar on my left eyebrow, my dead eyes. I dared my hard self to flinch. My mouth opened slowly and murmured an erotically morbid demand: "Don't return without fifty thousand dollars."

Stephen Crane describes a "delirium that encounters despair and death, and is heedless and blind to the odds." I knew that state. I'd surrender my fear of death to the bathroom mirror. Then, unafraid of consequences, I'd pick up my .357 Magnum, tuck it into the back of my trousers, draw a deep breath, then walk into those banks fully prepared for a final shootout with law enforcement if destiny decreed it.

But destiny never did.

I was arrested when a girlfriend informed on me. The FBI was waiting for me when I went to meet her at college. I was sitting outside the student union, sipping a cappuccino, reading the *Wall Street Journal*. The agents identified themselves. I leapt up and started swinging. It took eight men to subdue me.

I served seven years in prison—a biblical number. Seven dreary Christmases. Seven banal birthdays. The same inane banter on every prison tier for seven years. The tedium wore away the thug in me. I vowed never to return.

I was released six months ago. Adjustment is a bitch, especially with the recidivism statistics breathing down my neck. Close to 50 percent of all released inmates return to prison within three years.

BOX 10.1, continued

If prison has its tedium, the world outside has its terrors. Part of my anxiety has to do with the reckless pace of the world. I am accustomed to the opposite, to the methodical tempo of prison life. Mindless rapidity startles me and leaves me feeling off balance.

On the day of my release, I got a check for $150 and was shown to the gate. The change of rhythm was startling. The friend who picked me up is a monk, the abbot of his monastery. But even this usually reverent man was a terror on the road. Charging ahead in fits and spurts, he wove maniacally through highway traffic, cutting off slower drivers.

And then there are the everyday humiliations an ex-convict must endure in order to remain free. Poverty is one of them. The cash I left prison with seemed like a mockery: I owned nothing but the clothes on my back, no change of underwear, no soap or toothbrush, no bed. The shame of living off handouts made me wake up one morning at 3 o'clock with the old temptation tugging at me. I wanted to say, "Fuck patience." I wanted to just go out and take mine.

The pitfalls for me are the everyday indignities the rest of you have learned to accept. The car that cuts me off on the freeway. The woman who barges into me while I wait in a grocery line. The obnoxious clerk at the Department of Motor Vehicles.

Or my devious neighbor.

Her. The one who substituted her clothes in my washing machine because she was in a hurry. I found my clothes, sopping wet, atop the rumbling machine I'd placed them in. If someone had done that to me in prison, I would have confronted him with a sharpened piece of bed spring and made him regret his insult, his foolish underestimation of me. Instead, in my role as a "free man," I returned to my apartment and suffered what Crane called the "rage of the baffled." I became mousy.

I don't presume to recall my violent past as halcyon days. But I know I never would have allowed myself to be treated like this when my mien included menace. The truth is that I wanted to walk next door and say, "Hey, you crazy bitch, don't ever touch my fucking clothes again or you'll find yourself spinning in that fucking machine." But I didn't play the thug.

It is, then, in the sting of everyday disrespect that I can vividly recall the thrills of my adventurous days when I loathed the future and abandoned caution. When the adrenaline sped through my veins as I drove away from a bank, laughing at the local cops racing past me in the opposite direction, toward the scene of the crime.

I have a friend who used to suffer from severe manic depression. Gray, moody, Kafkaesque lows, hysterical highs. Now he tells me, with no trace of angst, that he manages his existence well in the boring hum of lithium normalcy. Yet he and I know that it's not just the highs and the lows the medicine has dulled: It is also his imagination. He went to the doctors for relief and was prescribed compulsory mediocrity.

I see sorrow in his tame liberation. Perhaps I see similarities in our freedoms. It's as if we have become slower versions of previous selves, lesser men.

I have had to learn to crawl to be free. It remains to be seen whether I can live without flying.

Source: Loya, 1997:27–29. Reprinted by permission of the author.

THE ROLE OF PAROLE SUPERVISION

Persons on conditional release are subject to differing levels of supervision by correctional officials. In the case of some provincial temporary absences, this supervision can take the form of periodic telephone calls to verify the offender's presence at home. At the other end of the spectrum, supervision can include a requirement that the parolee reside in a community-based residential facility with 24-hour monitoring and attend frequent face-to-face meetings with a parole officer. This condition is often imposed on high-risk federal sex offenders who are on one-chance statutory release.

The Correctional Service of Canada (CSC) directly operates 17 **community correctional centres** across the country and has contracts with private operators for beds in over 150 **community residential centres.** Federal inmates must apply to community residential centres and be accepted by centre staff. In every province/territory, there are parallel systems of residences, operated directly by the government or under contract with private operators. These facilities are collectively known as **community-based residential facilities** and are often referred to as halfway houses. There are also residential treatment centres and recovery houses that specialize in alcohol and substance abuse intervention. (The Maple Ridge Treatment Centre in British Columbia is profiled in Box 10.2.) As previously noted, most released offenders live on their own or with their family.

Community residential centre, suburban neighbourhood, Ontario

Offenders on parole are generally required to report regularly to a correctional agent such as a parole officer. All federal parolees are supervised by parole officers employed by or under contract to the CSC. By agreement, the CSC also supervises the provincial parolees released by the National Parole Board. In three jurisdictions—British Columbia, Ontario, and Quebec—provincial probation and parole officers provide supervision for offenders on parole and many of the inmates on temporary absence. In provincial/territorial corrections, there are few distinctions between parole and probation, with the exception of the provisions for enforcement. For example, while the breach of a probation condition is a new offence, the violation of a parole condition can (but will not always) lead to suspension of the release and a return of the parolee to custody.

The Dual Function of Parole Supervision

Like probation officers, parole officers have a dual role in their relationship with clients. The first role is as a resource person and confidant to counter the pains of re-entry. Supportive activities of parole officers can include job search advice, referral for counselling, and advocacy with welfare authorities. The second role involves surveillance and the enforcement of parole conditions

BOX 10.2

Maple Ridge Treatment Centre (British Columbia)

Maple Ridge Treatment Centre (MRTC) provides a residential addiction program that uses a holistic approach to promote healthy change. Individual treatment plans are developed that address the client's physical, emotional, social, intellectual, spiritual, and occupational needs. The program includes group therapy, educational and family programs, and aftercare, as well as recreational and fitness opportunities.

Clients at MRTC are introduced to six aspects of wellness. They use these to assess their current state and then, with help from the staff, develop personal treatment goals to move toward a balanced, healthy state. The overall goal of treatment is to increase self-awareness in such a way as to reinforce and deepen a client's commitment to change, and to offer tools which help to effect positive change. There are three phases of the treatment program:

Phase 1: Assessment and Stabilization, including orientation, education about addiction, introduction to recovery, and in-depth assessment using the wellness approach

Phase 2: Intensive Treatment, including group therapy, education and skill-building workshops, individual counselling, family workshops, and couples counselling

Phase 3: Aftercare Planning, including developing awareness of high-risk situations and how to deal with them, exploring ways of avoiding and dealing with relapse, and the development of an aftercare plan and support network

Source: Maple Ridge Treatment Centre (www.mrtc.bc.ca).

and includes contact with an employer to verify employment, periodic checks to ensure continued employment, home visits to verify residence or compliance with curfews, urinalysis tests, and checks with the police and/or the staff at treatment programs.

Ideally, a balance between the two roles is achieved, with more control/surveillance during the early phases of the release period and more assistance as the supervision period draws to an end. It is likely, however, that the majority of parolees view their parole supervisor as more of a watcher than a helper. High-risk offenders, such as sex offenders, may be unlikely to disclose their urges to reoffend to their parole supervisor for fear of being returned to custody.

The increasing emphasis on risk management in corrections (see Chapters 1 and 9) may transform the role of parole officers completely into one of monitoring and enforcing compliance with release conditions and periodically reassessing changes in risk and need. The paperwork burden of conducting these assessments and recording them in computerized, centralized databases has had a significant impact on the amount of time parole supervisors can spend in face-to-face contact with clients. A key objective of the federal case management strategy Operation Bypass (see Box 8.3 on page 296) is to decrease duplication in reports and the amount of time spent filling out forms and writing reports.

Intensity of Supervision

Not all offenders who are released into the community require the same level of supervision. The Community Intervention Scale (CIS) is used with every federal offender discharged on a conditional release and is readministered every six months to monitor any changes in the parolee's situation. The CIS classifies and rates the parolee in 12 areas of need (academic/vocational, employment pattern, etc.). Using specific guidelines, each area is rated as being (1) an asset to community adjustment, (2) no current difficulties, (3) some need for improvement, and (4) considerable need for improvement. The parole officer then categorizes the offender into one of three need levels: low, medium, or high.

The second part of the CIS is the criminal history risk rating. To achieve this rating, which is either low or high, the parole officer consults the offender's case record, including the Statistical Information on Recidivism Scale (discussed in Chapter 9). When juxtaposed, these two ratings indicate the intensity of supervision required (see Table 10.1). For example, a low-risk

Table 10.1 Risk/Needs Level and Minimum Frequency of Contact

| Criminal History Risk | Case Needs | | |
	Low	Medium	High
Low	1/month (periodic)	2/month (active)	4/month (intensive)
High	4/month (intensive)	4/month (intensive)	4/month (intensive)

Source: Motiuk and Nafekh, 1997:10.

offender with low needs requires only periodic supervision, about one contact per month. This allows parole officers to spend more time supervising high-risk and high-need offenders. Box 10.3 describes the activities of a CSC Team Supervision Unit that supervises high-risk offenders on statutory release in Metropolitan Toronto.

BOX 10.3

CSC Team Supervision Unit: A Night on the Town

CSC Parole Officers Sherri Rousell and Cathy Phillips buzz the apartment from the panel in the lobby; a female voice tells them to enter. They ride up the elevator and step out into a long corridor, at the end of which they see a woman. She's standing in an apartment doorway smiling and beckoning to them. It's not until they get closer that they see a man they know, Salvador, standing behind the smiling woman.

Salvador is not smiling. Salvador is standing silently with his head down and his arms folded, an expression of tight-lipped anger on his face. He doesn't acknowledge the two officers or look up at them. The woman, Salvador's wife, manages to make pleasant chit-chat with the two CSC officers, then bids them good evening and closes the door.

There was no exchange between Sherri, Cathy, and Salvador, but the two officers walk away satisfied. Their intent was to ensure that the Colombian immigrant is complying with his parole conditions, including a nightly curfew. A former cocaine trafficker with a history of narcotic-related and violent offences, Salvador must obey the imposed conditions or go back to prison. It's obvious to the officers that Salvador is not happy with this arrangement; he resents taking orders and being monitored, especially by two women.

This is just one of the stops that Sherri and Cathy will make during the late evening. They are part of a special Team Supervision Unit (TSU) handling high-maintenance, often repeat offenders on statutory release in Metropolitan Toronto. Because of the volatile nature of these individuals, team members always work in pairs, manage a smaller case load than most parole officers, and contact their "clients" more frequently than they would average parole cases. There are two teams in the TSU based at the Keele Community Correctional Centre, headed by Director Shelley Hassard and Parole Supervisor Curtis Jackson. Members of the second unit are parole officers Paul Lay and Angela Beecher.

BOX 10.3, continued

"The idea with team supervision units is stabilization," explains Curtis Jackson. "Guys come out of prison, we try to stabilize them. It requires intense supervision and we are held accountable for monitoring their behaviour. If they don't stabilize right away, they stay with us longer. Once we feel that they don't require such intensive supervision, we will transfer them to the jurisdiction of area offices."

Over the past 10 years, TSUs have proven to be highly effective. With increased monitoring, TSU officers can spot signs of deterioration in an offender's behaviour and quickly intervene. They identify factors that contribute to behaviour problems, provide access to counselling, and give practical advice that may head off trouble. "Some of these guys are fairly low functioning," says Curtis. "They have difficulty doing the things that most of us take for granted—finding a place to live, opening a bank account, managing their money. If we can teach them, for instance, not to blow all their money the first night out, then they won't immediately get into trouble looking for more."

Cathy and Sherri continue on their rounds, clocking mile after mile in their Corsica, heading east as far as Scarborough, then back in a big circle towards downtown. One night each week they spend five hours, usually from 7 p.m. until midnight, checking to see that clients have made their curfews. During the week they may pick up the phone, drop in to an offender's workplace unannounced, or call a parolee in for an office interview to verify that he is complying with parole conditions.

They reach the Sheppard and Warden area and knock on a townhouse door. A big fellow named Wayne appears barefoot, wearing a rumpled T-shirt and sweatpants. He's loud and abrupt with the officers; 16 years in Ontario's toughest maximum security prisons for armed robbery and murder haven't smoothed his abrasive personality.

Yeah, yeah, everything's okay, says Wayne. He's anxious to get out of the frosty air and get to bed. The officers let him go.

The next stop is Rick's place. Rick opens the door and Cathy and Sherri can see he has guests in the living room, glued to an action adventure on the television. The officers say hi, how's it going, meanwhile they're sniffing the air and casting sharp looks over Rick's shoulder into the kitchen, scanning for evidence of drugs or alcohol. There are no liquor bottles or drug paraphernalia in sight, only a child's stuffed toy lying on the table. Sherri asks if she can step inside. She takes a few steps towards the living room to get a better look at what's going on. She asks to speak with Rick's girlfriend, Brenda, who is supposed to be supporting him until he can find a job. Brenda gets up from the couch, happy to oblige, and they have a quick word in the kitchen. Yes, still working at the video store. Satisfied, Sherri and Cathy wish Rick a good night and continue on their way.

Finally, around midnight, after all 14 visits have been completed, they drive back to the office at the Keele Community Correctional Centre where they pick up a private vehicle and head home. It's late and the paper work can wait until morning.

Source: Correctional Service of Canada, 2001a.

Innovations in Parole Supervision

Restorative Parole Project (Manitoba)

The Restorative Parole Project, operated by the John Howard Society of Manitoba, applies the principles of restorative justice to the reintegration of parolees. The objective of the program is to give crime victims and the community a role in the development of an inmate's proposed parole release program. Restorative parole staff assist victims with their involvement at all stages of the process, including during parole hearings and following release. Some of the processes may include correspondence, direct victim–offender mediation, and healing circles. In these ways, victims are given an opportunity for direct but mediated involvement in the development and implementation of an offender's release plan.

Among the objectives of the program are (1) to assist the victims in bringing closure to the trauma of the crime, (2) to have the offender accept responsibility for the crime, (3) to lessen any fear the victims and the community have about the release of the offender, (4) to increase victim and community involvement in and satisfaction with the correctional process, and (5) to successfully reintegrate federal offenders into the community. The pilot project is designed to balance victim and community concerns about safety with the needs and responsibilities of inmates, while making use of community resources.

London Community Parole Project

The objectives of the London Community Parole Project are to increase public involvement in the federal correctional process and to harness the talents of volunteers to provide a quality service in a time of diminishing resources. The project recruits qualified volunteers from the London, Ontario, area and trains them to perform a variety of community-based tasks for the CSC, including interviewing, report-writing, and parole co-supervision. Volunteers are selected for their maturity, demonstrated writing skills, and desire to learn about corrections and to bring a community perspective to their contact with offenders.

The volunteers undergo a training course that acquaints them with basic information about the criminal justice system and specific information about the policies and procedures of the CSC. Offence-specific training is also provided for such topics as sexual offending and family violence. Upon completion of the training program, the volunteers are able to prepare post-sentence community assessments and interview newly admitted federal inmates at the local detention centre immediately after sentencing but prior to transfer to the Assessment Unit at Millhaven Institution near Kingston, Ontario.

The focus of the program is on the eventual release of the offender from confinement. For collateral information on the offender, volunteers interview community contacts, including the inmate's spouse or family members with whom the inmate may intend to live while out on parole, and the arresting police officer. In addition, volunteers play a key role in the reintegration process by co-supervising parolees to provide more face-to-face contact than would otherwise be the case. This project also uses an innovative strategy called circles of support with high-risk offenders who have reached warrant expiry (more on circles of support below).

Community Adult Mentoring and Support (CAMS)

Operated by the Pacific region of the CSC, the CAMS program was developed in collaboration with a church in Victoria. The objective of the program is to complement the work of parole officers and other community-based professionals by helping long-term offenders on statutory release cope with life in the community. Under the program, high-needs, high-risk offenders are matched with community mentors. A written document called a covenant sets out the expectations of the mentor and the offender and provides the framework for the relationship. Following a thorough selection and screening process, volunteers undergo a 10-week training course.

The Lifeline Concept

The Lifeline Concept identifies four stages that offenders serving lengthy sentences in prison must pass through: (1) adaptation (coming to grips with the reality of confinement), (2) integration into the prison environment (living within the context of that reality), (3) preparation for release, and (4) reintegration into the community.

The lifeline concept has three components: in-reach (discussed in Chapter 7), community resources, and public education. In-reach workers engage in long-term pre-release visits, aid release planning, and, where applicable, provide liaison with and support of the inmate's family. It is assumed that lifers who have themselves successfully reintegrated with the community would be the best in-reach workers. Most in-reach workers are employed by private agencies such as the St. Leonard's Society and visit long-term offenders in the federal facilities in their areas. LINC (Long Term Offenders Now in the Community), of Abbotsford, British Columbia, has two workers, serving over 300 offenders in eight institutions. In-reach workers also assist with correctional plan development, attend parole board hearings, and supervise escorted temporary absences as part of a guided social reintegration process.

One obstacle to providing specialized service in the community is that, upon release, offenders relocate across the country. In only a few locales is there a critical mass of long-term offenders sufficient to create services solely for this group. One program is the Life Line Residential Service in Windsor, Ontario, a residential facility, operated by the St. Leonard's Society, to which lifers on day parole can be released.

SPECIAL OFFENDER POPULATIONS ON PAROLE

As noted earlier in the chapter, offenders may vary in the specific types of problems they encounter upon re-entry in society. This disparity requires that correctional systems adapt policies and programs to meet the needs of special offender populations and to manage the risks they present.

Aboriginal Offenders

Clearly, the present parole system is not working for Aboriginal peoples and systematically discriminates against them.

—Hamilton and Sinclair, 1991:473

Although there are no differences in the rate of revocation for new offences among Aboriginal and non-Aboriginal parolees, only half of Aboriginal offenders reach their warrant expiry out of custody (LaPrairie, 1996; Solicitor General Canada, 1998). There are a number of factors that may hinder effective parole supervision. First, there are very few Aboriginal parole officers employed by the CSC and this often results in cultural and language barriers that may prevent the development of a good relationship between the parole officer and the Aboriginal parolee. Second, there is a lack of full-time parole officers in most remote and northern communities, and much of the supervision is carried out by volunteer parole officers who often have little training and few resources at their disposal.

Systems of corrections have recognized that Aboriginal communities should be encouraged to play a greater role in the reintegration of offenders. In recent years, a variety of community-based services and programs for offenders on conditional release have been developed in Aboriginal communities across the country. Many of these programs are rooted in traditional Aboriginal culture and spirituality and incorporate elements of the restorative/community justice initiatives discussed in Chapter 4. In addition, the CSC has established the Aboriginal Community Reintegration Program to enhance the role of Aboriginal communities in working with offenders on conditional release.

Two major issues that surround increased community involvement are ensuring that there is harmony between the needs of the offender and the concerns of the community and determining the specific role that communities will play in the supervision and treatment/healing of offenders (LaPrairie, 1996:107–8). Section 81 of the Corrections and Conditional Release Act authorizes the federal government to enter into agreements with Aboriginal communities whereby the community will take over the "care and custody" of some Aboriginal inmates, and section 84 states:

> *Where an inmate who is applying for parole has expressed an interest in being released to an aboriginal community, the Service shall, if the inmate consents, give the aboriginal community*
>
> *(a) adequate notice of the inmate's parole application; and*
>
> *(b) an opportunity to propose a plan for the inmate's release to, and integration into, the aboriginal community.*

In many cases, however, Aboriginal parolees take up residence in urban centres, where they are not able to benefit from the support of their home community or band. In some urban centres, there are specialized residential services for Aboriginal offenders on conditional release, several of which are described in Box 10.4.

The experience to date suggests that there is considerable potential for Aboriginal communities to facilitate the reintegration of Aboriginal offenders through the use of Elder counselling, traditional and cultural activities, and healing circles. Communities that have developed reintegrative programs and services have a greater understanding and awareness of the needs of federal offenders on conditional release and display a higher level of support for becoming involved in efforts to assist offenders (Saulis, Fiddler, and Howse, 2001).

BOX 10.4

Selected Community Facilities and Programs for Aboriginal Offenders

Community Training Residence (Saskatoon): Operated by the Elizabeth Fry Society, this facility takes referrals directly from the courts or on release from the provincial women's institution or from the Okimaw Ohci Healing Lodge, the federal institution for Aboriginal women. The programs in the residence are centred on holistic health and a variety of alternative therapies.

Circle of Eagles Lodge (Vancouver): A 10-bed transition residence for Aboriginal men on release that offers alcohol and drug counselling in individual and group sessions, including Alcoholics Anonymous programs. Sweat lodges and talking circles are used to explore Aboriginal traditions and spirituality.

Regina House (Regina): This facility is operated by the Native Clan Organization and offers services to both provincial and federal Aboriginal offenders. Treatment efforts in the 35-bed facility centre on relapse prevention, an Elder program, and teachings of the Medicine Wheel.

Waseskun House* (Montreal): This facility for Aboriginal men operates a 20-week residential program providing individual and group counselling with programs in life skills, conflict resolution, family systems awareness, and women's issues. Sweat lodges and talking circles are also used.

* More information on this facility is available online at www.waseskun.net.

Source: Nuffield, 1998:11–13. Reproduced with permission of the Minister of Public Works and Government Services Canada, 1999.

Female Offenders

Female offenders are, as a group, better release risks than men but require different types of assistance while on conditional release. More specifically, women have a higher level of health needs; are more likely to have experienced sexual or physical victimization prior to incarceration; and are more likely to be a caretaker parent for children (Conly, 1998). Finding employment may be even more challenging for women than it is for men because women are less likely to have completed their education, often have little job experience, and may have to find and pay for daycare. Compared with male offenders, female offenders also have greater needs in the areas of emotional stability, marital and family relations, and academic/vocational skills (Correctional Service of Canada, 1998: 5–6).

For inmate mothers, the challenges may include re-establishing contact with their children, finding suitable accommodation with sufficient space, and attempting to regain custody of their children if the children have been placed in care during the mother's confinement. Particularly in those cases in which the inmate mother is the sole caregiver, child protection authorities may require that the mother first obtain stable employment and suitable accommodation before being allowed to re-apply for custody. The frustrations that mothers may encounter upon release are reflected in the following comments of an ex-offender on parole in Ontario:

> *I took parole to get my kids back. Parole agreed to my present location, but now the Children's Aid Society is saying it's not suitable for the kids. I can't rent before I know whether I am going to get my kids, and I can't get them back until I rent. I can't get mother's allowance until I have my kids, and without it I can't rent. I never know what I have to do for who. There are just so many hoops to jump through. (cited in Wine, 1992:111)*

The likelihood of re-establishing a parental relationship with children will depend on the length of the absence, the ages of the children, and how close the mother and children have been able to remain during the mother's confinement. If the children have been in the care of a child protection agency (e.g., the Children's Aid Society in Ontario), she will have to satisfy the agency that the children will not be placed at risk if returned to her. In most provinces/ territories, parental rights can be terminated once children have been in care for two continuous years; the children may be subject to adoption.

A portion of the women released on parole have continuing mental-health needs that are the consequence of multiple or long-term traumas they have experienced as both children and adults (Rivera, 1996). As previously noted, a high proportion of incarcerated women have histories of sexual and physical abuse. Although it has not been isolated as a specific criminogenic risk factor, the long-term consequences of abuse can be manifested in behaviours that are dynamic risk factors that can and should be addressed. Comparing the literature on criminal risk and on the consequences of abuse for women, it is possible to identify the areas of greatest overlap: family support, education, employability, and, perhaps most significantly, substance abuse. Substance abuse treatment programs based on the 12-step model are readily accessible but have been criticized by feminists as disempowering and patriarchal.

Even if incarcerated women receive therapy while in the institution, the continuation of this work in the community is critical. Indeed, there is evidence to suggest that the community is the best setting in which to counsel female offenders. Therapy that probed painful past experiences was suspected to be associated with several suicides at the Prison for Women, and researchers have described how the prison experience can reproduce the experience of child sexual abuse (Heney and Kristiansen, 1997; Kendall, 1994).

The Task Force on Federally Sentenced Women (1990) advocated the creation of meaningful connections to community-based resources for women re-entering the community, which involves:

- ensuring the quality and timeliness of release planning and case preparation
- ensuring appropriate supervision and assistance in the community
- fostering women's connection to a network of resources that will be sustainable past warrant expiry (Correctional Service of Canada, 1998:5)

As they reintegrate, women are encouraged to foster their strength areas rather than focus solely on their problem areas. This is an approach that may one day find broader application with other offender groups.

Mentally Disordered Offenders

The mentally disordered parolee may require more assistance in the reintegration process. Five program elements have been found to be effective in supporting parolees with mental illnesses:

- *medical and therapeutic services:* prescription, administration, and monitoring of medication, along with individual and group psychotherapy
- *money management:* direct receipt of payments such as welfare, payment of fixed expenses (e.g., rent and utilities), and distribution of the residual to the client as a daily allowance as long as prescribed daily medication is taken
- *housing and other support services:* intensive case management to provide directly for basic needs, including housing and monitoring by periodic home visits
- *close monitoring:* daily reporting to a clinic for medication, disbursement of allowances, and observation and interaction with staff to identify changes needed in medication and to track down those who fail to attend

- *participation:* combination of support and the legal authority to revoke release to ensure that clients maintain medication regime and other treatment measures (McDonald and Teitelbaum, 1994)

In Calgary, a community residential facility called Robert's House provides services for offenders with mental-health issues. It is operated in conjunction with the Canadian Mental Health Association.

Sex Offenders

No group of offenders has attracted more public interest than sex offenders. Their release from prison is often front-page news in the local press or even announced over the Internet (see Box 10.5). Sex offenders now compose an increasing portion of the federal offender population. Despite the extensive literature on sex offenders, there are many unresolved issues in the treatment and prediction of recidivism among this group of offenders. For example, opinion is mixed over whether their rate of recidivism is high or low, but it most likely varies by category of offence and by how recidivism is measured (Doren, 1998; Hanson and Bussiere, 1998; Prentky et al., 1997).

The successful reintegration of sex offenders may be assisted by relapse prevention programs, in which the offender identifies both the patterns of his offences and the distorted rationalizations used to justify them. The offender is then taught to avoid the situations in which he is most likely to reoffend, especially the sequence of events that, once started, he may not be able to stop. For example, if an offender has a history of befriending prepubescent boys in parks, he must learn never to go to parks and to resist the sometimes convoluted thinking that can lead him to think he absolutely has to go to the park today on his way home from the local parole office. A convicted rapist-murderer who is on parole for life reveals his technique for avoiding situations that may trigger a relapse:

> *Sometimes when I'm driving down the road and I see some well-developed fifteen-year-old and I think, "Oh yeah, she's cute," I kind of mentally give myself a slap and say, "Yeah, she's cute. Let her stay cute, you stupid bastard." I have to give myself the height of shit…. I'm motivated by her memory not to do that sort of garbage. (cited in Murphy, Johnsen, and Murphy, 2002:117)*

The general approach of correctional systems is to use a variety of techniques to *manage* the risk of this offender group. These techniques include treatment, drugs such as antiandrogens to reduce sex drive, community notification, registration, and supervision and monitoring strategies that can include polygraph testing (English, 1998; Harris, Rice, and Quinsey, 1998; Wilson et al., 2000). Ontario and Alberta are among those provinces considering the use of the satellite-based Global Positioning System (GPS) to supervise and control high-risk offenders in the community.

The federal government and several provinces (including British Columbia and Ontario) have established sex offender registries to track high-risk sex offenders. Sex offenders must generally register 15 days prior to release into the community (or upon conviction if they receive a noncustodial sentence) and re-register annually as well as 15 days prior to any change of address. The register database includes information on the offender, such as name, date of birth, current address, and identifying marks, as well as photographs. Offenders remain on the registry indefinitely unless they are acquitted upon appeal or receive a pardon.

Judicial Recognizances for Sex Offenders

Federal sex offenders not released on either parole or statutory release remain in custody until warrant expiry. These offenders are then released "cold turkey" and are not obliged to inform law enforcement or correctional agencies of their location. One response to this problem is the use of **community notification,** which is discussed below. Another is the use of section 810.1 of the Criminal Code to force the individual to enter into a **judicial recognizance,** often referred to in this context as a peace bond.

Judicial recognizance is most commonly used with pedophiles who have reached warrant expiry but who remain at a very high risk of offending against children under 14 years of age. This response is unusual as the applicant, who can be a police officer, need only have reasonable grounds to fear that the subject of the order may commit one of the designated offences in the near future. In other words, it is applied proactively for offences that may be committed rather than in reaction to offences that have been committed.

The application is heard in a provincial court, where the judge can order the subject to enter into a recognizance to comply with set conditions, which can include a prohibition from engaging in any activity that involves contact with persons under the age of 14. For example, the subject would not be permitted to visit a daycare centre, school ground, playground, or any public park or swimming area where children are present or can reasonably be expected to be present. This order can be in effect for up to 12 months. A person who refuses to enter into the recognizance can be sent to prison for up to 12 months for the refusal, and an offender who violates a condition of the order commits an offence for which he is liable for up to two years in prison.

Community Notification

The use of community notification (CN) is relatively new in Canada but is widely employed in cases involving sex offenders and other high-risk offenders released on parole in the United States. In Canada, CN is possible because local police departments are always notified by the CSC of the impending arrival of federal parolees in their jurisdictions. Motivated in part by fear of exposure to lawsuits, most provinces have developed policies designed to facilitate police decision making with respect to the release of identifying offender information. Nova Scotia, for example, has developed a protocol for the release of high-risk offenders (available online at www.gov.ns.ca/just/hro.htm) that includes guidelines on the use of community notification.

Decisions about CN are most often made by a committee. In Manitoba, the first province to establish a CN program, the police refer the cases of high-risk sex offenders to the Community Notification Advisory Committee, which comprises a private citizen, a specialist in medical/therapeutic interventions, and representatives from the RCMP, the police services of Winnipeg and Brandon, Manitoba Justice, Manitoba Corrections, and the CSC. The committee reviews all of the information about the offender—including criminal record, participation in treatment programs, age and gender of past victims, proposed release plan or living arrangement, and support network—and then determines the type and scope of information to be released. The protocol also involves listing the designation on the Canadian Police Information Centre and notifying past victims of the release. The community notification process in Manitoba is illustrated in Figure 10.2. Further information on the province's CN process is available online at www.gov.mb.ca/justice/safe/pubnote.html.

There are several models of community notification, but all involve a public announcement, usually made by the police, that a high-risk offender has taken up residence in the area. CN can involve proactive measures, such as distribution of leaflets door-to-door, or it can be passive, involving posting the information on the Internet to be accessed by interested parties. In Canada, provincial authorities and police departments periodically place public warnings on their websites. The RCMP news release reproduced in Box 10.5 was posted on the Alberta Solicitor General website.

The issue of CN remains intensely controversial. It is often framed as one of a balance of rights: the community to protection and the offender to privacy. In actuality, Canadians do not enjoy an absolute right to privacy, and even protection of privacy statutes permit release of personal information in the public interest. See the following At Issue.

Figure 10.2

The Community Notification Process in Manitoba

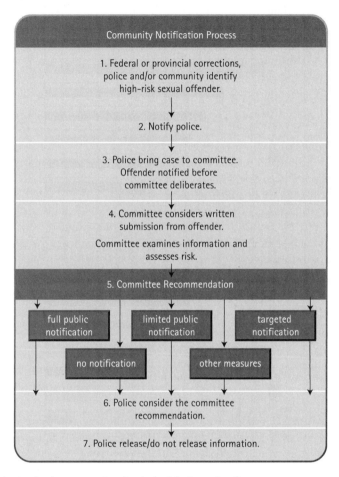

Source: Manitoba Justice (www.gov.mb.ca/justice/safe/pubnote.html).

AT ISSUE

COMMUNITY NOTIFICATION OF SEX OFFENDERS

Proponents of community notification make one primary argument: that CN will alert the neighbourhood to a potential risk, thereby reducing the likelihood of another offence.

More specifically, it is argued:
- Public safety overrides any expectation the offender has for privacy.
- Information on convictions is in the public domain.
- The protection of potential victims is an important goal for society.
- Offenders have forfeited the expectation of privacy by virtue of their offences and the risk they pose. Indeed, the poor record of sex offender treatment and high like-lihood of recidivism are arguments recognized even by those who are concerned about the civil rights of the identified offenders.

Opponents of community notification counter:
- Politicians support CN laws to exploit public fear of crime for their own political ends.
- There is no evidence that it is effective.
- The cost of conducting proactive CN is high and means that resources are diverted from other more useful activities.
- It can engender an exaggerated sense of security.
- Conversely, it can increase public fear and paranoia.
- The overuse of CN would result in too many false positives.
- Vigilantism against identified offenders (and those who bear a resemblance to their pictures) is possible.
- Individuals intent on reoffending can simply visit or move to another area.
- The stress of CN could increase a sex offender's propensity to recidivate in much the same way that stress increases relapse among substance abusers.
- CN makes it difficult for some offenders to reintegrate into the community because they can find it difficult to secure employment or accommodation.
- If offender has served to warrant expiry, thereby paying the entire "debt to society," CN could be construed as a punishment inflicted after a punishment.

The Research Evidence

Community notification laws have proliferated despite the lack of any evidence of effectiveness. In the only empirical study ever conducted, community notification did not affect the likelihood of re-arrest for a sexual offence in Washington State (Schram and Millroy, 1995). In a group of 125 Level III sex offenders about whom the commu-nity was notified, 14 percent were re-arrested for a sex offence during the follow-up period. Interestingly, many arrests occurred outside the police jurisdiction where the offender was registered (19 percent) or outside the state altogether (19 percent), and only half of the arrests resulted in a conviction. The offending of this sample was then compared with that of a matched sample from before the enactment of the community notification law. Using a statistical technique that controlled for differential follow-up periods, it was estimated that 19 percent of the CN group would be re-arrested for a sex offence within 54 months, compared with 22 percent of the control group—not a significant difference.

However, there is anecdotal indication of some unanticipated benefits in the United States, including the prospect of CN acting as a catalyst for offenders to enter treatment or take other measures to avoid being the subjects of a CN, increasing public knowledge about sex offences, improving collaboration among criminal justice sectors, and involving criminal justice employees with the community.

QUESTIONS

1. Would you want to be notified of the presence of a sex offender in your neighbourhood? Why or why not? If so, what would the knowledge cause you to do differently?
2. Does your province have a community notification law? Check the statute books because several do and more are planned. Check out the website of your local police. Many now have community notification pages.

Sources: British Columbia Civil Liberties Association, 1996; Kabat, 1998; Schram and Millroy, 1995; United States Department of Justice, 1998; Washington State Institute for Public Policy, 1998.

BOX 10.5

High-Risk Offender Community Notification

Royal Canadian Mounted Police   Gendarmerie royale du Canada

NEWS RELEASE

FOR IMMEDIATE DISTRIBUTION

August 15, 2001

The Royal Canadian Mounted Police is issuing the following public information and warning with the consent of Mr. Arthur Cyr in regard to his release as a provincial inmate, in the interest of public safety.

Mr. Arthur Paul Cyr has been released from Stave Lake Correctional Centre, British Columbia, on having served a sentence of 2 years less one day for indecent assault contrary to 271 of the Criminal Code. This offence involved a 10 year old male victim. Mr. Arthur Paul Cyr has a criminal record of previous convictions for sexual assault and breach of probation involving males ages 9 to 16 years old. These offences took place in British Columbia. Information contained in his file indicates that this individual represents a significant risk for sexual offences against children.

Mr. Arthur Paul Cyr is described as a 52 year old white male, 168 cm (5'6"), 59 kg (131 lbs), brown eyes and short brown hair. Mr. Arthur Paul Cyr is presently residing in the Town of Strathmore, Alberta.

BOX 10.5, continued

Upon his release Mr. Arthur Paul Cyr will be on probation for 3 years and further prohibitions for 25 years. Significant conditions of his probation and prohibition are that he not have contact directly or indirectly with persons under the age of 16 years unless he is in the company of a person over the age of 16 years who has been previously approved of by the Probation Officer. In addition he is prohibited for twenty-five (25) years from attending any public park or public swimming area where persons under the age of fourteen years are present or can reasonably be expected to be present or a daycare centre, school ground, playground or community centre.

With the written consent of Mr. Arthur Paul Cyr, The Royal Canadian Mounted Police is issuing this information and warning after careful deliberation and consideration of all related issues, including privacy concerns, in the belief that it is clearly in the public interest to inform the members of the Community of the release of Mr. Arthur Paul Cyr. The Royal Canadian Mounted Police believe that there is a risk of significant harm to the health and safety of the public, and in particular, any children.

Members of the public are advised that the intent of the process is to enable members of the public to take suitable precautionary measures and not to embark on any form of vigilante action.

Note: This information is released under the authority of the Privacy Act, R.S. 1985 c. P-21 and the Freedom of Information and Protection of Privacy Act, S.A. 1994 c. F-18.5.

Further information contact: S/Sgt. Glenn DeGoiej, the Strathmore Detachment RCMPolice.

Source: Retrieved August 19, 2003, from the Alberta Solicitor General website: http://www4.gov.ab.ca/just/ims/client/upload/cyr.pdf.

Circles of Support

Sex offenders who have reached warrant expiry are the most likely targets of judicial recognizances and community notification. As noted in Chapter 9, offenders detained during the period of statutory release are subsequently released cold turkey. Also of concern are the sex offenders who have been on conditional release but whose period of supervision has expired at the end of the sentence. When sex offenders who have been in treatment with correctional staff reach warrant expiry, the contact with the therapist must effectively be severed because a continuing relationship could leave the CSC legally liable for any offences the offenders commit.

To assist in the reintegration of high-risk sex offenders who have reached warrant expiry, many communities have developed circles of support. Any offender who participates in the program does so on a voluntary basis because there is no legal mechanism that can compel him to be subject to monitoring. Offenders may choose to participate because they lack any other support system and/or wish to avoid police harassment and media attention (Cesaroni, 2001:91–92).

A circle of support is a team of five or six volunteers assigned to an offender to assist him as he takes up residence in their community. They assist in all facets of reintegration, including housing, employment, budgeting and financial management, spiritual development, and moral support. The offender may call only in times of stress or may have daily contact with the circle members. Circle members can also mediate between the offender and the community, as suggested in the conceptual model in Figure 10.3. Mediation took place in the case of Joe, whose arrival in the community was the subject of a community notification (see Box 10.6).

Figure 10.3

Conceptual Model of a Circle of Support: Relationships of the Circle within the Community

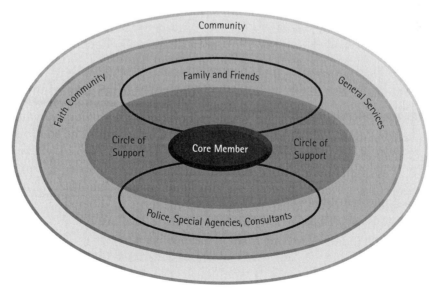

Source: Heise et al., 1996:14. Reprinted by permission.

In Ontario, the Mennonite Central Committee operates the Community Reintegration Project (CRP), which provides the Circles of Support and Accountability program—circles of support for sex offenders who are released from federal institutions at warrant expiry. The CRP uses a reintegrative/restorative approach in which community members play an active role in providing assistance to—and a measure of control over—persons who present a risk to the community. An individualized agreement called a covenant is negotiated between the volunteers in the group and the offender. The covenant sets out the roles and responsibilities of each party. Core volunteers in the group, for example, may agree to maintain the confidentiality of information about the offender and to assist the offender, while the core member (offender) may agree to develop a relapse prevention plan and to be open and honest in his communications with the group (Petrunik, 2002).

Most volunteers in the CPR's Circles of Support and Accountability program are from the faith community; other participants include teachers, social workers, police officers, and local businesspersons. The positive view of the program held by offenders is related to the fact that it is operated by a private, philanthropic organization rather than by the CSC. This suggests that church-based organizations and community groups have the potential to play a significant role in the reintegration process.

BOX 10.6

Joe and His Circle of Support

It began with a telephone call. "Can you help me?" the caller asked. "I'm just out of prison, and the police have already been warning everyone that I am in town. Where am I going to find a quiet place to live?" Joe, 54, had been released at Warrant Expiry from prison after serving a 6-year sentence for sexual assault against a child. It was his 8th conviction.

Joe wanted to come to our city for several reasons. He knew us, he had met public resistance in another town when he attempted to settle there before his parole was [revoked], and he suspected that he could get help in relapse prevention. We agreed to help him find accommodation, help him to find a job, and try to build a Circle of friendship and support in his new city. We thought of people that we knew who could help him in each of these areas and who would be willing to work with us. We also agreed to make contact with the police.

The detectives, when we met with them, candidly said, "We don't want him here." Based on institutional reports, the police felt that Joe was likely to reoffend. There had been a lot of negative publicity recently about released prisoners reoffending, and they didn't want any of that kind of publicity for their department.

When Joe came to stay with us for the weekend while beginning the apartment search, the police quickly made his picture available to the media and warned the community of his presence among us.

The media descended upon us because we had been identified as providing support for Joe. Pickets of irate and concerned parents arrived in front of our home. After a number of angry and threatening phone calls, we finally bought a telephone answering machine.

The police mounted a plan of surveillance. They felt sure he would reoffend within a short period. They were concerned about the safety of the children in the neighbourhood, but they also wanted to ensure Joe's safety.

One of the neighbours had called the police and had a lengthy discussion with the detective. She later called to talk with me. Ann had small children and was very concerned for their safety and that of the many other children living in the area. After a discussion with her, and later with Joe, we agreed that he would meet with her to discuss her concerns. Lengthy negotiations ensued, finally resulting in a meeting proposed in a neutral site, and several other neighbours were invited to participate. The police detectives would also be present. They would be there not only as a resource, but as people who could add to the participants' feelings of security.

Joe, accompanied by two of his friends, was the first to arrive at the meeting and take a seat on the far side of the room. Soon the neighbours began to arrive. Then the detectives entered. The ground rules of the meeting were outlined. We would go around the circle to allow everyone an opportunity to share their first name and a particular concern they brought with them. We would have a statement from the neighbourhood group, followed by an opportunity for Joe to share, and from there we would move to addressing the issues presented. Only one person at a time would speak, and they would follow our direction and instructions for the orderly addressing of the issues. Before the end of the meeting, we would decide together what of this meeting would be appropriate to share with other people, outside of this meeting.

As we began to go around the circle, the first person began by saying how much she appreciated the willingness of Joe and his friends to attend such a meeting. Ann outlined the questions she had heard the others discussing with her. There was a long list of questions: they wanted to know what had happened, what the sentence

BOX 10.6, continued

was, what treatment he had obtained, and what treatment he planned to receive now that he was released. "From your experience, what is the best way to avoid the behaviour you were charged with?" "How do you plan to deal with the negative reactions and anger of some individuals in the community?"

Joe responded, outlining in general terms his offences. Appreciation was expressed for the constructive method the residents had chosen to address their concerns, which he acknowledged was understandable. He indicated that he had received some treatment while in the institution and was planning to arrange suitable community-based therapy and had indeed made arrangements for that already. He had also set up an accountability system through his Circle of Support, by which he had daily contact with us, and we were able to make inquiry as to his faithfulness to his commitments in specific relevant areas.

We talked, and the earlier tension in the room eased as we got on with the task of problem-solving around the various issues at hand. Though all the questions were not answered, by the end of the 2½-hour meeting, there was a feeling of accomplishment and a readiness to move on.

Out of that meeting and others we had, some bridges were built. Neighbourhood residents, some of whom were vocally angry, began to see Joe as a person and recognized the difficulties with which he coped.

Throughout this time, Joe's Circle of Support met regularly with him. At least one of the Circle Members contacted him every day. After a year, we still talk to him daily. We took him to do his laundry, to shop for groceries and furnishings for his apartment.

The police have been partners with us in Joe's Circle of Support. Without the patient, humorous, understanding commitment of the detectives with whom we dealt most frequently, our efforts might not have reached this point. They came to our Circle meetings. They checked in with us frequently and we trusted their openness with us. Similarly, the police served as a buffer with the community, correcting rumours and diffusing problems.

Joe's life has settled into a comfortable pattern. He maintains a clean, comfortable apartment and has developed some close relationships. He is finding ways to spend his time and is slowly developing a small network of friends, although trust takes a long time.

Source: Heise et al., 1996:5–7. Reprinted by permission.

FAILURE ON CONDITIONAL RELEASE: GOING BACK

Even the most institutionalized state-raised inmate does not leave a correctional institution with the intent of returning. And correctional systems have as a primary objective the reduction of recidivism among offenders released into the community. Statistics indicate that the majority of offenders successfully complete conditional release and do not reoffend prior to warrant expiry. More specifically, in 2001–02:

- total new convictions by federal offenders on conditional release accounted for less than .5 percent of total adult convictions in Canada
- practically all offenders (99.8 percent) who had been granted temporary absences, ranging on average from a few hours to 60 days, successfully completed these absences from institutions

As a proportion of all crimes reported to the police in 2000, federal offenders re-admitted with a new conviction were responsible for about one of every 1,000 federal statute offences, including:

- 1.3 of every 1,000 violent offences
- 0.7 of every 1,000 sexual offences
- 1.2 of every 1,000 drug offences
- 1.1 of every 1,000 property or other federal statute offences (Motiuk, Boe, and Nafekh, 2002)

Unfortunately, as noted in Chapter 3, it is the relatively small number of released offenders who commit heinous crimes that receives the attention of the media and may have a significant impact on correctional policy and practice, from changes in sentencing laws to the decision making of parole boards. The "silent majority" of offenders who successfully complete conditional release is invisible to the community. When asked about the connotations attached to the word *parolee*, community residents may respond in one of two ways: "got out too soon" or "dangerous to the public." These responses reflect the fact, noted in Chapter 3, that most citizens get their information on crime, criminal justice, and corrections from the media.

The media's focus on the more sensational features of corrections and offenders further distorts the perceptions of the public. This sensationalism is reflected in the headline "Missing Parolee Killers Criticized" in an Ontario newspaper, relating to a story about the approximately 700 federal offenders who had violated the conditions of their parole and were at large, their whereabouts unknown (Fazari, 1999). The group included 34 persons who had been convicted of murder or manslaughter. Although newsworthy, such reporting is not balanced by headlines such as "One Hundred Parolees Celebrate Successful Completion of Conditional Release." Consider the last time you heard on television or radio or read in the newspaper a news story that focused on the positive achievements of offenders on conditional release.

Contrary to what media reports would lead one to believe, the rate of re-conviction for violent offences for offenders under community supervision has declined in recent years. In the period between 1994–95 and 1999–2000, the rate of violent offences per 1,000 offenders supervised in the community by the CSC declined by approximately 35 percent, from 40 to 26 per 1,000 offenders supervised (Correctional Service of Canada, 2002:8). The highest failure rate is among those offenders who are not granted parole but are released on statutory release by the CSC after serving two-thirds of their sentence. As a group, these offenders are at high risk to reoffend, which is one reason they may not have been granted release on parole.

Those offenders who successfully complete their parole and continue on to live a law-abiding life may apply for a pardon. Persons convicted of summary offences may apply for a pardon three years after the completion of their sentence, while persons convicted of an indictable offence may apply five years after the end of their sentence.

The charts in Figure 10.4 show the outcome rates for federal offenders on day parole, full parole, and statutory release for the period 1994–95 to 2001–02. The outcome rates indicate that:

- offenders released on day parole had significantly higher completion rates than offenders released on full parole or statutory release
- offenders released on statutory release had the lowest rate of successful completion of parole and were more likely to commit a violent offence while under supervision than offenders on day parole and full parole

The charts in Figure 10.5 present the outcome rates for provincial offenders on day parole and full parole for the five-year period 1997–98 to 2001–02. The outcome rates indicate that:

- provincial offenders on full parole had higher successful completion rates than offenders on day parole
- provincial offenders on day parole were more likely than offenders on full parole to have their parole revoked for a breach of condition

Suspension of Conditional Release

Failing to abide by any of the set conditions, including committing a new criminal offence or failing to adhere to the conditions of the parole certificate, may result in a **suspension of conditional release.** This is a "limbo situation" during which the offender is placed in temporary detention in local custody. Parolees suspected of committing a new offence can be suspended as well, but

Figure 10.4

Federal Outcome Rates for Day Parole, Full Parole, and Statutory Release, 1997/98 to 2001/02

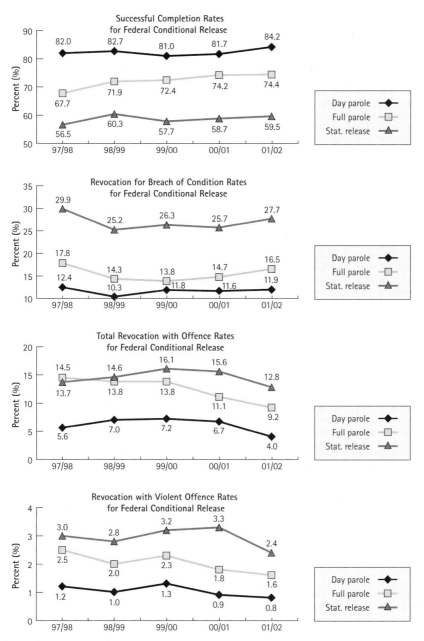

Source: National Parole Board, 2002:94–95.

Figure 10.5

Provincial Outcome Rates for Day and Full Parole, 1997/98 to 2001/02*

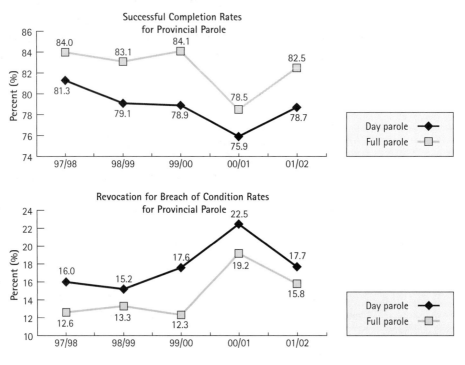

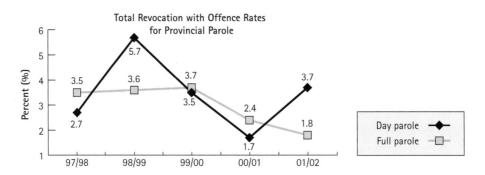

*Note: For provincial offenders released by the NPB in provinces/territories without a provincial parole board (all except British Columbia, Ontario, and Quebec).

Source: National Parole Board, 2002: 96.

most suspensions are for technical violations. When a parolee is suspended, there are two possible outcomes: (1) the parole supervisor can cancel the suspension and release the person from custody or (2) the case can be referred back to the National Parole Board for a hearing to determine whether there should be a **revocation of conditional release** (usually meaning a transfer back to a federal correctional facility). In those cases in which federal parole officers suspend the release, it is most often for a breach of a parole condition or to prevent the breach of a condition.

There is a specific rationale behind suspending a parolee for a technical violation. If release conditions are established in order to reduce or manage the risk of reoffending, a violation of these conditions might cause the parole board to re-assess the original decision. In other words, if attendance at a treatment program is a release condition for a parolee, the parole board should be notified if the offender has dropped out of the program.

To suspend a release, a parole supervisor issues a warrant of apprehension and suspension of conditional release, which empowers the police to arrest the parolee and place him or her in the local lockup. Parole officers have considerable discretion in the use of suspension. The law states that officers "may" suspend a parolee for violations of parole conditions and when new offences are alleged. The number of cases in which technical violations occur or new offences are alleged but a suspension is not imposed is unknown. Concern has been expressed that federal parole officials are being encouraged to look the other way when violations occur in order to improve the rates of parole completion (Cairns, 1999).

Those who violate parole by absconding become the subjects of arrest warrants. Their status is recorded in the Canadian Police Information Centre, a centralized, computer-based information system linked to municipal/provincial police forces and the RCMP. For these offenders, the sentence stops running until they are arrested. In Ontario, a Fugitive Apprehension Squad operates under the umbrella of the Criminal Intelligence Service Ontario, which coordinates the activities of municipal and regional police forces and the Ontario Provincial Police. Box 10.7 describes the execution of a warrant of suspension and apprehension on a federal offender by a CSC Team Supervision Unit in Ontario.

Post-Suspension Hearing

Offenders who have had their conditional release suspended are returned to the correctional facility to await a post-suspension hearing before the parole board.

BOX 10.7

CSC Team Supervision Unit: Execution of a Warrant of Suspension and Apprehension

Jeff had violated the terms of his parole—missed his curfew, neglected to report in for several days—and now he's on the phone to Parole Officer Angela Beecher, sounding contrite and asking for her guidance. He admits he'd been on a cocaine binge over the last few days and is, by his own description, "extremely messed up." Angela is surprised to hear from him; she figured he had gone on the run days ago. A warrant of suspension and apprehension was issued the night before and the police are now on the lookout for Jeff. Once they find him, he'll have to go back to prison.

Angela calmly speaks with Jeff. It's a touchy situation and she knows from experience that if she says the wrong thing, a man in Jeff's shaky condition might be tempted to disappear. Finally, she convinces him to meet her that same evening at his home.

As soon as she hangs up the phone, she contacts the Toronto Police, 42nd Division and requests backup. A meeting is quickly arranged. Officers from the Major Crime Unit are gathered by the time Angela and Paul Lay, her co-worker, arrive at 42nd Division. They discuss how to apprehend Jeff if he is still at home when they arrive. It's necessary to somehow get Jeff out on the street so they can make a legal arrest; without a search warrant, it's illegal to enter his home.

They plan for possible scenarios: Jeff's not home when they arrive; Jeff panics and runs; Jeff pulls a gun, resists arrest and tries to take Angela hostage. They decide that Angela and Paul should go to the door alone while police officers conceal themselves nearby, ready to move in. Angela and Paul will try to draw the offender out of his house and down the driveway where their car will be parked.

On the way to Jeff's house, Angela calls to confirm that he's still there. She's relieved when she hears his voice and tells him she will be there soon. Angela and Paul pull up in front of the parolee's house with the plainclothes police officers not far behind. To their surprise, Jeff is outside waiting for them, a dishevelled and solitary figure at the edge of his driveway. Angela gets out of her car and has a few words with him. As they speak, Jeff sees men approaching from the corner of his eye. He immediately understands what is happening. He wavers momentarily and Angela sees that his eyes have suddenly welled with tears but he stands his ground. In a gentle voice, one officer asks Jeff if he knows why they are there. Jeff nods and offers no resistance. They lead him off to the waiting cruiser.

Later on, Paul and Angela go over the evening's events. "It couldn't have gone better," comments Paul. "I think Jeff knew what was going to happen and was ready for it. It was a perfect execution of a warrant; nobody was injured, safety wasn't compromised and the rule of law was followed."

"Right now, I feel very happy about the way things were accomplished," says Angela. "However, I won't lie, early on I was apprehensive. At one point, I thought it was going to get out of hand, but given how the situation was dealt with, I'm pleased. I couldn't ask for a better resolution. It was a learning experience too. There's no written policy about what to do in a situation like this, so you have to improvise as you go along." She pauses, thinking for a moment, then continues. "The fact that Jeff phoned me this afternoon and was willing to co-operate, that told me he wanted help. So I did my best to get him the help he needs."

Source: Correctional Service of Canada, 2001b.

Two key documents in the deliberations of the parole board are the critical incident report and the post-suspension report prepared by the supervising parole officer. These reports set out the circumstances surrounding the alleged violations of the conditional release or statutory release, consider the viability of the original release plan, and generally include a recommendation as to whether the offender's release should be revoked, terminated, or reinstated.

A report of a critical incident (key identifiers removed) involving an offender on day parole with electronic monitoring is presented in Box 10.8. In this report, the supervising parole officer has written to the parole board to express concerns that the offender is not abiding by the conditions of the parole certificate. To the officer's knowledge, no new offences have been committed. The parole board must decide whether to issue a warning letter to the parolee or to issue a warrant of suspension that would result in the offender being apprehended and returned to the prison to await a post-suspension hearing before the board.

As discussed earlier, a parole supervisor may suspend the conditional release for technical violations or if there is reason to believe that the offender has committed or will commit a criminal offence. If the parole supervisor does not cancel the suspension, the case goes forward to a revocation hearing before a parole board. On any given day, there are hundreds of offenders awaiting a decision about revocation.

BOX 10.8

Critical Incident Report (B.C.)

BRITISH COLUMBIA

████, 2002

Office of the Chair
BC Board of Parole
#303-960 Quayside Drive
New Westminster, BC V3M 6G2

RE: CRITICAL INCIDENT REPORT
████████
DOB: ████████
CS#:   ██████
FPS#: ████

Mr. John ██████ has reported to this ██████ Probation Office on Wednesday afternoon on ████ 26, 2002, not on ████ 27, 2002 by 2:00 pm as was indicated on Condition 1 of his parole Certificate. Mr. ██████ had telephoned from Vancouver Island on ██████ 25, 2002 in the afternoon stating that he was unable to attend this ██████ office by closing time at 5:00 pm. Probation Officer ████ received the phone call and directed Mr. ██████ to attend this ██████ Office the next day during the morning. Mr. ██████ failed to report during the morning but later telephoned this office to state that he will arrive to this office 'shortly'. When Mr. ██████ finally did arrive, it was at 4:00 pm. When questioned about why he did not attend the office the day before, he stated that he did not have enough time, but when questioned further, he admitted that he was released from the Institution the previous day at 10:00 am in the morning.

Condition 8 of Mr. ██████'s Parole Certificate states that he is to reside at ██████████ , BC, *and thereafter obtain permission from the Parole supervisor for*: 8(i) *a change in address or residence*. During his first appointment, Mr. ██████ informed this writer that he has already made plans to reside with his girlfriend, ██████, and would like to move to ██████ immediately. This writer informed Mr. ██████ that he was granted permission to reside at his mother's residence based on several reasons, which included a technical suitability report that was conducted and submitted to the Parole Board. Mr. ██████ was informed that if he wanted to move to ██████, there would have to be another technical suitability report conducted, and that the Board will be contacted for direction. Mr. ██████ was directed to remain at his residence until further notice. It should be noted that Mr. ██████ girlfriend, ██████, has a criminal history.

Ministry of Public Safety & Solicitor General	Community Corrections	Mailing Address: Corrections Branch

Telephone:

Facsimile:

Mr. ▆▆▆ was also connected up to the Electronic Monitoring equipment and was asked to return to his residence and plug in the equipment. Central Monitoring Unit (CMU) was contacted and Mr. ▆▆▆ curfew was logged in. Mr. ▆▆▆ left this Office at 5:15pm, however, did not return to his residence, which is approximately twenty minutes away from this office. CMU contacted his residence at least three times and was told that he had not yet arrived. Eventually, at 7:15pm, Mr. ▆▆▆ returned to his residence.

Mr. ▆▆▆ also stated that he needed a letter of permission to be outside his residence for the purpose of employment, as indicated on Condition 10(k). He stated that as indicated on his release application, he would be starting his employment with his stepfather right away. A letter of permission was provided to him indicating that he will leave the residence at 5:00am and return no later than 7:00pm. These times were confirmed by Mr. ▆▆▆ mother, Ms. ▆▆▆, who stated that these times are consistent with the hours her husband leaves for work in the morning and returns back in the evening. However, when a telephone call was made to the residence this morning, Ms. ▆▆▆ informed this writer that Mr. ▆▆▆ had not left for work in the morning with her husband, but instead was sleeping. When Mr. ▆▆▆ woke up, he telephoned this writer and indicated that he did not to go work because he needed to buy work equipment and he inquired about going on a shopping trip. This writer is concerned that Mr. ▆▆▆ has not followed through with attending his employment and is already requesting permission to vary his curfew restrictions.

Mr. ▆▆▆ has informed this writer that he has already established that he would be moving in with his girlfriend to ▆▆▆, and trying to seek different employment. It is clear that Mr. ▆▆▆ has planned to deviate from his original release application immediately upon release on parole. This writer is seeking direction from the Board as to whether Mr. ▆▆▆ new plans comply with the Conditions of his Parole.

Sincerely,

▆▆▆▆

Parole Supervisor.

Ministry of Public Safety & Solicitor General   Community Corrections   Mailing Address: Corrections Branch   Telephone:

Facsimile:

In a post-suspension hearing, a parole board has several options: (1) cancel the suspension, (2) revoke the release, or (3) terminate the release (for federal and Ontario provincial parolees). This last option is selected when there is a need to end the conditional release for reasons beyond the control of the individual offender, such as if the community residential facility where the offender was living burned down. If the board felt that this person could not be on conditional release without a residency requirement, it would terminate the release until new accommodation could be secured. In the federal system, two additional options are available: (1) issue a reprimand to the offender and cancel the suspension or (2) cancel the suspension but order a delay in its taking effect for up to 30 days, which can only be imposed for a second or subsequent suspension. In neither case will the release be revoked.

The charts in Figures 10.4 and 10.5 indicate that most offenders whose releases are revoked have committed technical violations—that is, they have violated the general and/or specific conditions attached to their conditional release. These violations include having a positive urinalysis test, being in an unauthorized area, and making contact with prohibited persons. About 10 percent of cases involve a revocation for a new offence. It is important to note, however, that this does not mean that only 10 percent of those on conditional release commit new offences. It is unknown how many offences are committed but not discovered by the police or correctional authorities, how many offences are discovered but are classified as technical violations because such charges are more easily proved, or how many suspensions are cancelled for other reasons, when in fact an offence has been committed.

In reality, it can be difficult to revoke a release for the commission of a new offence because a parole board hearing is not the appropriate venue to determine a person's guilt or innocence of a criminal charge. In most such cases, the offender has been charged with a crime but has not yet been convicted. However, a federal offender who has been convicted of an indictable offence will automatically have the release revoked.

THE EFFECTIVENESS OF PAROLE

The task of measuring the effectiveness of parole is complicated by the following factors:

- Many offenders (up to 85 percent in some provincial correctional institutions) do not apply for parole, but rather serve their time until their release at discharge/remission.
- Offenders on conditional release may be suspended and subsequently have their conditional release revoked for violations of the conditions of their release certificate and without having committed a new crime.

This may include such minor incidents as having a beer with friends and violating the condition to abstain from alcohol and drug use.

- Most studies of conditional release follow offenders for only brief periods following completion of their sentence.
- There is no measure of the offender's subsequent quality of life, personal and family stability, substance use/abuse, or progress in addressing other need areas. The only concern is whether the offender comes to the attention of the criminal justice system and is committed to custody.
- The most common measure of recidivism used is re-admission—that is, the number of offenders who re-enter prisons for a subsequent conviction who have been there before. Offenders who have moved to other jurisdictions or who have been deported to their home country and may have become involved in criminal activity are not counted.

In Quebec during 2001–02, 23 percent of offenders on parole had their release subsequently revoked for violating a condition of their release, while 7 percent committed a new offence (www.msp.gouv.qc.ca). Figures on recidivism for provincial offenders in British Columbia, presented in Figure 10.6,

Figure 10.6

Recidivism in British Columbia, 1980–1995

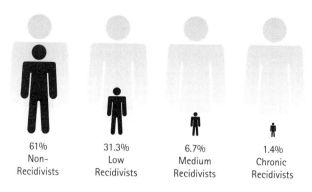

| 61% | 31.3% | 6.7% | 1.4% |
| Non-Recidivists | Low Recidivists | Medium Recidivists | Chronic Recidivists |

- A chronic recidivist is an offender who has been convicted 10 or more times.
- A medium recidivist has been convicted 5 to 9 times.
- A low recidivist has received 2 to 4 convictions.
- A non-recidivist is an offender who has not received a subsequent conviction.

Source: Justice Institute of British Columbia, 2002:6.

reveal that 61 percent of the offenders who had served time in custody were not reconvicted of an offence during the period 1980–1995; note that these figures do not indicate whether those offenders who relapsed into criminal behaviour were on some form of conditional release. The Ontario Parole and Earned Release Board uses three performance measures to gauge recidivism rates. As Table 10.2 illustrates, the board exceeded its performance targets for the period 2000–01.

Table 10.2   Performance Measures for the Ontario Parole and Earned Release Board

Performance Measure	2000–2001 Target	2000–2001 Actual
Percentage of parolees who reoffended while on parole	No greater than 4.5%	3.5%
Percentage of parolees suspended for serious reoffending	No greater than 2%	0.7%
Percentage of parolees who reoffend within two years of release	No greater than 25%	18%

Source: Ontario Parole and Earned Release Board (www.operb.gov.on.ca/english/intro.html).

VICTIM NOTIFICATION AND OFFENDERS ON CONDITIONAL RELEASE

As noted in Chapter 9, the victims of incarcerated offenders have the right to request that they be informed of the timing of release. In some cases, this information can assist the victims to take the necessary steps to ensure their safety. The large majority of crime victims are not harassed or threatened by offenders on conditional release; however, some victims are at great risk. It is in these cases that victim notification is most crucial, for both officially sanctioned releases and unauthorized absences from community supervision.

QUESTIONS FOR REVIEW

1. Identify the key challenges confronting systems of corrections in developing effective reintegration policies and programs.

2. Discuss the pains of re-entry experienced by inmates released from confinement.

3. Identify the survival needs of parolees.

4. Describe two mandatory and two additional conditions that can be associated with a federal parole release.

5. Define the concept of technical parole violation and explain why it might trigger a suspension of conditional release.

6. Describe the dual functions of parole supervisors and provide examples.

7. Describe one innovative program for parole supervision.

8. Identify the major problems encountered by (a) Aboriginal, (b) female, and (c) mentally disordered parolees.

9. Summarize the arguments of proponents and critics of community notification.

10. Describe and discuss the goals of circles of support.

REFERENCES

Auditor General of Canada. 1996. "Correctional Service of Canada—Reintegration of Offenders." *Report of the Auditor General to the House of Commons, Chapter 30*. Ottawa: Minister of Public Works and Government Services Canada.

British Columbia Civil Liberties Association. 1996. *BCCLA Privacy Positions: Community Notification Regarding Released Sex Offenders*. Vancouver: British Columbia Civil Liberties Association.

Cairns, A. 1999. "Victims Groups Rip Push for Parole." *The Toronto Sun* (February 18):1.

Caron, R. 1978. *Go-Boy! The True Story of a Life behind Bars*. Toronto: McGraw-Hill Ryerson.

Cesaroni, C. 2001. "Releasing Sex Offenders into the Community through 'Circles of Support': A Means of Reintegrating the 'Worst of the Worst.'" *Journal of Offender Rehabilitation* 34(2):85–98.

Conly, C. 1998. *The Women's Prison Association: Supporting Women Offenders and Their Families*. Washington, D.C.: National Institute of Justice, U.S. Department of Justice.

Correctional Service of Canada. 1998. *Community Strategy for Women on Conditional Release: Discussion Paper*. Ottawa: Correctional Service of Canada.

———. 2001a. "CSC Team Supervision Unit: A Night on the Town." *Let's Talk* 26(2). Retrieved from www.csc-scc.gc.ca/text/pblct/letstalk/2001/no2/4_e.shtml.

———. 2001b. "CSC Team Supervision Unit: Execution of a Warrant of Suspension and Apprehension." *Let's Talk* 26(2). Retrieved from www.csc-scc.gc.ca/text/pblct/letstalk/2001/no2/6_e.shtml.

———. 2002. *2002–03 Estimates. Part III—Report on Plans and Priorities.* Ottawa: Solicitor General Canada.

Doren, D.M. 1998. "Recidivism Base Rates, Predictions of Sex Offender Recidivism, and the 'Sexual Predator' Commitment Laws." *Behavioral Sciences and the Law* 16(1):97–114.

English, K. 1998. "The Containment Approach: An Aggressive Strategy for the Community Management of Adult Sex Offenders." *Psychology, Public Policy and Law* 4(12):218–35.

Fazari, L. 1999. "Missing Parolee Killers Criticized." *The London Free Press* (January 10):A7.

Hamilton, Associate Chief Justice A.C., and Associate Chief Judge C.M. Sinclair. 1991. *Report of the Aboriginal Justice Inquiry of Manitoba: The Justice System and Aboriginal People.* Vol. 1. Winnipeg: Queen's Printer.

Hanson, R.K., and M.T. Bussiere. 1998. "Predicting Relapse: A Meta-Analysis of Sexual Offender Recidivism Studies." *Journal of Consulting and Clinical Psychology* 66(2):348–62.

Harris, G.T., M.E. Rice, and V.L. Quinsey. 1998. "Appraisal and Management of Risk in Sexual Aggressors: Implications for Criminal Justice Policy." *Psychology, Public Policy and Law* 4(12):73–115.

Heise, E., L. Horne, H. Kirkegaard, H. Nigh, I.P Derry, and M. Yantzi. 1996. *Community Reintegration Project.* Toronto: Mennonite Central Committee.

Heney, J., and C.M. Kristiansen. 1997. "An Analysis of the Impact of Prison on Women Survivors of Childhood Sexual Abuse." *Women and Therapy* 20(4):29–44.

Irwin, J. 1970. *The Felon.* Englewood Cliffs, N.J.: Prentice-Hall.

Justice Institute of British Columbia. 2002. *Facts about Adult Corrections in British Columbia.* New Westminster, B.C.: Corrections and Community Justice Division, Justice Institute of British Columbia.

Kabat, A.R. 1998. "Scarlet Letter Sex Offender Databases and Community Notification: Sacrificing Personal Privacy for a Symbol's Sake." *American Criminal Law Review* 35(2):333–70.

Kendall, K. 1994. "Creating Real Choices: A Program Evaluation of Therapeutic Services at the Prison for Women." *Forum on Corrections Research* 6(1):19–21.

LaPrairie, C. 1996. *Examining Aboriginal Corrections in Canada.* Ottawa: Aboriginal Corrections, Ministry of the Solicitor General.

Loya, J.S. 1997. "Life after Hard Time: An Ex–Bank Robber Reflects on Freedom's Down Side." *Utne Reader* (May/June):27–29 [reprinted from *L.A. Weekly*, January 31, 1997].

McDonald, D.C., and M. Teitelbaum. 1994. *Managing Mentally Ill Offenders in the Community: Milwaukee's Community Support Program.* Washington, D.C.: National Institute of Justice, U.S. Department of Justice.

Motiuk L. 1997. "The Community Risk/Needs Management Scale: An Effective Supervision Tool." *Forum on Corrections Research* 9(1):8–12.

Motiuk, L., R. Boe, and M. Nafekh. 2002. "The Safe Return of Offenders to the Community: Statistical Overview." Ottawa: Research Branch, Correctional Service of Canada. Retrieved from www.csc-scc.gc.ca/text/faits/facts08-03_e.shtml.

Murphy, P.J., L. Johnsen, and J. Murphy. 2002. *Paroled for Life: Interviews with Parolees Serving Life Sentences*. Vancouver: New Star Books.

National Parole Board. 2002. *Performance Monitoring Report, 2001–2002*. Ottawa: Solicitor General Canada. Retrieved from www.npb-cnlc.gc.ca/reports/pdf/pmr_2001_2002/index_e.htm.

Nuffield, J. 1998. *Issues in Urban Corrections for Aboriginal People*. Ottawa: Solicitor General Canada.

Petrunik, M.G. 2002. "Managing Unacceptable Risk: Sex Offenders, Community Response, and Social Policy in the United States and Canada." *International Journal of Offender Therapy and Comparative Criminology* 46(4):483–511.

Prentky, R.A.L., F.S. Austin, R.A. Knight, and D. Cerce. 1997. "Recidivism Rates among Child Molesters and Rapists: A Methodological Analysis." *Law and Human Behavior* 21(6):635–59.

Rivera, M. 1996. *"Giving Us a Chance": Needs Assessment, Mental Health Resources for Federally Sentenced Women in the Regional Facilities*. Ottawa: Correctional Service of Canada.

Saulis, M., S. Fiddler, and Y. Howse. 2001. *Release Potential of Federally-Sentenced Aboriginal Inmates to Communities: A Community-based Research Project*. Ottawa: Research Branch, Correctional Service of Canada. Retrieved from www.csc-scc.gc.ca/text/rsrch/reports/r110_e.pdf.

Schram, D.D., and C.D. Millroy. 1995. *Community Notification: A Study of Offender Characteristics and Recidivism*. Olympia: Washington State Institute for Public Policy.

Solicitor General Canada. 1998. *CCRA Five-Year Review: Aboriginal Offenders*. Ottawa.

Task Force on Federally Sentenced Women. 1990. *Creating Choices: The Report of the Task Force on Federally Sentenced Women*. Ottawa: Correctional Service of Canada.

Thurber, A. 1998. "Understanding Offender Reintegration." *Forum on Corrections Research* 10(1):14–18.

Travis, J. 2000. "But They All Come Back: Rethinking Prisoner Reentry." *Sentencing and Corrections: Issues for the 21st Century*. Washington, D.C.: U.S. Department of Justice, National Institute of Justice. Retrieved from www.ncjrs.org/pdffiles1/nij/181413.pdf.

United States Department of Justice. 1998. *National Conference on Sex Offender Registries: Proceedings of a BJS/SEARCH Conference*. Washington, D.C.: Office of Justice Programs, U.S. Department of Justice.

Washington State Institute for Public Policy. 1998. *Sex Offenses in Washington State: 1998 Update*. Olympia: Washington State Institute for Public Policy.

Wilson, R.J., L. Stewart, T. Stirpe, M. Barrett, and J.E. Cripps. 2000. "Community-based Sex Offender Management: Combining Parole Supervision and Treatment to Reduce Recidivism." *Canadian Journal of Criminology* 42(2):177–88.

Wine, S. 1992. *A Motherhood Issue: The Impact of Criminal Justice System Involvement on Women and Their Children*. Ottawa: Solicitor General Canada.

APPENDIX A

CHRONOLOGY OF EVENTS IN CANADIAN CORRECTIONS

1754 to 1867

1754	The first Canadian workhouse is constructed in Nova Scotia.
1791	The Constitutional Act divides the country into the provinces of Upper and Lower Canada, both of which utilize English criminal law.
1792	The first Parliament of Upper Canada passes legislation providing for the construction of a courthouse and a jail in each of the region's districts.
1800	Legislation reducing the severity of punishments for many criminal offences is passed.
1826	A proposal to construct a penitentiary in Upper Canada is presented to the House of Assembly.
1830	Corporal punishment for incarcerated women is abolished.
1831	Report of H.C. Thomson documenting the need for a penitentiary is accepted by the House of Assembly.
1832	*Report of the Commissioners on Penitentiaries*, issued by H.C. Thomson, recommends the construction of a penitentiary based on the Auburn model.
1834	The recommendations of Thomson are embodied in the Penitentiary Act of 1834.
1835	Canada's first penitentiary opens in Kingston, Ontario.
1838	The Gaol Construction Act is passed by the Parliament of Upper Canada, marking the first attempt to legislate control over local jails.
1843	A penitentiary opens in Halifax.
1848	A Royal Commission of Inquiry (Brown Commission) is appointed to investigate charges of corruption and mismanagement at Kingston Penitentiary.

1851   The Penitentiary Act of 1851 provides for reforms at Kingston Penitentiary, including an end to the practice of allowing the public to buy admittance to view the inmates.

1857   The Prison Inspection Act provides for the construction of a separate facility for mentally disordered convicts and the building of a reformatory for young offenders.

1858   The first reformatory for juvenile boys opens on Isle aux Noix in Lower Canada.

1859   A reformatory for juvenile boys opens in Penetanguishene, Upper Canada.

1867 to 1900

1867   The British North America Act gives the federal government control over making criminal laws and the provinces responsibility for the administration of justice.

1868   The federal Department of Justice is created and given responsibility for federal penitentiaries.

               The Penitentiary Act of 1868 brings the pre-Confederation prisons in Kingston, Halifax, and Saint John under federal jurisdiction, thereby creating the federal penitentiary system.

               The province of Ontario passes the Prison and Asylum Inspection Act, which provides for the inspection of provincial jails.

1873   The provincial boys' reformatory in St. Vincent de Paul, Quebec, becomes a federal penitentiary.

1875   The Supreme Court of Canada is established.

1877   Manitoba Penitentiary opens near Winnipeg.

1878   British Columbia Penitentiary opens in New Westminster.

1880   Dorchester Penitentiary opens in New Brunswick.

1886   The Act Respecting Public and Reformatory Prisons provides for the operation of provincial correctional facilities.

               The Penitentiary Act of 1886 provides for federal–provincial agreements relating to the transfer of prisoners and giving provinces the authority to establish prisons for offenders under provincial jurisdiction.

1887   Victoria Industrial School for Boys opens near Toronto.

1889   The Act to Permit the Conditional Release of First Offenders in Certain Cases provides for the placement of offenders on "probation of good conduct."

1891   The *Report of the Commissioners Appointed to Enquire into the Prison and Reformatory System of the Province of Ontario*, chaired by J.W. Langmuir, documents the continuing problems of provincial and local institutions, including the lack of classification, poor physical facilities, and inadequate management.

1892   The Criminal Code is enacted.

1895   Legislation is passed that abolishes systems of contract labour, authorizes the use of solitary confinement cells, and reinforces the use of the silent system.

1899   Parliament enacts the Act to Provide for the Conditional Liberation of Penitentiary Convicts (Ticket of Leave Act). Under the Act, the governor general could allow offenders to be at large under certain conditions and under the supervision of police officers.

1900 to 1960

1904   Penetanguishene Reformatory for Boys is closed.

1906   The Penitentiary Act of 1906 includes provisions for the administration of the federal penitentiary system, conditions for earned remission, powers and duties of prison inspectors, and the removal of youthful inmates and the mentally disordered from general penitentiary populations.

The Prison and Reformatories Act requires separation of youth and adult offenders.

The first dominion parole officer is appointed.

1907   Alberta Penitentiary is constructed.

1911   Saskatchewan Penitentiary opens near Prince Albert.

1934   The federal Prison for Women opens in Kingston, Ontario.

1936   The Royal Commission on the Penal System of Canada (Archambault) is appointed to investigate federal prisons.

1938   The report of the Archambault commission recommends reform of the federal prison system.

1945   The rule of silence is abolished in federal institutions.

1956   *Report on a Commission Appointed to Inquire into the Principles and Practices Followed in the Remission Service of the Department of Justice* (Fauteux) recommends the adoption of a correctional philosophy centred on the treatment of offenders.

1958   The Ticket of Leave Act is replaced by the Parole Act, which establishes the National Parole Board (NPB) and gives the NPB exclusive jurisdiction to grant, refuse, or revoke parole. The authority of the NPB extends to all federal inmates and to provincial inmates in provinces that do not subsequently create their own parole boards.

1960 to Present

1961   The Penitentiary Act of 1961 establishes procedures for the operation of penitentiaries, authorizes statutory remission and the granting of temporary absences, and permits the transfer of inmates.

1963   A 10-year plan for federal penitentiary construction is initiated; 10 new prisons, of varying size and security classifications, are ultimately built.

1965   The first Citizen's Advisory Committee is created.

1966   The Organization Act creates the federal Ministry of Solicitor General of Canada, responsible for federal police, penitentiaries, and parole.

1968   The first community correctional centre opens in Montreal.

1969   The Canadian Committee on Corrections (Ouimet) presents recommendations for the development of a unified federal justice system.

            Day parole is created through an amendment to the Parole Act.

            The living unit concept, based on a therapeutic community model, is implemented on an experimental basis and subsequently adopted in federal penitentiaries.

1970   Amendments to the Parole Act provide mandatory supervision for inmates who were released prior to the completion of their sentence under earned remission and who were not granted parole.

1971   Bail reform legislation that is designed to reduce the interference with freedom of persons awaiting trial and to encourage the use of summonses in place of incarceration is enacted.

   Restriction and censorship of inmate correspondence is reduced and provision is made for inmates to correspond with a wide range of persons outside the prison.

   The federal solicitor general contracts with private, not-for-profit organizations to operate community-based residential centres for federal offenders.

1972   Corporal punishment (whipping) as a punishment for disciplinary offences in federal penitentiaries is abolished.

   The federal solicitor general enters into contracts with provincial and aftercare agencies for case preparation and parole supervision. Under these agreements, provincial correctional agencies and private-sector organizations conduct community assessments and supervise inmates released on full parole, day parole, mandatory supervision, and unescorted temporary absences.

   The first regional psychiatric centre opens to provide treatment for federal offenders who are mentally disordered and/or emotionally disturbed.

1973   The Task Force on the Release of Inmates (Hugessen) examines the procedures for the release of offenders from institutions prior to the completion of their sentence. It recommends the creation of five regional parole boards at the federal level and the appointment of part-time board members.

   The first federal Correctional Investigator is appointed to act as a prison ombudsman, hearing prisoner complaints and making recommendations to the federal government.

1974   Five regional districts of the federal parole system (Atlantic, Quebec, Ontario, Prairies, Pacific) are created.

1976   Capital punishment is abolished by a free vote in Parliament and is replaced by a mandatory sentence of life imprisonment.

Mandatory sentences of 25 years minimum are introduced for certain types of crimes.

Bill C-51, the Peace and Security Bill, is enacted in an attempt to reduce violent crime. It creates the category of "dangerous offenders" who can be subjected to indeterminate prison sentences.

1977   An amendment to the Parole Act gives provinces the authority to create their own parole boards with jurisdiction over provincial inmates. Three provinces—Ontario, Quebec, and British Columbia—create boards.

The Parliamentary Sub-Committee on the Penitentiary System in Canada (MacGuigan) inquires into the operation of federal maximum-security institutions and makes 65 recommendations for reform. The federal solicitor general accepts the majority of the recommendations in the MacGuigan report.

The Task Force on the Creation of an Integrated Canadian Corrections Service recommends the merger of the National Parole Service with the Canadian Penitentiary Service to create the Correctional Service of Canada. The task force also concludes that rehabilitation is an unrealistic goal of incarceration and that incarceration should constitute the sole punishment of offenders sentenced to prison.

The first Special Handling Unit, designed to confine inmates with a history of violence, opens at Millhaven Institution, a maximum-security facility west of Kingston, Ontario.

The National Advisory Committee on the Female Offender (Clark) identifies the need to create more community-based residences, recommends closing the Kingston Prison for Women, and proposes that the federal government construct small facilities for female offenders in each region of the country or give the provinces authority to confine federal female offenders.

1978   Inmate committees are established in federal institutions.

The National Planning Committee on the Female Offender is created to assess the Clark report. The final report supports the closure of the Kingston Prison for Women and the building of regional facilities.

1980	A 12-week, full-time training course with a 24-month probationary period is introduced for all correctional officer recruits.
	A family visitation program, which allows inmates with long sentences to spend up to three days with family members in a home-like setting, is implemented at the maximum-security Millhaven Institution.
1985	Legislation is enacted that gives the National Parole Board the authority to prevent the mandatory release of inmates believed to be dangerous.
1987	A motion to reinstate the death penalty is defeated in a free vote in Parliament.
1996	Bill C-41, which contains numerous sentencing reforms (including the creation of conditional sentences), is passed.
	The Commission of Inquiry into Certain Events at the Prison for Women in Kingston (Arbour) issues a report that is highly critical of the Correctional Service of Canada.
	The federal government opens several small, regional facilities for federally sentenced women.
1998	An Aboriginal band and the federal government sign the first agreement providing for the delivery of correctional services to Aboriginal offenders by the band.
1999	The Correctional Service of Canada implements Operation Bypass, an initiative to streamline the case management process.
2000	The Kingston Prison for Women is closed.
	A get-tough, no-frills approach to corrections, reflecting the punishment-oriented American model, emerges in Ontario.
2002	The Supreme Court of Canada strikes down a law that prohibited federal offenders from voting.
	Canada's first privately operated correctional institution opens in Ontario.

APPENDIX B

GLOSSARY OF KEY TERMS

accelerated parole review: A process defined in the Corrections and Conditional Release Act in which some first-time federal offenders are fast-tracked for parole consideration. The intent is to expedite the release of inmates who have committed less serious offences.

actuarial prediction: A prediction scheme based upon analysis of a large number of previous cases.

additional conditions: Conditions attached to a probation order, a conditional sentence order, or a parole certificate that are designed to meet the specific needs of the offender.

aggressive precautions: Inmate strategies for avoiding violence and victimization, including developing a tough attitude, being physically strong, and keeping a weapon. See also *passive precautions*.

alternative sanctions: See *intermediate sanctions*.

Auburn model (for prisons): A system that allowed prisoners to work and eat together during the day and provided housing in individual cells at night. A strict silent system, which forbade prisoners from communicating or even gesturing to one another, was enforced at all times. The Auburn system was the model upon which most prisons in the United States and Canada were patterned. See also *Pennsylvania model*.

banishment: Historically, the practice of sending offenders away to another location permanently or for a specified period. In more contemporary times, the prison is used as a form of banishment.

Basic Case Management Program: The training program for federal correctional personnel who have been appointed to positions involving case management.

Bloody Code: Legislation during the late 1700s in England, under which over 350 offences were rendered punishable by death.

Canadian Charter of Rights and Freedoms (1982): The primary law of the land that guarantees basic rights and freedoms for citizens (including those convicted of criminal offences) and includes sections on fundamental freedoms, legal rights, equity rights, and enforcement.

carceral: That portion of systems of corrections relating to confinement in correctional institutions. Broadly defined, it includes sentencing judges, superintendents and wardens, inmates, correctional officers, program staff, volunteers, the offender's family, treatment professionals, health-care providers, and spiritual advisers such as chaplains and Aboriginal Elders.

Career Management Program: A core component of the human resources policy of the federal CSC that provides employees with the opportunity to establish and pursue career goals with the service.

case management: The process by which identified needs and risks of inmates are matched with selected services and resources.

circle sentencing: A restorative justice strategy that involves a collaborative effort on the part of community residents (including the crime victim and the offender) and justice system personnel in order to reach a consensual decision through a process of reconciliation, restitution, and reparation.

classical school: A perspective of crime and criminals set out in the writings of Cesare Beccaria and Jeremy Bentham in the 1700s. Among the basic tenets of this perspective are (1) criminal offenders exercise free will and engage in criminal behaviour as a consequence of rational choice, and (2) to be effective, punishment must be certain and must fit the crime.

classification: The process by which inmates are categorized through the use of various assessment instruments. Classification is used to determine the appropriate security level of the inmate and program placement.

clinical prediction: A prediction scheme that involves mental-health professionals conducting assessments and making recommendations.

cold turkey release: Discharge of an offender at the end of the sentence when no conditional release or supervision is possible. For federal offenders, this only occurs when statutory release is denied and the inmate serves the entire sentence in confinement. For provincial offenders, for whom cold turkey releases are far more common, this occurs when they have reached the two-thirds point in the sentence if they have not lost any remission. However, if the sentencing judge orders probation to follow imprisonment, some provincial offenders will immediately begin a period of probation supervision.

commissioner's directives: In the federal system of corrections, the rules for the management of service delivery and for implementing the provisions of the Corrections and Conditional Release Act.

community assessment: A document prepared by parole officers for the parole board and containing information on the feasibility of the inmate-applicant's proposed community plan in terms of the level of supervision required and the availability of community resources.

community-based residential facilities: Community-based facilities for federal offenders that are operated either directly by the government or by private contractors.

community correctional centres: Community-based residential facilities operated by the Correctional Service of Canada.

community corrections: A generic term used to denote correctional programs that are delivered in community settings.

community holistic healing: A restorative justice approach that is embodied in the Community Holistic Circle Healing Program operated by Hollow Water First Nation (Manitoba). This program involves the use of traditional healing practices in an attempt to restore community, family, and individual peace and harmony.

community notification: The practice, usually carried out by police agencies, of making a public announcement that a high-risk offender has taken up residence in an area.

community residential centres: In Ontario, community-based residential facilities, usually operated by private agencies, that house special-needs inmates on temporary absences.

community sanctions: See *intermediate sanctions*.

conditional release: A generic term for the various means of leaving an institution before warrant expiry whereby an offender is subject to conditions that can, if breached, trigger revocation of the release and return to prison.

conditional sentence: A sentence imposed on an offender who would otherwise be incarcerated for a period of less than two years but whose risk to the community is deemed by the court to be so low that the offender can serve the term at home, abiding by prescribed conditions and subject to imprisonment should the conditions be violated.

conservative correctional ideology: A perspective of criminality and corrections that focuses on free will and the lack of discipline as causes of crime and holds offenders responsible for their behaviour.

Constitution Act (1867): Formerly known as the British North America Act (1867), this legislation includes provisions that define the responsibilities of the federal and provincial governments in the area of criminal justice. The federal government is assigned the authority to enact criminal laws and procedures for processing criminal cases, while the provinces are assigned responsibility for the administration of justice.

continuum of correctional institutions: A term used to describe the differences in institutional environments among correctional institutions located at either ends of the security spectrum—maximum to minimum. While all correctional institutions are total institutions, some are more "total" than others.

correctional camps/farms/day detention centres/treatment centres/community residences: Correctional facilities that generally house low-risk inmates in a minimum-security setting.

correctional centres/reformatories/établissements/penitentiaries: Correctional facilities that are generally used to confine sentenced offenders.

correctional plan: A key component of the case management process that determines the offender's initial institution placement, specific training or work opportunities, and preparation for release.

Correctional Service of Canada (CSC): The federal system of corrections in Canada.

Correctional Training Program: The basic training program for federal correctional officers.

corrections: The structures, policies, and programs that are delivered by governments, nonprofit agencies and organizations, and members of the general public to punish, treat, and supervise, in the community and in correctional institutions, persons convicted of criminal offences.

Corrections and Conditional Release Act (1992): The primary legislation under which the federal system of corrections operates. The Act covers all facets of managing and supervising federal offenders.

Criminal Code: Federal legislation that sets out the criminal laws of Canada and the procedures for the administration of justice.

criminogenic factors: Risk/needs factors that contribute to a person's propensity to commit criminal offences, including the acceptance of antisocial values and substance abuse problems. See also *dynamic risk factors*.

critical incident stress (among correctional officers): The consequence of exposure to incidents, including disturbances and riots, hostage-takings, murder, and inmate self-mutilation and suicide. See also *post-traumatic stress disorder*.

critical incident stress debriefing: A procedure for assisting correctional officers following a critical incident that includes debriefing by a trained intervenor, identifying the symptoms of stress, and providing the officer with stress management strategies.

cross-gender staffing: The practice of staffing correctional institutions with both male and female officers. Most often discussed in terms of the issue of whether male correctional officers should work inside correctional facilities for women.

dangerous offender (DO): A designation made by the judge after conviction (or up to six months later in some cases) that results in an indeterminate term of federal imprisonment. It is not commonly used and can be ordered only if the person poses such a clear danger to the community that preventive detention is justified. Dangerous offenders can be released by the National Parole Board only when they no longer constitute a danger to the community.

day parole: The authority granted by a parole board for inmates to be at large in order to prepare for full release (e.g., for job search) while returning at night to the institution or, more typically, to a community residential facility. Day parolees can seek full parole when they reach their parole eligibility dates. Day parole does not apply to provincial offenders.

denunciation: A retributive goal of sentencing designed to express disapproval of the offender's behaviour.

deprivation theory: An explanation which holds that the inmate social system develops as a consequence of inmates' attempts to mitigate the pains of imprisonment.

detention during the period of statutory release: A decision by the National Parole Board (after an application by the CSC) that a federal inmate be denied statutory release and be detained in the institution until warrant expiry.

determinate sentence: A prison term in which the release date is specified but the inmate may earn remission. Often referred to as a "flat sentence."

differential amenability to treatment: The notion that, for a variety of reasons, not all inmates are receptive to treatment and/or require interventions tailored to meet their specific needs, abilities, and interests.

differential supervision: The practice of providing differing levels of supervision and control of probationers, depending upon their level of risk.

differential treatment availability: The recognition that within systems of corrections not all inmates have equal access to treatment programs.

differential treatment effectiveness: The requirement that, to be effective, treatment interventions must be multifaceted and matched to the specific needs of individual offenders.

diversion programs: Those programs that are designed to keep offenders from being processed further into the formal criminal justice system. May operate at the pre-charge, post-charge, or post-sentencing stage.

dynamic risk factors: Attributes of the inmate that can be altered through intervention, such as level of education and cognitive thinking abilities. Unlike static criminal history factors, dynamic factors can be changed (for the better or, if not addressed, for the worse).

dynamic security: A variety of ongoing, meaningful interactions between staff and inmates, including officers making suggestions, assisting with problems, and speaking with inmates on a regular basis. See also *static security*.

ecological fallacy: A common problem in the prediction of recidivism in corrections whereby data on the performance of a group of offenders is used to predict the performance of an individual offender.

electronic monitoring (EM): A correctional strategy that involves placing an offender under house arrest and then using electronic equipment to ensure that the conditions of supervision are fulfilled. May be used as either an alternative to confinement or following a term of incarceration in a provincial correctional facility.

exchange of service agreements: Arrangements for the delivery of services made between the federal and provincial/territorial systems of corrections. Among the more common are transfer agreements whereby federal offenders are allowed to complete their sentence of incarceration in a provincial/territorial facility.

expressive violence: Violence between inmates that is neither planned by the perpetrator nor deliberate. Rather, it is a result of specific problems that the inmate-initiator is experiencing, such as stress or difficulties in coping with life inside the institution.

faint-hope clause: The provision for judicial review set out in section 745 of the Criminal Code. Allows offenders who are serving life sentences with no eligibility for parole for at least 15 years to apply to the court for a reduction of the parole eligibility period.

family group conferences: A restorative justice approach, first developed in New Zealand, that brings together justice personnel, the crime victim, the offender, and, when appropriate, their families. A coordinator facilitates the conference, during which consensual decisions are made in an attempt to redress the harm caused by the offence while providing for the reintegration of the offender.

full parole: The authority granted by a parole board for an inmate to be at large during the last part of his or her sentence. A term of full parole can begin as early as the one-third point in a sentence and will run until warrant expiry if not revoked. Provincial offenders on full parole give up their earned remission.

general deterrence: An objective of sentencing designed to deter others from engaging in criminal conduct.

hulks: Old sailing vessels that had been converted into floating prisons, anchored in rivers and harbours, used to confine inmates during the 1700s.

importation theory: An explanation that holds that the inmate social system develops as a consequence of pre-prison attitudes and behaviours that are brought by inmates into the institution.

incapacitation: A utilitarian goal of sentencing designed to prevent crimes that the offender would have otherwise committed if out of custody.

indeterminate sentence: A prison term in which the release date is not specified by the judge but is determined by an administrative body such as a parole board.

inmate code: A key component of the inmate social system composed of a set of behavioural rules that govern interaction among the inmates and between inmates and correctional staff. Among the tenets of the code are (1) do your own time, (2) never rat on a con, (3) don't weaken, and (4) don't steal from cons.

inmate social system: See *inmate subculture*.

inmate subculture: The patterns of interaction and the relationships that exist among inmates confined in correctional institutions.

institutionalized: A term used to describe those inmates who have become so immersed in prison life (prisonized) that they are unable to function in the outside, free community.

institutional parole officers: Staff in federal correctional institutions who are primarily responsible for case management.

instrumental violence: Violence between inmates that is the result of planned or deliberate action on the part of the inmate-perpetrator and most often used to gain status or to intimidate other inmates in order to secure illicit goods and services.

intensive supervision probation (ISP): An intermediate sanction (between the minimal supervision of traditional probation and incarceration) that generally includes reduced caseloads for probation officers, increased surveillance of probationers, treatment interventions, and efforts to ensure that probationers are employed.

intermediate sanctions (also known as alternative sanctions or community sanctions): A term used to describe a wide variety of correctional programs that generally fall between traditional probation and incarceration (although specific initiatives may include either of these penalties as well). Includes fines, community service, day centres, home detention and electronic monitoring, intensive probation supervision and boot camps.

jails and detention centres: Correctional facilities that are generally used to house short-term inmates and those offenders on remand awaiting sentencing or appeal.

judicial determination: When a sentencing judge orders that a person being sentenced to a federal term must serve one-half of the sentence before being eligible to apply for parole. It is possible only for certain offences, specifically serious interpersonal offences and drug offences as specified in Schedule I and II of the Corrections and Conditional Release Act.

judicial recognizance: An order of the court, often referred to as a peace bond (section 810 of the Criminal Code), that requires the subject of the order to adhere to set conditions such as avoiding places where children may be present. It is frequently used for high-risk sex offenders who reach warrant expiry.

judicial review: A process authorized by section 745 of the Criminal Code whereby those serving life sentences for murder can, after serving 15 years, apply to a court and jury to have their period of parole ineligibility reduced.

liberal correctional ideology: A perspective on criminality and corrections that focuses on the role of poverty, racism, and social injustice as causes of crime and on the treatment and rehabilitation of offenders.

long-term offenders: A designation under section 752 or 753 of the Criminal Code that requires the offender to spend a portion of time under supervision following the expiry of sentence. Long-term supervision orders may prescribe a period of supervision up to 10 years.

mandatory conditions: Standard conditions—such as obeying the law and keeping the peace—contained in a probation order, a conditional sentence order, or a parole certificate.

mature coping: A term coined by the criminologist Robert Johnson to describe a positive approach to adjusting to life inside correctional institutions. The three components of mature coping are (1) dealing with problems in a straightforward manner, (2) avoiding the use of deception and violence in addressing problems, and (3) being altruistic.

maximum-security institutions: Federal correctional facilities with a highly controlled institutional environment.

medical model of corrections: A perspective on corrections that emerged in the post–World War II period. The medical, or treatment, model held that the offender was ill—physically, mentally and/or socially—and criminal behaviour was a symptom of this illness. As in medicine, diagnosis and treatment were thought to ensure the effective rehabilitation of the offender.

medium-security institutions: Federal correctional facilities that have a less highly controlled institutional environment than maximum security institutions and in which the inmates have more freedom of movement. These institutions generally have high-security perimeter fencing.

minimum-security institutions: Federal correctional facilities that allow unrestricted inmate movement, except during the night. These institutions generally have no perimeter fencing.

moral architecture: The term used to describe the design of the first penitentiary in Canada, the intent of which was to reflect the themes of order and morality.

mortification: A term coined by the sociologist Erving Goffman to describe the process by which new inmates are transformed from "free" citizens into inmates.

multi-level institutions: Federal correctional institutions that contain one or more security levels (minimum, medium, maximum) in the same facility or on the same grounds.

National Parole Board (NPB): A federal agency that makes conditional release decisions for federal inmates as well as for inmates in provincial/territorial facilities, except those in of British Columbia, Ontario, and Quebec, which have provincial parole boards. Members of the National Parole Board are appointed by orders-in-council.

need principle: The notion that, to be effective, treatment interventions must address the needs of inmates. The most amenable to treatment are the inmate's criminogenic needs, including substance abuse, relations with peers, and attitudes toward and experience with employment.

net-widening: A potential, unanticipated consequence of diversion programs in which persons who would otherwise have been released outright by the police or not charged by Crown counsel are involved in the justice system.

niches (of inmates): The friendship networks among inmates in correctional institutions. These networks may be based on previous associations, shared ethnicity or culture (e.g., Aboriginal), or length of sentence (e.g., lifers).

NIMBY (Not In My Back Yard) syndrome: A term used to describe the resistance of community residents and neighbourhoods to efforts of systems of corrections to locate programming and residences for offenders in the community.

noncarceral: That portion of systems of corrections relating to supervision, control and the provision of services for offenders in non-institutional settings. Broadly defined, it includes sentencing judges, probation officers, probationers, staff of not-for-profit organizations such as the John Howard Society, parole board members, parole officers, offenders released from confinement on parole, and staff in community halfway houses.

occupational subculture: The concept that correctional officers, similar to police officers, share a solidarity due to the specific nature of their job. One component is a normative code of conduct, which includes such tenets as (1) always assist other officers, (2) don't become overly friendly with the inmates, (3) don't backstab your colleagues, and (4) defer to the experience of veteran officers.

Office of the Correctional Investigator: The agency charged with investigating problems experienced by inmates in the federal correctional system. Investigations are initiated in response to complaints made by inmates.

one-chance statutory release: The result of a detention hearing when the National Parole Board orders that a federal inmate can be released at the statutory release date. Should that release be revoked, however, the inmate would be disqualified from release until warrant expiry.

pains of imprisonment: The deprivations experienced by inmates confined in correctional institutions, including the loss of autonomy, privacy, security, and freedom of movement and association.

pains of re-entry: The difficulties that inmates released from correctional institutions encounter in attempting to adjust to life in the outside, free community.

parole eligibility date: The one-third point in a sentence (except for lifers and those federal offenders whose parole eligibility has been delayed by judicial determination).

passive precautions: Inmate strategies for avoiding violence and victimization, including spending time in cells and avoiding certain areas of the institution. Generally used by older, socially isolated inmates serving long sentences. See also *aggressive precautions*.

Pennsylvania model (for prisons): A separate and silent system in which prisoners were completely isolated from one another, including being kept out of eyesight of one another. Inmates ate, worked, and slept in separate cells. The Pennsylvania system became the model for prisons in Europe, South America, and Asia. See also *Auburn model*.

pillory: A solid wood frame punctured with holes through which the head and hands of the offender were placed. This punishment device was used in Lower Canada until 1842.

positivist school: A perspective of crime and criminals set out in the writings of Cesare Lombroso, Enrico Ferri, and Raffaelo Garofalo in the 1800s. A basic tenet of this perspective is that criminal behaviour is determined by biological, psychological, physiological, and/or sociological factors that can be studied and understood by application of the scientific method.

post orders: In the federal system of corrections, in-depth guidelines that outline the responsibilities for staff in specific locales (or posts) in the institution.

post-traumatic stress disorder (PTSD): An extreme form of *critical incident stress* that includes nightmares, hypervigilance, intrusive thoughts, and other forms of psychological distress.

pre-sentence report (PSR): A document prepared by probation officers for the sentencing judge that contains information on the convicted offender, including sociobiographical information, offence history, and risk assessments. May also include a sentence recommendation, which is not binding on the judge.

prison-industrial complex: A term coined by American journalist Eric Schlosser to refer to the bureaucratic, political, and economic interests that encourage increasing spending on imprisonment, regardless of the actual need.

prisonization: A term coined by the criminologist Donald Clemmer in 1940 to describe the process by which new inmates are socialized into the norms, values, and culture of the prison.

private family visits: A program operated by the federal CSC that allows inmates to have periodic visits from family members in private quarters on prison grounds for up to 72 hours.

probation: A sentence imposed on an offender by a judge in the criminal court that provides for supervision of the offender in the community by a probation officer. All probation orders contain *mandatory conditions* that the offender must adhere to and may also contain *additional conditions* tailored to meet the specific needs and requirements of the individual probationer.

program drift: The extent to which a treatment program as delivered has moved away from the original model, with a potential impact on program effectiveness.

program fidelity: The extent to which a treatment program is delivered in accordance with the original program design.

provincial ombudsman: Provincial office with the authority to investigate citizen complaints (including inmate complaints) against the decisions and actions of provincial government agencies and employees (including the system of corrections and correctional personnel).

radical correctional ideology: A perspective of criminality and corrections that views the capitalist system, exploitation, and the gap between rich and poor as the causes of crime and systems of corrections as instruments of repression of the lower classes. Highlights the role of economics and politics in the administration of justice and the response to offenders.

recidivism rates: The traditional method used to determine success in correctional treatment. The number of offenders who, once released from confinement, are returned to prison either for a technical violation of a condition of their parole (or statutory release) or for the commission of a new offence.

regional instructions: In the federal system of corrections, directives issued by Regional Headquarters that elaborate on commissioner's directives or address specific regional issues.

rehabilitation: An objective of sentencing designed to address the underlying causes of the offender's behaviour.

reintegration: The process whereby an inmate is prepared for and released into the community after serving time in prison.

remand: The status of persons who have been charged with a criminal offence and are in custody awaiting a court appearance, or who have been convicted and are awaiting sentencing.

remand centres: Correctional facilities that generally house offenders awaiting trial.

remission/discharge: Provincial/territorial inmates can have up to one-third of their sentences remitted, often called "good time." In practice, this means that inmates who serve two-thirds of their sentence in prison are discharged free and clear and are not subject to parole supervision. Remission can be lost for institutional misconduct.

responsivity principle: The notion that treatment interventions must be matched to the learning styles and abilities of individual inmates.

restorative/community justice: An approach to the administration of justice based on the principle that criminal behaviour injures not only the victim, but communities and offenders as well. A key feature of the restorative justice approach is the attempt not only to address the specific criminal behaviour of the offender but also to broaden the focus to consider the needs of the victims and the community.

retribution: An approach to the administration of justice based on the ancient "eye for an eye" philosophy of punishment. The sentence is imposed to make the offender "pay" for the criminal behaviour.

revocation of conditional release: A decision by a releasing authority, such as a parole board, made in connection with an offender whose release has been suspended. When a release is revoked, the offender begins to serve the sentence on the inside again. A re-application to the parole board would then be necessary before another parole release would be granted.

rigorous custody programs: The Canadian version of boot camps, these secure custody programs for young offenders emphasize discipline and a highly structured regimen, with a focus on behaviour modification, community service, and personal accountability.

risk principle: The notion that treatment interventions have a greater chance of success when they are matched with the risk level of the offender. Research studies suggest that high-risk inmates are more likely to benefit from intensive treatment programs than low-risk inmates.

sentencing disparity: When similar offenders who commit similar offences receive sentences of different severity.

social (or argot) roles: The various roles in the inmate social system, including "square john," "right guy," "rat," and "politician." These roles are based on the inmate's friendship networks, sentence length, current and previous offences, and extent of participation in illegal activities such as gambling and drug distribution.

Special Handling Unit: A federal correctional facility that houses inmates who pose such a high risk to inmates and staff that they cannot be confined in maximum-security institutions.

specific deterrence: An objective of sentencing designed to deter the offender from future criminal conduct.

split personality of corrections: A term used to describe the conflicting objectives—protection of society vs. treatment of the offender—that systems of corrections are asked to pursue.

Staff Application, Recruitment, and Training (START): The training program for provincial correctional officers in Ontario, consisting of three components: (1) admission process, (2) pre-employment training, and (3) institutional orientation.

standard operating procedures (also known as standing orders): In the federal system of corrections, directives that (1) repeat or elaborate on commissioner's directives and regional instructions, and (2) provide procedural instructions for specific activities within the institution.

state-raised offenders: Inmates who have spent the majority of their adult (and perhaps youth) lives confined in correctional facilities and, as a consequence, may have neither the skills nor ability to function in the outside, free community. For these offenders, prison is "home."

static risk factors: The offender's criminal history, including prior convictions, seriousness of prior offences, and whether the offender successfully completed previous periods of supervision in the community. These variables predict the likelihood of recidivism but are not amenable to change.

static security: Fixed security apparatus in a correctional institution, including perimeter fencing, video surveillance, alarms, and fixed security posts wherein correctional officers are assigned to and remain in a specific area, such as a control room. See also *dynamic security*.

status degradation ceremonies: The processing of offenders into correctional institutions whereby the offender is psychologically and materially stripped of possessions that identify him or her as a member of the "free society."

statutory release: A type of conditional release that allows incarcerated federal offenders to be released at the two-thirds point of their sentence and to serve the remaining one-third under the supervision of a parole officer in the community.

stocks: A punishment device consisting of a wood structure with holes for arms and legs in which offenders were seated. Stocks were widely used in Upper Canada until 1872.

suspension of conditional release: A process typically initiated by a parole supervisor (but sometimes directly by the parole board) in which an offender's release is suspended and he or she is taken back into local custody to await a further decision. In most cases, the parole board will reconsider the case, and may release the inmate or revoke the release. A decision to revoke the release would result in the person returning to federal or provincial/territorial custody.

temporary absence: A type of conditional release that allows an inmate to participate in community activities, including employment and education, while residing in a minimum-security facility or a halfway house.

total institution: A term coined by the sociologist Erving Goffman to describe prisons, mental hospitals, and other facilities characterized by a highly structured environment in which all movements of the inmates/patients are controlled 24 hours a day by staff.

transportation: A practice common in the 1800s that involved sending offenders—many of whom had been sentenced to death—to confinement in hulks in England or to other locations, including Australia and Bermuda.

two-year rule: The division of correctional responsibility between the federal and provincial governments whereby those offenders who receive sentences of two years or longer fall under the jurisdiction of the federal government, while those offenders receiving sentences of two years less a day are the responsibility of provincial correctional authorities.

unit management system: The model on which many federal and provincial/territorial institutions are structured. Among the features of this system (ideally) are a decentralized approach to inmate management, clear lines of authority, an emphasis on staff cooperation, and an integration of case management and security activities at the line and administrative levels.

unit management team: The correctional staff in the unit management system, which generally includes case management officers (or, in federal institutions, Institutional Parole Officers), correctional officers, and correctional supervisors.

victim–offender mediation (VOM): A restorative justice approach in which the victim and the offender are provided with the opportunity to express their feelings and concerns and, with the assistance of a third-party mediator, to resolve the conflict and consequences of the offence.

victim–offender reconciliation program (VORP): See *victim–offender mediation*.

warrant expiry date: The last day of a prison term as ordered by the sentencing judge.

COPYRIGHT ACKNOWLEDGMENTS

Grateful acknowledgment is made to the copyright holders who granted permission to use previously published material. Where it was not possible to provide acknowledgment in the chapters, provision is made on this page, which constitutes an extension of the copyright page.

Box 1.1, p. 9: © Her Majesty the Queen in Right of Canada. All rights reserved. Source: http://www.csc-scc.gc.ca, Correctional Service of Canada, 2001–2002. Reproduced by permission of the Minister of Public Works and Government Services Canada, 2003; **Box 2.3, p. 50:** © Her Majesty the Queen in Right of Canada. All rights reserved. Source: "Symbol of Discipline: The Bell," by C. Blanchfield, 1985. From 10(1) *Crime and Punishment: A Pictorial History*, Part III. *Let's Talk*. Special Report. Ottawa: Correctional Services Canada, 1985. Reproduced by permission of the Minister of Public Works and Government Services Canada, 2003; **Box 2.4, p. 51:** © Her Majesty the Queen in Right of Canada. All rights reserved. Source: "Symbol of Discipline: The Bell," by C. Blanchfield, 1985. From 10(1) *Crime and Punishment: A Pictorial History*, Part III. *Let's Talk*. Special Report. Ottawa: Correctional Services Canada, 1985. Reproduced by permission of the Minister of Public Works and Government Services Canada, 2003; **Fig. 3.1, p. 71:** © Queen's Printer for Ontario, 1995. Reproduced with permission; **Fig. 3.2, p. 72:** © Her Majesty the Queen in Right of Canada. All rights reserved. Source: *Corrections and Conditional Release: Statistical Overview*, p. 17, Solicitor General Canada, 2002. Reproduced with the permission of the Minister of Public Works and Government Services, 2003; **Fig. 3.3, p. 73 (top):** © Her Majesty the Queen in Right of Canada. All rights reserved. Source: *Corrections and Conditional Release: Statistical Overview*, pp. 1, 9, Solicitor General Canada, 2002. Reproduced with the permission of the Minister of Public Works and Government Services, 2003; **Fig. 3.3, p. 73 (middle):** Adapted from the Statistics Canada publication "Crime Statistics in Canada, 2001," Catalogue 85-002, vol. 22, no. 6 (17 July 2002), pp. 6, 8; **Fig. 3.3, p. 73 (bottom):** © Her Majesty the Queen in Right of Canada. All rights reserved. Source: *Corrections and Conditional Release: Statistical Overview*, pp. 9, 21, Solicitor General Canada, 2002. Reproduced with the permission of the Minister of Public Works and Government Services, 2003; **Fig. 3.4, p. 74:** © Her Majesty the Queen in Right of Canada. All rights reserved. Source: *Corrections and Conditional Release: Statistical Overview*, p. 4, Solicitor General Canada, 2002. Reproduced with the permission of the Minister of Public Works and Government Services, 2003; **Fig. 3.5, p. 78:** Adapted from the Statistics Canada publication "Crime Statistics in Canada, 2001," Catalogue 85-002, vol. 22, no. 6 (17 July 2002), p. 3; **Fig. 3.6, p. 80:** Adapted from the Statistics Canada publication "Crime Statistics in Canada, 2001," Catalogue 85-002, vol. 22, no. 6 (17 July 2002), p. 10, 82, 74, © Her Majesty the Queen in Right of Canada. All rights reserved. Source: *Corrections and Conditional Release Statistical Overview*, p. 5, Solicitor General Canada, 2002. Reproduced with the permission of the Minister of Public Works and Government Services, 2003; **Fig. 3.8, p. 84:** © Her Majesty the Queen in Right of Canada. All rights reserved. Source: *Corrections and Conditional Release: Statistical Overview*, p. 15, Solicitor General Canada, 2002. Reproduced with permission of the Minister of Public Works and Government Services, 2003; **Box 3.4, p. 93:** Reprinted by permission – Torstar Syndication Services; **Box 3.5, p. 93:** Reprinted by permission of Manitoba Justice; **Box 4.5, p. 123:** Reprinted by permission of the National Post; **Fig. 4.1, p. 128:** T.F. Marshall (1999), *Restorative Justice: An Overview*. Home Office Occasional Paper 48. London: Home Office. Reprinted with permission; **Box 4.7, p. 131:** © Her Majesty the Queen in Right of Canada.

PHOTOS

INDEX